AN
ENGLISH PANJABI DICTIONARY

AN
ENGLISH PANJABI DICTIONARY

BY

T. GRAHAME BAILEY

GYAN

Published by

GYAN

Gyan Publishing House
5, Ansari Road
Daryaganj, New Delhi-110002
Phone: 011-47034999, 9811692060
E-mail: books@gyanbooks.com

Distribution Network
gyanbooks.com
India, USA, Canada, UK, Australia, France

ISBN : 978-81-212-4341-4 (PB)

2nd Impression 2020

Printed at: Gyan Press, Delhi.

TABLE OF CONTENTS

ABBREVIATIONS

A , App. refers to Appendix II, Additions to Vocabulary.
acc., accus., accusative.
adj., adjective.
adv., adverb.
aux. v., auxiliary verb.
bet., between.
caus., causal.
d., *dēṇā*.
educ., used in schools.
f., fem., feminine : f. pl., feminine plural : f. m., feminine or masculine.
fr., from.
G., refers to the last or Grammar section of the "Panjabi Manual and Grammar."
gen., in general, generally.
H., word used by Hindus.
h., *hōṇā* : *-h.*, e.g., *jārī-h.*, see Introduction, Explanation of Contractions, p. vi.
inf., infin., infinitive.
infl., inflec., inflected.
interj., interjection.
int., intransitive.
k , *karnā* : *-k.*, e.g., *natthī-k.*, see Introduction, Explanation of Contractions, p. vi.
K., khansama's language.
leg., legal language.
loc., locative case.
M. (alone), word used by Muhammadans.
M. followed by number refers to the earlier parts of the "Panjabi Manual and Grammar."
m., masculine : m. pl., masculine plural : m. f., masculine or feminine.
metaph., metaphorical.
neg., negative.
obj., object.
obl., oblique.
occ., occasionally.
pa. p., past participle.
pl., plur., plural.
prep., preposition
pres., present.
pron., pronoun.
pronom. suff., pronominal suffix.
rel., relig., religious.
Rom. Cath., Roman Catholic.
sthg., something.
tr., transitive.
U., word or expression borrowed or altered from Urdu, Urduised Panjabi.
v., verb.
verb subst., verb substantive, the same as auxiliary verb.
W., see Weights and Measures in Appendix

PRONUNCIATION.

CONSONANTS.

b, *g*, *j*, *m*, *n*, *s*, *z* are nearly as in English.

d, *t* are made with the tongue covering the inner side of all the upper teeth, both front and side teeth.

c, *j* are approximately as in English, but the tongue is further forward, and *c* is unaspirated.

The cerebral letters *ḍ*, *ṭ*, *ḷ*, *ṇ*, *ṛ* the tongue strikes or touches the hard palate rather far back.

kh is approximately the *gh* in Irish "lough" or the *ch* in Scotch "loch": *g* is the same sound voiced.

l is nearly as in English "willing."

ñ is like *ñ* in Spanish "señor" or *gn* in Italian and French words, practically the same as *ni* in English "lenient."

ṅ is like *ng* in "singing."

r is made with a single tap of the tongue, like the so-called trilled *r* in Scotland. In genuine Panjabi words it is never found doubled.

w has hitherto been described by all writers (including myself) as a bilabial letter made by the lips without the use of the teeth. It is not bilabial; it is made by the contact of the upper teeth with some part of the lower lip, either where it is visible or lower down, but the contact is so faint that the acoustic effect is quite different from that of English *v*. *f* is the same letter unvoiced.

y is like English *y*, but when doubled tends towards an attenuated *zh*, written phonetically *J*.

h:—(i) *h* is like English *h* when it occurs in *ch*, *kh*, *ph*, *th*, *ṭh*; in the word *āho*, yes; and occasionally in *āhā̃*, no; *oe hoe*, alas or oh; *āe hāe*, alas or oh; *īho*, this very one; *ūho*, that very one; and possibly two or three more words.

(ii) *h* coming after, even though not immediately after, the vowel of an accented syllable is not pronounced, but gives the high-falling tone to the syllable.

(iii) *h* coming before, even though not immediately before, the vowel of an accented syllable, is not pronounced, except when it stands alone, but gives to the syllable the low-rising tone. When the *h* is alone, i.e. without another consonant, it is faintly pronounced as a sonant *h*, and the syllable has the low-rising tone.

Tones.—Panjabi is a tone language like Chinese, but the tones do not play so important a part in speaking. There are four tones :—

(i) level tone found in about 75% of the words. It might also be described as absence of tone.

(ii) high-falling. The syllable is begun about six or seven semitones above the lowest note that the speaker can reach, and falls about two semitones. If no pause follows, the fall is in the following syllable.

(iii) low-rising. The syllable is begun about a tone above the lowest note that the speaker can reach, and rises one or two semitones. If no pause follows, the rise is in the following syllable.

(iv) A combination of low-rising and high-falling, the former always coming first. See "Panjabi Manual," pp. xvii–xix.

The following points connected with consonants are worth remembering :—

(1) The surd letters *c*, *k*, *p*, *t*, *ṭ* must be kept unaspirated (unlike the corresponding English letters which always have slight aspiration). *ch*, *kh*, *ph*, *th*, *ṭh*, are strongly aspirated.

(2) Some letters when occurring undoubled after a vowel are frequently, but not always, changed to certain others. Thus *g* becomes *g̱*; *tag̱ṛā* strong, not *tagṛā* : *kh* becomes *k̲h̲*, as *āk̲h̲dā* saying for *ākhdā* : *nj* becomes *ñ*, as *aiñ*, thus, rather than *ainj* : *s* becomes English *h*, as *maĩ tenū̃ dahnā̃ dah paihe ditte hāhū*, I tell you he gave ten pice. This is extremely common in rapid conversation, but Panjabis have not, as a rule, observed it themselves and most of them will not admit that they pronounce in this way. A little careful listening will convince the student that they do.

(3) Foreigners have a strong tendency to allow the letters *r*, *ṛ*, *ḍ*, *ṭ*, *ṇ*, *ḷ* to alter the sound of vowels immediately preceding or following. This must be avoided. They have no effect upon vowels.

Vowels.

ă, *a* are like *u* in "mutton" when stressed, and like *a* in "along" when unstressed.

ā, *ī*, *ū* are like Italian *a*, *i*, *u*, and approximately like English *a* in "calm," *ee* in "seen" and *u* in "rule."

ē is between French *é* and *è*, not unlike the Scotch vowel in "lane."

e, *ĕ* are the same but shorter.

ō is approximately like *o* in Scotch "mote," not like the English diphthongal sound. *o* is the same but shorter.

i is like English *i* in "linen."

u is like *u* in pull. Scotch and North Irish speakers should note that it is quite different from *ū* which is like *u* in "rule" or *oo* in "pool."

ai is almost identical with *a* in English "man," i.e. it is longer than the same vowel in "mat." It is far removed from the vowel in "height," "like," "side," etc.

au is not far from *aw* in "shawl." More exactly it begins with the vowel of "shawl" and goes on with the "*o*" in "O'Neill," the two being combined into a diphthong. It is utterly unlike the English diphthong in "how," "mound," "shout," etc. The *au* in *maulwī* is practically the same as that in English "maul."

Nasal vowels are as in French except that nasalisation does not change the vowels.

I have gone more fully into the question of pronunciation in my "Panjabi Phonetic Reader." (See back of Title-page).

ERRATA.

jamhā (*karnā*), add, collect, is preferably *jamhā*, not *jamā*.

likhṇā, write, is *likhṇā*, not *likhṇā* or *likkhṇā*.

To express the idea of drawing or painting (pictures, maps, etc.) the Panjabi tendency is to use *baṇāṇā*, make, and to reserve *khiccṇā* for photographs, a distinction being made between what is done by hand and what is mechanical.

The short *a* usually written in the following words is better omitted: *barkhlāf*, contrary: *kīmtī*, costly: *baṇāwṭī*, counterfeit, etc.: *nazāktā*, *nazāktī*, see delicacy, delicate: *dadēhs* and *paṭēhs*, see father: *saltnat*, kingdom.

p. 153, *wajjṇā*, strike, be struck, normally has past part. *wajjeā* or *wajjā*, but when it means "o'clock" it is *wajeā*: *ikk wajeā e*, it is one o'clock: *trai waje*, at three o'clock.

augur: *for* augur *read* auger.
bean: ,, *bin* ,, *bīn*.
p. 15, quail: ,, *batērā* ,, *baṭērā*.
shrike: ,, *latōr* ,, *laṭōr*.
bit: ,, *kaṛe ālā* ,, *kaṛeāḷā*.
bitterly: ,, *ṛōṇā* ,, *rōṇā*.
blow (1): add *dhapphā*, m., slap.
brain: *omit* "2nd and."
calm: for *kaṛnā* read *karnā*.
careless: add "*see* thoughtless."
conspire: for *pākāṇī* read *pakāṇī*.
coronation: ,, *gaddī* ,, *gaddī*.
cotton: *waṇēwā*, add "or *waṛēwā*, m."
cultivator: *for* leg, *read* leg.
cupola: ,, *gumbaz* ,, *gumbaz*.
dark, of colour, add "*kāḷī bhai mārdā e*: see somewhat."
depth: for *dūṅghiāī* read *ḍuṅghiāī*.
dislocated: after *ṭalṇā* insert comma.
district: *taihsīl*, add "or *tasīl*."
door: for *bhītt* read *bhitt*.
entrust: for *de peṭe*, *de pāṇā* read *de peṭe pāṇā*.
excitement: for *macṇā* read *macnī*.
family: ,, *munde* ,, *muṇḍe*.
grand-daughter; add "*see* grand-son."
grand-mother: ,, "*see* grand-father."
grave (1): for *khāngāh* read *khāngāh*.

hollow: after *khoḷā* insert comma.
house: for *baṅgḷā* read *baṅglā*.
impress upon: add *jhī karnī* (*nū̃*).
instrument: for *ṛacch* read *racch*.
invite: „ rotī „ roṭī.
kitchen: „ He's „ H.'s.
layer: after *raddā* add "or *radā*."
marry: *duhā̃jū*: I have heard a fem. *duhā̃jaṇ*.
milk: for *bauhlā* read *bauhḷā*.
moustache: „ *daṛhī* „ *dāṛhī*.
passenger: note that *suārī* is fem.
rainbow; for *piṅgh* read *pīṅgh*.
sailor: after *beṛīwāḷā* insert comma.
sauce: for *grēbbī* read *grēbbī*.
shoe: *tehrī*, *cauhdī juttī*: they also say *tehrā*, *cauhdā*, *pair*.
signal: for *hōṇā ḍauṇ h. hatth*, read *hōṇā*, *ḍauṇ h.*: *hatth*.
sponge: for spane read *spanc*.
stair: „ paurī „ *pauṛī*.
stick (1): „ *dāṅg* „ *ḍāṅg*.
tattoo: after *ukkhaṇṇā* insert comma.
test: for *tēst* read *ṭēsṭ*.
thread: omit comma after *paṛkatteā*.
tune: for *thīk* read *ṭhīk*.
vaccinate: add *ṭīkā ukkhaṇṇā*, see inoculate, tattoo.

English—Panjabi Dictionary

A

a, an, omit or use *ikk*, one: *koī*, some.

abandon, *chaḍḍṇā*: (an idea) *dilõ kaḍḍhṇā*, or *bhulāṇā*.

abate, *see* lessen.

ability, *liākat*, f.: *jinnī pujj e*, up to one's: *jinnā sare*, as far as one can financially.

(1) able, *laik*, *tagṛā*: able for, *de jogā*, or *jogā* w. inflec. infin., G. 95.

(2) able, to be, *sakṇā*, *koḷõ* w. tr. passive or int. or inflec. inf., G. 66, 96, 97. 112.

ablution, perform (relig.) *wuzū karnā* (M.), *ashnān karnā* (H.): *see* wash.

abnormal, *see* strange, wonderful.

abolish, *maukūf k.*: *band k.*: *band karāṇā*.

abominable, *burā*, *ghinaoṇā*, *makrūh*.

abound, *bauht hōṇā*: *see* much.

(1) about, *eddhar oddhar* (here and there): *see* round, approximately, concerning.

(2) about to do, verb w. *wāḷā*, *ḍigganwāḷā*, a. to fall: G. 44, 45, 98. 99: sometimes w. *caleā*, G. 67: a. to go, come, *ṭureā*, *āyā cāhndā e*, G. 112: *see* ready.

above, prep., *de utte*, *de te*, *te*: *see* upon: adv., *utte*: *see* up: from a., *uttõ*: by way of a., *uttõ dī*.

above-mentioned, use *jihdā utte zikar hoeā* or *āyā e*.

abroad, *pardēs*, m., foreign country: *wilait*, f., Europe, America.

abrogate, *see* abolish, cancel, repeal.

abscond, *nass jāṇā*, *bhajj jāṇā*.

absence, *gair-hāzrī*, f.: in my a., *mere picche*, *merī gair hāzrī wicc*: *see* back.

absent, adj., *gair-hāzar*.

absolute, *jihnū sārā ikhtyār e*.

absolutely, *ukkā*, *atte*, *aslõ mūḷõ*, *bilkul*. A.

abstain (from forbidden food), *thõ parhēz* (m.f.) *k.*: (from defiled food), *thõ choh karnī*: (give up doing sthg.), *muṛnā*, *chaḍḍṇā*.

abundant, *see* much.

abuse, n, v., *gāḷ* (plur. *gāhḷā*) *kaḍḍhnī* (gen. indecent); be abused, *gāḷ laiṇī*, *khāṇī*; *gāḷ paiṇī* (*nū*), M. 125. 9: (very bad) *phakkaṛ tōlṇā*: (very mild) *phiṭak dēṇī*; be a., *phiṭak laiṇī*, *khāṇī*: use badly, *see* injure, spoil.

abusive, *gandī zabān-wāḷā*, *baṛīā gāhḷā kaḍḍhaṇwāḷā*, *trakkī hoī zabān-wāḷā*.

acacia (various kinds), *kikkar*, m.: *kikkrī*, f.: *phulāh*, f.: *sharīh* (siris), m.

accent (in language), *laihjā*, m. : (stress), *zōr*, m. (*d*).
accept, *manzūr k.*, *kabūlṇā*, *kabūl k.* : *see* agree, assent.
acceptable, use like.
acceptance, *manzūrī*, f.
accident, *hādsā*, m. (U.) : use injury.
accidental, *takdīrī*, *itfākī*, *itfāk dā*.
accidentally, *sbabb nāḷ*, *aīwē*, *ēwē*, *takdīr nāḷ*, *itfāk nāḷ*.
accommodation, *gunjaish*, f. : place, *thā*, m. f. : *jaghā*, f.
accompany, *de nāḷ jāṇā* or *calṇā*.
accomplice, *bhētī*, m. : *nāḷ raḷeā hoeā*.
accomplish, *mukāṇā* (int. *mukkṇā*) : *kar laiṇā*, *kar chaḍḍṇā* : *see* finish, complete.
accomplished, *see* learned, able.
accomplishment, *hunar*, m. : *ilm*, m. (knowledge).
according to, *de mūjab*.
accordingly, *so*, *bas pher*.
account (money, etc.), *lēkhā*, m. : *hisāb*, m. : settle a., *hisāb k.* or *mukāṇā* : to his account, *ohde peṭe pāṇā* : *see* responsibility : (narration), *bēān* (m.) *k.* : on no a., *kadī nehī*, *kise tarhā nehī* : on a. of, *see* because of.
account-book (village) *behī*, f. : *wehī*, f. : (gen.) *hisāb dī kitāb*, *f.*, or *pōthī*, f.
accountable, *see* responsible.
accountant, village, *paṭwārī* : his business, *paṭwār*, f. : head a., *gardaur*, *kānūgo* : his business, *gardaurī*, f.
accumulate, *katthā k.*, *jamā k.*
accurate, *ṭhīk*, *durust*.
accuse, **accusation**, *ilzām lāṇā* (*utte*) : *cuglī khāṇī* or *k.* (*dī*): *bhanḍī karnī* (*dī*) : *nindyā karnī* (*dī*) : *bhanḍṇā* (*nū*) : *shikait karnī* (*dī*, lit. complaint) : *see* slander.
accused, *mulzam*.
accuser, *ilzām lānwāḷā* : (in court) *nālish karnwāḷā*.
accustom, v. tr., *haḷāṇā*, *gijhāṇā*.
accustomed, become, *gijjhṇā* (pa. p. *giddhā*, *gijjheā*), *hilṇā*, both w inflec. inf. as *iṭṭā ḍhōṇ hiḷeā hoeā e*, or *gijjhā e*, he is a. to transporting bricks; state of being a., *gējh*, f., *hiḷtar*, f. : *see* habit.
ache, *see* pain, hurt.
acid, sour, *khaṭṭā*.
acidity, *khaṭeāī*, f.
acknowledge (saint, prophet, ruler, error, sin) *mannṇā*.
acquaintance (person), *jāṇū*, m.f. : *see* information, knowledge.
acquire, *see* obtain.
acquit, *chaḍḍṇā*, *barī k.* : be a., *chaḍḍeā jāṇā*, *barī h.*, *k͟halāsī hōṇī* (*dī*).
acquittal, *k͟halāsī*, f.
acre, *ghumā*, m. : *ēkaṛ*, m. : *see* App. weights and meas.
acrobat, *see* tumbler.
across, *-ō pār*, *de pār*, *de parle pāse* : *see* crosswise.
(1) **act**, v., drama, *see* imitate.
(2) **act**, n. (law), *kānūn*, m. : of God, *K͟hudā dā kamm*.
action, *fēhl*, m. : *kamm*, m : *amal*, m. : *karam* m. : *see* deed.
active, *kamm karnwāḷā*, *tagṛā*, *cust*.
actual, *aslī*.
actually, *asl wicc*; *saccī muccī* (truly).

acute (severe) *sakht* : (clever) *siāṇā*, *aklwāḷā*.

Adam's apple, *ghaṇḍī*, f.

add, *jōṛnā*, *jamā k.*

(1) address (residence), *patā*, m. : on letter, *patā*, m. : *sarnāmā*, m. : short, relig. a., *nasīhat*, f. (*k.*) : *see* sermon, lecture, speech.

(2) address, v , *kise nāḷ gall karnī*.

adhere (of stamp, etc.) *laggṇā* ; to opinion, *apṇī gall nā chaḍḍṇī* : to someone, *cambaṛnā* (*nū̃*).

adherent, *see* follower.

adhesive, *lēslā*.

adieu, *see* farewell.

adjacent, *nāḷ dā*.

adjoin, *see* adjacent.

adjourn, *chaḍḍṇā* (for two days, *dūh dinā̃ wāste*, etc.) : *see* postpone : (legal), *pher tarīk pai geī e*, another date fixed.

adjure, *see* conjure.

administer, *bandobast karnā* (*dā*), *intizām karnā* (*dā*) : *see* arrange, settle, oath.

admire, *wēkhke khush hōṇā*, *acchā* or *sohṇā laggṇā* (*nū̃*) : *see* praise.

admit (acknowledge), *mannṇā* : (person) *wāṛnā*, *andar aun d.* : not be admitted, *ḍhoī nā hōṇī* or *milṇī* (women's talk).

admittance, *ḍhoī*, *f.* (*milṇī*).

admonish, *samjhāṇā*, *nasīhat dēṇī* (*nū̃*) : *see* reprimand.

adopt (boy) *putrēla banāṇā* : (girl) *dhī karke rakkhṇī*.

adopted son, *putrēlā* : daughter, *dhī karke rakkhī hoī* or *pāḷī hoī*.

adore, no good word, use worship.

adorn, *sajāṇā* (int. *sajjṇā*) : *sajāwat karnī* (*dī*).

adorned, *sajjeā hoeā*.

adult (man) *gabbhrū*, *juān* : (woman) *muṭeār*, *juān* : *see* young.

adulterate, *ohde wicc pāṇī*, *trāmma*, etc., *raḷāṇā* or *pāṇā*, a. w. water, copper, etc. A.

adulterated, *raḷā miḷā*, *nakhā-khrā nehī*.

adulterer, fornicator, *zanāhī*, *harāmkār*.

adultery, fornication, *zanāh karnā* (*nāḷ*), *burāī karnī* (*nāḷ*), *haramkārī karnī* (*nāḷ*).

advance, *trakkī karnī*, *agā̃ waddhṇī* : (money) *pēshgī dēṇī* (int. *milṇī*) : *see* earnest.

advantage, *fāidā*, m. (*uṭhāṇā*) : *nafā*, m. (*uṭhāṇā*) : *see* profit, good : a. and disadvantage, *nafā nuksān*, m.

advantageous, *mufīd*, *fāidewāḷā* : *see* useful.

adversary, *see* enemy : man of other side, *dujjī dhir dā*, *dujje pāse* or *dhaṛe dā*.

adversity, *see* misfortune, poverty.

advertise-, -ment, *ishtihār dēṇā* (*dā*).

advice, advise, *matt*, f. : *salāh*, f. : *nasīhat*, f. : *hidait*, f. : (all w. *dēṇī* and *nū̃*) : *see* consult.

advisable, *cāhidā* w. inf., G. 67, 96 : *see* necessary, duty, require, have to.

adze, *tēsā*, m.

aeroplane, *jahāz*, m. : *hawāī jahāz*, m.

aesophagus, *shāh rag*, f.

affair, *gall*, f. : *bāt*, f. : *kamm*, m. : *muāmlā*, m.

affection, *see* love, friendship.

affix, *lāṇā* (int *laggṇā*).

affliction, *see* grief, pain, misfortune.

afford, *dē saknā, sarnā* (*nū̃*), M. 248. 6.
affray, *fasād*, m. : *dangā fasād*, m.
aforesaid, *see* above-mentioned.
afraid, *see* fear.
afresh, *nawī̃ suannī*, *nawē sireõ* : *see* beginning.
after, *de picche, de magar* : from a., *de picchõ, de magarõ* : after all, *aksar* : *see* behind, finally.
afterwards, *magarõ*, *picche*, *picche nū̃*, *picchõ*.
afternoon, *pishlā paihr*, m : divisions w. approximate times (which vary with the season) are :—*kaccī pēshī*, 1-0 P.M. ; *pēshī*, 2-0 ; *nikkī ḍīgar*, 3-0 ; *ḍīgar* 4 or 5 ; *laudheweḷā*, 5 or 6 : in the a., *pishle paihr*, *ḍīgarī*, *pēshī*, *laudhewēḷe*, etc. : *see* morning, evening, A.M.
again, *muṛ*, *phēr*, *watt* ; a second time, *dujje phēre*, *dujjī wārī* : *see* repeatedly.
against, *de khalāf, de barkhlāf*.
age, *umar*, f. : present a., *hāl dā zamānā* : past a., *purāṇā z.* : old age, *see* old : of same a., *see* equal : *see* hair.
aged, *buḍḍhā*, *buḍhṛā* : *see* old.
agent (advocate, lawyer) *wakīl*, *mukhteār*, *mukhtār* : (land -a., etc.) *gumāshtā* : a. in gen., verb w. ending *-wāḷā*, G. 44, 45, 98, 99, or *-ū*, G. 45.
agitation, be in state of, *taṛapṇā*, *dil taṛapṇā* (or *taṛafṇā*).
agitate, *see* excite, incite, shake.
agitator, *lokā̃ nū̃ bhaṛkāṇwāḷā* or *cukkaṇwāḷā*.
ago, five years ago ; *panjā̃ warheā̃ dē gall e paī*, *panj warhe hoe ne paī* : *see* since.
agree, *mannṇā*, *manzūr k.*, *rāzī h.* : a. w., *itfāk k.* (*nāḷ*), *see* assent : a. to take, pay money, *karnā*, M. 119. 38 : G. 118.
agreeable, *dil nū̃ cangā laggṇā* ; *suādḷā* (tasty).
agreement, *itfāk*, m. : *mēḷ*, m. : written a., *karārnāmā* : written reconciliation, *rāzīnāmā*, m. : *see* settle, covenant.
agriculture, *wāhī*, f. : *khētī*, f. : *khētī bāṛī*, f. : *see* plough.
agriculturist, *zamīndār* : *wāhī karnwāḷā* : (legal) *kāshtkār*.
ague, *kāmbū*, m. : *kāmbū tāp*, m. (both *caṛhnā*, *nū̃*).
ahead, *see* front.
aim, *irādā*, m. : *matlab*, m. : *manshā*, f. : a. at target, etc., *nishānā*, m. (*mārnā*) : *see* intention, object, interest.
(1) air, *wā*, f. : *hawā*, f. : in the open a., *waule* : airs, give oneself, *nakhre karne* : *nazākatā karnīā̃* : *shēkhī mārnī* : *ākaṛnā* : *see* conceit, show, tune. [*sukṇe pāṇā*.
(2) air (clothes, etc.) *sukāṇā*,
airing, go for, *wā bhakhṇī*.
alarm, *see* fear, start, startle.
alarming, *ḍaraoṇā*, *ḍarnwāḷā*, *ḍarāṇwāḷā*.
alas ! *hāe hāe*, *āe hāe*, *hoe hoe*, *oe hoe*.
alert, *hushyār*, *cukannā*, *khabardār*.
alight, *laihṇā* (pa. p. *latthā*), *utrnā*.
alike, *ikse kism de*, *ikkojehe*, *āpe icc raḷde ne*.
alienate (person) *apṇe wallõ dil khaṭṭā k.* (*kise dā*).
alive, *jiūndā*, *jiūndā jāgdā*.
all, *sabbh*, *sāre*, *sārā*, *sāre de*

sāre: not at all, *ukkā nā*, *atte nā*: nothing at all, *kujjh wī nehī*.
allay, *see* lessen, quench.
alliance, *aihd*, m.: *dōstī*, f.
alligator, *sansār*, m.: *magarmacch*, m. (U).
allow, *dēṇā* w. inflec. inf., G. 66: *ijāzat dēṇī* (*dī*).
allowance (food) *rāsan*, m.: *rasad*, m.: food a. in travelling, *bhattā*, m.: travelling a. (money), *safar kharc*, m.: famine a., *mahṅgāī*, f. (pron. *manghāī*): *see* famine.
allude, *ishārā karnā* (*ohde wall*, to him): hit at someone, *nōk lāṇī* (*nū*), *see* hit.
almanac, *jantrī*, f.
almond, *badām*, m.; w. thin shell, *kāgzī badām*, m.: colour, *badāmī*.
almost, *karīb*: *see* approximately: a. falling, *ḍigg caleā e*, G. 67.
alms, give alms, *khair*, m. (*pāṇā*, M.), *khairāt*, f. or *kharait*, f. (*d.*, M.), *lutāṇā*, G. 109: *dāt*, f. (*dēṇī*, M.), *dān*, m. (*d.*, H.): *dānpun*, or *pundān* m. (*d.* or *k.* H.)
aloe, *keoṛā*, m.: soft kind, *kuār gandal*, f.
alone, *kallā*, *chaṛā*, *kall mukallā*, *chaṛā muṛā*, *chaṛā chāṇḍ*, *dam dā dam*: *see* unmarried.
along (road, bank, etc.), locative case repeated; a. bank, *daṇḍe dande* or *kandhe kandhe*: a. road, *sarke sarke*: a. side, *nāl*, *nālo nāḷ*
aloud, *ūccī*: *see* loudly: ideas hardly distinguished.
alphabet, *allaf bē*, f.
also, *wī*, *bī*: *see* moreover.
alter, *see* change.
altercation, *see* quarrel.
alternate, on a. days, *dujje dujje dihāṛe*, *ikk ikk din chaḍḍke*.
alternately, *wārī wārī*, *wāro waṭṭī*.
alternative, *koī hōr tajwīz* (f.) or *gall* (f.)
although, *bhāwē*, *bhāwē pīkar*, *hālā*: conjunct. part. of verb, as *sārī gall wekhke wī nehī mureā*, he did not desist a., he had seen the whole thing.
altitude, *see* height.
altogether, *kull*, *sārā*, *sāre dā sārā*: *see* absolutely.
alum, *phaṭkaṛī*, f.
always, *hamēshā*, *hamēsh*, *sadā*, *nitt*: *see* continuously.
amass, *see* collect.
A.M., P.M., use *rāt de*, *shām de*; *din de do waje*, 2 P.M.; M. 61.
amazed, *harān*, *hakkā bakkā*: *see* astonished.
amazement, *harānī*, f.: *see* astonishment.
ambassador, *wakīl*: *ēlcī* (U.).
ambiguous, *shakkī*, *dūh maihneā wāḷī gall*, *gōḷ mōḷ*: *see* obscure.
ambition, no word: use *waḍḍe waḍḍe khyāl karne*, have high thoughts: *waddhaṇ dī baṛī kōshish karnī*, try to increase.
amble (of horse), *rawhāḷ calṇā*.
amend, *see* improve.
amiable, *khushmizāj*, *khushtabīat*.
amicable, *see* friendly.
amidst, *de wicc*, *de wishkār*, *de darmiān*: *see* between.
amiss, take, *burā mannṇā* (*gall nū*).
amnesty, *muāfī*, f.: general a., *ām muāfī*.

among, *see* amidst.
amount, n., *rakam*, f.: a. to, *bannā*, *h*.
amputate, *waḍḍhṇā*.
amulet, *tawīt*, m.: *tāwīz*, m. (U.).
amuse, *dil parcāṇā* (int. *parcṇā*): *dil bhulāṇā* (int. *bhullṇā*): *khush k*. (int. *h*.): *mauj karnī*: *bullhe luṭṭne*: *lillā luṭṭṇīā*: *noshe luṭṭne*: *see* delight, charm.
amusement, *tamāshā*, m. (often suggests dancing girls): *mauj mēlā*, m.
amusing, *hasāṇwāḷī gall*: *see* amuse.
anarchy, *mulkh wicc gaṛbaṛī* (*paiṇī*), *hanēr* (*macṇā*).
ancestors, *pyōdādde*, *waḍḍe*, *waḍēre*, m. pl.
anchor, *langar*, m.: weigh a., *cukkṇā*: let down, *saṭṭṇā*.
ancient, *kadīm*, *muṇḍh kadīm dā*, *purāṇe zamāne dā*.
and, *te*, *nāḷe*: both this and that, *nāḷe eh te nāḷe oh*, *eh wī te oh wī*.
anecdote, *see* story.
angel, *farishtā*, m.
angle, corner, *nukkar*, f.: *guṭṭh*, f.
anger, *gussā* (*k*. and *h*.): *tā*, m. (heat, *auṇā*): *lāl h*., *lālo lāl h*.: God's wrath, *kahr*, m.: swallow down one's a., *gussā pī laiṇā*: *see* angry, flare, rage.
angry, *gussā auṇā* or *caṛhnā* (*nū̃*) M. 117. 3: G. 117: *gusse h*., *saṛnā*, *baḷṇā*, *lūsṇā*: *see* annoy, displease, frown. A.
animal, *hawān*, m.: *jānwar* or *janaur*, m. (gen. means bird).
animosity, *see* enmity, envy.
aniseed, *saū̃f*, f.
ankle, *giṭṭā*, m.
anklet, *kaṛī*, f.: *toṛa*, m. A
anna, *ānnā*, m.: two a., *duānnī*, f.: four a., *paulī*, *paulī*, f., *cuānnī*, f.: eight a., *dhēllī*, f., *aṭhiānnī*, f.: half a., *ṭaga*, m., *adhiānnī*, f.
annihilate, *fanā k*.: *see* exterminate.
announce, *khabar dēṇī*: *itlāh dēṇī*: *see* proclaim, inform.
annoy, *satāṇā*, or *satā mārnā*, *dikk k*. *ḍicc k*., *tang k*., *akāṇā*, *chēṛnā*: int. *satnā*, *dikk h*., *ḍicc h*., *akkṇā*, also *wiṭarnā*, *kiṛnā*, *ciṛhnā*: *see* tease, displeased, angry, bore.
annual, *see* year, yearly.
anoint, *lēp karnā* (*tē*): *copaṛnā*, put on oil, *ghi*, butter, etc.: *see* ointment, apply, rub.
anonymous, *gumnām*.
another, *ikk hōr*, *dujjā*.
answer, *juāb*, m. (*d*.): flat refusal, *sukkā juāb*: know the a., *juāb auṇā*, (*nū̃*). M. 117. 2, G. 117. *see* refusal.
ant, *kīṛī*, f.: whiteants, *syōk*, f. or *simak*, f. (used collectively in sing.).
antagonist, *see* enemy, adversary.
antagonism, *mukhālfat*, f. (*k*): *wair*, m. (*k*.): *dushmaṇī* (*k*.), 2nd and 3rd mean enmity: *see* enmity, envy.
antelope, *harn*. fem. *harnī*.
antecedents, *paihlā hāl* or *cāl caln*.
antimony, *surmā*, m., *kajjal*, m.
anvil, *airan*, f., *aihran*, f.
anxiety, *waswās*, m.: *fikr*, m.: *andēshā*, m.: *sōc*, f. (thought)

any, anyone, *koī*. [*tarhā*.
anyhow, *ēwē*, *aīwē*, *kiwē*, *kise*
anything, *kujjh*.
anywhere, *kitale*, *kite*.
apart, adv., *nawēklā*, *pasittā*, *alagg*, *ikk pase*, *alaihdā* : see separate.
aperient, *see* purgative.
apologise, *muāfī mangṇī*. A.
apostle, *rasūl*, m.
apostleship, *rasālat*, f.
apparatus, *samān*, m.
apparent, *zāhr* ; *see* appear, seem, visible.
apparently, *wēkkhan wicc* : of person's professions, *uttō-wālī*, *uttōdī*.
appeal (legal), *apīl*, f. (*k.*) : as interj., *duhāī* : *duhāī Rabb dī*, I a. to God : *see* ask, beseech.
appear, *see* seem, visible.
appearance, *sūrat*, f. : *shakl*, f.: *rang rūp*, m. : *see* form.
appease, *manānā*, *rāzī k.* A.
appetite, no word, use *bhukkh*, f., hunger : *shauk*, m., desire, liking.
apple, *syō*, m. : crab-a., *cōṭā*, m. : custard a., *sharīfā*.
applicant, *umēdwār*, *jihdī dar-khāst e*, etc. : *see* beggar.
apply (ointment, varnish, etc.), *lāṇā* (int. *laggṇā*) : *see* anoint, ointment : apply to, use ask, speak to, write to.
appoint (servant) *rakkhṇā* : sometimes *lāṇā*, M. 196. 18 : (*see* servant) : (day) *din mitthṇā* : (date) *tarīk* or *tārīkh pāṇī* (int. *paiṇī*) or *rakkhṇī*.
appointment, *naukrī*, f.
apprentice, *shagird*, m.
approach, *nēṛe auṇā* : *ḍhukkṇā* (esp. of marriage procession, or ox to yoke).
approximately, *nēṛe trēṛe*, *nēṛe*, *aṭā saṭā*, *aṭkal paccū*, *duāle* : *koī*, *ko* and *ku*, as *koī trai*, *trai ku*, about three. G. 87.
apricot, *khurmānnī*, f.
April, *aprail*, m. : *ēpril*, m. : *wasākh*, m. (about Apr. 13 to Mar. 12).
apt to, *see* prone.
arbiter, *tarfain*, m. : *see* mediator.
arch, n., *dāṭ*, f.
arena, *akhāṛā*, m. : *piṛ*, m.
argue, *baihsṇā*, *baihs karnī*, *dalīlā chāntṇīā*, *dalīlī laggṇā*, M. 131. 8.
argument, *dalīl*, f. : quibble, *hujjat*, f., *see* quibble.
argumentative, *hujtī*, *baih-sanwālā*, etc. : *see* argue.
arid, *sukkā*, *jitthe pāṇī nehī*.
arise, *utthṇā* : *see* stand, happen, rise.
arithmetic, *hisāb*, m. : (educ.) *riāzī*, f., (mathematics).
arm (whole), *bāh*, f. : fore-a., *wīṇī*, f. : upper, *ḍaulā*, m. : *see* biceps : a. of river, *shākh*, f. : in arms (of child) *kucchaṛ* (m.) *wicc*. : *see* arms, tie. A.
armpit, *kacch*, f.
arms, *hathyār*, m.
army, *fauj*, f. : *lashka*[illegible].
around, *see* round.
arouse, *see* wake, incite, excite.
arrange, arrangement, *ṭhīk ṭhāk k.* : *sajāṇā* (adorn), *sāmbhṇā* or *sambhāḷṇā* (look after) : a. about, *āhr karnā*, *āhr pāhr karnā* (*dā*) : *intizām karnā* (*dā*) : *bandobast karnā* (*dā*) : *tajwīz kaṛnī* (*dī*) : make some arrangement or other, *koī bhantṛik karnā* : *see* settle : a. to pay, take money, *see* agree.

arrears, *bakāyā*, m.
arrest, *phaṛnā*.
arrival, *auṇā* (come) : news of a., *awāī*, f.
arrive, *appaṛnā*, *auṇā*, *paūhoṇā*, *ḍhukkṇā* (esp. of marriage procession).
arrow, *tīr*, m.
artery, *nāṛ*, f. : (also vein, sinew).
artful, *calāk*, *hīlebāz*, and words for deceitful.
artifice, *see* trick, deceit.
artificer, *kārīgar*, m.
artificial, *baṇāwṭī* (also of made-up story or excuse).
artillery, *tōpkhānā*, m.
as, adj., *jehā*, *jaisā* : adv. *jīkaṇ*, *jīkar*, *jīkarā*, *jiwē*, *jis tarhā*, *jiñ* (rare) : as if, *jiwē*, *goyā*, *jāttā*, *jāṇo*.
ascend, *caṛhnā*, *uṭā jāṇā* (tr. *cāṛhnā*, *caṛhāṇā*).
ascent, *caṛhāī*, f.
ascertain, *see* discover, investigation.
ashamed, *sharmindā*, *lāzam* (both gen. of actual shame, not shyness) : *see* shame, shy.
ashes (from fire) *sāh*, f., *suāh*, f. : (still hot) *bhubbal*, f. : (from decomposition), *see* dust.
aside, *see* apart, aside.
ask (question), *p u c c h ṇ ā*, *pucchṇā gicchṇā* : *suāl karnā* (also make petition) : ask for, *maṅgṇā*, (*see* beg); ask after health, *see* inquire : *see* beg, beseech.
aslant, *see* slanting.
asleep, *suttā hoeā* ; while people are a., *suttī bandī*, G. 78 : half a., *jāggo mīṭī* : a. (of limb) *suttā hoeā*, *sunn* : *see* numb, sleepy.
aspire, *see* ambition, desire.
ass, *khōtā*, fem. *khōtī* : *waihtar* m. (any beast of burden) : *see* horse, mule.
assafoetida, *hiṅg*, *f*.
assault (leg.), *mār piṭṭ*, f. : *see* attack.
assemble, *katthā k.* (int. *h.*) : *jamā k.* (int. *h.*).
assembly, *majlis*, f. : *jalsā*, m. (of large a.) : *manḍlī*, f. (company) : *see* company, meeting.
assent, *hā karnī*, *huṅgārā bharnā*, *mannṇā*.
assert, *zōr nāḷ ākhṇā*, *takīd nāḷ ākhṇā*.
assess (of land), *muāmlā lāṇā* : *see* settlement, tax.
assessment, *muāmlā*, m.
assist, *see* help.
assistant, *madadgār*, m. : Asst. Commissioner, *Ashṭanṭ Sāhb*.
associate, n., *see* companion : v., *milṇā julṇā* (*nāḷ*), *wartṇā* (*nāḷ*), *wāh paiṇā* (*nāḷ*).
assure, *tsallī duāṇī*, *yakīn duāṇā* : *see* insure.
astonish, *harān k.* : *hakkā bakkā k.* : astonished, be, *harān h.*, *hakkā bakkā h.* : *tajjab k.*, *h.* and *acarj h.* (mildly) : *see* wonderful.
astonishment (mild), *tajjab*, m. : (great) *harānī*, f. : interj. of a., *balle balle*, *bāī bāī*.
astray, go, (*rāhō*) *khunjhṇā* or *ghussṇā*, *kurāhe* or *kurāh paiṇā* : *see* way, seduce.
astrologer, *ramlī*, m. : *najūmī*, m. : *jōtshī*, m.
asylum (lunatic), *pāgalkhānā*, m.
at, *wicc* : at well, shop, tank, railway station, etc., *te* : for at often use loc., G. 9, 10,

77: at of time, loc. G. 10, 34, 78.
atheist, *daihrīā*.
athlete, *see* wrestler, tumbler.
atone, atonement, *kafārā*, m. (*d.*, *h.*)
attach, *lāṇā* (int. *laggṇā*): *see* file (papers), tie, apply.
attachment, *see* love.
attack, *hamlā*, m. (*k.*, *utte*) : of dog, *paiṇā* (*nū*), G. 120, M. 125. 8.
attain, *see* obtain, reach.
attempt, *see* try.
attend (to someone), *dhiān karnā* (*de wall*) : a. upon, serve, *ṭaihl karnī* (*dī*), *khidmat karnī* (*dī*): *see* serve: a. sick person (of doctor), *ilāj karnā* (*dā*).
attendance (being present), *hāzrī*, f. (*lāṇī*, to enter attendance in book, int. *laggṇī*) : *see* call.
attendant, *see* servant.
attention, *dhiān*, m. (also meditation).
attentive, use *dhiān nāḷ*, *dil nāḷ*, *dilō wajhō hōke*.
attribute, *see* quality.
auction, n., *lalāmī*, f. : v., *lalām-k.* (*nū*)
audience (people present), *hāzrīn*, m. pl. (U.): *jehṛe hāzir* or *baithe ne*: *jamāt*, f. : *see* congregation, spectator.
audit, *paṛtāḷ k.* (*dī*, rarely *nū*).
augur, *warmā*, m.
August, *agast*, m. : *bhādrō*, m. (about 13th Aug. to 12th Sep.).
aunt, father's sister, *phupphī*, *bhūā* : mother's sister, *māssī* : father's elder brother's wife, *tāī* : father's younger brother's wife, *cāccī* : mother's brother's wife, *māmmī* : wife's or husband's aunt, *see* father.
auspicious, *nēk* (M.), *mubārak* (M.) : *shubh* (H.), *mahūrat caṅgā* (H.) : *see* fortunate.
author, (*kitābā*) *likkhaṇwāḷā*.
authorise, *ikhtiār dēṇā*, *mukhtār rakkhṇā* or *banāṇā* (*see* advocate) : *hukam dēṇā* (order) : *ijāzat dēṇī* (permit).
authority, *ikhtiār*, m. : *ijāzat*, f. (permission): *hukam*, m. (order) : *hakk*, m. (right) : *kadr*, m. f. (value, i.e. who was he to do so and so ?) : *tākat*, f. (power).
avarice, avaricious, *see* covetous, covetousness.
avenge, *see* revenge.
average, n., *ausat*, *aust*, f. : adj., *wishkārle mēḷ dā* ; strike an a., *aust kaḍḍhṇī* : *see* approximately, mediocre.
avert, *ṭāḷṇā*, *rōkṇā*, *rafā dafā k.* (int. *ṭaḷṇā*, *rukkṇā*, *rafā dafā h.*).
avidity, *see* desire, wish, long.
avoid (food, actions), *parhēz* (f. m.) *k.* (-*ō*, *te*) : avoid meeting someone, *matthe nā laggṇā* (*de*), *neṛe nā jāṇā* (*de*) : *see* escape.
avow, *see* admit, confess.
await, *see* wait.
awake, adj., *jāgdā* : v., *see* wake.
aware, *patā h.* or *laggṇā*, *khabar hōṇī*, *mālūm h.* (all *nū*).
away (from home on visit) *wāhndā* : begone! *jā parā*, *parā hō*, *dūr hō*, *radd hō*, *dafā hō* ; *jā*, *ṭur jā* : (*see* rise) : (to dog) *dūr dūr*, *dūre* : (to cat) *chir chir*, *chire*.
awe (person's influence), *rohb*, m. : *see* fear.

awkward, *bhaddā*, *kōjhā*, *kuḍhabbā*.

awning (over shop), *chappar*, m. (strictly thatch) : (kind of large tent), *shāmiānā*, m.

axe (large) *kuhāṛā*, m. : (small) *kuhāṛī*, f.

axle, *dhurā*, m.

azure, *asmānī* (*rang*. m.).

B

baby, *baccā*, m. (*kucchaṛ wicc*. in arms).

bachelor, *kuārā* : *charā* (alone).

(1) back, *pitth*, f. : upper b., *kanḍ*, f. : lower, *lakk*, m. (*see* waist) : b. of shoulders, *maur*, m. : *see* spine : b. of book, paper, *pusht*, f. : behind one's back, *picchō kanḍī*, *pitth picche* : *see* absence : (carry) on one's b., *kandhāṛe*, shoulders : at the b. of, *see* behind, after. A

(2) back, adv. (as send b., go b.), *partāke*, *partke* : *see* return.

(3) back out of, *phirnā*, *thiṛnā*, *pasrnā*.

backbite, *see* tale, slander, accuse.

bad, *burā*, *kharāb*, *mandā*, *bhaiṛā*, *raddī* : rotten, *trakkā hocā* ; slightly, *musscā hocā* : go bad, *trakkṇā*, *see* rot ; slightly, *mussṇā* : (of milk) *see* sour : *see* worthless, useless : a bad business, *matthī gall*, *burī gall*, *mandī gall* : (of land) *niras*, *raddī*, *karlāthī* : *see* coin, evil, soil, sin.

badness, *burāī*, *bureāī*, f. : *kharābī*, f. : *see* sin.

badge, *nishān*, m. : (for *caprasī*) *caprās*, f.

baffle, *see* bewilder.

bag (large) *thailā* : (small) *thailī*, f. : for schoolbooks, *bastā*, m. : *jhōḷī*, chudder or front of shirt used as b. : *see* purse, sack : b. and baggage, *gandh gaṭṭhṛī*, *grām gaṭṭhṛī*, f. : *bistrā bōriā*, m. : *bhānḍā ṭinḍar*, m. : *bā bistar*, m. : (all w. *bannhṇā*, tie up).

baggage, *samān*, m. : *asbāb*, m. : *see* bag and baggage.

bail, *zamānat*, f. (security) : release on b., *zamānat te chaḍḍṇā* ; person going b., *zāman*, m

bake, *pakānā*, *bēk k*. (K).

baker, *roṭiāwāḷā*, or as U *roṭīwāḷā* : village b., *māchī*, fem. *māchaṇ* : *nānwāī*, no fem.

balance, *see* scales : (financial) *bakāyā*, m.

bald, (head b. and face bare) *rōḍḍā* : b. through disease (favus), *ganjā* : *see* hairless.

ball (for play), *khehnū*, m. : *gēnd*, m. : *bīl*, m. : *khiddo*, m. (made of cloth) : bullet, *gōḷī*, f. : cannon-b., *gōḷā*, m.

bamboo, *wanjh*, m. : *bās*, m.

banana, *kēlā*, m. : more often *phaḷī* or *kēle dī phaḷī*, f.

band (music) *wājewāḷe*, m. pl. : *see* company.

bandsman, *wājewāḷā*, m.

bandage, *paṭṭī* f. : (v., *paṭṭī bannhṇī*) : over ointment. etc., *phāh*, m. (*lāṇā*).

bangle, *see* bracelet.

banish, *mulkhō* or *watnō bāhr kaḍḍhṇā*.

banjo, *see* guitar.

bank (of river, lake, etc.) *kanḍhā*, m : *dandā*, m. : (for money), *bank*. m. : (actual building) *bank-ghar*. m.

banker (Hindu) *shāh*, *shāhūkār* : (European) *bankwālā*.

banknote, *nōṭ*, m.

bankrupt, become, *duālā nikḷnā* : he has become b., *ohdā duālā nikḷeā e* : he claims to be b., *oh duālā kaḍḍh baiṭhā e*.

banner, *see* flag.

banquet, *khāṇā*, m. : invite to, *dāwat karnī* : *see* invite.

banyan tree, *bōṛh*. f.

baptise, *baptismā* (m.) *d.* (*nū̃*) : be b., *baptismā h.* (*dā*) or *laiṇā*.

bar (for door), *hohṛkā*, m. : *hohṛā*, m. : *arl*, m. : *see* rod.

barbarian, *waihshī*, *jāṅglī* : original inhabitants of canal districts called *jāṅglī*.

barber, *naī*, fem. *naın*.

bare, *naṅgā* : barefooted, *naṅgī pairī* (G. 10. 78), *pairā̃ tō wāhṇā* : bareheaded, *naṅge sir* : lay bare, *naṅgā k.* : lay bare thoughts, *thullnā* : matter, *phōlnā*.

barely, *see* scarcely.

bargain, *saudā*, m. : good b., *caṅgā saudā* : a b. *i.e.* cheap, *sastā*.

(1) **bark**, v., *bhauṅknā*.

(2) **bark**, n., *see* tree.

barley, *jaū*, m. : barley and wheat, *gojī*, f.

barracks, *bārak*, f.

barrel (of gun) *nāḷī*, f. : (cask) *pīpā*, m.

barren (land), *kallar*, *banjar* : (of tree) *apphaḷ* : (woman) no good word, say *baccī baccā* or *dhī puttar koī nehī̃*, etc. : *autrī nakhattrī* means either barren or children dead : often as abuse.

barrow, *reṛhī*, f. : *see* cart.

barter, exchange, *waṭāṇā*.

(1) **base**, adj., (low family or ideals) *kamīnā* : (evil) *see* bad, wicked.

(2) **base**, n. (plinth) *kursī*, f. : *see* foundation.

bashful, *see* shy, shyness.

basin, *cilamcī*, f.

bask (in sun) *siyā sēkṇā* : *siye* or *dhuppe baihṇā* : *dhupp sēkṇī*.

basket, *ṭōkrā*, m. : *ṭōkrī*, f. : *caṅer*, f. : for winnowing, *chajj*, m. : for fruit, vegetables, sweets, *chābṛī*, f. : of fruit, vegetables, presented to superior, *ḍāhḷī*, f. : in scales, *chābbā*, m.

bastard, *harām dā*.

bastion, *burj*, m.

(1) **bat** (animal) *cāmcṛikk-* or *-ī*, f. : *cāmciṭṭh*, f.

(2) **bat**, for playing, *ballā*, m. : *bait*, m. : village bat and ball, *khehnū̃ ṭallā*.

bath, n. (the article) *ṭapp*, m. : *see* cistern : Turkish b., *hamām*, m. : *see* boiler, bathe : bathroom, *gusḷkhānā*, m.

bathe, *nhauṇā* (pa. p. *nhātā*), *gusl-karnā* : b. someone else, *nalwhāṇā*, *nuhāṇā*, *gusl dēṇā* (*nū̃*) : *see* wash, ablution.

battalion, *baṭālyan*, f.

bawl, *see* scream, shout.

battle, *laṛāī*, f. : *see* war.

bay (of horse) *kumaid*, *kumait*.

bayonet, n. and v., *saṅgīn mārnī* (*nū̃*).

bazar, *bazār*, m.

be, to, verb subst., am, was, etc., only pres. and past : G. 50, 55, 56 : become, *hōṇā* : let it be, *raihṇ dē* : *see* mind.

bead, *maṇkā*, m.

beadle, *caprāsī*, m.

beak, *cunjh*, f. : *cinjh*, f. : *see* peck.

beam, large, *shatīr*, m. : small, *shatīrī*, f. : *ballā*, m. : small cross bit in ceiling, *kaṛī*, f. : *see* log.

bean, *sēm*, f. : French, *frās* [*bin*, f.

(1) bear, n., *ricch*, m : fem. *ricchṇī* : sometimes *bhālū*, m.

(2) bear, *see* endure : b. children, *jamṇā* : b. young (cattle) *sūṇā* (int.) : in gen. *baccā dēṇā* : *see* born.

beard, *dāṛhī*, f.

bearded, *dāṛhīwāḷā*, m.

beardless (because too young), *alū̃* : (older person) *khōddā* : gen., *andāṛhīā* : *see* bald, hairless.

bearer (servant), *baihrā*, m.

beast, *hawān*, m. (not much used, if possible name animal) : *jānwar*, *janaur*, m. (nearly always means bird).

beat, *mārnā*, *kuṭṭṇā*, *phaṇḍṇā*, b. w. shoe, stick, blows of fist, etc., *mārnā* w. word for shoe, stick, etc., and *nū̃* of person struck : *see* blow, strike : rush at to strike, *ṭuṭṭke paiṇā* (*nū̃*), G. 120, M. 125. 14, *mārn paiṇā* (*nū̃*), G. 120, M. 125. 13 : drum, *wajāṇā* : carpets, *phaṇḍṇā*, *phaṇḍākā mārnā* : whisk eggs, *phēṇṭṇā*.

be beaten, *mār khāṇī*, or passive of *mārnā* or *phaṇḍṇā* ; *khāṇā* w. word for shoe, stick, etc., or these words w. *paiṇā* and *nū̃* of person beaten. [(U.).

beautiful, *sohṇā* : *khūbsūrat*

beauty, *suṇh-ippaṇ*, *-appaṇ*, m.

because, *kyū̃ jo*, *ēs wāste pai*, *ēs karke pai*, *ēs lai pai*, *kyū̃ pai* : *jo* as enclitic, M. 221. 12.

because of, on account of, *de sadkā* : G. 37, 38 : *de sabb*, *de sbabbō̃* : *dā mārā*, *de māreā* (last two of intellectual condition), G. 37, 38.

beckon, *hatth nāḷ saddṇā*, *sainat karnī* (*nū̃*) : *see* wink.

become, *hōṇā*, *ho jāṇā* : *see* suit, suitable. [able.

becoming, *see* beautiful, suit-

(1) bed, *manjī*, f. : (large) *palaṅgh*, m. : side-piece, *hī̃*, f. : end-piece, *sērū*, m. : head, *sarhāndī*, f. : foot, *puāndī*, f. : make b., *wachauṇā* or *bistrā wachāṇī* : sometimes *bistrā k.* : bedding, *sōt*, f., *wachauṇā*, m., *bistrā*, m : bed-room, *sauṇā kamrā*, m.

(2) bed *see* flower-bed.

bee, *mākhyō̃ dī makkhī*, f.

beef, any word for meat w. *waḍḍā*, big, or *gōkā*, cow's, or *gā̃ dā*, cow's, prefixed : also *bīf*, m. (K.).

beer, *bīr sharāb*, m. (K.).

beetle for levelling road, *durmaṭ*, m. : *damūsā*, m.

beetroot, *cakundar*, m.

before, adv. of time (both previously and in future), *agge*, *agge nū̃* : (previously only), *paihlā̃*, *paihle*, *paihlū̃*, *paihle nū̃*, *agētre*, *agdū̃* : adv. of place, *agge*, *sāhmṇe* : forward, *agā̃* : from before, from in front of, *aggō̃*, *sāhmṇeō̃* : by way of in front, *aggō̃ dī*, *sāhmṇeō̃ dī*.

prep., *de agge*, *de sāhmṇe* : one in front of the other, *agge picche*, *aggaṛ picchaṛ* : *see* front, face :

conj., inflec. inf. w. *tō̃* or *thō̃* or *thī̃* or *-ō̃* followed by *agdū̃* or *paihlū̃* : G. 95.

befriend, *see* help.

beg, *mangnā*, *suāl karnā* : *see* ask, beseech.

beggar, *manganwālā*. *suālī*, *mangtā*, *fakīr*, fem. *fakīrnī*.

beggary, *see* poverty.

begin, *laggnā* (pa. p. *lagā*, when unemphatic, and *laggā* when stressed) w. inflect. inf.: *shurū k.* (w. inf. agreeing w object): to begin w., *paund satte.* [*lagā*.

beginner, *aje hune sikkhan*

beginning, *shurū*, m. : from the b., *mundhō*: from b. to end, *alfō laike yē tōṛī* : *mundhō laike akhīr tōṛī*.

begone, *see* away.

behalf, on my, etc., *mēre wallō* from me: *mērī khātar*, for my sake: *mēre laī*, *mēre wāste*, for me: *see* for.

behaviour, *see* character.

behead, *sir waḍḍhṇā* (*dā*).

behind, adv., *picche*, *pichēre*, *pishēre* : *see* afterwards: towards behind, *pishā̃* : from b., *picchō*, *pichēreō*, *pishēreō*, prep., *de picche*, *de magar* : sheltered b. or hidden b., *de ohle* : pass b., *picchō dī* or *magarō dī laṅghṇā* : *see* after, before.

belie, *jhūṭhā k.* or *baṇāṇā*.

believe (a fact) *mannṇā*, *yakīn k.* or *h.* or *auṇā* (M. 153. 30, 31) : b. in (God, Christ, etc.) *īmān leauṇā* (*utte*), M. 154. 33-6, 155 : *see* faith, trust, confide, reliance.

bell, large, *ghaiṇṭā*, m., *ṭall*, m. : gong, *ghaṛeāl*, m. : iron bar, *ghaiṇṭī*, f. : bicycle, dinner bell, *ṭallī*, f.: tongue of b., *dur*, m. : ring b., strike gong, *wajāṇā* : (*ṭallī*) *chankāṇī*, *wajāṇī*, int. *chaṇakṇī*, *wajjṇī* : tiny bells on hands, feet, neck of horses, etc., *ghuṅghrū*, m. (*chaṇakṇā*).

belly, *see* stomach.

beloved, *pyārā* : *see* lover.

below, adv., *hēth*, *hēṭhā̃*, *thalle*, *hēṭhle pāse* : downwards, same words : from b., *hēṭhō*, *thalleō* : prep. *de hēṭh*, etc. same words: pass b., *hēṭhō dī*. *hēṭh dū*, *thalleō dī*, all w. *laṅghṇā*.

belt, *pēṭī*, f. : *bilṭ*, m. (*k*): *see* badge.

bench, *banc*, f. : *see* seat, chair.

bend, *lafāṇā* : be bent, *lifṇā* : b. head, *sir jhukāṇā* : *see* crooked, stoop.

beneath, *see* below.

benediction, *barkat dā kalmā* (pronounce, *suṇāṇā*) : *see* blessing. [(kind).

benefactor, *murabbī*, *mehrbān*

beneficial, *see* advantageous.

(1) benefit, v. tr., *fāidā*, m. (*karnā*): int. *fāidā h.* (*dā*) : arrogantly claim to have benefited someone, *ahsān* (pron. *as-hān*) or *ṭhāhrā cāṛhnā* (*utte*) : admit being benefited, *ahsān* or *ṭhāhrā mannṇā* (*dā*) : *see* obligation.

(2) benefit, n., *fāidā*, m. : *ahsān* m. (kindness) : *see* profit.

benumbed, *see* numb.

bequeath, *wasīat karke d.* : *wasīatnāme wicc d.*

beseech, *tarle karne*, *tarlā karnā*, *minṭā karnīā*, *mint tarlā k.*, *mint mājrā karnā* (all w. gen.) ; *hatth bannhke arz karnī* (*de agge*) : *see* ask.

(1) beside, *see* near.

(2) besides, *ehnū chaḍḍke*, *ehde suā* : *see* without.

besiege, *ghērnā*, *muhāsrā karnā* (*dā*). [*laggṇī*.

bet, *shart*, f.: v., *lāṇī*: int.

best, *sārcā tō* or *sāreā wiccō caṅgā*: best man, *sarbāhlā*, m.

betel-leaf, *pān*, m.:—nut, *sipārī*, f.

between, *wishkār*, *de darmiān*: *see* through: go-between, *see* mediator.

bewilder, v. tr., *ghabrāṇā*: be b. *ghābbarnā*.

bewitch, *see* charm.

beyond, adv., *pare*, *parle pāse*, *pār*: towards b., *parā̃*: prep., *de pare*, *de parle pāse*, *de pār*.

Bible, *baibal*, f.: *Khudā dī* (*dā*) *kalām*, or *dī kitāb*, f.: *see* Testament.

bhang, *bhaṅg*, f.: *cars*, f. (a preparation of b.): man who uses b., *bhaṅgī*.

bias, *see* partiality.

biceps, triceps, *ḍaule dā paṭṭhā*, m.

bicycle, *baiskal*, m.: among children, *aṅgrēzī ghōṛā*, m.

bid (at auction), *bōlī ḍēṇī*.

big (age, size) *waḍḍā*, G. 34: *see* great; so b., *ēḍḍā*, *ōḍḍā*: how b., *kēḍḍā*: as b., *jēḍḍā*: as b as I, *mēre jēḍḍā*: G. 91, 92.

bigoted, *tassabī*.

bigotry, *tassab*, m.

bill (of exchange), *hunḍī*, f.: *see* cheque, beak.

bind, *see* tie: b. books, *jild bannhṇī* (int. *bajjhṇī*).

binoculars, *dūrbīn*, f.

bird, *jānwar*, m.: *janaur*, m.: *painchi*, f.: *pakhērū*, m.: small, *ciṛī*, masc. *ciṛā* (esp. sparrow): *see* fledgling.

List of Common Birds.

Great confusion exists in the nomenclature, and Panjabis are certain of none but the best-known.

babbler (seven sisters) *sehṛ*, f.

bee-eater, *harī ciṛī*, f.

bulbul, *bulbul*, f.

cock, *kukkaṛ*, m.

crane, *kūnj*, f.

crow, *kā̃*, m.

crow, jungle, Indian corby, *pahāṛī kā̃*.

cuckoo, pied crested, *bambīyā*, m.

dabchick, *ḍubkū*, m.; *jalkukkaṛ*, m.

dove, ring-, *ghuggī*, f.

dove, little brown and red turtle, *ṭotrū*, m.

duck, *baṭakh*, f., masc. *baṭkhī*.

duck, wild, *mugrāī*, *murgābī*, f.

duck, Brahminy, *nikkā maggh* or *maṅgh*, m.

eagle, *bāz*, *ukāb*, m.: often *ill*, f.

falcon (lugger), *lagaṛ* (often used for tawny eagle).

flamingo, *lamḍhīng*, f.

goose, *baṭakh*, f.: rare, *hans*, m.: wild g., *maggh*, *maṅgh*.

goshawk, *bāz*, f.

grebe, *see* dabchick.

grouse, *bhaṭittar*.

hen, *kukkṛī*, f.

heron, pond, *baglā*, m.

heron, grey, *waḍḍā baglā*; *naṛī*, f.

hoopoe, *cakkī rāh*, m.

ibis, black, *bōjā*, m.

jay, *see* roller

kestrel, *cūhe mār*, m.

king-crow, *lāṭ*, f.: *kāḷ kṛiccī*, f.: *kāḷ klīccī*, f.

king-fisher, *macchī mār*, m.
kite, *ill*, f.
koel, *koēl*, f. : *kōl*, f.
lapwing, *ṭaṭaulī*, f.
lark, *canḍōl*, m.
merlin, *turmtī*, f. : *turmcī*, f.
minivet, *lāl*, m. : *surkh*, m.
myna, common, *lāllī*, f.: *lālṛī*, f.
myna, bank, *shārk*, f.
nightjar, *cabākhī*, f.
owl, *ullū*. [f.
owlet, *bilbatauṛī*, f. : *cabākhī*,
paddy bird, *see* pond heron.
parrot (rose-ringed paroquet), *tōttā*, m.
parrot (large Indian paroquet), *rā tōttā*, m.
partridge, *tittar*, m. : *bhaṭiṭṭar*, m.
peacock, *mōr*, fem. *mornī*.
pigeon, *kabūt-ar*, m., fem. *-rī*.
pigeon, hybrid (tame), *khumrī*, f., *kumrī*, f.
pipit, same as lark.
quail, *baṭērā*, m.
raven, *ḍhoḍḍar kā*, m., *ḍhoḍḍrī*, f.
redstart, same as robin.
robin, and any bird like it, *piddī*.
roller, *lalāṛan*, f.: *garaṛ pōpō*, m., *garaṛ*, m.
sandpiper, *kakaūā*, m.
shikra, *shikrā*, m.
shrike, bay-backed and rufous-backed, *syōṇ ciṛī*, f. *sōṇ ciṛī*.
shrike, grey, *latōr*, f.
sparrow, *ciṛī ghar dī ciṛī*, f.: masc., *ciṛā*.
starling, common Indian, *tilyar*, m.
starling, rose-coloured, *gulābī tilyar*.
stork, *lamḍhīṅg*, f.
swallow, *abābīl* f.
swift, *abābīl*, f.
tern, *jhiūrī*, f.: wrongly *ṭaṭaulī*, f.
tree-pie, often *bambīyā*, m.
turkey, *pērū*, m.
vulture, any large v., *girjh*, f.
vulture, Egyptian (larger white scavenger), *ganjā*, m.: sometimes *baggī ill*, f. : or simply *nikkī girjh*, f.
wagtail, *mamōlā*. m.
warbler, particularly ashy wren w., *camūṇā*, m.: *ṭimmā*, m.
woodpecker, golden backed, or any large w. *ṭōkkā*, m : *tarkhāṇ*, m.
woodpecker, pied, *nikkā ṭōkkā*, *nikkā tarkhāṇ*.
birth, *jamm*, m. : *paidāish*, f.: when was she (he) born, *oh kadō dī (dā) jamm e?*: *see* bear, born.
birthday, *janam din*, m.
biscuit, *biskuṭ*, m. : very thin, *tunkī*, f.: Indian, *khatāī*, f.
bit, *see* piece, mouthful: horse's, *kaṛe ālā*, m : *see* bridle.
bite, *waḍḍhṇā*, *waḍḍh khāṇā*: *dandīā waḍḍhṇīā*: of horse, *cak mārnā* (all *nū*) : of rats, mice, *ṭukkṇā*, *kutarnā*: *see* gnaw, attack (dog).
bitter, *kauṛā* : of person, *kauṛā*, *saṛeā baleā*: *see* annoy: of mind, *khaṭṭā*: *see* embitter.
bitterly, *saṛke*: weep b., *uccī uccī*, loudly, or *bauht*, very much, &c., *rōṇā*.
black, *kālā* : *see* jet-black.
blackness, *kālakh*, f. (especially from soot, smoke).
blackguard, *badmāsh*, *sharīr*, immoral, *luccā*.

blacking, for boots, *syāhī*, f. *see* polish.

blacksmith, *luhār*, fem. *luhārī*.

blade, of knife, etc., *phal*, m.

bladder, *bhakānnā*, m.

blame, *ilzām lānā*, (*utte*): *pēṭe gall pāṇī* (*de*): *see* reprimand, accuse, sit upon.

blameless, *bēkasūr*, *bēgunāh*: *see* sinless, innocent.

blank (paper), *kōrā*: *see* unused.

blanket, *kambal*, m.: *jhull*, f.: *loi*, f. (fine): *bhūrā*, m. (esp. for horses, cattle): *see* quilt, sheet, shawl.

blaspheme, blasphemy, *kufar*, m.: (*baknā*, *bōlnā*).

blasphemer, *kāfar*, M.: *kufr bakaṇwālā*: *see* atheist, unbeliever.

blaze up, *bhakhṇā*, *bhakh paiṇā*: *see* burn, heat.

bleat, of sheep, goats, *maīkṇā*.

blemish, *nuks*, m.: *dāg*, m. (spot, stain): *aib*, m.

bless, blessing, God to man *barkat dēṇī*: *asīs dēṇī* (H.): man God, *see* praise: man man, *duā dēṇī*: see benediction, curse.

blessed, *mubārak*, *dhann*.

blind, *annhā*: (title by courtesy), *hāfaj* (for *hāfiz*,: *see* Quran): of one eye, *kāṇā*: *see* see.

blindly, *annhe wā* or *wāh*.

blindness, at night, *artānnā*, m. *andhrātā*, m.

blister, *chāllā*, m. (*paiṇā*): *see* water.

blood, *ratt*, f.: *khūn*, m.: *lahū*, m.

bloody, *ratt nāl bhareā hoeā*.

blossom, n., *kalī*, f.: *phull*, m. v.: *see* flower.

blot, *dāg*, m.: moral, *dhabbā* m.: *see* disgrace, delete.

blotting paper, *syāhīcat*, m., *blātin*, f.

(1) **blow**, n., *satt* (*laggṇī*, *wajjṇī*: tr., *lāṇī*, *mārnī*): *see* wound: b. w. fist, *hūrā*, m., *ghasunn*, m., *gubbh*, f.: slap, *capēr*, f.: w. stick, *hujj*, f. (*see* prod), or *sōṭī* f.: w. shoe, *chittar*, m., *juttī*, f.: verb for all, *wajjṇā*. *khāṇā*, *paiṇā*; tr. *mārnā*: *see* beat: come to blows, *hatthī paiṇā*: struggled w. me, tried to strike me, *mērī hatthī peā*: G. 120, M. 125. 7.

(2) **blow**, v., *phūk mārnī*: trumpet, bugle, &c., *wajāṇā*: of wind, *wagṇā*: b away (of wind), *uḍāṇā*.

blue, light, *asmānī* (*rang*): darker, *līllā*, *nīllā*: very dark, *kālā*.

blunt, *khunḍhā*.

boar, same as pig: wild, *bēlle dā*.

board, large, *phaṭṭā*, m.: *takhtā*, m.: small, *phaṭṭī*, f., *takhtī*, f.

boast, *phaṛā mārnīā*: *baṛīā gallā karnīā*: *shēkhī mārnī*.

boat, *kishtī*, f., *bēṛī*, f.: *bēṛā*, m. (esp. raft).

boatman, *mallāh*, m.: *mānjhī* (Hindu caste).

body, *pinḍā*, m.: *jussā*, m.: *wujūd*, m.: *jism*, m.: *badan*, m.: *sarīr*, *sharīr*, m.: one's form, outline, *but*, m.: *see* corpse, carcase.

(1) **boil**, n., *phōṛā*, m.: small, *phimhṇī*, f.: *gaṛ*, m.: in armpit, *kachrāḷī*, f.

(2) **boil**, v. tr., *kāṛhnā*, *khulāṇā*, *ubāḷṇā* (make bubble): (int. *kaṛhnā*. *khaulṇā*, *ubbaḷṇā*):

cook, *rinnhṇā* (pa. p. *riddhā*) (also stew : int. *rijjhṇā*).
(3) boiled, *kaṛheā hoeā*, *riddhā hoeā*.
(4) boiler, for heating water, *hamām*, m.
(5) boiling, *khauldā*.
bold, *see* brave, forward.
boldness, including forwardness, *jurat*, f. : *dalērī*, f.
bolt, n., *ciṭkhanī*, f. : screw-b., *kāblā*, m. : v., *ciṭkhanī mārnī* or *lāṇī* (int. *wajjṇī*, *laggṇī*).
bomb, *bamb*, m.
bond, *karār*, m. : *likhat paṛhī*, f. : *see* agreement, covenant.
bondage, *see* slavery, imprison.
bone, *haḍḍī*, f.
(1) book, *kitāb*, f. : *pōthī*, f. (esp. relig. H.) : note-b., copy-b., *kāpī*, f. : b.-language, *kitābī bōlī* : *see* account [f.
bookcase, (*kitābā wālī*) *almārī*,
bookseller, *kitābā wēccaṇwālā*, *kutub-farōsh* (U.).
(2) book, v., ticket, *ṭikaṭ laiṇā* : seat, *thā rakhāṇā* : b.-ing office, *ṭikṭā dā daftar* : b.-ing clerk, *ṭikṭā wālā bābū* : b. luggage, *asbāb tulāṇā* (have weighed), *buk karāṇā*
boot, *see* shoe.
booty, *luṭṭ dā māl*, m.
border, *see* boundary, edge, skirt.
bore, *mōrī kaḍḍhṇī* or *karnī* : *chēk kaḍḍhṇā* : (worry) *akāṇā*, (int. *akkṇā*) ; *sir khapāṇā* : *see* annoy.
borer, *see* auger.
born, be, *jammṇā*, *paidā h.* : b. (blind), *jamāhndrū* (*annhā*).
borrow, *udhār laiṇā* (money) *karz cukkṇā* (money) : *mang leauṇā* (gen.).
borrowed, *udhār*, *udhārā* (money) : *māngwā* (gen.).
both, *dowē* : *see* also.
bottle, *bōtal*, f. : small, *shīshī*, f.
bottom, of vessel, box, almirah, *thallā*, m. : *see* foot.
boundary, *hadd*, f. : narrow, bet. fields, *bannā*, m., *bannī*, f., *waṭṭ*, f., *see* path : b. pillar, *buttī*, f. ; bet. three villages, *tarhaddā*.
boundless, *bēant*, *bēbahā*.
(1) bow, for arrows, *kamān*, f. : b. and arrow, *tīr kamān*, f. : for pellets, *gulēl*, f. : *see* sling, pellet.
(2) bow, v., *matthā ṭēkṇā* (esp. relig.), *see* salute, stoop.
bowels, *āndrā*, f. pl.
(1) bowl, n., *pyālā*, m. : *bōl*, m. (K.).
(2) bowl, v., (cricket) *bāl dēṇā*.
box, *sandūk*, m. : *sandūkṛī*, f. : *bakas*, m. : *pēṭī*, f. (esp. wooden) : rough wooden, *khōkhā*, m. : steel, *taraṅk*, m. : very small, *ḍabbī*, f. : for measuring *kaṅkar*, lime, etc., large, *sandūkṛī*, f. : small, *ḍaggā*, m.
boy, *munḍā*, *kākkā*, *jātak* : *see* child, son.
boyishness, *munḍpunā*, m. : *munḍeā-* or *aṅāṇeā-wālī tabīat*, f.
bracelet, *cūṛī*, f. : *cūṛā*, m. : *waṅṅ*, f. : *gajrā*, m. : *kaṅṅaṇ*, m. : *gokhṛū*, m. : *parībān*, m. : *pauncī*, f., *juṭ*, m. A.
braces, *gālas*, f.
brackish, *kauṛā*, *khārā*.
brain, *bhējā*, m. : *magz*, m. : *damāg*, m. : (2nd and 3rd gen. of conceit) : *see* sense, intelligence, conceit, pride.
brake-van, *birk*, m. : *brēk*, m.

bran, *cōkar*, m. (wheat and gram) : *chāṇ*, m. : *see* straw.
branch, large, *ḍāhṇ*, m. : *ḍāhḷ*, m. : smaller, *ṭāhṇī*, f. : *ḍāhḷī*, f. : small switch, broken off, *chamak*, f. : shoot, *gullā*, m. : thorn b., *mōṛhā*, m. : *mōṛhī*, f. : *ḍhīṅghṛī*, f.
brand, *dāg*, (*lāṇā*) : morally *dhabbā*, (*lāṇā*) : int. *laggṇā*.
brandy, *brāṇḍī*, f.
brass, *pittal*, m. : b. worker, *ṭhaṭhyār*. [age.
brave, *bahādar*, *dalēr* : *see* cour-
bravo ! *sadke*, *balle balle*, *shābāse*, *shāhbā*, *bāī bāī*.
bray, of ass, *hīṅgṇā*.
bread, *rōṭī*, f. : made of maize, millet, *ḍhōḍḍā*, m. : *see* loaf, food.
breadth, *pēṭ*, m. : *cuṛāī*, f.
break, *bhannṇā* (int. *bhajjṇā*) : *tōṛnā*, *trōṛnā* (int. *ṭuṭṭnā*) : b. into bits, *ṭōṭe ṭōṭe k.* : b. against, *see* knock : b. open (box, etc.), *jandrā trōṛnā* : b. down (become ill) of well, cart, man, animal (not woman), *hanēkeā jāṇā*, M. 118. 32 : into house, *sannh mārnī* : b. fast, at right time, *rōzā kholhṇā* : at wrong time, *see* fast : b. in for ploughing, *hāḷī kaḍḍhṇā* (*nū̃*) : for burdens, *lādū kaḍḍhṇā* (*nū̃*) (int. of both *nikḷṇā*) : b. off habit, *ādat chaḍḍnī* (for someone else, *chuḍāṇī*).
breakfast, *hāzrī*, f. : early b., *chōṭī hāzrī*.
breast, *hikk*, f. : *chātī*, f. (U.).
breath, breathe, *sāh*, m. (*laiṇā*, also stop talking) : *dam laiṇā* : *see* rest : out of b. become, *happ jāṇā*, *sāh caṛhṇā* (*nū̃*).

bribe, *waḍḍhī*, f. : take b., *laiṇī*, *khāṇī* : give b., *dēṇī* : *rishwat*, f. : taker of b's *waḍḍhīkhōr*, *rishwatkhōr* (U.).
brick, *iṭṭ*, f. : well-baked, *pakkī* : half-baked, *pillī* : sun-dried, *kaccī* : broken bit, *rōṛā*, m. ; small, *rōṛī*, f. : b-powder, *surkhī*, f. : b-maker, *pathērā*, m. : b-making, *pathēr*, f. : b-layer, *rāj*, m. : *see* layer.
bride, use *kuṛī*, girl. A. [man.
bridegroom, *lāṛā*, m. : *see* best
bridge, *puḷ*, m. : make b., *puḷ bannhṇā* : (int. *bajjhṇā*).
bridle, *lagām*, f. (*cāṛhnī*).
brief, *mukhtsar*, *thoṛeā lafzā wicc*.
bright, *baṛī lō*, *baṛā cānaṇ* or *cānnā*, *baṛī rōshnī* : *see* shine : colour, *gūṛhā*, *shōkh*, *tēz*.
brim, *kandhā*, m. : of hat, *kannī*, f. : *see* edge.
bring, *leauṇā*, *laiāuṇā* : pa. p. *le-*, *lai-āndā* or *-āyā* : take w. one, *khaṛnā* : b. near of cattle to yoke, *ḍhōṇā* (int. *ḍhukkṇā*) : cause to be brought, *aṇwāṇā*.
brinjal, *see* egg-plant.
brink, *see* edge.
brittle, *ṭuṭṭaṇwāḷā* : *see* crisp.
broad, *cauṛā*, *caiṛā* : broadways, across, *cauṛe dā*.
broad-cloth, *banāt*, f.
broker, *dalāl*.
bronze, *kaīh*, f. [*nadī*, f.
brook, *nāḷā*, m. (wet or dry) :
broom, *jhāṛū*, m. : *bauhkar*, f. : *bahārī*, f. : *kharkṇā*, m. : *mānjā*, m. : *see* sweep.
broth, *shurūā*, m.
brother, *bhrā*, *bhāī* : full b., *sakkā bhrā* : step b., *matrēā bhrā* : wife's b., *sāḷā* : *sāḷā's*

wife, *sāḷihār*, *sāḷihāj*: sister's husband, *bhanūjā*: husband's elder b., *jēṭh* (*jēṭh's* wife, *jaṭhāṇī*): husband's younger b., *deōr* (*deōr's* wife, *darāṇī*): *jēṭh's* son, *jaṭhuttar*: husbands of two sisters are *sāṇḍhū* to each other: *see* sister.
brotherhood, *bilādrī*, f.
brown, *bhūslā*, *bhūrā*: *badāmī*, almond colour: *khākī*, dust-colour: *naswārī rang*, snuff colour.
brush, n., v., *burs*, *bursh* (*karnā*, *nū*): *see* sweep, broom.
bubble, *bulbuḷā*, m.
bubo, *phōṛā*, m.: *gilṭī*, f.: *phimhnī*, f.
bucket, *bāḷṭī*, f. (pail): leather b., *bōkkā*, m.: iron, *ḍōl*, m.
buckle, *bagsūā*, m.
bud (flower) *kalī*, f.: tiny shoot, *kōpal*, f.: *see* sprout, branch.
buffalo, *sandhā*, m.: *majjh*, *maīh*, f.: gen. *mehrū*, m.: b.-calf, *jhōṭṭā*: smaller, *kaṭṭā*: adj., *mājhā*.
bug, *khaṭmaḷ*, m., *caṛ*, f.
bugle, *bigal*, m. (*wajāṇā*, *wajjṇā*).
build, *banāṇā*: raise walls, *usārnā*, (int. *usrnā*).
building, *makān*, m.: large, *hawēlī*, f.: *amārat*, f. (U.).
bull, *ḍhaggā*, *balḍ*: for breeding, *sāhn*: *see* calf, ox.
bullet, *gōḷī*, f.
bullock, *see* bull, calf.
bundle, *gandhṛī*, f.: of corn, etc., *pūḷī*, f., *thabbā*, m., *bharī*, f., *panḍ*, f.
bunch, of flowers, grapes, keys, *gucchā*, m.
burden, *see* load, weight.
burdened, *bhār hēṭh dabbeā hoeā*.
burn (as fuel), *bāḷnā*, int. *baḷnā*: b. up, *sāṛnā*, int. *saṛnā*: *phūkṇā*: *see* firewood.
burning, n., *sāṛā*, m. (fire, also feeling mental or physical).
burrow, *see* hole.
burst, *pāṭṇā* (tr. *pāṛnā*): by crushing, squeezing, *phissṇā* (tr. *phehṇā*).
bury, *dabbṇā*: *dafn k.* (U.).
bush *jhāṛī*, f.
busy, be, *rujjhṇā* (pa. p. *ruddhā*, *rujjhā*): being b., n., *rujjh*, f: b., adj., *ruddhā hoeā*, *laggā hoeā*.
butcher, *kasāī*, fem. *kasaiṇ*.
but, conj. *par*: *see* only, except.
butt, v., *mārnā*, *sing mārnā*.
butter, *makkhan*, m.: *see* ghee.
butter-dish, *makkhanḍān*, m.
butterfly, *bāhmaṇ baccā*, m. A.
buttermilk, *lassī*, f. A.
button, *bīṛā*, m.: *baṭan*, m. (*mēḷnā*, *mārnā*, rarely *band k.*): unbutton, *bīṛā kholhṇā*: put on b., *bīṛā lāṇā*: *see* stud: b.-hole, *kāj*, m.
buy, *mull laiṇā*: *kharīdṇā* (U.): *see* purchases.
buyer, *gāhk*, *laiṇwāḷā*.
buzz, of bees, mosquitoes, etc., *ghankūr*, f., *shukāṭ*, f.
by (agent), use agent case, G. 8, 74: *koḷō*, G. 66, 90, 112: by himself, *see* alone: of himself, *see* spontaneously; one by one, *ikk ikk karke*: ten by ten, *das das karke*.
by and by, *see* afterwards.
byre, *kuṛh*, f.

C

cabbage, *gobhī*, f.: *band gobhī*: *ganḍh gobhī*.

cactus, flat, *chillar thōhr*, m.: round, *thōhr ḍanḍā*, m.

cage, *pinjrā*, m. [*gācī*, f.

cake, *kēk*, m. (K.): of soap,

calamity, *balā*, f.: *āfat*, f.: *biptā*, f.: *musībat*, f.: *ā<u>kh</u>ar* (*auṇī*).

calculate, *lēkhā lāṇā*: *hisāb karnā*: *kiās karn-ī*, *-ū*: *see* guess, approximately, count, estimate.

calf, *wacchā*, m.: bigger, *waihṛā*: *see* buffalo: calf of leg, *pinnī*, f.: *pinnī dī machlī*, f.

caligraphy, *<u>kh</u>att*, m.: *<u>kh</u>ush-<u>kh</u>attī*, f.: -ist, *<u>kh</u>ush nawīs*

call, *saddṇā*, *kuāṇā*, *bulāṇā*: *wāz*, or *awāz mārnī* (*nū*): *see* name, remember: c. out, *see* shout, scream, proclaim: pay a call, *miln jāṇā*: *mulākāt wāste jāṇā*: c. attendance, *hāzrī laiṇī* or *lāṇī*.

(1) calm, adj., of water, *khlōtā hoeā*: of person, neg of excited, or use calmly: *see* still, quiet.

(2) calm, v. tr., *phēr rāzī k.*, *ṭhanḍā k.*, *gussā ṭhanḍā* or *maṭṭhā karnā*: *see* peace, quiet, appease.

calmly, *hausle nāḷ*, *saihe nāḷ*, *saihj nāḷ*, *amn nāḷ*.

calumniate, *see* slander.

camel, *ūṭh*, fem. *uṭhṇī*, *ḍācī*, *sāhnnī*: young c., *bōttā*, m.

camp, *kampū*, m.: *see* tent.

camping ground, *paṛā*, m.

camphor, *kāfūr*, m.

can, *see* tin.

canal, *naihr*, f.: branch c., *sūā*, m.: channel made by farmers, *mohgā*, m.: *khāḷ*, m.: to make such, *khāḷnā*: c. bank, *paṭrī*, f.

cancel, order, *hukm band karnā*: name, *nā kaṭṭṇā*.

candidate, *umēdwār*, m.: in exam., *imtihān deṇwāḷā*.

candle, *mōmbattī*, f.

candle-stick, *battīdān*, m.

candour, *safāī*, *sāfdilī*, *sāf sāf ākhṇā*.

cane, *baint*, m. (*mārnā*, *nū*): *see* sugar-cane: be caned, *baint khāṇā*, *paiṇā*.

canister, *see* tin.

cannibal, *ādam<u>kh</u>ōr* (U.): *bandeā dā gō<u>sh</u>t khāṇwāḷā*.

cannon, *tōp*, f. (*calāṇī*, int. *calṇī*).

canopy, *see* awning.

canter, (horse) *poīā calṇā*.

cantonment, *chāoṇī*, f.

cap, *ṭōpī*, f.

capable, *laik*: *see* able.

capacious, *mōkḷā*.

capacity, *gunjaish*, f.: *samāī*, f.: *see* ability.

capital, *pūṅī*, f., *sarmāyā*, m., *rās*, m., *rupayye*, m. pl.: chief town, *dār ul <u>kh</u>alāfa*, m. (U.).

captive, in war, *asīr*: prisoner, *kaidī*: take c., *phaṛnā*, *kaid k.*

captivity, *kaid*, f.: *asīrī*, f. (U.).

caravan, *kāflā*, m., *kārawān*, m., *ṭollā* m., *ṭollī*, f.

carcase, *murdār*, m. (collective term): *lōth*, f.: *see* corpse.

(1) card, v., cotton, etc., *piññā*, *jhambhṇā*. A.

(2) card, n., post-c., *kāṭ*, m.: *<u>kh</u>att*, m.

cards, *tā<u>sh</u>*, m. (*khēḍṇā*).

cardamum, *lācī*, f.

care, *see* anxiety, look after, protect, like: take c., interj., *backe*, *<u>kh</u>abardār*, *sambhaḷke*. I don't care, *menū koī parwāh nehī*.

caretaker, *rakhwālā*, *rakhwāl*, *caukīdār*.
careless, *lāparwāh*, *bēparwāh*.
carelessness, *lā-* or *bē-parwāhī*, *gaflat*, f.
caress, *pyār dēṇā*; *see* fondle, kiss.
carpenter, *tarkhāṇ*: fem. *tarkhāṇī*.
carpet, *darī*, f.: rug, *galīcā*, m.
carriage, driving, *bagghī*, f.: *tamṭam*, f.: (tonga) *ṭāṅgā*, m.: phaeton, *fiṭn*, f.: (railway) *gaḍḍī*, f. (also train): *see* class: ladies only, women only, *zanānī gaḍḍī*: servants, *sarwanṭī*, f.: act or price of carrying, *see* cartage.
carrion, *murdār*, m. (including animal dead, not killed).
carrot, *gājar*, f.
carry, *cukkke* or *uṭhāke khaṛnā* or *laijāṇā*: c. bricks, earth, *ḍhōṇā*: be carried, *hūṇṭe* or *hūhṇṭe laiṇe* (M. 122. 34: tr. *dēṇe*), *see* ride, swing, back: c. on work, *kamm ṭōrnā* or *calāṇā* (int. *ṭurnā*, *calṇā*).
cart, for two bullocks, *gaḍḍā*, m.: for one bullock, handcart, wheel-barrow, *reṛhī*, f.
cartage, act or price, *ḍhuāī*, f.
cartridge, *kārtūs*, m.
carve, *ghaṛnā*.
case, *see* cover: lawcase, *mukadmā*, m.: bring c. ag., *kise te arzī pāṇī* or *dāhwā karnā* or *nālish karnī*: in this c., *es hālat* or *sūrat wicc*: in no c., *cāre banne* w. neg., or *kise sūrat wicc* and neg.: *see* lose.
cash, *nakad*, m.; v., *ṭōṛnā*. A.
cask, *pīpā*, m.
cast, *see* throw, lots.
caste, *zāt*, f.: *gōt*, f. (division of c.): low, *nīwī*: high, *uccī*: put out of c., *chēkṇā*, *hukkā pāṇī band k.* (*dā*).
castor-oil plant, *harnōḷā*, m.
cat, *billā*, fem. *billī*.
cataract (in eye) *mōtīā*, m. A.
catarrh, *sardī*, f.: *zukām*, m.
catastrophe, *see* calamity, accident.
catch, *phaṛnā*, *phagaṛnā*: ball, etc., *jhōpṇā*, *jhaṛapṇā*: *see* seize: allow oneself to be caught, *phaṛā dēṇā*, *phaṛāī dēṇī*: G. 74, 75. A.
catch, n., in door, window, *huḍhkā*, m., *billī*, f.
catechumen, *mutlāshī*, m.
caterpillar, *suṇḍī*, f.: *bhaṅgū kuttā*, m., *bhaggū kuttā*.
cattle (horned), *māl*, m.: *ḍaṅgar*, m.: *caukhar*, m.
cauliflower, *phull gobhī*, f.
(1) cause, n., *wajhā*, f. (reason): *sbabb*, m.: *see* reason, purpose: causeless, *see* reason, useless.
(2) cause, v., use causal vv. w. direct acc. or *kolō* of agent: G. 41-3, 109, 110: *see* force.
caution, *hōsh*, f., *hushyārī*, f. *khabardārī*, f.
cautiously, words for caution w. *nāl*: *samjhke*.
cavalry, *risālā*, m.
cave, *khundhar*, f.: *gār*, f. (U.).
ceaselessly, *see* continuously.
cedar, *diār*, m.: *biāṛ*, m.
ceiling, *chatt*, m.: thin planks, *pakkhar*, m.
celebrated, *see* famous: be c., of fair, festival, *laggṇā*, *manneā jāṇā*.
cement, *see* mortar, glue.
cemetery, *see* graveyard.

centre, *markaz*, m. (U.): adj., *wiclā*, *wishkārlā*: *see* middle.
ceremony, *rīt*, f.: *rasm*, f.
certain, *pakkā*, *yakīnī*: a. c. man, *fulāṇā*.
certainly, *bĕshakk*, *nishang*, *zarūr*, *lājarūr*; *hōr kī?* *te hōr?* *hā̃ te*.
certainty, *yakīn*, m.
certificate, *saṭifkaṭ*, m.; *sanad*, f.
certify, *zimewār* or *zimmewār h.*, *guāhī dēṇī*, *tsallī dēṇī*.
chafe, *see* rub, annoy, grief: be chafed (of skin, etc.) *ucchṇā*, *ambṇā*.
chaff, of rice, barley, etc., *phakk*, f.: *see* bran: chopped straw from wheat, *tūṛī*, f., *ciṭṭā bhoh*: from gram, etc., *bhoh*, m., *missā bhoh*. A.
chain, *sangaḷ*, m.: smaller, *sangḷī*, f.: very small, *zanjīrī*, f., *e.g.* watch-c. A.
chair, *kursī*, *khursī*, f.: low, all wood, *caukī*, f.: of reeds, *mūṛhā*, m.: easy c., *arām kursī*, f.: *see* stool, seat.
chalk, *cāk*, m., *khaṛīā miṭṭī*, f.
chamber, *see* room: c. pot, *pāṭ*, m.
champ (horse) *cabakṇā*.
chance, *sbabb*, m.: by c., *sbabb nāḷ*, *ēwē*, *aīwē*, *kār e kazā*.
(1) change, *tabdīlī*, f.: *see* difference: for rupee, etc., *bhanghaṛ*, m., *bhān*, m., but *see* rupee: whole unchanged rupee, *baddhā rupayyā*.
(2) change, v., *badalnā*: c. person, animal, regiment for other, *badlī karnī* (int. *hōṇī*): *see* exchange: c. several things, *adal badal k.*: c. notes, rupees, *tōṛnā*: get them changed *tuṛānā* (int. *tuṭṭṇā*): give back, *partāṇā*: c. opinions, *phir jāṇā*, *dalīl badalnī*.
changeable, *kacce khyāl dā*, *dudilā*: *see* vacillate.
channel, *nāḷā*, m.: small, *nālī*, f.: *see* stream, drain, brook.
chap, (hands, feet) *biāī pāṭnī* [(*dī*).
chapter, *bāb*, *m*.
character, no good word, use adj. describing person, or word for disposition, temperament: of good moral c., *nēkcalan*: of bad, *badcalan*: *see* good: life and actions. *cāl calan*, m.
characteristic, *sift*, f.
charcoal, *koḷā*, m.: *koḷe*, m. pl.: *lakkaṛ de koḷe*, m. pl.: *see* coal: small broken bits, *kērī*, f.
charge, give into c., *de hawāle k.*: *de pēṭe pāṇā*: give over c., *cāraj d.*: take over c., *cāraj laiṇā*: c. price, *lāṇā* (int. *laggṇā*): M. 122. 27: *see* cost.
charity, *see* alms.
charm, please, *baṛā khush k.*: bewitch, *jādū k.* or *pāṇā* (*utte*), *mantar paṛhnā* (*utte*): *see* amuse, delight.
charmer, *see* magician, snake.
chase, *see* pursue, hunt.
chaste, *pāk*.
chatter, foolishly, *yabbhā̃ mārnīā̃*, *yabbhṇā*, *bakṇā*, *cilkṇā*: of birds, *cī cī karnī*: of teeth, *dandoṛikke wajjṇe* (*de*): *see* talkative.
cheap, *sastā*, *suwallā*.
cheat, *rupayye* or *paise mārne*, M. 123, 46: *see* deceit, deceive.
check, *see* hinder, stop, compare, examine.

cheek, *gallh*, f.
(1) cheer, *see* amuse, comfort.
(2) cheers, applause, *cirs dēṇe*: *see* clap.
cheerful, *khush*.
cheese, *panīr*, m.
cheque, *cikk*, m.: *see* bill.
cherish, *see* support.
chess, *shatranj*, m. (*khēḍṇā*).
chest, (body), *hikk*, f.: *chātī*, f. (U.): of drawers, *almārī*, f.: *see* drawer, box.
chew, grain, etc., *cabbṇā*: suck, *cūpṇā*.
chick, *see* chikk.
chicken, *cūccā*, m.: for table, *see* fowl.
chief, chieftain, *sardār*, fem *sardārnī*.
chikk, hanging screen, *cikk*, f.: *cikh*, f.
child, *baccā*, m., *bāl*, m.: *añāṇā*, m.: *bacṛā*, m.: European, *bāwā*. fem. *bāwī*: plur., *dhī puttar*, m.: *dhīā puttar*, m. pl.: *muṇḍe kuṛīā*, m. pl.: *see* descendants.
childish *muṇḍeāwāḷā*, *añāṇeāwāḷā*.
childishness, *see* boyishness.
childless, *dhī puttar nehī*: *autrā* or *autrā nikhattrā* is mild abuse or self pity.
chimney, of lamp, *cimnī*, f.: for fire, *dhūkash*, m.: for sugarcane furnace, *lūhmbā*, m.: *see* funnel.
chimneypiece, *parchattī*, f.
chin, *ṭhōḍḍī*, f.
china (ware), *cīnī*, f. (*de bhāṇḍe* or *bartan*). [m.
chip, of wood, *sakk*, m. *sakṛā*,
chocolate, *caklēṭ*, f.: *see* cocoa.
choice, use *marzī*, f. (will): *see* select.
choke (food going wrong way), *athrū auṇā* (*nū*): from disease, *galghōṭū hōṇā*: v. tr., *see* smother, strangle, hang: by pressure, *saṅgh ghuṭṭṇā*.
cholera, *haizā*, m. (gen. merely severe vomiting).
choose, *see* select.
(1) chop, n., (meat) *cāp*. f. (K.).
(2) chop, v. tr., wood, *lakkaṛ dalṇi*: cut long piece into thick bits, *mōche pāṇe*: into long thin bits, *phāṅgā karnīā*.
chopper, farmer's, *ṭōkkā*, m.: kitchen, *cāpaṛ*, m. (K.).
Christ, *Masīh*.
Christian, *Isāī*, *As-hāī*, fem. *Isain*, *As-hain*.
Christmas Day, *waḍḍā din*.
chudder, *see* veil.
church; building, *girjā*. m: congregation, *jamāt*, f.: many congregations, *kalīsyā*, f.
chutney, *caṭnī*, f.
cinnamon, *dālcīnī*, f.
circle, *ghērā*, m., *dāirā*, m. (educ.) [round.
circuit, *cakkar*, m.: *see* tour,
circuitous, use *waḷā paiṇā*: *see* round.
circular, *gōl*: *see* roundness.
circumcise, *suntī bahāṇā* (*nū*): be c., *suntī baihṇā*.
circulate, (money), *calṇā* (tr. *calāṇā*): *see* pass: (story) *dhummṇā* (tr. *dhumāṇā*).
circumstance, *gall*, f.: *wākiā*, m.: *hāl*, m.: *hāl hakīkat*, f.: in no c.: *see* case.
cistern, *hauz*, m.: *hauzī*, f.: (also place for bath in bathroom).
citizen, *shaihrīā*, *shaihrī*, *shaihrdār* (all city-dweller): *see* subject.

citron, *khattā*, m.
city, *shaihr*, m.
civil, not military, *mulkhī*: not criminal, *duānī*: *see* polite.
civilised *muhazzab* (U.).
claim, *dāhwā*, m. (*k.*).
claimant, *mudaī*, m. (leg.).
clandestine, *see* secret.
clap hands, *māhngā mārnā* (approval, applause): *taurī mārnī* (derision).
class, in school, *jamāt*, f.: of people, railway, *darjā*, m: first c., *paihlā darjā*, *fast klās* (*see* excellent); second c., *dujjā darjā*, *sikand klās*, *sěkand klās*, m.: intermediate, *deodhā darjā*, *intar*, m.: third c., *trījjā* or *tīsrā darjā*, *thadd klās*, m.
claw, *naūh*, m.: whole foot, *panjā*, m.
clay, *mittī*, f.: *see* mud.
clean, *sāf*, *suthrā*: ceremonially, *see* holy: *see* scrub, wash, pure.
cleanliness, *safāī*, f.: *see* purity.
clear (water, sentence, meaning) *sāf*: (water) *nitreā hoeā*: v., water, meaning, etc., *natārnā* (int. *nitrnā*): *see* evident, acquit: c. up (weather), *see* weather; (difficulty, *see* solve: c. away table), *see* table.
clerk, *munshī*, *bābū*, *klārak*.
clever, *see* able, intelligent: *hushyār*, *kārīgar*, *ustād*, *siānā*: (bad sense) *calāk*, *hikmatī*, *catur*.
cleverness, *hushyārī*, f.: *hikmat*, f.: *kārīgarī*, f.: *ustādī*, f.: bad sense, *calākī*, f., *catrāī*, f.: *see* intelligence, ability.
climate, *hawā*, f.: *āb hawā*, f.
climb, *caṛhnā* (*utte*): climbing plant, *wěl*, f.: *walī*, f.
cling to, *cambaṛnā* (*nū*).
clip (w. scissors) *katrnā* *see* prune.
clique, *dhaṛā*, m.: *see* party.
cloak, *cogā*, m.: *see* coat: v., *paṛdā pānā* (*utte*): *see* screen.
clock, *ghaṛī*, f.: *see* o'clock.
clockmaker, *ghaṛīsāz*, m.
clod, *dhehm*, f., *dhīhm*, f.
clogged, dirty, *jaddā*.
(1) close, v. tr., door, window: *phērnā*, *dhoṇā*, *bhīṛnā*: *see* shut: w. closed doors, *wajjī būhī*, G. 78: *see* shut.
(2) close, adj., *see* near.
cloth, *kapṛā*, m.: *see* sheet, skirt, shawl, etc.: c.-merchant, *bazāz*: trade of selling c., *bazāzī*, f.
clothe, oneself, *kapṛe pāṇe*: another, *kapṛe pāṇe* (*nū*): make him put on clothes, *kapṛe puāṇe*: in gen. clothe, *kapṛe dēṇe*.
clothes, *kapṛe*, m. pl.
cloud, *baddal*, m.: clouds all over, *jhaṛ*, m., *baddal ghuleā hoeā e*: c-less, *see* weather.
clove, *laung*, f.
clown, *see* jester.
club (building) *kalafghar*, m.: wooden, *see* stick.
clue, *patā*, m.: *see* discover.
clumsy, *see* awkward.
cluster, *see* bunch.
coach-house, *bagghī-khānā*, m.
coagulate, *jammṇā* (tr. *jamāṇā*).
coal, *patthar dā kōlā*: *see* charcoal: live coal, *bhakheā hoeā kolā*, m.: small broken bits, *kērī*, f.
coarse, not fine, *mōtā*.
coast, *samundar dā kandhā* or *dandā*, m.

coat, *kōṭ*, m.: servant's double breasted, *aṅgā*, m.: *see* overcoat, waterproof. [*cāṇā*.

coax, *khush karke manāṇā*: *par-*

cob of maize, *challī*, f.: without grain, *tukkā*, m.

cobbler, *mōcī*, fem. *mōcaṇ*.

cobweb, *jāḷā*, m.: single thread, *tār*, f., *cinākh*, m.

cock (bird) *kukkaṛ*, m.: of gun, *ghōṛā*, m.

cocoa, *kōkō*, f.: *see* chocolate.

cocoanut, whole, *nanyēr*, m.: half of kernel, *ṭhūṭhī*, f.: *khōppā*, m.: kernel in gen., *garī*, f. (cf. *girī*, f., kernel of other fruit, pith).

coffee, *kāfī*, f.: -pot, *kāfīdān*, m.

coffin, *sandūk*, m.: *see* shroud.

coin, no word, use rupee, pice, etc., good, *kharā*: bad, *khōṭā*.

coincide, *raḷṇā*, *miḷṇā*.

cold, n., *pāḷā*, m.: *sardī*, f.: *sīt*, f.: *ṭhanḍ*, f.: feel cold, *pāḷā*, etc., w. *laggṇā*, G. 108: hands, feet feel c., *hatth*, *pair ṭharne*: air get c., *pāḷā uttō paiṇā*: catch c., *sardī laggṇī*, *zukām hōṇā* or *laggṇā*.

colic (*dhiddh wicc*) *waṭṭ*, m.

collar, *kālar*, m.

collect, *kaṭṭhā k.*, *jamā k.*: money, *ugrāhṇā* (int. *ugharnā*).

college, *kālij*, m.

coll-ide, -ision, *ṭakkar khāṇī*, *mērī ṭakkar wajjī* (*nāḷ*); tr. *mērī ṭakkar mārī* (*nāḷ*): *see* knock.

colloquial, *ām bōl cāl dī*.

colonel, *karnail*.

colonise, *see* people (2).

colony (canal), simply *naihr*, f.: in the c., *naihr te*.

colour, *raṅg*, m.: dark, *see* dark in A.: *see* light, fast, bright: faint, *maddham*.

coloured, *raṅgdār*, *raṅgwāḷā*: many-c., *raṅg baraṅgī*.

colt, *wachērā*, m.

comb, *kaṅghī*, f.: of cock, *kalgī*, f., *pagg*, f.

come, *auṇā* (pa. p. *āeā*): c. in, *see* enter: c. out, *nikḷ auṇā*; of sun fr. clouds, *dhupp nikḷṇī*; of stain, *see* delete.

comet, *bōdī āḷā tārā*, m.

comfort, *tsall-ī* or *-ā dēṇī nū*: be c.-ed., *tsallī hōṇī* (*nū*): *see* ease, condole, soothe.

Comforter (Holy Spirit), *Tsallī Dēṇwāḷā*.

command, *hukm* m. (*d.*): unwarrantably, *hukm cāṛhnā*.

commander-in-chief, *jaṅgī lāṭ*.

commemoration, *yādgārī*, f.

commence-, -ment, *see* beginning.

commend, *see* recommend, praise.

commentary, *tafsīr*, f.

commerce, *see* trade, intercourse.

commercial, *tajārtī*: c. usage, *sudāgrī* or *bazār dā dastūr*.

commission (discount, percentage) *dastūrī*, f.: (written authority), *sanad*, f.; *see* order: seller on c., *āhṛtī*, *āhṛtalī*: his c. is *āhṛtal*, f.: (a committee) *kamēṭī*, f.

committee (of all kinds, relig. and secular) *kamēṭī*, f.: c-meeting, *kamēṭī*, f.

common, *ām*, *mamūlī*; *see* much: shared by others, *sāñjhā*: c. village land, *shāmlāṭ*, f.: c. people, *ām lōk*, *kamīne lōk* (low), *see* everyone, people.

commonly, *aksar*.
commotion, *see* disturbance.
communication, *see* intercourse, information.
communion, *see* intercourse: Holy C., *Ashū Rabānī*, f.: celebrate H. C., *karnī*. take, *lainī*.
companion, *sāthī*, *jōṛīdār*, *mēre nāḷ dā*: bet. men, *yār*: bet. women, *sahēlī*, f.: *see* partner, equal.
company, of people, *katth*, m.: *ṭōllā*, m., *ṭōllī*, f.: *jatthā*, m.: *taraṇḍī*, f.: *taraṇḍā*, m.: *see* assembly, congregation: business c., *kaumpanī*, f.: good or bad c., *baihṇī*, f.: M. 127. 3: G. 121.
compare, *raḷāṇā*, *miḷāṇā*, *mukāblā karnā*: c. weights, size, etc., *hāṛnā*: comparison of size, cost, etc., *see* time, G. 23: compared w., *ohde mukāble wicc*.
compass, *kutabnumā*, m.
compassion, *see* pity.
compassionate *raihm-dil*, *tars karnwāḷā*: God, *rahīm*.
compatriot, *see* fellow-countryman.
compel, *see* force, cause.
compensation, *harjānnā*, m.: *iwzānnā*, m.: in c. for, *ohde*, *badle*: *see* loss, damage in A.
compet-e, -ition, *see* emulate.
competent, *laik*, *samajhdār*, *khabardār*: *see* able, clever.
complain-, -t, *shikait*, f. (*k.*, *dī*): *faryād*, f. (*k.*, *dī*): leg. *nālish*, f. (*k.*, *utte*).
complainant, *see* plaintiff.
complete, *pūrā*, *mukammal*: *see* finish.
complex: *see* intricate.
complexion, *rang*, m.

complication, *see* intricate, entangle.
compliment, *see* praise: present my compliments, *mēre wallō salām ākhṇā* or *hatth bannhṇā*.
comply, *see* agree, assent.
composed of, *dā baneā hoeā*.
compromise, leg., *rāzīnāmā*, m.
compulsion, *see* force.
compulsory, subject in exam., *lāzmī*.
comput-ation, -e, *see* calculate, count.
comrade, *see* companion, friend.
conceal, *see* hide.
conceit, *baṛī mizāj*, f.: *baṛā damāg*, m.: *see* pride, sense.
concentrate, *see* attend.
concerning, *dī bābat*, *de bāre wicc*.
concession, *riait*, f.: adj. *riaitī*.
conciliate, *razī k.*, *manāṇā*.
concise, *see* brief.
conclude, draw conclusion, *natījā kaḍḍhṇā*: *see* settle, finish.
concussion, *ṭakkar*, f.: *see* collide.
condemn, *mujrim k.*, *baṇāṇā*: be c., *mujrim h.*, *jurm sābit hōṇā*: *see* guilt.
condemnation, *sazā dā hukm*, m.
condition, *hāl*, m.: *hālat*, f.: *hāl hakīkat*, f.: *hawāl* m. (often story): make c., *eh shart e*: on c. that, *es shart te paī*.
conditional, *shartī*.
condole, (go to), *mukāṇī jāṇā*: *see* comfort, mourn-, -ers, -ing, sympathise.
conduct, *see* character, lead.
confectioner, *halwāī*, fem. *halwaiṇ*: *mithāī-wāḷā*.

confederate, *see* partner.
conference (meeting) *kamēṭī*, f.: (consultation) *salāh mashwarā*, m.
confess, *mannṇā*: c. under torture, *bakṇā* (tr. *bakāṇā*): force to c., without torture, *dhakke nal* or *zōre manāṇā*.
confidant, *bhēṭī*, m., fem. *bhēṭan*.
confide, *wasāh karnā* (*dā*): *wasāh hōṇā* (*menū̃ ohdā*): *see* trust.
confidence, *wasāh*, m.: lack of c., *bēwasāhī*, f.
confidently (speak), *dāhwe nāḷ*.
confirm, *pakkā k.*: *see* ratify.
confiscate, *ghar kurk* (*k.*, *h.*), house confiscated: *ghar dī kurkī* (*k.*, *h.*), furniture, etc., c-ed.
conflicting, *āpe wicc nehī̃ raḷde*.
confront, *mū̃h te ākhṇā*: *see* face.
confuse, things, *rauḷā mārnā*: *gaṛbaṛī pāṇī*: persons, *ghabrāṇā*, *ghabrā chaḍḍṇā* (int. *ghābbarnā*, *ṭhiṭhambarnā*): *see* perplex.
confusion, *gaṛbaṛī* f.: mistake, *ṭapḷā*, m.: *see* disorder.
confute, *jhūṭhā sābit k.*
congeal, int. *jammṇā*: tr. *jamāṇā*.
congratulate, *mubārakbādī dēṇī*: *see* bravo.
congregation, *jamāt*, f. (either audience or settled c.).
conjecture, *see* guess, calculate, estimate, approximately.
conjectural, *kiāsī*.
conjure, adjure, *saū̃h duāṇī* (*nū̃*).
conjurer, *madārī*, fem. *madāran*.
connection, *tallak*, m.: *wāstā*, m. (both *menū̃ ohde nāḷ*): *see* relative, relationship.
conquer, *jittṇā*, *fatā-karnā* (*fatā* used alone is fem.): *see* possess, defeat.
conscience, *dil*, m.
conscious, *hōsh wicc*: *see* aware, remember.
consciousness, *hōsh*, f. (also sense).
consecrate, *Khudā de hawāle k.*, *makhsūs k.* (U.) *bilkull Khudā dā samjhṇā*: give in charity, *Khudā de nā dēṇā*.
consecutive, *suāhrā*, or use *nā chaḍḍṇā*. [assent.
(1) consent, v., *see* agree, assent.
(2) consent, n., *razāmandī*, f.: *manzūrī*, f.: *marzī*, f.: *razā* f.: w. c. of all, *sāreā̃ dī razā* or *marzī nāḷ*.
consequence *natījā*, m.: of no c., *koī gall nehī̃*, *see* matter: *see* useless, worthless.
consider, *sōcṇā*, *gaur karnā*.
consideration, *sōc*, f.: *gaur*, m.: *dhiān*, m.: out of c. for, *ohdā lihāz karke*: *see* concession, esteem, partiality, deference.
considering, conj., *see* since.
consist, *see* composed.
console, *see* comfort, condole.
conspicuous, *jehṛā sāf disse*, etc.: *see* visible.
conspire, *de khalāf gall pakāṇī* (int. *pakkṇī*).
constant, *see* faithful, resolute, continuous, repeatedly.
consternation, *harānī*, f.: *see* astonish-, -ishment.
constipation, *kabzī*, f.: the pain and straining, *maroṛā*, m.
consult, *salāh karnī* (*nāḷ*): *mashwarā karnā* (*nāḷ*): *rā pucchṇī* (*dī*).

consum-e, -ption, *kharc karnā* (int. *h.*) : *see* waste, phthisis.
contagious disease, *lagganwālī bimārī*, f.
contain, be contained, *aunā* (come) : *see* room.
contaminate, *see* defile, unclean. [sider.
contemplate, *see* think, con-
contemplation (relig.) *dhiān*, m.
contempt, *hikārat*, f. : *see* despise, scorn.
contemptible, *kamīnā*, *burā*.
contend, *see* argue, fight.
content, *rāzī*, *khush*.
contentious, *see* argumentative, quarrelsome.
contents, *jehṛā wicc e* : (of letter, book) *mazmūn*, m.
continual-, -ly, *see* always, repeatedly, daily.
continue, *raihṇā* : c. throwing, *sattdā rehā*, *sattī geā* : G. 68.
continuously, *barābar* : *see* continual. [*see* settle.
(1) contract, *ṭhēkā*, m.(*d.*, *laiṇā*) :
(2) contract, v., *see* shrink.
contractor, *ṭhēkedār-*, fem. *-nī*.
contradict, *jhūṭheā k.* : *gall mōṛnī*.
contrary, *de khalāf*, *de barkhalāf*, *de ulṭ* : *see* opposite : on the c., *sagō*, *sagō*.
contrast, *fark*, m. : *see* compare.
contribution, *madad*, *madat*, f. : *rupayye*, m. pl. : *candā*, m.
contriv-e, -ance, *see* arrange : c. w. difficulty : *taradad*, or *taraddad*, m. (*k.*), *taragas*, m. (*k.*).
control, *kābū*, m. : *ikhtiār*, m. : *wass*, m. : *hatth*, m (all w. *wicc rakkhṇā* or *h.*) : self-c., *hauslā* : *see* patience.
controversy, *see* argu-e, -mentative, quarrel-, -some.

convalescent, *kujjh wall*, *wall hōṇ lagā e*.
convene, *karāṇā*, *jamā k.* (both w. word for meeting as object).
convenien-ce -t, -tly, *see* ease, inconvenience: use *je taklīf nā hōwe*, *lokā wāste eh welā ṭhīk e*, etc., *see* inconvenience.
conversational, *bōl cāl dā*.
convers-e, -ation, *gall katth*, f. : *gallā katthā*, f. pl. (*k.*) : *carcā* f m. (*k.*) : *bāt cīt*, f. (*k.*) : *gallā*, f. pl. (*k.*).
conversion (rel.) *dil dā badalnā*, *nawē sireō jammṇā*, *dil dī tabdīlī*.
(1) convert, v. (make) *banāṇā* : to Christianity, etc., *Isāī k.* (often used of baptism) : be converted, *see* conversion.
(2) convert, n., *Isāī*, *Musalmān*, *Āryā*, etc., *ho geā*.
convey, *see* carry.
conveyance, *see* carriage, cart.
(1) convict, *kusūr*, m. : *gallī*, f. (etc. all w. *sābit k.*) : *see* condemn, convince.
(2) convict, n., *kaid-ī*, fem. *-aṇ*.
convince, *kail k.*, *manāṇā*, *yakīn karāṇā*. [*lāngrī*.
(1) cook, n., *khānsāmā*, *bāorcī*,
(2) cook, v., *pakāṇā* (int. *pakkṇā*) : roast, *bhunnṇā* (int. *bhujjṇā*) : bread, *pakāṇā*, *lāṇā*, M. 121. 10 (int. *laggṇā*.) A. : c. in pot, *rinnhṇā* (pa. p. *riddhā*, int. *rijjhṇā*) : put on pot, put on to c., *cāṛhṇā* (int. *caṛhṇā*) : M. 118. 23, 26 : ready cooked, *pakkā pakāeā*.
cool, *see* cold : nice and cool (wind, water, etc.) *ṭhaṇḍā ṭhaṇḍā*.
coolie, *kulī*, *mazdūr*.

co-operate, *nāḷ raḷke kamm k.*
copper, *trāmmā*, m.
coppersmith, *ṭhaṭhiār*
copse, few trees, *jhaṅghī*, f.
copy, n., *nakl*, f. : sample, *namūnā*, m. : (book), *kāpī*, f. : v., *nakl k.* : boy at school, *nakl mārnī* : *see* imitate.
copyist, *kātib*, *naklnawīs*.
cord, of leather, *waddhrī*, f. : *see* string, rope.
cordial-, -ity, use love, friendship.
coriander, *dhanīā*, m.
cork, *ḍaṭṭ*, m. (any stopper, plug) : *kāg*, f. : of maize-cob, *tukkā*, m.
corkscrew, *pēckass*, m.
(1) corn, on toe, etc., *caṇḍī*, f : on sole, *bhaurī*, f. [wheat.
(2) corn, *see* grain, maize, oats,
corner, of room, box (outside or in), *nukkar*, f. : *guṭṭh*, f. : four -ed, *caunukrā*, *cauguṭṭhā* : c.-dish, *ḍōṅghā*, m.
coronation, *tājpōshī*, f. : of raja, *gaddī te bahāṇā* (int. *baihṇā*).
corpse, *lōth* f. : *murdā* (dead person) : *see* carcase.
corpulent, *mōṭā* jocular, *ḍhiḍḍhū*, *ḍhiḍḍhaḷ*.
correct, *ṭhīk* (*k.*) : *durust* (*k.*) : c. character, *sudhārnā* : *see* rebuke, reprimand, improve.
correspond, *raḷṇā*, *milṇā* : (write letters) *ikk dujje nū̃ ciṭṭhīā̃ likhṇīā̃* : *khaṭṭ kitābat karnī* (U.).
corrupt, v. tr., *wigāṛnā*, *kharāb k.* (int. *wigaṛnā*, *kharāb h.*) : adj., *wigṛeā hoeā* : *see* bad, bribe.
cost, n., *mull*, m. : *kīmat*, f. : costs (leg.) *kharcā*, m., *kharc*, m. : v., how much c. ? *kinnā mull e*, *kinnā laggā*, *kinne tō̃ āeā* : *see* spend, expense.
costly, *baṛe mull dā*, *kīmatī* : *maihṅgā* (dear). [hut.
cottage, *nikkī kōṭhī*, f : *see*
cotton, growing, *kapāh*, f., *phuṭṭī*, f : wool, *rū̃*, m. : c.-seeding machine, *welṇī*, f. : c.- seed, *waṛēwā*, m.
couch, *see* sofa.
cough, n., *khaṅgh*, f. : v., *khaṅghṇā*, *khaṅgh auṇī* (*nū̃*) : severe c. and sneezing, *dhrañṇā*, *dhrāsṇā*.
council, *kamēṭī*, f. : *kaunsal*, f.
count, *giṇṇā*, *gintrī karnī* : *see* calculate.
countenance, *see* face.
counteract, *see* hinder.
counterfeit, *baṇāwaṭī*, *naklī* : forged, *jāhlī* : (coin) *khōṭā*.
countermand, *see* cancel.
countless, *see* innumerable.
country, *mulkh*, *muḷkh*, m. : *dēs*, m. : native c., *watan*, m. : in c. (not town) *piṇḍā̃ wicc* : adj., not foreign, *dēsī*.
countryman (fellow), *mērā watnī*, *mēre dēs* or *mulkh dā*.
couple, *jōṛā*, m. : *jōṛī*, f.
courage, *bahādrī*, f. : *dalērī*, f., *see* boldness : patient c., *himmat*, f., *hauslā*, m.
courageous, *see* brave : patiently c., *himmatwāḷā*, *hauslewāḷā*.
course, *see* method, arrangement, way, path : of c., *hōr kī*, *bēshakk*, *nishaṅg*, *hā̃ te*. G. 94 : of c. (concessive), *hā̃*.
court, of law, *kacaihrī*, f. : official, royal, raja's darbar, *darbār* m. : person w. right to sit in darbar, *darbārī* : court dress, *darbārī kapṛe*.

courteous, no real word, use *ashrāf*, or kind, good: *see* polite.
courtesy, *see* favour, kindness.
courtier, *see* court.
courtyard, *waḷgan*, m.: *walgaṇ*, m.: *wehṛā* m.
cousin, use brother: on father's side, *cācce bābbeõ bhrā*: mother's, *māmmeõ bhrā*, etc.
covenant, *kaul karār*, m.: *aihd*, m.: *shṭāmp*, m.: *rajisṭrī*, f.: *see* agreement, bond.
(1) **cover**, v. *kajjṇā*, *ḍhakkṇā*: *see* hide, screen.
(2) **cover**, n. (also lid) *ḍhakkaṇ*, m.: *ḍhakknā*, m.: for earthen pots, *capṇī*, f., *chūṇī*, f., *chūṇā*, m.: of dried earth, *cāppaṛ*, m.: for umbrella, hat, pillow, *uchāṛ*, m.
coverlet, *see* quilt.
covet-, **-ousness**, *lālac*, m. (*k.*): *tamā*, m. (*k.*): *see* desire, greed.
covetous, *lālcī*.
cow, *gā̃*: adj., *gōkā*: -dung, *gohā*, m. [*wāḷā*.
coward, *ḍarākaḷ*, *ḍarū*, *ḍarn-*
cowherd, *chēṛū*, *wāggī*.
cowhouse, *kuṛh*, f.
coxcomb, *see* fop.
crack, n., *trēṛ*, f.: v., *trēṛ paiṇī* (*nū̃*): of glass, *tiṛakṇā*: china, *līk paiṇī*: wood, *kaṛkṇā*: (split, *pāṭṇā*, tr. *pāṛnā*).
cradle, *paṅghūṛā*, m.
craft, *see* cleverness, deceit, profession
cram, *tunnṇā*.
(1) **cramp**, get, *bakhōṛ paiṇā*: *nāṛ caṛhnī*.
(2) **cramped** (no room), *sauṛā*, *taṅg*, *bhīṛā*.

crash, *ḍiggaṇ*, etc. *dā khṛāk*.
crawl: creeping things, use *ḍhiḍḍh parne ṭurnā*: child, *riṛhnā*: go very slowly, *jū̃ dī ṭōr calṇā*: *see* creep.
crazy, *see* mad.
creak, *cī cī karnī*, *cīkṇā*: *see* squeak.
cream, *malāī*, f.
crease, *bhann*, f. (*paiṇī*): *see* fold.
create, *paidā k.*
creation, *khalkat* f.: *makhlūk*.
Creator, *Paidā karnwāḷā*, *Khālik*: *see* God.
credible, *mannanwāḷī gall*.
credit, *see* belief, trust: on c., *udhār*, *see* borrow, debt.
creditor, *laiṇdār*, or use *laiṇā*.
credits, *laihṇā*, m.
credulous, *shtābī mannanwāḷā*, *siddhā* (simple).
creed, *akīdā*, m.: *imān*, m.: brief M. sentences, *kalmā*, m.
creep, *see* crawl: -ing plant, *wēl*, f., *wall*, f.: -ing things: *see* insect, ant.
crest, on bird, *kalgī*, f.: *see* comb.
cricket, insect, *bīṇḍā*, m.: game, *kirkaṭ*, m.
crime, *jurm*, m.: *see* sin.
criminal, *see* guilty, prisoner: adj. (leg.), *faujdārī*, *see* civil.
crimson, *kirmzī*, *kirmcī*: *see* red.
cripple, *lunjā*, *lūhlā*,: lame, *laṅgā*: *see* hand.
crisp, *kṛākēdār*.
crisis, *nāzak wakat*, m.
critical, *see* critical, crisis, delicate.
criticise, *nuks kaḍḍhṇā*, *nuktācīnī karnī*, *ghutklā̃ chēṛnīā̃* or *kaḍḍhṇīā̃*.
crocodile, *see* alligator.

crook, shepherd's, *ḍhāṅgā*, m.: *kalpā*, m.
crooked, *ḍiṅgā*, *ḍiṅg phaṛiṅgā*: bent at end, *muṛeā hoeā*: c. matter, *puṭṭhī* or *kuāsī* or *kasūtī gall*: *see* intricate.
crookedness, *ḍiṅg*, m.: *ḍiṅg phaṛiṅg*, m.
crop, n., *fasl*, m.: spring c. (*rabī'*), *hāṛhī*, f.: autumn c. (*kharīf*), *sauṇī*, f.: *see* produce.
crop-eared, *buccā*.
cross, *salīb*, f.: *sūḷī*, f. (lit stake): c. temper, *kauṛī tabīat*, f.
cross-examination, *jarhā*, f. (*k.*)
cross-legged, *caukṛī mārke baihṇā*: *see* squat.
crossroads (four), *curastā*, m., *curāhā*, m.; *caūk*, m. (in town).
crosswise, *cauṛē dā*: M. 128. 8: G. 122: *see* direction.
crow, v., *bāṅg dēṇī* (of cock).
crow-bar, *bārī*, f.
crowd, *katth*, m.: *baṛā mulkh*. m.: *baṛā ādam*, *baṛī khalkat*: *jhurmaṭ* (*pāṇā*): *see* company.
crown, *tāj*, m.
crucify, *sūḷī* or *salīb utte cāṛhnā*.
crude, of word, *ḍagg*.
cruel, *bĕraihm*, *zālim*, *sakht*, *betars*.
cruel-ly, -ty, *bĕraihmī*, f.: *betarsī*, f.: *sakhtī*, f.: all w. *k.*, and *nāḷ*: *see* oppression.
crumble, (e.g. food, bricks, earthen pots), become powder, *bhurnā*: tr. *bhōrnā*.
crumb, *bhōrā*, m.: *krām*, collective term (K.).
crunch, *see* gnaw.
crush, *citthṇā*, *ghōṭṇā*, *dabāṇā*, *mandhāṛnā*: *see* squeeze, trample, pound, beetle.

crust, *krās* (K.).
cry, *see* call, weep, shout, scream.
crystal, *bilaur*, m.
cubit, *hatth*, m.
cucumber, *tar*, f., *khīrā*, m.
cud, chew, *ugāḷī karnī*.
cudgel, *see* stick.
cuff, *kaff*, f.: *see* blow (1).
culprit, *see* guilty.
cultivate, *wāhī karnī*, *khētī karnī*: *wāhṇā* (int. *waggṇā*): *see* plough.
cultivation, *wāhī*, f.: *khētī*, f.: leg, *kāshtkārī*, f.
cultivator, *wāhk*, leg, *kāshtkār*: *see* farmer.
cunning, *see* clever, deceitful.
cup, *pyālā*, m.: *see* drinking-vessel.
cupboard, *almārī*, f.
cupola, *gumbaz* m.
curb, *see* bit, bridle, restrain.
curdle, *jammṇā* (tr. *jamāṇā*): *see* rennet.
curds *dahī*, m.: *see* rennet.
cure, *wall k.*: *caṅgeā k.*: *see* treat.
curious, *see* strange.
curly, *challeāwāḷe wāḷ*: *see* hair.
(1) curry, food, *kārī*: c. and rice, *kārī cauḷ*, m. pl.
(2) curry, curry-comb (horse), *kharkṇā phērnā*.
curse, *bad duā dēṇī* (*nū̃*): of God, *lānat karnī* (*nū̃*).
cursed, *lāntī*.
cursory reading, etc., *sarsarī nazr mārnī* (*te*).
curtain, *paṛdā*, m.: *see* screen, mosquito, cikk.
curved, *gōḷ* (round), *see* crooked.
custodian, *see* guardian, watchman.
(1) custom, gen., *dastūr*, m., *riwāj*, m.: esp. rel. *rīt*, f. *rasm*, f.: *see* habit, rule.

customer, *gāhk*, m. : *laiṇwāḷā*, m.

(2) customs, *maihsūl*, m. : *cuṅgī*, f. (octroi) ; *see* tax.

cut, gen., *waḍḍhṇā* : clip w. scissors, *katrnā* : hair, *katrnā* (get cut, *katrāṇā*) : pay, *kaṭṭṇā* : grass, *mārnā* (int. *marnā*), *khōtarnā* : teeth, *dandīā nikḷṇīā* (tr. *kaḍḍhṇīā*) : c. up fodder, *kutrnā* : c. up wood, *see* chop : *see* prune. A.

cutting (of flowers, trees for sowing), *kalam*, f. : of pay, *see* deduction.

cymbal, *channā*, m.

D

dagger, *khanjar*, m. : *churā*, m.

dacoit, *ḍākū*, m.

dacoity, *ḍākā*, m. (*mārnā*).

daily, *rōz*, *rōz dihāṛī*.

dam, n., *bann*, m.

damage, *nuksān*, m. : *see* loss, injure, hurt : leg., *see* A : v., *nuksān k.* (*dā*), be damaged, *nuksāneā jāṇā*, *nuksān h.* (*dā*).

damp, n., *sill*, f. · *sējjal*, f. : *see* moisture, wet : adj., *gillā* : become d., *sill* or *sējjal caṛhnī* (*nū̃*) : *sill ghattṇā*.

dance, gen., *naccṇā* : special d., *bhaṅgṛā* (*mārnā*) or *dhamāḷ* (*pāṇī*). [*ḍāṇḍī*, f.

dandy, *see* fop. : sedan chair,

danger, *khatrā*, m.

dangerous, *khatrewāḷā*.

dare, *dalērī karnī*, *jurat karnī*.

dark, n. and adj., *hanērā* : get d., *hanērā paiṇā* : at d., *hanēre paie* : very d., *ghupghēr*, m. : d. of colour, *see* A.

darling, *see* dear : rather spoilt, *lāḍḷā*.

dash, *see* run, throw.

(1) date, fruit ; dried, *chuhārā*, m. : green, *khajūr*, f. : tree, *khajūr*, f.

(2) date, time : *tārīkh*, f. : *tarīk*, f. : *see* appoint : useful dates for computing middle-aged and old persons' age : *maiṇe wāḷā sāl*, Apr. 1877 to Apr 1878 : mutiny, *gadar*, m. (1857) : *Sikkhā dā rāj*, rule of the Sikkhs, later forties : *see* era, year.

daub, *see* plaster, smear.

daughter, *dhī* : leg. document, *bint* (always called *bannat*) : European's, *bāwī*, *miss bāwā* : d. in-law, *nūh*.

dawn, day, *diṇ* or *dihāṛ caṛhnā*.

day, *dihāṛā*, m. (gen.) : *wār*, m. (day of week) : *diṇ*, *din*, m. (d a y l i g h t, also 24 hours) : *rōz*. m. (rare except meaning daily) : *aṭṭh paihr*, eight watches, one day : d.'s work or wages, *dihāṛī*, f. : in course of day or less, *sādihāṛī* : by day, *diṇe* : day and night, *rātī diṇe*, *dēh rātī* : long days of hot weather : *mōkḷe dihāṛe*, *lamme dihāṛe*, *mōkḷī bahār*, f. : next d., *agle bhaḷak*, *dujje bhaḷak* : few days ago, *agle dihāṛe* or *diṇ* (the other day) : *see* time, year : that d., *ōddiṇ* : what d., *kiddiṇ ?* which d., *jiddiṇ* : (or *ōddihāṛe*, etc.) : d. for, fever, *wārī*, f. (turn). [die.

dead, *moeā hoeā*, *murdā* : *see*

deadly ; disease, *marnwāḷī*, *mautwāḷī* : snake, *zaihrī* : *see* fatal.

deaf, *ḍōrā*, *bōḷā* : *uccā suṇṇā*,

M. 129. 24: ears stopped, *jhappe aune* (*nū*), M. 117. 8.

deal, *see* associate.

dealings, *laihṇā dēṇā*, m., *lāho deī*, f., *laihṇ dēṇ*, m.: *kamm*, m.

dear; loved, *pyārā*, *azīz* (U.): money, *maihṅgā*, *pyārā*, *tēz*.

dearness, money, *maihṅgāī*, f. (pron. *maṅghāī*): *see* rise.

death, *maut*, f.: *see* die

debar, *see* forbid hinder.

debauchee, *sharābī*, *nashebāz*, *nashaī*, *luccā*.

debris, *malbā*, m. (also wood. bricks of house).

debt, *karz*. m.: get into d., *karz cukknā*, *de sir karz caṛhnā*: M. 118. 20: *see* owe.

debtor, *karzāī*.

decadence, *raunak ghaṭṇī*; *zōr*, etc., *ghaṭṇā*.

decamp, *cupp capītā nass jāṇā*.

decapitate, *see* behead.

decay, *trakkṇā*: *see* bad: get soft, *gaḷṇā*: get spoiled, *wigaṛnā*: *see* decadence.

deceased, *see* dead, late.

deceit, deceive, *dhōkhā*, m. (*d.*, *nū*): *farēb*, m. (*k.*, *nāḷ*): *dhroh*, m. (*k.*, *nāḷ*): *ṭhaggī*, f. (*k.*, *nāḷ*): *ṭhaggṇā*, *luṭṭṇā* (both lit. rob): *see* trick: be d., *dhōkhā khāṇā*, *farēb khāṇā*: *see* put off.

deceitful, *dhōkhebāz*, *farēbī*, *dhrohī*, *ṭhagg*: *see* double (-tongued).

deceitfulness, *dhōkhebāzī*, f.

December, *dasambar*, m.: *poh*, m., about Dec. 13 to Jan. 12.

decide, *faislā karnā*: *see* settle, arrange, umpire.

decline, day, *din ḍhaḷṇā*: *see* sink: in years, *umr ḍhaḷṇī*; *see* old: *see* refuse (1), decadence, lessen.

decorate, *see* adorn.

decrease, *see* lessen, decadence.

decree, *ḍigrī*, f.: *see* lose, command, regulation, law.

deduce, *natījā kaḍḍhṇā*.

deduct, *mujrā* m. (*mujre laiṇā*, *d.*): d. pay, *see* cut: *see* subtract.

deduction, of pay, *kāṭ*, f. (*k.*).

deed, *see* action: *amal*, m.: *kartūt*, f. (gen. bad).

deep, *ḍūṅghā* (water, thoughts, matters), *gaihrā* (thoughts, matters, U): *see* cunning.

deer, *harn*, fem. *harnī*.

defame, *see* accuse, slander.

defeat, v. int. *hārnā* (tr. *harānā*): n., *hār*, f.: *see* conquer, vanquish.

defect, *nuks*, m., *aib*, m., *kasr*, f.: *see* fault.

defective, *nākas*.

defence, *bacā*, m.

defenceless, *māṛā* (weak): *hathyār nehī*.

defend, *bacānā* (save): *hifāzat karnī* (protect).

deference, *lihāz*, m.: *ādar*, f.: *izzat*, f.: *see* consideration, favour, partiality.

deficient, *ghaṭṭ*, *kassā*, *kam*: *see* paucity.

defile (dirty) *maiḷā k.*: ceremonially, *palīt k.*: *bhēṭ chaḍḍṇā* (int. *bhiṭ jāṇā*): *choh chaḍḍṇā* (only by touch, int. *choh ghaṭṭṇā*): *see* unclean, abstain.

deformed, *see* cripple, hunchback.

defraud, *hakk dabāṇā* or *mārnā*, M. 123. 46.

defy, *laṛn nū teār k.*: *see* disobedient.

degrade, in rank, *trōṛnā*, *lōṛnā* (int. *tuṭṭnā*).
degree, rank, *darjā*, m.: by degrees, *hōndeā̃ hōndeā̃*, *hōndeā̃ hawāndeā̃*, *hauḷī hauḷī*.
delay, *cir lāṇā* (int. *laggṇā*): *ḍēr lāṇī* (int. *laggṇī*): *ḍhill karnī*, *ḍhill maṭṭh karnī*.
delete, *ḍhāṇā*, *miṭāṇā*, *lāhṇā* (int. *ḍhaiṇā*, *miṭṇā*, *laihṇā*): strike off name, *kaṭṭṇā*, *khārij*.
delegate, *wakīl*; *ēlcī*, (U.). [*k*.
deliberately, *jāṇke*, *sōc samjhke*, *jāṇ bujhke*, *aĩwē nehī*: *see* purposely.
delicacy, esp. affected, *nazākatā̃*, f. pl. (*k*): *nakhre*, m. pl. (*k*.): *nakhrebāzī*, f. (*k*.): real, use *bimār raihṇā*, *tagṛā nā raihṇā*, *nāzak*.
delicate, matter, person, *nāzak*: *see* delicacy, weak: affectedly, *nazākatī*, *nakhrebāz*.
delicious, *suādlā*, *mazedār*.
delight, (int. sense,) *suād auṇā* (*nū̃*), *khush h*., *rāzī h*.: tr., *khush-k*., *rāzī-k*.: *see* charm, rejoice.
delightful, *see* good, beautiful, delicious, etc.
delinquent, *kusūrwār*, *see* guilty.
delirious (raving) *bĕhōshī wicc bakṇā*.
deliver, *chuḍāṇā*: d. address, *d*., *k*., etc., or *suṇāṇā*: of midwife, *jamāṇā*.
deluge *see* flood.
delusion, *waihm*, m: *see* deceit.
demand, *see* ask, claim: commercial d., *māg*, f.; *wikrī*, f. (sale).
demolish, *ḍhāṇā*, *ḍēgṇā*: *see* destroy.
demoralised, become, *wigaṛnā*.
demur, *cū̃ carā karnī*, *kusakṇā*: *see* refuse (1).
den, animals, *khundhar*, f.
dense, trees, population, *sañhṇā*: *see* stupid.
dent, in metal, soft brick, *cibb*, m., (*paiṇā*, tr. *pāṇā*; *see* straighten): in wood, *ṭoā*, m. (*paiṇā*, tr. *kaḍḍhṇā*).
deny, *mukkarnā*, *inkārī karnī*, *namukkar jāṇā*, *nāh karnī*.
depart, *ṭur jāṇā*, *Allāh Belī h*.; *alī panj h*.: *see* start, farewell.
department, *maihkmā*, m.: of education, *sarishtā e tālīm*, m.
depend, *see* confide, trust: my visit d. upon my getting leave, use "if" clause, or *shart*, f., condition: *see* condition. [*e*.
deplore, *menū̃ ohdā baṛā afsōs*
deport, *see* exile, banish.
deposit, n., *amānat*, f.: v., d. in bank, *jamā k*., *rakkhṇā*.
depressed, *see* sad, sorry.
deprive, *khohṇā*: *see* defraud.
depute, *mukhtār banāṇā*: *wakīl karke ghallṇā*.
depth, *duṅghiāī*, f.
deputy, *wakīl*, *naib*.
deride, *see* ridicule.
derogatory, *eh de wicc sāḍḍī bĕiztī e*.
descend, *laihṇā*, G. 64: *utrnā*, *ḍhalṇā*.
descendant (s), *aulād*, f., *uḷād*, f.: *āl aulād*, f., *aṇs*, f., *aũs*, f., *nasl*, f.: of Muhammad, *sayyad*, fem. *sayyadzādī*: *see* tree.
descent, *lahāī*, f.: *utrāī*, f.
describe, *bĕān karnā* (*dā*).
(1) desert, n., *rēgistān*, m.; *ujāṛ*, m.: *barētā*, m., *barētī*, f., bit of dry sand in water: *see* waste: -ed, *ujjaṛeā hoeā*.

(2) desert, v., *nass jāṇā, chaḍḍṇā.*
deserve, *oh dā hakk e.*
design, *matlab*, m., *wiclā matlab* ; *see* intention : drawing, *nakshā*, m. (*baṇāṇā*).
desire, n., *cāh*, f. : *hirs*, f. : *shauk*, m. : *khāhsh*, f. : *rījh*, f. : *see* taste : v., above nouns w. *hōṇā* : *jī*, m., *rūh*, m., *dil*, m., all w. *karnā* (M. 119. 35, 37) : *cāhṇā* G. 67 : *auhlṇā* (w. hesitation) : *pucchaṇ pucchaṇ* (etc.) *k.*, d. but hesitate to ask, G. 112 : cause to d., afflict, *tarsāṇā* : I wish for, want, *mēnū̃ cāhīdā e*, or *lōṛīdā e*, G. 67 : *see* long.
desist, *muṛnā*, *chaḍḍṇā*.
despair, *nāumēdī*, f. (*h.*) : *udāsī*, f., (*h.*).
desolate (place) *ujāṛ*, *wīrān* : *see* desert (1).
despatch, *see* send.
despise, *kujjh nā samjhṇā*, *jutte de barābar samjhṇā* : *see* contempt, scorn.
despot-, -ic, *see* cruel.
destiny, *see* fate.
destitute, *see* poor.
destroy, *barbād k.*, *kharāb k.*, *nās karnā* (*dā*), *cauṛ k.*, *cauṛ capaṭṭ k.* ; *traṭṭī cauṛ karnī* (*dī*) : lay waste, *ujāṛnā* (int. *ujjaṛnā*) : money, *phūkṇā*, *uḍāṇā* : *see* demolish, devastate, waste, downfall, perish, ruin.
detail, n., *tafsīl*, f. : in d., *sārīā gallā̃*, *tafsīlwār* (U.), *mufassal* (U.) : v., *see* relate.
detain, someone, *bahāī rakkhṇā*, *khalhārī rakkhṇā*, *jāṇ nā d.*
detect, *tāṛ laiṇā*, *wēkh laiṇā*, *jāc laiṇā*, *samjhṇā* : *see* trace, discover.
detective, *khufyā pulswālā*.
detenu, *nazrband*, m. : *see* surveillance.
deteriorate, *wigaṛnā*, *kharāb hōjāṇā*.
determin-ation, - e, *pakkā irādā karnā* : *see* inten-d, -tion, purpose.
dethrone, *takhtō haṭāṇā*, *gaddīō lāhṇā*.
devastate, *wirān k.*, *ujāṛnā* (int *ujjaṛnā*) : *see* destroy, waste, desert (1).
devi-ce, -se, mechanism, *kalā̃*, f., *kalā*, f., : *see* arrange, plan, trick.
devil, *shatān*, m.
devote, time, *lāṇā*, *kharc k.* : *see* consecrate.
devoted, *see* love.
devour, *khā laiṇā*, *rugaṛ laiṇā*.
devout, *see* religious.
dew, *trēl*, f. (*paiṇī*).
dhak, tree, *chichrā*, m.
dialect, *bōlī* f.
dialogue, *see* conversation.
diamond, *hīrā*, m.
diarrhoea, *baṛe dast*, m. pl. (*laggṇe*, *nū̃ auṇe*, motions) : *see* dysentery. [f.
dice, *dāṇā*, m. : *pāshā*, m. : *nard*,
dictat-e. ion, (in school) *imlā likhāṇī* : gen., *kise nū̃ koī gall likhāṇī*.
dictionary, *lugāt*, f. : *ḍikshnarī*, f. (educ.).
(1) die, v., *marnā*, *guzar jāṇā*, *pūrā h.* : trees, plants, *sukkṇā*, *marnā* : *see* death.
(2) die, n., *mohr.*, f. (*lāṇī*) : *see* dice.
diet, *khurāk*, f. : *gazā*, f.
differ, *nā ralṇā*, *nā milṇā* : words for difference w. *hōṇā*.
difference, *fark*, m. : *wērwā*. m. :

great d., *zamīn asmān dā fark*: slight d., *rawāḷ jehā fark.*

different, *wakkhrā, hōr*: *see* differ, separate.

difficult, *aukkhā, mushkil, sakht.*

difficulty, *aukh*, m.: *aukhat*; f.: *mushkil*, f.: *aukkaṛ*, f.: *see* inconvenience, trouble; straits: w. d., adv., words for difficulty, trouble, etc., w. *nāḷ*: also *masā, masā masā, kiwē, aukkheā hōke, marke, see* scarcely.

dig, *puṭṭṇā*: *see* hoe, weed: d. hole, *ṭoā kaḍḍhṇā.*

digested, be, *pacṇā, hazm h.*, (tr. *k.*).

digestion, *hāzmā*, m.

dignity, (honour) *izzat*, f.: (rank) *darjā*, m. [*wāḷā.*

diligent, *mehntī, kamm karn-*

dim, *matthā, maddham*: sight, *matthī, māṛī.*

dine, *khāṇā khāṇā*: -ingroom, *khāṇā kamrā*, m.

dinner, *khāṇā*, m.

direct, adj., *see* straight: v., *rāh pāṇā* or *dassṇā* (*nū̃*).

direction, in what d.? *kehṛī gutthe, kehṛe pāse, kehṛī sehde*: *see* north, south: lengthwise, *lamme dā*, M. 128. 8: crosswise, *cauṛe dā*: in this way, *ēs dā.*

dirt, *gand*, m: *maiḷ*, f.: in well, *jīndar*, f.: *see* rubbish.

dirty, *gandā, maiḷā*; *see* bad: of water, *see* muddy: of machine, *see* clogged: v., *gandā k., maiḷā k.*

disabled, well, cart, animal, man, but not woman, *hanēkeā jāṇā*: for woman use ill, injured, etc.

disadvantage, *nuksān*, m.: *see* defect.

disaffected, *badniyyat, badkhāh* (U.): *see* disloyal.

disagree, *khiāl nā raḷṇā*: *rā nā raḷṇī*: food, *menū̃ muāfik nehī̃, mere laī caṅgā nehī̃.*

disagreeable, affair, *matthī* or *burī* or *mandī* or *kauṛī gall.*

disagreement, *see* discord, quarrel.

disappear, *disṇō raih jāṇā, gaib hōjāṇā*: *see* run, visible.

disappoint, no exact word, *nāumēd k., umēd jāndi rehī, umēd pūrī nehī̃ hoī.*

disapprove, *caṅgā nā laggṇā* (*nū̃*).

disaster, *hanēr*, m.: *see* calamity.

discharge, gun, arrow, etc., *see* fire: debt, *see* pay: servant, *juāb d.* (*nū̃*): *see* dismiss.

disciple, *cēllā* (H.): *murīd* (M.): *shagird*: *see* pupil scholar.

discipline, *intizām*, m. (arrangement).

discomfort, *bēarāmī*, f.: *taklīf*, f.: *see* inconvenience.

discontented, *rāzī nehī̃*: *see* displeased.

discord (tune), *see* tune: unfriendliness, (*see* tune), *nāitfākī*, f.: *phuṭṭ*, f.: *wigāṛ*, m.: *see* enmity, quarrel

discordant, *see* tune.

discourage, *dil tōṛnā* (int. *ṭuṭṭṇā*), *bedil k.* (int. *h.*): be d., *hauslā chaḍḍṇā, dil chaḍḍṇā.*

discover, *malūm k.*: *daryāft k.* (inquire): by asking, *patā karnā*: by looking for oneself, *patā lāṇā* (int. *laggṇā*).

discuss, *gall karnī, salāh karnī,*

salāh mashwarā karnā : *see* argue.

disease, *rōg*, m. : *bamārī*, f. : *marz*, f : contagious or infectious, *lagganwālā*.

disembark, *see* land.

disgrace, *beiztī* f., *bepatī*, f., (both *k.*, *h.*, *dī*) : *namōshī*, f. (*h.*, *dī* or *aunī nū*, M. 117. 3) : *see* dishonour.

disgraceful, *sharm dī gall* : *see* bad, mean.

disguised, *bhēs badalke.*

disgust, *krīc*, f. : *kraiht*, f. : *nafrat*, f. : all w. *aunā* and *wallō*, *tō*, M. 117.3 : or *k.* and *nāl*.

dish, *bhāṇḍā*, m., *bartan*, m., *dīs*, m. (K.) : *kunāl*, m., *kunālī*, f. : *see* plate.

dishcloth, *jhāṛan*, m.

disheartened, *see* discourage.

dishonest, *beīmān*, *badniyyat* (in intention)

dishonour, *pat lāhnī* (int. *laihṇī*, *dī*, M. 121. 19 : 122. 32) : *beiztī k.*, *dī* : *izzat lāhṇī* (int. *laihṇī*, *dī*) : *see* disgrace.

disinclined, *see* sick of.

disinfect, *pōcā pherṇā* (plaster) : *fanail chiṇkṇī* or *traūkṇī* (phenyle) : *see* fumigate.

dislike, *burā laggṇā* (*nū*, M. 121. 11) : *caṅgā* or *acchā nā laggṇā* (*nū*) : *see* disgust, annoy, displeased.

dislocated, be, of joint, *ṭalṇā laihṇā*, *utrnā* : adj., *ṭaleā hoeā.*

disloyal, *khairkhāh nehī* : *see* disaffected.

dismay, v., tr. *ghabrāṇā*, *ghabrā dēṇā* : int. *ghābbarnā.*

dismiss, *kaḍḍhṇā*, *tōr d.*, *juāb d.*, (*nū*) : permit to go, *rukhsat-karnā* (*nū*). A.

disobedient, *ākkhe nā laggṇā* : *gall na mannṇī* : *hukm nā mannṇā.*

disobliging, no word, say *putthā ādmī* ; *kise dā faidā nehī cāhndā* ; *badniyyat.*

disorder, *gaṛbaṛī*, f. : *beintizāmī*, f. : *bētartībī*, f. : *see* confus-e, -ion, tidy, untidy.

dispensary, *haspatāl*, m. : *see* hospital.

disperse, *khalārnā*, *ēddhar ōddhar k.*, *urā parā k.*

display, *see* show.

displease, *narāz k.* : -d., *rinj*, *narāz*, *wiṭreā hoeā*, *mūh waṭṭṇā* (*mēre wallō*) : *see* angry, annoy.

disposition, *tabīat*, f. : *mizāj*, f. : *see* pride.

disprove, *jhūṭhā* or *galt sābit* [*k.*

disqualify, *nā kaṭṭṇā* (*dā*). A.

dissension, *see* discord, quarrel, disturbance.

dissuade, *mōṛnā*, *manā k.*, *samjhāṇā.*

distance, *paiṇḍā* m. : *wāṭ*, f. : *witth*, f. (very small space) : *dūh pailīā dī wāṭ*, two fields' d. : *kukkaṛ uḍārī*, f., cock-fly, short d. : *see* near.

distant, *durāḍḍā* : *dūr* (fem., as *kinnī dūr* how far ?) : *see* far.

distinct, *see* different, separate.

distinguish, *nakhēṛā karnā*, *fark kaḍḍhṇā*, *pachāṇṇā* (pa. p. *pachā-ttā*, *-neā*) : *tamīz karnī* (U.).

distinguished, *see* famous.

distressed, be, (heat, worry) *hussaṛnā* : *see* worry, trouble.

district, gen., *alākā*, m. : small, *tappā*, m., *halkā*, m. : Govt. d., *zilā*, m. : *taihsīl*, f. : *pargana*, m. : *zail*, f.

disturbance, *rauḷā*, m. : *raṭṭā*, m. : *rēṛkā*, m. : *rappha*ṛ, m. : *bakhēṛā*, m. (all w. *pāṇā*, int. *paiṇā*, *h.*) : *halcal*, f. (*paiṇī*, *h.*) : *rohḷī*, f. (*macāṇī*, int. *macṇī*) : serious d., *fasād*, m. (*k.*, *h.*) : *daṅgā fasād*, m. (*k.*, *h.*) : *see* quarrel, noise, excitement, riot.

ditch, *ṭoā*, m. (*kaḍḍhṇā*) : *see* pit.

dive, *cubbhī mārnī* : go under accidentally, *gōtā khāṇā*.

diver, *ṭōbhā*, m.

divert, *dil parcāṇā* (int. *parcṇā*) : *dil bhulāṇā*, int. *bhullṇā* : *see* delight, please, game.

divide, *waṇḍṇā*, *taksīm-k*.

division, *taksīm*, f. : of school class, *farīk*, m. : *see* part.

divorce, paper of, *'likhat*, f. (M.) : *tiāg pattrī*, f. (H.), *tiāg pattar*, m. (H.) : v. tr., *likhat dēṇī* (*nū̃*) : *tiāg dēṇā* (*nū̃*) : *tiāgṇā*, *talāk dēṇī* (*nū̃*).

divulge, *bhēt dassṇā*, *zāhr k*.

dizz-y, -iness, *nhērnī auṇī* (*nū̃*), *bhuāṭṇī auṇī* (*nū̃*), *sir cakrāṇā*, *sir cakkar khāṇā*, *akkhīā agge nhērā auṇā*.

do, *karnā* (pa. p. *kītā*) : *see* accomplish, finish, work : d. without, *ohde bājhō guzārā karnā* or *kamm calāṇā*.

docile, animal, *asīl*.

doctor, *ḍāgdār*, m. : *ḍākṭar*, m. : *hakīm*, m. : d.'s work, practice, *ḍākṭarī*, f.

doctrine, *tālīm*, f. (teaching) : *akīdā*, m. (creed) : *maslā*, m. (one point of d.).

dog, *kuttā*, m. : *see* puppy.

doll, *guḍḍī* f.

dome, *gumbaz*, m.

donation, *candā*, m.

donkey, *see* ass.

dooly, *ḍōlī*, f.

door, *būhā*, m., *darwāzā*, m. : rough wooden, *bhitt*, m. and *khiṛk*, m. : one side of double door, *bhitt*, m. : w. open doors, *latthī būhī*, G. 78 : w. shut d., *wajjī būhī* : indoors, *ghare*, *andar* : d.-frame, *cugāth*, m. : side of d., *muhāth*, f. : wood above, *sardal*, m. : below, *brū̃*, f. : lean against doorpost, *muhāṭhī laggṇā* (M. 120. 5) : through door, *būhe rāh* : *see* socket, pivot.

dot, *nukhtā*, *nuktā*, m.

double (size, price, distance, etc.) *dūṇā* : (two layers, etc.), *dohrā* : on both sides, *duallī*, thus *dūṇī sazā*, double punishment; *duallī sazā*, punishment to both parties : *see* fold, time : v. tr., *dūṇā k.*, *dohrā k.* : d.-entendre, *domaihnī gall*, f. : double-tongued, *duragā*, *dubājrā* : *see* deceit-, -ful.

doubt, *shakk*, m. (*k.*, *h.*).

doubtful, *shakkī*.

doubtless, *beshakk*, *nishaṅg*.

dough, *tauṇ*, f., *guddhā hoeā āṭā* : for pudding, cake, scones, *māwā*, m.

dove-cot, *kābuk*, f. : in ground, *ghumaiḷ*, f. : roost, *chatṛī*, f.

down-, -wards, *see* below.

downfall, *nās*, m. : *barbādī*, f. : *see* destroy.

dowry, *dāj*, f. : *see* marr-y, -iage.

dozen, *darjan*, m.

drag, *dhrūhṇā*, *ghasīṭṇā* : d. in, *see* rake up.

drain, *waihṇī*, f. : *nāḷī*, f.

drama, *nāṭak* m.

draught, rough, of deed, etc., *masaudā*, m. (*baṇāṇā*).

draw, *khiccṇā* : *see* drag : d. water, *bharnā*, rarely *kaḍḍhṇā* : of tea, *rang auṇā* (*nū̃*, M. 50. 4) : *see* drawing.

(1) **drawer**, *drāz*, f.

(2) **drawers**, *drāz*, f. sing. : very small, *jāṅghīā*, m. sing.

drawing, *taswīr*, f. (*khiccṇī*) : plan, map, *nakshā*, m. (*baṇāṇā*).

drawingroom, *gōḷ kamrā*, m.

dread, *see* fear.

dream, *khāb* f. m. : *sufnā*, m. (both *auṇā*, M. 117. 6, and *wēkhṇā*).

dress, n. v. : *see* clothes, clothe : lady's d., *drēs*, m. : d. wound, *paṭṭī bannhṇī*, *phāh lāṇā* (int. *laggṇā*) : *see* ointment. [m.

dressingroom, *saṅgār-kamrā*,

drill n., *kawaid*, f. (*k.*).

drill (hole) *chēk kaḍḍhṇā*.

(1) **drink**, *pīṇā* (pa. p. *pītā*) : caus. *piāṇā*, *piāḷṇā*.

(2) **drink**, intoxicating, *sharāb*, m. : *nashā*, m. (both w. *pīṇā*) : *see* drunk-, -ard.

(3) **drinking-vessel**, *channā*. m. : *kaul*, m. : *kaṭōrā*, m. : *gaṛwā* m. : *gaṛwī*, f. : *gilās*, m. : *see* cup.

drip, (of vessel, house. water), *cōṇā* : (of vessel, water), *wagṇā* : *see* ooze, trickle.

drive, horse, etc., *tōrnā*, *calāṇā* : d. fast, *bhajāṇā* : d. on or away, *hikkṇā* : *see* hammer.

drizzle, *phak*, f. : *phūhr*, f. (both *paiṇī*).

(1) **drop**, n., *būnd*, f. : *chiṭṭ*, f. (fr. splashed or falling water), both *paiṇī*.

(2) **drop**, v., *ḍiggṇā*, *paiṇā* : let fall, *ḍiggaṇ d.* : *see* drip.

drought, *rōṛā*, m. : *auṛ*, f. : *sōkā*, m. (all w. *laggṇā*).

drown, *ḍubbke marnā*, *ruṛhke marnā* (in flowing water) ; tr. *ḍōbṇā*.

drowsy, *see* sleepy.

drum, *ḍhōl*, m. : smaller, *ḍholkī*, f. : double, *tablā*, m. : all w. *wajāṇā* (int. *wajjṇā*).

(1) **drunk**, *matwālā*, *nashe wicc*.

(2) **drunkard**, *nashebāz*, *nashaī* (both also of drugs), *sharābī*.

drunkenness, *nashebāzī*, f.

dry, *sukkā* : d. bread, *rukkhī rōṭī*, f., bread alone : *sukkī rōṭī*. actually dry : *see* insipid.

due, n., *hakk*, m. : adj., d. to me, *menū̃ aundā e* (money) : train due, *gaḍḍī āī cāhndī e*. (G. 112), *huṇ āī khlōtī e*.

dumb, *gūṅgā*.

dumbbell, village, *bugdar*, m. : *muṅglī*, f., Indian club.

dung, horse, ass, *lidd*, f. : cattle, *gohā*, m., *gohā gaṭṭā*, m. : sheep, camel, rats, mice, *meṅgṇā*, f. pl. : dogs, human, *gūh*, m. : birds, *wiṭṭh*, f. (all w. *k.*).

dunghill, *rūṛī*, f.

dupe, *see* prey.

durable, *see* lasting.

dusk, *muhānjlā*, *mūh anhērā* m.

dust, n., *dhūṛ*, f. : *dhuddaḷ*, f. : *ghaṭṭā*, m. : of decayed body, *khāk*, f. : *miṭṭī*, f. : v., *jhāṛnā*, *jhāṛ pōc karnī* (*dī*) : *see* sweep.

duster, *jhāṛan*, m.

duty, *farz*, m. (*pūrā k.*) : of work, *naukrī* (*laggṇī*, M. 121. 7) : *dyūṭī*, f. (*h.*).

dwarf, *giṭh miṭhīā*, *ṭhiṅgṇā*, *ṭhiṅgṇā*, *gīṇḍhā*, *wauṇā* (all for very small man).

dwell, *wassṇā*, *raihṇā* (pa p. *rehā*) : *see* resident.

dye, n., *rang*, m.: for hair, beard, *wasmā*, m. and *kalf*, f., indigo: *mehndī*, f., red dye, (all with *lāṇā*): v., *rangṇā*.
dyer, *lalār-ī*, fem. -*an*.
dysentery, *pēcish*, f.: griping pain, *marōṛā*, m.: *see* diarrhoea.

E

each, *see* every: two e., three e., etc., *dō dō*; *trai trai*, etc., G. 24: at certain rate for e., *sētī*, *picche*, *fī* (U.): *e.g.* *jaṇe sētī*, per man: *see* per.
eager, *see* desire.
ear, *kann*, m.: w. cropped ears, *buccā*: poison ears, *see* incite.
early, *sawēḷe*, *sājhre*, *sawakhte* *see* morning.
earn, *khaṭṭṇā*, *kamāṇā*: *see* deserve, obtain.
earnings, *khaṭṭī*, f.: *kamāī*, f.: *see* advantage, profit.
(1) earnest, *sargarm*, *jōshwāḷā*: in e., truly, *saccī muccī*.
(2) earnest money, *sāī*, f.
earth, *see* world, soil: filling up w. e., *bhartī*, (*pāṇī*): e. coloured, *ghasmailṛā*, *khākī*.
earthquake, *bhucāḷ*, m.
ease (rest), *arām*, m.: (easiness), *sukhall*, m., *asānī* f., at e., *maze wicc*, *maze nāḷ*: *see* rest, convenience.
easily, *saukh nāḷ*, *asānī nāḷ*, *cuṭkī wicc*; *hāī māī*, used only in neg. sentences.
east, *caṛhdā*, m.: *caṛhdā pāsā*, m.: e.-wards, *caṛhde wall*.
easy, *sukhallā*, *saukkhā*, *saihl*, *asān*: *see* chair.
eat, *khāṇā*, pa. p. *khādhā*: e. greedily, *ragaṛnā*: e. orange, lime, lemon, mango, sugar-cane, *cūpṇā*: parched grain, *cabbṇā*.
eavesdropping, *cōrī suṇṇā*: *see* overhear.
eccentric, *laihrī*.
echo, *dūhrī awāz*, f. (*auṇī*).
eclipse, *cugarn*, m.: solar, *sūraj* or *diṇ dā*: lunar, *cann dā*: among educated people, *graihṇ*, e. (gen.); *cugarn*, lunar e.
economy, *sarfā*, m. (*k.*): *ghaṭṭ kharc*, m. (*k.*)
edge, of instrument, *dhār*, f.: of river, lake, etc., *kaṇḍhā*, m., *danḍā*, m.: of garment, *kannī*, f.: raised e. round roof, *banērā*, m.
educat-e, -ion, *see* teach: educated, *paṛheā likheā*.
efface, *see* delete: mental, *dūr k.*, *haṭāṇā*.
effect, *asar*, m. (gen.).
efficacious, *asarwāḷā*: *see* advantageous.
efficacy, *see* effect, advantage.
efficient, *see* able.
effort, *kōshish*, f. or *kōsht*, f. (*k.*): *ṭill*, m. (*lāṇā*, int., *laggṇā*): great e., *jataṇ*, m. (*k.*); *zōr*, m. (*lāṇā*): w. an e., *ṭill nāḷ*, *zōr nāḷ*: *see* difficulty.
egg, *āṇḍrā*, m.: *āṇḍā*, m.: (lay, *d.*,): white of, *safēdī*, f.: yellow, *zardī* f.: hatch e., *bacce kaḍḍhṇe*: e.-shell, *chill*, f.
egg-plant, *baṭāū*, m., *waiṅṅaṇ*, m.: *bhaṭṭhā*, m.
eight, *aṭṭh*: eighth, *aṭṭhwā̃*: G. 19-24: eighth part, *see* time, wts. and meas.
eighteen, *aṭhārā̃*: -th, *aṭhāhrwā̃*: eighteen-finger shoe, *aṭhāhrī juttī*, f., G 19-24, 123.
eighty, *assī*: -one, *ikāsī*: -two,

beāsī: three, *tirāsī*: -four, *curāsī*: -five, *panj-* or *pac-āsī*: -six, *cheāsī*: -seven, *sat-āsī*: -eight, *athāsī*: -nine, *unānwe*: G. 19-24, 123: ordinals: 80, *assīwā̃*: 81 to 88 end in *-āhsīwā̃* with high tone or occ. *āsīwā̃*: -nine, *unāhn-wewā̃*: G. 22, 123.
either..or, *cāhe..cāhe, yā̃..yā̃ bhāwē....bhāwē.*
eject, *see* expel.
ekka, *yakkā*, m.
elapse, time, *laṅghṇā.*
elastic, *lifṇwāḷā.*
elbow, *ark*, f.
electric-, -ity *bijlī*, f.: e. light, *bijlī dī battī.*
elder, *waḍḍā, thō̃ waḍḍā*: *see* old: church-e., *ēldar*, m.
electroplate, *gilṭ*, m.
elephant, *hāthī*, fem. *hāthṇī.*
eleven, *yārā̃*: -th, *yāhrwā̃*: G. 19-24, 123.
eliminate, *kaḍḍhṇā.*
elope, of woman, *uddhalṇā, nikḷ jāṇā*: of man, *udhāḷṇā* w. woman as obj.
elopement, *udhāḷā*, m.
else (e.g., who e., what e.) *hōr*: *see* otherwise, course.
elude, *ḍhōkhe nāḷ nikḷṇā* or *bacṇā.*
emaciated, *baṛā māṛā* or *patlā.*
embankment, *bann*, m
embark, *jahāz utte suār-h.* or *caṛhṇā.*
embers, *see* coal, ashes.
embezzle, *rupayyā khāṇā (bei-mānī nāḷ).*
embitter, *ohdā dil mere wallō̃ khaṭṭā k.*
embrace, *gaḷ nāḷ* or *hikk nāḷ lāṇa* (int. *laggṇā*, M. 1.2. 31): *japphā, japphī mārn-ā, -ī, nāḷ*: *kaḷāwē wicc laiṇā.*
embroil, *phasāṇā* (int. *phasṇā*) w. word for quarrel.
emerge, *nikḷṇā.*
emergency, *see* crisis.
emigrate, *dujje mulkh wicc jāke wassṇā* or *raihṇā.*
emperor, empress, *see* king, queen.
(1) **emphasis,** particle of, *ī, hī*: also expressed by *chaḍḍṇā* (*chaṛnā, saṛnā*), *dēṇā, laiṇā, suṭṭṇā, jāṇā* compounded w. verbs, G. 65, 110, 111: never by repetition of words, G. 71: *see* very.
(2) **emphasise,** *zōr dēṇā* (*utte*).
empower, *see* authorise.
empty, *sakkhṇā* (*k.*), *khālī* (*k.*): e. handed, *sakkhṇe hatth*: *see* unoccupied.
emulate, *rīs*, f. or *barābrī*, f. (*k.*).
enable, *es gall jogā k.* or *baṇāṇa*: *tākat dēṇī (nū̃).*
enamel, gen. *lohā*, m. (iron).
encamp, *ḍērā* or *tambū lāṇā* (int. *laggṇā*): *see* tent, camp.
enclose, a place, *duāḷe wāṛ dēṇī* or *jaṅglā baṇāṇā*: *see* shut up, hedge, railing.
enchant, *see* charm.
encourage, *dil wadhāṇā*: *see* comfort.
end, *akhīr*, m.: *ant*, m.: *natījā*, m. (result): to the e., *tōṛ tīkar*: in the e., *see* finally: *see* head, foot, object, edge, boundary.
endanger, *khatre wicc leauṇā.*
endeavour, *see* try.
endless, *beant, bēbahā, behadd, jehṛā nā mukke.*
endow, paraphrase, or *wazīfā dēṇā* (scholarship): *rupayye ḍēṇē*, etc.
endure, *jhallṇā, jhāgṇā, saihṇā,*

jarnā : *bhugtṇā* (go through w.) : *see* remain, lasting, strong.

enemy, *wair-ī*, fem. *-an* : *dushmaṇ, dōkh-ī*, fem. *-aṇ* : deadly e., *jānī dushmaṇ* : *see* enmity, envy.

energetic, *cust, mehnti, himmatwāḷā.*

enervate, *see* weaken.

enforce, *zōre karāṇā* : *see* force.

engage, servant, *naukar rakkhṇā* : e. a seat, *thā rakhāṇā* : (but keep seat, *rakkhṇā*) : be e. to be married, *see* fiancé : be e. in work, *ḍaihṇā* (pa. p. *ḍehā*) : G. 67, 68.

engagement, (marriage), *kuṛmāī*, f. : *maṅgṇī*, f.

engine, *iñaṇ*, m. : small mechanical contrivance, *kalā*, f., *kalā*, f.

engrave, *ghaṛnā* : signet, *ukkarnā* (caus. *ukrāṇā*), *ukkhaṇṇā* (caus. *ukhṇāṇā*).

enjoy-, -ment, *suād*, m. : *mazā*, m. (both *auṇā*, *nū̃*) : *see* amuse, delight.

enlist, tr., *bhartī-k.* (int. *h.*) : *nāwā̃ likhāṇā*, have one's name entered

enmity, *wair*, m. : *dushmaṇī*, f. : mutual ill-feeling, *aṇ baṇ*, f. : *see* envy.

enough, *bas*, *kāfī* (U.) : words for much : *jinnā lōṛīdā e* or *cāhīdā e* : *jinnī lōṛ e.*

enrage, *baṛā gussā duāṇā* (*nū̃*) : *see* excite, incite : be e., *baṛā gusse h.* : *see* angry, displeased, rage.

enquire, etc., *see* inquire, etc.

entangle, *phhāṇā, phasāṇā* (int. *phasṇā*).

enter, *waṛnā* (tr. *wāṛnā*) : *andar jāṇā* : e. name, *nā likhṇā* (caus. *likhāṇā*) : e. pupil in school, *dākhil h.* (of pupil) ; *dākhil k.* (of teacher) ; *dākhil karāṇā* (of guardian).

enteric, *mohrkā tapp*, m.

entertainment, *tamāshā*, m. : w. name, as *bhanḍā dā*, clowns' : *madārīā dā*, conjurers' : otherwise dancing-girls suggested : *see* amuse, delight.

enthusiasm, *jōsh*, m. : *sargarmī*, f.

enthusiastic, *baṛī cāh rakhdā e, baṛā shukīn.*

entice, *hirs*, f., or *tamā*, m., or *lālac*, m., *kujjh duāke manāṇā.*

entire, not broken or incomplete, *sābit* : *see* all, bag and baggage.

entitled, *see* right.

entrance fee, *see* fee.

entrails, *āndrā*, f. pl.

entreat, *see* beseech, ask.

entrust, *kōḷ chaḍḍṇā*, *de pēṭe*, *de pāṇā*, *hawāle k.*

envelope, *lafāfā*, m.

envy, *khār*, f. (*h. nāḷ*) : *kiṛ*, f. (*k. nāḷ*) ; *mērā sāṛā* (*ohnū̃ paiṇā*) ; *dukh*, m. or *dukhwaidā*, m. (*h nāḷ*) ; *cōbh*, f. (*h. nāḷ*) ; or *mērā dukh k.* or *mēre nāḷ dukh rakkhṇā*, or *ohnū̃ mērā dukh e* : this last also means sympathise : M. 130. 33-6 : *see* enmity.

epilepsy, *mirgī*, f.

equal, *barābar, barabbar, barōbbar* : in age, *hāṇī*, m., fem. *hāṇnaṇ* : *mēre iehā* (like), *jēḍḍā* (size), *jinnā* (amount, number), G. 91.

equality, *barābrī*, f.

equip, *sārā samān d.*, etc.

equipage, *see* retinue.

era, *sammat*, m., esp. that of

Wikrama Ditya, in which 1975 = Apr. 13, 1918 to Apr. 12, 1919: year A.D., *san Iswī*: *see* date.
eradicate, *see* expel, annihilate, destroy, exterminate.
erase, *see* delete.
erect, *khalhārnā*: *see* build.
err, error, *see* mistake.
escape, *bacṇā, bac nikḷnā, chuṭṭṇā, mal jāṇā; phaṛā nā dēṇā, phaṛāī nā dēṇī*: *see* run.
escort, *see* retinue.
especial, *khāss*: -ly, of set purpose, *ucēcā*.
espionage, *jāsūsī*, f.: *mukhbarī*, f.: *see* spy.
essence, *asl* f.
essentially *asl wicc*: *see* real, necessary.
establish, *kaim k.*: *see* build, found.
estate, landed, *malkīyat*, f.: *jagīr*, f. (given as reward): *jāēdāt*, f. (property).
esteem, *izzat*, f. (*k.*): *ādar*, f. (k.): *acchā* or *nēk samjhṇā*: *see* consideration, partiality.
estimate, n., *takhmīnā*, m. (of cost, *banāṇā* or *lāṇā*): *jāc*, f. (*k.*, less formal, v., *jācṇā*): *see* calculate, guess, approximately.
estrangement, *see* discord, quarrel, enmity.
eternal, *hamēshā dā, azlī* (without beginning), *sadā dā, abdī* (without end): *see* life.
eternally, *azlõ abad tīkar*: *hamēshā toṛī*, etc.
etiquette, *see* custom, rule.
Eurasian, *dōglā*: (jocular), *bēṛṛā*, m.
evacuate, *see* empty, leave.
evade, *see* escape, put off.
evaporate, *sukk jāṇā*.
evasion, *see* evade.
even, not odd, *jist*: *see* level, smooth.
even, adv. *sagō, wī, bī*: *see* emphasis.
evening, *shām*, f. (sunset: in e., *shāmī*): *tarkāḷā*, f. pl., about half hour after sunset: *khaupīyyā*, m., time of e. meal, about 8: *sōtā*, m., sleeping time, about 9 or 10: *dūṅghī shām*, when full darkness comes: *see* afternoon.
event, *wākiā*, m: *gall*, f.
ever, *kade*: for e., *see* always, eternal.
every, as in e. eighth day, *aṭṭhī dinī, aṭṭhwē* (or *aṭṭhwē de aṭṭhwē*) *dihāṛe*.
everyone, *har koī, sabbh koī, hamā shamā, jaṇā khaṇā*: *see* all, people, common.
everything, *sabbh kujjh*.
everywhere, *sabbhnī pāsī, sabbh dare, sabbhnī thāī*: *see* side.
evidence, *guāhī*, f. (*d.*, *dī*): *sabūt*, m. (proof, *d.*, *dā*).
evident, *zāhr, sāf zāhr, ujāgar*: self-e., *apū malūm hondā e.*
evil, adj., *see* bad: n. *bureāī*, f.: *burāī*, f.: *kharābī*, f.: *badī*, f.: *see* sin.
evil eye, be injured by; *nazreā* or *nazrāṛeā jāṇā, nazr* or *nazrāṛ ghattṇā*: *tērī ohnū nazr laggī*.
exact, *ṭhīk, bilkul ṭhīk*.
exact, v., *zōre laiṇā* or *ugrāhṇā*.
exactly, *hū bahū, aiṇ*.
exaggerate, *wadhāṇā*.
examin-e, -ation, in school, etc., *imtihān laiṇā* (*dā* of person, subject): be e., *imtihān d.* (*dā* of subject): e. books, *paṛtāl* or *paṛtāl karnī* (*dē*): e.

school, *muāīnā karnā* (*dā*) : inspect (medical and in gen.) *mulāhzā karnā* (*dā*, U.) : cross-e., *jarhā karnī* : *see* pass, test.

examiner, *imtihān laiṇwāḷā*.

example, *namūnā*, m., moral, also pattern, sample : in grammar, etc., *misāl*, f. : for e., *maslan* : make e. of, say *dujjeā nū̃ wī mat āwe*.

excavate, *see* dig.

exceedingly, *see* very.

excellent, *see* good : also *baṛā abbal*, *baṛā ḍabal* (strong, big), *fasṭ klās*, *baṛ umdā sohṇā* (*baṛ* for *baṛā*).

except, *de bā̃jhõ*, *de suā*, *nū̃ chaḍḍke*, *de bagair* (U.).

exception, *kaide de khalāf*.

excess, *bakāyā*, m. : *jinnā waddhe* : *lōṛ tõ waddh* : amount in e. or defect, *wādhā ghāṭṭā*, m.

excessive, *haddõ waddh* : -ly, *sakht* (for something undesirable) : *see* very.

exchange, *waṭāṇā* : *see* change : in e., *ohde thā̃* or *badle* : that may be e., *waṭāwā̃*.

excise, v., *waḍḍhṇā*.

excite, *jōsh duāṇā* (*nū̃*) : *ghabrāṇā* (confuse) : *see* incite, induce : be e.-ed, *jōsh wicc auṇā* : *ghābbarnā* (dismayed) : *halcal macṇī* (tr. *macāṇī*, lot of people).

excitement, *jōsh*, m., *hal cal painī* or *macṇā* among lot of people : *see* disturbance.

exclud-e, -ing, *see* except, expel

excommunicate, *chēkṇā*, *zātõ chēkṇā* : *hukkā pāṇī band karnā* (*dā*, int. *h*.) : remove ban, *hukkā pāṇī kholhṇā*, (int. *khulhṇā*).

excrement, *see* dung.

exculpate, *barī k.* : *see* acquit.

excursion, *sail*, m. or *sair*, m. or *sail sapaṭṭe wāste jāṇā*.

excuse, v., from doing, *muāf k.*, int. *h.* (*thõ*) : *see* forgive : n., *uzar*, m. : you've no e., *terā koī caṅgā uzar nehī̃* : what e. have you ? *wajhā kī e* : a mere e., *huṭṭar*, m., *hīlā*, m., *jugat*, f. (quibble) : *see* pretence.

execrate, *nā̃ suṇke saṛnā* : *see* curse.

execute (hang), *phā̃he d.* (*nū̃*) : *see* do, finish, behead.

executive, *intizāmī*.

exempt, v. tr., *muāf k.* (int. *muāf h.*, *thõ*).

exercise, bodily, *warzish*, f. (*k.*) : *kasrat*, f. (*k.*) : practice, *mashk*, f. : e. book, *kāpī*, f.

exert, *see* effort.

exhausted, *see* faint.

exhibit-, -ion, *see* show, spectacle.

exhort, *nasīhat dēṇī* (*nū̃*) : *see* incite, encourage.

exile, v. n. : *see* banish and add : *mulkhõ paṛ mulkh* (*karnā*, int. *hōṇā*).

exonerate, *see* exculpate, acquit.

exorbitant, *see* dear.

exorcist, *see* magician.

expect, *umēd*, f. (*h.*, *k.*) : person, *uḍīkṇā*.

expedient, *see* means, plan.

expedition, military, *lām*, m. (*laggṇā*, sometimes f.).

expel, *kaḍḍhṇā*, *bāhr dhikkṇā*, *banne saṭṭṇā* : see turn out.

expend, *see* spend, expense.

expense, *kharc*, m. : *lāgat*, f. :

see cost : at my e., *mēre pēṭe, mēre palleõ*, G. 34 : M. 129. 20 : marriage expenses paid to inferior castes, *lāg*, m.

expensive, *see* costly.

experience, *tajrabā*, m. (*k.*, *dā*).

experiment, science, *tajrabā*, m. (*k.*) : *see* test.

expert, *see* clever-, -ness.

explain, *samjhāṇā, bēān karnā, matlab dassṇā, suṇāṇā.*

explicit-, -ly, *sāf, sāf saf, safāī nāḷ.*

expression, favourite, constantly used, *takīā kalām* m.

expressly, *see* especially, explicitly.

exquisite, *ḍāhḍā sohṇā* : *see* excellent.

extensive, *mōkḷā, waḍḍā.*

exterminate, *aslõ* or *mūḷõ kaḍḍhṇā* : *see* destroy, annihilate, uproot.

extinguish, lamp, fire, *bujhāṇā*, (int. *bujjhṇā*) : for lamp also *waḍḍā k.*, G. 113.

extort, *see* force, confess.

extraordinary, *see* strange, wonderful.

extract, v., *kaḍḍhṇā* : n., from book, *ibārat*, f.

extraction, *kāḍh*, f.

extravagance, *fazūl kharcī*, f.

extravagant, *fazūl kharc.*

extremity, of trouble, heat, etc., *ākhar āī hoī e.*

exude, *see* ooze.

eye, *akkh*, f. (pl. *akkhīā*) : have bad eyes, *akkhīā auṇīā* (*dīā*), M. 116. 1 : evil e. *see* evil : pupil of, *dhīrī*, f. : healed ulcer in, *phōllā* (*paiṇā*), *ciṭṭā* (*paiṇā*).

eyebrows, *bharwaṭṭe*, m. pl.

eyelash, *pipṇī* f.

eyelid, *chappar*, m.

eye-witness, use *akkhī ḍiṭṭhī gall*, f. : *see* witness.

F

fable, *see* story.

face, *mūh*, m. : *muhāndrā*, m. : *see* appearance : f. to f., *mūh drūhī* : *āhmo sāhmṇe, āhmṇe sāhmṇe* : to his f., *ohde mūh te* : f. downwards, *mūhdā, mūhdṛe mūh, mūhdṛe mūh* : (fall) on f., *mūh parne* : faces, *see* grimace.

facilitate, words for easy w., *karnā.*

fact, *saccī gall*, f. : *asl gall, wākiā*, m. (U.).

fail, gen. *ukkṇā* : (exam.) *fēhl h.* (*wicc*) : other things, *raih jāṇā, kujjh nā baṇṇā* : *see* bankrupt, deficient.

faint, *behōsh h.* ; feel f., *dil chappṇā* or *chōṭā h.*, *dil ghaṭṇā* : M. 128. 10 : exhausted through heat, thirst, etc., *hussaṛnā, ghābbarnā* : adj., of colour, *maddham, phikkā* : of light *maddham.*

fair, complexion, *gōrā* : f.-haired, *kakkā.*

faith, *imān*, m. : *see* believe, trust, confide, reliance, religion.

faithful, *namak-halāl, imān-wāḷā.*

fall, v., *ḍiggṇā, girnā* : something big, *ḍhaiṇā* : house, *ḍiggṇā, ḍhaiṇā*, (collapse, *baihṇā*) : hair, leaves, fruit, *jhaṛnā* : evening, darkness, night, dew, drops of rain, *paiṇā.*

fallow, *peā hoeā.*

false, *jhūṭhā* : *see* deceitful : coin, *khōṭā* : forged, *jāhlī* : *see* mistake : f. story, *gapp*, f. (*mārnī*).

falsely, *kuṛī mucci*, *jhūṭhī mūṭhī*.

fame, *nā̃*, m. (name) : *see* famous.

familiar, too ; cheeky, *bhūhe h.* or *caṛhnā*.

family, *ṭabbar*, m. : *bāl bacce*, m. pl. : *munde kuṛīā̃*, m. pl. : *kabīlā*, m. (U.) : *horī* may be used, G. 82 : wide sense, *khāndān*, m. : f.-man, *bāl baccedār*, *ṭabbarwāḷā* : *see* tree.

famine, *kāḷ*, m. : f.-allowance, *maihṅgāī*, f. (pron. *maṅghāī*), *kaihtsālī*, f., *kaiht*, m.

famous, *mashāhūr*, *manneā parwanneā*.

fan, *pakkhā* m. : *see* punkah.

fancy, silly, *waihm*, m. : person w., *waihmī*.

far, *see* distant : far side, *see* further.

fare, *bhāṛā*, m. : *karāyā*, m.

farewell, say f. to, *widyā-k.* (int. *widyā h.*) : *see* leave, dismiss, salute.

farmer, (caste), *jaṭṭ*, *jaṭṭ būṭ*, *zamīndār*, *wāhī karnwāḷā* (actual farmer) : leg. *kāshtkār*.

(1) **fast**, *see* swift : tight, *kasseā hoeā* : of colour, *pakkā*.

(2) **fast**, n., *rōzā*, m. (M.) : *wart*, m. (H.) : keep f., *rakkhṇā* : break f. at wrong time, *rōzā tōṛnā* or *bhannṇā* ; at right time, *rōzā kholhṇā*.

fasten, *see* tie, shut : button, *bīṛā* or *baṭaṇ mēḷṇā* or *mārnā*.

fat, n., *carbī*, f. : adj., *mōṭā* : *see* grease, corpulent.

fatal, *marnwāḷā*, *jis thō̃ mar jāīdā e* : *see* deadly.

fate, *takdīr*, f. : *kismat*, f. : *nasīb*, m (all M.) : *lēkh*, m. (H.).

fated, *likheā hoeā*.

father, *pyō*, *caccā* : f. in law, *sauhrā* : married woman's f.'s house or family, *pēke*, m. pl. (adj., *pēkā*) : f. in law's f., *dadiauhrā* : f. in l.'s mother. *dadēhas* : f. in l.'s brother, *patiauhrā*, *patrauhrā* : *patiauhrā's* wife, *patēhas* : f. and mother of bridegroom are *kuṛm* and *kuṛmṇī* to f. and mother of bride, and vice versa.

fatigue, *thakewā̃*, m. : *see* tired.

fault, *kasūr*, m. : *see* mistake, defect, guiltless.

favour, *ahsān* (pron. *as-hān*) m. : *mehrbānī*, f. : out of deference to you, *tērā lihāz karke* : *see* grace.

favouritism, *see* partiality.

fear, n., *ḍar*, m. : *khauf*, m. : v., *ḍarnā*, *saihmṇā* : *ḍar laggṇā* or *auṇā* (*nū̃*) : (tr., *ḍarāṇā*) : be afraid and confused, *ghābbarnā*, (tr. *ghabrāṇā*).

fearless, *see* venturesome.

feast, *ziāfat*, f. : *khāṇā*, m. : *see* festival, invitation.

February, *farwarī*, f. : *phaggaṇ*, m. (about Feb. 13 to Mar. 12).

fee, fees, *fīs*, f. : entrance fee, *dākhlā*, m.

feeble, *māṛā*, *kamzōr* : *see* weak, ill, delicate.

feed (v. tr.), *khuāṇā* (gen.) : poultry, int., *cuggṇā* (tr. *cugāṇā*) : *see* graze. A.

feel, by touching, *ṭohṇā*, *chohṇā*. *hatth lāṇā* (*nū̃*) : *see* cold, hot, hunger, thirst : f. angry, etc., simply use *be* angry, etc. : f. pulse, *nabz wēkhṇī*.

feeling, without f. in skin, etc., *sunn* : salvation not dependent on f., *najāt es gall wicc nehī pai sānū̃ baṛī khushī malūm howe yā̃ nā howe.*

fellow-countryman, *watnī*, *mēre watan* or *dēs* or *pinḍ dā.*

female, adj., *zanānā* : of sex (animals), *madīn* : *see* sex.

fence, *see* hedge, railing, enclose.

ferrel, at end of stick, *shām*, f.

ferry, *pattaṇ* m. : f. -train, *ṭhēllā*, m., *ṭhehlā*, m.

fertile, *see* soil (good).

festival, *īd*, f. (M.) : *tyohār*, m. (H.) : *see* holiday, keep.

fetch, *see* bring.

fetter, *bēṛī*, f.

fever, *kass*, f. : *tāp*, m. : *bukhār*, m. : get f., these words w *caṛhnā* (*nū̃*) : f. go off, *laihṇā* : f.-heat, *bhakhā*, m. A.

few, *thōṛe*, *ṭā̃wā ṭā̃wā*, *wirlā wirlā*, *koī koī*, *ghaṭṭ waddh* (G. 28).

fez-cap, *turkī ṭōpī.*

(1) **fiancé**, *mangeā hoeā.*

(2) **fiancée**, *mang.*

fickle, *see* changeable, vacillate.

fie! fie! *tobā tobā.*

field, *paiḷī*, f. : *khēt*, m. (U.) : part of, *kiārā*, m. : division of arable land, *wanḍ*, f.

fierce, *ḍāhḍā*, *sakht*, *waihshī*, *ḍarāṇwāḷā muhāndrā* (*see* face).

fife, *wanjhḷī*, f. : *bā̃srī*, f.

fifteen, *pandrā* : -th, *pandhrawā̃* : fifteen finger long shoe, *pandhrī juttī* : G. 19-24, 123.

fifty, *panjāh* : -one, *ikwanjā* : -two, *bawanjā* : -three, *tarwanjā* : -four, *curinjā* : -five, *pac- pach-wanjā* : -six, *chawinjā*, *chiwanjā* : -seven, *satwanjā* : -eight, *aṭhwanjā* : -nine, *unāhṭh* : ordinals add -*wā̃*, 51 to 58 add also high-tone h, *ikwanjhawā̃*, etc., G. 19-24, 123.

fig, fruit and tree, *phagwāṛā*, m., *phagwāṛī*, f., *anjīr*, m.

fight, *laṛnā* : *see* quarrel : *bhiṛnā* (gen. of buffaloes) : n., *laṛāī*, f.

figure, *sūrat*, f. : *shakl*, f. : in arithmetic, *hinsā*, m. : *see* form, face.

file, n., *rētī*, f. : v., *rētṇā* : file papers, attach to file, *natthī k.* [*bharke.*

fill, *bharnā* : one's f., *ḍhiḍḍh*

filth, *see* dirt, dirty, rubbish.

final, *chēkaṛlā*, *ākhrī*, *ōṛak dā.*

finally, *chēkṛe*, *chēkaṛ nū̃*, *ōṛak nū̃*, *nihait nū̃*, *ākhar.*

find, *labbh laiṇā* : int. *labbhṇā*, as *menū̃ labbhā*, I found it; *milṇā* (*nū̃*) : f. out, *see* discover.

(1) **fine**, n., *ḍann*, m. : *caṭṭī*, f. : *jarīmānā*, m. : impose, f., *lāṇā*, int. *laggṇā.*

(2) **fine**, adj., *see* beautiful, good : not coarse, *mhīn*, *barīk* : f. fellow (ironical) *hazrat*, *bātshāh.*

finger, *ungaḷ*, f. : little f., *cīcī*, f. : *see* thumb, toe.

finish, *mukāṇā*, *pūrā k.*, *khatam k.*, *nabēṛnā* (settle) : *bhugtāṇā* (go through w.) : int. *mukkṇā*, *pūrā h.*, *khatam h.*, *nibbaṛṇā*, *bhugtṇā.* Also by adding to root of verb *baihnā*, *raihṇā*, *cukṇā*, *haṭṇā* ; G. 66 : or *chaḍḍṇā*, *dēṇā*, *laiṇā*, *suṭṭṇā*, *jāṇā*, G. 65, 110, 111 : it's all over, *syāpā mukk geā*, *khalāsī mukk geī* : the food is finished, occ. *waddh geā*, G. 114.

(1) fire, n., *agg*, f. : light f., *agg bālṇī* (int. *balṇī*) : set on f., *agg lāṇī* (*nū̃*, int. *laggṇī*, catch f.) : *see* flame : slow fire, *see* slow.

(2) fire, v., gun, etc., *calāṇā* : missile, *mārnā*, *calāṇā* (bullet, arrow) : *see* stone, throw. A.

firefly, *ṭaṭāṇā*, m. *ṭanāṇā*, m.

fireplace, for fire or cooking, *aṅgīṭhī*, f. : *culhā*, m.

firewood, *bāllaṇ* (note *l* in *bāllaṇ*, *ḷ* in *bāḷṇā*, light).

fireworks, *astbāzī*, f. : *ātashbāzī*, f. : fire off f., *calāṇā*, *chaḍḍṇā*, int. *calṇā*, *chuṭṭṇā*.

firm, stand, fixed, *ḍaṭṭṇā*.

first, *paihlā* : leader, *āggū*, *mohrlā* : at f., *paihlā*, *paihlū̃*, *paihle* : at f. go off, *paund*, *paund saṭṭe* : fr. the f., *muṇḍhō̃*, *shurū tō̃*.

firstborn, *pahlēṭhī dā* (pron. *palēṭhī*, *paḷēṭhī*).

fish, *macchī*, f. : catch f., *macchīā̃ pharnīā̃*.

fisherman (water-carrying caste), *māch-ī*, fem. *-aṇ* (M.) : *jhiūr-*, fem. *-ī* (H.).

fist, *muṭṭh*, f., rarely *muṭṭhī*, f. : close f., *muṭṭh ghuṭṭṇī* : *see* handful

(1) fit, v., key, *see* key : clothes, shoes, etc., *pūrā auṇā* or *h.* (*nū̃*).

(2) fit, *see* able : f. for me, etc., *de laik*, *de jogā* (G. 38) : *de gōcrā* (G. 38) : *jogā* w. infl. inf., G. 95 : *see* proper, suitable.

fitting, *see* suitable.

five, *panj* : fifth *panjwā̃* : G. 19-24 : fifth part, *see* time : two-fifths and three-fifths in land tenure, *panj-duanjī*.

fix, in ground, *gaḍḍṇā* : f. day, date, *see* appoint.

flag, *jhaṇḍā*, m. : small, *jhaṇḍī*, f.

flame, *lāṭ*, f. : *lamb*, f. : *bhāhmbaṛ*, m. : in lamp-chimney, *lāṭ*, f. : flame up (lamp), *lāṭ nikḷṇī* : fire, *bhaṛk uṭṭhṇā*, *bhāhmbaṛ uṭṭhṇā*.

flank, *pāsā*, m. : of animal, *wakkhī*, *pāsā*.

flannel, *falālain*, f.

flare up, *see* flame : get angry, *gussā bhaṛkṇā* (*dā*) : *see* angry.

flash, n., *lishk*, f. : *camak*, f. : *jhalak*, m. : v., *lishkṇā*, *camkṇā*.

flat, *cauṛā*, *caiṛā* : *see* level, plain.

flatter, *cāplūsī karnī* (*dī*).

flaw, *see* defect.

flax, *aḷsī*, f.

flea, *pissū*, m., *pissū̃*, m.

fledgling, *bōṭ*, m.

flee, *see* run.

flesh, *mās*, m. . *gōsht* or *gōshat*, m. : for food, *see* meat, beef, mutton.

flexible, *lifaṇwāḷā*.

flinch, *sī karnī*.

float, *pāṇī utte tarnā*.

flock, sheep, goats, *ijjaṛ*, m. : birds, *ḍār*, m. : *taraṇḍā*, m. : *see* herd, swarm.

flog, *kōṭle mārne* (*nū̃*).

flood, *kāṅg*, f. : *haṛh*, m. : Noah's f., *Nūh nadī*, f. : *Nūh dī parlo*, f.

floor, *farsh*, m.

flour, *see* meal.

flourish, town, etc., *baṛī raunak*, etc.

flower, *phull*, m. : v., *phullṇā*, of crops, vegetables, *nissarnā*.

flower-bed, *khēḷ*, f., *kiārī*, f.

flower-pot, *gamḷā*, m.
fluctuate, *waddhṇā ghaṭṇā*.
fluent, *far far karke boldā e*.
flute, *wanjhḷī*, f. : *bā̃srī*, f. : double f., *jōṛī* f.
flutter, *phaṛkṇā* : of distress, *taṛafṇā*.
(1) fly, *uḍḍṇā*.
(2) fly, n., *makkhī*, f. : blue bottle, *makkh*, m.
foal, *wacherā*, *m*.
foam, *jhagg*, f.
fodder, *paṭṭhe*, m. pl. : *paṭṭhā daṭṭhā*, m. : very common kinds, *maiṇā*, m., *sinjī*, f.
fog, *dhundh*, f. (mist) : *gaihr* or *ghaihr*, m. (haze).
(1) fold, v., make f. in, *bhann pāṇī* (*wicc*), *bhannṇā* (*nū̃*) : f. in folds, *taih-k.* : roughly *kaṭṭhā k.*, *thappṇā* : f. double, *dohrā k.*, treble, *trehrā k.*, four fold, *cauhrā k.* : above four, *ehde panj*, *che taih kar*, (or fem., *ehdīā̃ taihā̃*), fold it five, six fold : f. up, *waḷhēṭṇā* : *see* wrap, single.
(2) fold, n., in cloth, paper, *bhann*, f. : sheep, etc., *wāṛā*, m.
follow, *magar jāṇā*, *picche jāṇā* : worryingly, *magar paiṇā* : f. Christ or relig. leader, *pairwī karnī* (*dī*) : f. Christ, *Masīh de magar magar jāṇā*.
follower, *murīd* (M.) : *cēllā* (H.) : *mannaṇwāḷā*.
folly, *see* foolishness.
foment, limb, *sēk karnā* (*nū̃*), *see* toast (contrast word).
fond-, -ness, *see* like, desire.
fondle, *lāḍ k.* (*nū̃*) : *pyār d.* (*nū̃*) : *see* love, spoilt.
food, *khāṇā*, m. : *ṭukkar*, m. : *ṭukkar cappā*, m. : *rōṭī*, f. : *bhōjan*, m. (H.) : *ann pāṇī*, m. : *bhattā*, m. (midday meal taken to workers) : *see* diet : special for cattle, *guṭāwā*, m. (mixture of straw, chaff, oilcake, water, meal) : for horses, *nihārī*, f.
fool, *aihmak*, *aihmakh*, *bewakūf* (last never to be used in address), *balēllaṛ*, *wāhyāt*, *bā-* or *mat-* or *hōsh-* or *akl-mārea*, *jhallā* : *see* mad, ignorant, stupid.
foolishness, *bewakūfī*, f. : *jhall-puṇā*, m. : *beaklī*, f. : *nadānī*, f.
foot, *pair*, m. . w. claws, *panjā*, m. : *see* paw, claw : crooked footed, *phiḍḍā* : on f., *ṭurdā*, *paidal* (U.) : fall at one's feet, *carnī ḍiggṇā*, *pairī paiṇā* : footfall, *pairā̃ dā khṛāk* : f. of bed, *puāndī*, f. : feet of bed, table, etc., *see* leg : f. of page, *hēṭhḷā pāsā*, m. ; *see* bottom : f. of 12 inches, *fuṭ*, *fiṭ*, m. : *see* rule, tiptoe, wts. and meas.
fop, *bā̃kā*, *shukīn*, *jēnṭal-main* : *ākkaṛ khā̃*.
for, *nū̃*, *wāste*, *laī*, *khātar*, *jogā*, *gōcrā* : *see* behalf, suitable, sake : gone for milk, *duddh nū̃ geā* : for of price, *tō̃*, *thō̃*, *thī̃*, G. 89, or loc. G. 9, 11, 78.
forbid, *manā k.* : *see* hinder, stop : forbidden food, etc., *harām* or use *saūh*, oath : M. 107. 17-9.
(1) force, n., *see* power, oppression, effort : by f., *bado badī*, *maḷo maḷī*, *zōrī*, *zōro zōrī*, *zabardastī*, *majbūr karke*, *majbūrī gall*. *zōrī gall*,

dhakke nāḷ : f.-ed labour, *wagār*, f. *wagyār*, f. : f.-ed labourer, *wagārī*, *wagyārī*.
(2) force, v. tr., *majbūr k.*, or causal v. w. word for "by force," G. 110 : f. him to do, *oh de kōḷō zōre karā*, etc. : *see* cause.
forenoon, about 8 or 9, *chāhwēḷā* : 10, *kūḷā bhattewēḷā* : 11, *bhattewēḷā* : 10 or 11, *rōṭī wēḷā* : *see* noon, morning.
forehead, *matthā*, m.
foreign, *horī mulkh dā*, *pardesī*, *ōprā*. *parāyā* : *see* strange.
foreknowledge, *see* prescience.
foremost, *āggū*, *mohrlā* : *see* first.
foresight, *dūrandesh-ā*, m., *-ī*, f.
forest, *ujāṛ*, m., *jaṅgaḷ*, m.
forged, *jāhlī*.
forgery, *jāhlsāzī*, f.
forget, *wisārnā*, *wissarnā*, *bhullṇā* ; last two mean forget of person, or be forgotten of thing. A.
forgetfulness, *see* mistake.
forgive, *muāf k.*, *bakhshṇā chaḍḍṇā*, *jāṇ d.*, *muāfī dēṇī*.
fork, for table, *kāṇṭā*, m. : f.-ed stick, *dusāṅghī*, f. : f.-ed tree, *dusāṅghā*.
form, *shakl*, f. : *ḍauḷ*, f. : outline of body, *but*, m. : *see* shape, face, appearance, system.
former, *see* previous.
formerly, *see* before.
fornicat-ion, -or, *see* adulter-y, -er.
fort, *kilhā*, m.
fortification, *kilābandī*, f.
fortress, *see* fort.
fortunate, *karmāṅwāḷā*, *caṅgē bhāgāṅwāḷā* (H.), *nasīb caṅge*, *kismat caṅgī* : *see* auspicious, unfortunate.
fortune, *see* fate : good f., *khush-kismatī*, f., *khush-nasībī*, f : *caṅge nasīb*, m. pl. : bad, *badkismatī* or *badnasībī*, f. : *bure nasīb*.
fortune-teller, *najūmī*, *ramḷī*, *majūsī*.
forty, *cāḷī* : -one, *iktāḷī* : -two *batāḷī* : -three, *tartāḷī* : -four, *cutāḷī* : -five, *paītāḷī* : -six, *chatāḷī* : -seven, *saītāḷī* : -eight, *aṭhtāḷī* : -nine, *uṇwanjā* : ordinals add *-wā̃* w. high tone h, *cāhḷīwā̃*, *iktāhḷīwā̃*, *uṇwanjhawā̃*, G. 19-24, 123.
forward, *agā̃*, *agge* : *see* before : cheeky, *athrā̃*, *ḍhīṭh* : *see* impertinent, familiar.
forwardness, *see* boldness.
foundation, *nīh*, f. : *bunyād*, f. (latter word also metaphorical)
founder, *bānī*. [owner).
foundling, *lawāris* (without
fountain, *see* spring : artificial, *phuhārā*.
four, *cār* : -th, *cauthā* : fourth part, *see* time.
fourteen, *caudā̃* : -th, *cauhdawā̃* : G. 19-24, 123 : fourteen finger long shoe, *caudhī juttī*.
fowl, for table, *kukkaṛ*, fem. *kukkṛī* : *see* cock, hen, chicken.
fox, *lūmb-aṛ*, fem. *-ṛī*.
frame, for door, picture, *cugāṭh*, f. : hanging f., for clothes, *taṅgṇā*, m.
fraud, *see* deceit, clever.
free, adj., *azād* : v. tr., *chuḍāṇā*, *chaḍḍṇā* : *see* leisure, gratis, liberty, release. A.
freeze, *jammṇā* : hands, feet, *see* cold

frequented, to be, of road, *wagṇā*. [ly.
frequently, *see* often, repeated-
fresh, *sajrā*, *tāzā* : green, *harā*.
fretful, *see* irritable.
friction, *see* discord : use *aṛnā*, *khaihke laṅghṇā*, *ragaṛke laṅghṇā*.
Friday, *jumā*, m.: *sukkar*, *shukkar*, *sukkarwār*, *shukkarwār*, (last four H.).
friend, *sajjaṇ*, *mittar*, *dōst*, *yār* (only one man of another), *bēllī* : *see* companion.
friendship, *dōstī*, f.: *yārī*, f. (between men): strong f., *gūṛhī dōstī* : make friends w., *dōstī*, *yārī*, *pyār*, m., all w. *pāṇā* and *nāḷ* (int. *paiṇā*, *nāḷ*): M. 120. 27 : 243. 5 : *dōstī rakkhṇī* (*nāḷ*), be friendly w.
frighten, *see* fear.
frill, *jhāllar*, f.
from, *tō*, *thō*, *thī*, -*ō*, G. 13, 36, 37, 88, 89 : fr. person, animal, *koḷō*.
front, in, adv. *agge*, *mohre*, *agēre* : adj., *mohrlā* : prep. *sāhmṇe* : *see* face, forward, before.
frost, hoar, *kakkar*, m. : *see* freeze.
frontier, *sarhadd*, f. : adj., *sarhaddī*.
froth, *jhagg*, f.
frown, *treoṛhīā* or *ghurākīā* or *ghūrīā*. all with *waṭṭṇīā* : *ghurākī wekhṇā*, look angrily : *see* angry.
frozen, *see* freeze.
fruit, *phaḷ*, m.: raisins, etc., *mewā*, m.
fruitful *phaḷwāḷā*.
fruitless, tree, *apphaḷ* : *see* useless, vain.
fryingpan, *fraīpān*, m. (*K.*), Indian, *kaṛāhī*, f.
fuel, *see* firewood.
fugitive, *nasseā hoeā*.
fulfil, *see* finish.
full, *bhareā hoeā* : f. of Holy Spirit, *Pāk Rūh nāḷ bhareā hoeā* : f. brother, etc., *sakkā*
fumigate, *dhūkh* or *dhūf dēṇā* : *guggaḷ dhukhāṇā* : *gandhak* (sulphur) *dhukhāṇī* : *see* disinfect.
fun, *see* entertainment.
funeral, *janāzā*, m. (*paṛhnā*).
funnel (engine, steamer, brick-kiln), *cimṇī*, f.
fur, *jatt*, f.
furious, *baṛe gusse wicc*, *bhakheā hoeā* : *see* anger, rage.
furlong, *farlāṅg*, m.
furnace (with boiler) *bhaṭṭhī*, f.: for sugarcane juice, *cumbā*, m. [m. : *raihl*, f.
furrow, including ridge, *siāṛ*,
furniture, *mēz kursīā*, f. pl., *asbāb*, m. : old f.-seller, *kuāṛīā*, *kabāṛīā*.
further, *zyādā dūr*, *waddh dūr*, *paindā waddh e* : on far side, *parlā*, *pailā* : *parle* or *paile pāse* : *see* distant : moreover, *nāḷe*.
fuss, *raṭṭā* or *rēṛkā pāṇā* (int. *paiṇā*) : *see* disturbance, quarrel.
future, *agge nū̃*, *agge wāste*.

G

gain, *see* advantage, profit, obtain, earn, reach, succeed, win.
gait, *ṭōr*, f. : *cāl*, f.
gale, *see* storm.
galled, be (horse ass, mule) *lāggā laggṇā* (*nū̃*) : M. 121. 14.

gallop, gentle, *poīā turnā*: vigorous, *sarpatī turnā*. A.
gallows, *sūlī*, f.: *see* hang, crucify.
gamble, *jūā khēḍṇā*: gambling, *jūā*, m.
gambler, *juārīā*, m.
game (gen.), *khēḍ*, f.: single g. or match, *bāzī*, f.: win g., *bāzī jittṇī*: lose g., *bāzī hārnī*, *bāzī ohde sir hōṇī*, *bāzī caṛhnī* (*nū̃*, M. 118. 24).
gaol, *see* prison.
gap, *khappā*, m., *witth*, f.
garden, *bāg*, m.: public g., *kaumpṇī bāg*: g.-walk, *rāk*, m.: g.-bed, *khēḷ*, f.: *kiārī*, f.
gardener, *māl-ī*, fem. *-aṇ*: caste, *arāī*, fem. *arāiṇ*; *maihr-*, fem. *-ī*.
garlic, *thōm*, f.
garrulous, *see* talkative
gasp, in death, *saihkṇā*: *see* pant; breath, out of.
gate, *phāṭak*, m.: *see* door.
gather, *see* collect, infer.
gender, *jiṇs*, f.
(1) general, n., *jarnail*.
(2) general, adj., *ām*, *mamūlī*.
generally, *aksar*, *ām*, *bauht karke*.
generation, *pīṛhī*, f.
generosity, *sakhāwat*, f. (U.).
generous, *sakhī*.
genius, *pujjke akl-wāḷā*: *see* sense.
gentle, no good word, *sharīf*, *ashrāf*, *bhalāmāṇas*: animal, *garīb*, *sāū*.
gently, *saihje saihje*, *saihe saihe*, *saihje nāḷ*, *saihe nāḷ*, *hauḷī hauḷī*: *see* quietly, slowly: speak g. *hauḷī*, *nimmhī*.
gentleman, *sāhb*, *sharīf*, *sharīf* or *ucce khāndān dā*: *see* gentle.
genuine, *see* real.
get, *see* obtain: g. something done, *see* cause.
ghee, *ghyō*, m., occ. *thindhā*, m., [*cōpaṛ*, m.
ghost, *bhūt*, m., *jinn*, m. (M.): Holy Ghost: *see* spirit.
giant, no word, *baṛā lammā*, etc.
gibberish, *ēwē bakṇā*.
gibe, *see* taunt.
giddy, *see* dizzy.
gift, to superior, *nazr*, f., *ḍhoā*, m., *ḍāhḷī*, f.: to inferior, *inām*, m., *bakhshīsh*, f.
gild, *mulammā-k.*: *gilṭ-k.*
ginger, *adhrak*, f.: *sunḍh*, f. (dry).
girdle, *see* belt, griddle.
girl, *kuṛī*, *kākkī*, *jātkṛī*, *laṛkī*: occ. *bālṛī*: European, *miss bāwā*: *see* daughter.
girth, of saddle, *taṅg*, m.
gist, *khulāsā*, m.: *matlab*, m.
give, *dēṇā* (pa. p. *dittā*), *bakhshṇā*: g. in, admit defeat, *hār mannṇī*: lose heart, *see* discourage.
glad, *khush*, *rāzī*.
gladly, *khushī nāḷ*, *khush* or *rāzī hōke*.
glance, at book, letter, etc., *nazr mārnī* (*te*): just a g., *sarsarī nazr*, f.
glass, *kac.*, f.: *shīshā*, m.: drinking g., *gilās*, m.: *see* mirror, drinking vessel.
glimmer, *thōṛī lishk* or *camak*, f.
glimpse, get g. of, *zarā nazrī paiṇā* (*ohdī*, &c.).
globe, of lamp, *hānḍī*, f.
glory, *jalāl*, m.: *see* splendour.
glove, *dastānā*, m.: G. 74.

glowworm, *ṭaṭāṇā*, m., *ṭanāṇā*, m.

glue, *sarēsh*, f. : v., *sarēsh lāṇī*, *sarēsh nāḷ jōṛnā* : *see* gum, paste. [frown.

gnash teeth, *dand pīhṇē* : *see*

glutton, *see* greedy.

gnaw, of rodents, *kutarnā*, *ṭukkṇā* : bone (dog), *khāṇā* : crunch, *kuṛkāṇā*.

go, *jāṇā* (pa. p. *geā*), *ṭurnā*, *calṇā* ; g. away, *ṭur jāṇā* *wag jāṇā*, *see* rise : g. out, *nikḷṇā*, *banne jāṇā* : g. in, *waṛnā* : *see* start, walk, off.

goad, ox-, wooden, *parāṇī*, f. : v., *parāṇī nāḷ hujj mārnī* (*nū̃*) ; *see* prod : metaph., *see* incite, urge.

goal, football, hockey, polo, etc., *gōl*, m. : *see* aim, object.

goat, *bakr-ā*, fem. *-ī* : long-haired, *kāgānī bakrā* · adj., *bākrā* : *see* kid.

gobble, *see* devour.

God, *Khudā*, *Rabb*, *Maulā* (all M.) : *Parmēshwar*, *Īshwar*, *Bhagwān* (H.) : god, *māhbūd*, m. (object of worship, M.), *dēotā*, m. (H.).

goddess, *dēwī*.

goitre, *gillhar*, m. : man w. g., *gillhaṛwālā*.

gold, *syōnā*, m. : *sōnā*, m.

golden, *syōne dā*.

goldsmith, *sunyārā*.

gong, *see* bell.

(1) good, *caṅgā*, *acchā*, *umdā*, *wall*, *baṛā waddhīā* : *kharā* (genuine) : of character, *caṅgā*, *acchā*, *nēk*, *bhalāmāṇas*, *ashrāf* : of soil, *see* soil : coin, *see* coin : *see* excellent, very : interj., *caṅgī gall*, *kharī gall* n., God seeks our good, welfare, *bhalā*, m. : *see* welfare.

goodness, *nēkī*, f. : *bhaleāī*, f. : *bhalmaṇs-āī*, f., *-āū*, m.

goodbye, *see* farewell.

(2) goods, *asbāb*, m. : *laṭar paṭar*, m. : *nikk shukk*, m. : *see* property bag and baggage.

gooseberry, cape, *ṭipārī*, f.

Gospel, *Injīl*, f. : *Anjīl*, f. (the book) : G. message, *najāt dī khabar*, f.

gossip, *see* conversation, chatter.

govern, *hukūmat karnī*, *bādshāhī karnī*, *rāj karnā*.

governor, *hākim* : Lieutenant G., *lāṭ sāhb*.

grace, *fazl*, m. (M.) : *dayā*, f. (H.), *kirpā*, f. (H.).

gradually, *hundeā̃ hundeā̃*, *hundeā̃ hawāndeā̃*.

graft, n. (plant), *pyōnd-karnā*.

grain, *dāṇā* m. : *dāṇā phakkā* : wheat and barley, *gōjī*, f. : wheat, barley and gram, *bēṛrā*, m. : receptacle for, *bhaṛohlā*, m., *bhaṛohlī*, f., *kōṭhī*, f.

gram, *chōlle*, m. pl.

granary, *see* grain.

granddaughter, son's daughter, *pōtrī* : daughter's, *dohtrī*.

grandfather, paternal, *dāddā* : maternal, *nānnā* : *dadda's* father, *paṛdāddā* : *dadda's* mother, *paṛdāddī* : *nannu's* father, *paṛnānnā* : *nannu's* mother, *paṛnānnī* : *dadda's* house or family, *dādke*, m. pl. : *nanna's* house or family, *nānke*, m. pl. : adjj., *dādkā*, *nānkā*.

grandmother, paternal, *dāddī* : maternal, *nānnī*.

grandson, son's son, *pōtrā* : daughter's son, *dohtrā* : *potra's* son, *parpōtrā* : *potra's* daughter, *parpōtrī* : *dohtra's* son, *pardohtrā* : *dohtra's* daughter, *pardohtrī*.

(1) grant-in-aid, *grānt*, f. : *imdād*, f. : in receipt of g. (institution), *imdādī*.

(2) grant, *see* allow, give.

grape, tree and fruit, *dākh*, m. : *angūr*, m.

grasp, *hatth nāl pharnā* or *phagarnā*.

grass, *ghāh*, m. : special kinds, *khabbal*, m. : *dīlā*, m. : *dabb*, f.

grasshopper, *tridd*, m., *triddī*, [f.

grateful, *dā shukrguzār* : *see* thank.

grating, small iron, *janjrīā*, f. pl., *jhajjrīā*, f. pl. : larger bars, *jharne*, m. pl.

grat-is, -uitous, *muft*, *mukhat*, *muft dā*.

(1) grave, M. *kabr*, f. : saint's, *khāngāh*, f. : H. *marhī*, f. : *samādh*, f.

(2) grave, *see* serious, sober.

graveyard, *kabristān*, m.

gravel, single stone, *gītī*, f. : collective, *bajrī*, f., *kankrī*, f.: *see* pebble.

gravy, *grēbbī*, f. (K.).

graze, v. int. *cugṇā*, *chirṇā* (go out to g.) : tr. *cārnā*, *cugāṇā*, *chērṇā*.

grease, *thindheāī*, f. : *ciknāī*, f. (both words mean greasiness) : *see* fat.

greasy, *thindhā*, *ciknā*.

great, of size, age, dignity, *waddā*, otherwise *barā* ; *see* very : G. 34.

greed- -y ; *see* covet-, -ous : *ohdī nazr bhukkhī e.* : great eater, *barā khāū* or *khāṇwāḷā*.

green, *harā*.

greengrocer (woman) *araīn* f. : *see* gardener. [-*ṇā*, *allhar*

greenhorn, *añāṇā*, *siddhā*, *kac-*

greenness, *hareauḷ*, f.

greet, *see* welcome, salute.

gregarious, *katthe raihṇwāḷe*.

grey, *see* brown : green grey, *sāwā* : of hair, *see* hair.

greyhound, *tāzī kuttā*. [m.

griddle, girdle, *tawā*, m. : *tajāl*,

grief, *dukh*, m. : *jhorā*, m. : *afsōs*, m. : *gam*, m. : *ranj*, m. (all w. *h.*, *afsōs* also w. *k*).

grieve, *jhurnā* : (*dā*) *dil dukhī hōṇā* : tr. *dil dukhāṇā* (*dā*) : *see* regret.

grimace, make to annoy, *cinghē lāṇe* : *dandīā cinghāṇīā* : bad taste in mouth, etc., *bhairā mūh baṇāṇā*.

grin, *dand kaḍḍhne*, *mūh aḍḍṇā*, *guṭak paiṇā*.

grind, fine, *pīhṇā* (int. *pisṇā*) : coarse, *daḷnā* : g.-ing board, *sil*, f. : roller, *waṭṭā*, m. : *see* mill, grindstone, pin.

grindstone (for knives, etc.) *sāṇ*, f. : v., *sāṇ te lāṇā*.

grizzled, *see* hair.

groan, *arāṇā hūngṇā*.

grocer, *pasār-ī* fem. -*an*.

groom, *sīs* (often pron. w. low tone, *s-hīs*).

groove, *nāḷī*, f.

ground, *zamīn*, f. (*zimī*, *jīwī*, *jiwī*) : on the g., *bhuñē*, *bhūē* : *see* soil, foundation. [*nehī*.

groundless, *ehdī bunyād koī*

grow, *waddhṇā* : plants, *uggṇā*, begin to grow : *see* sprout.

growl, *hūngṇā*

grudge, *see* envy.
grudgingly, *see* reluctant.
grumble, *ū ū karnī*, *kuṛhnā*, *buṛ buṛ* or *bhus bhus karnī*.
(1) guard, *rakhwālī* or *rākhī karnī* : *caukīdārī karnī* : protect, *hifāzat karnī* (all *dī*) : be on g. against, *ohde wallō hushyār raihṇā* : *see* preserve, save.
(2) guard, in train, *gāḍ*, *see* sentry.
guardian, of things, *rākkhā*, *rakhwālā*, *caukīdār* : of persons, *sarprast*, *walī wāris* : leg. *wāris*, *see* saviour.
guess, *tukk lāṇī* : *ṭēwā lāṇā* : g. prove correct, *tukk ṭhīk wajjṇī* : *see* calculate, estimate, approximately.
guest, *parauhṇā*, m.
guide, *rāh dassṇā* or *wakhāṇā* set one on one's way, *rāhe pāṇā*.
guilt, *jurm*, m. : *see* fault.
guiltless, *bēgunāh*. *bēkasūr*, *see* innocent, acquit.
guilty, *mujram*, *kasūrwār*.
guitar, *sitār*, f. : *see* plectrum.
gulf, *khalīj*, m.
(1) gum, *gūnd*, f. : v., *gūnd lāṇī*, *gūnd nāḷ jōṛnā* : *see* paste, glue.
(2) gum (mouth), *masūṛā*, m. (gen. plur.). [*calnī*) : *see* fire.
gun, *bandūk*, f., (*calāṇī*, int.
gunpowder, *barūd*, m.
gush (water) *zōr nāḷ wagṇā*.
gust, *see* storm.
gutter, *see* drain.
gyve, *see* handcuff.

H

habit, *hiṭṭar*, f., *gējh*, f.. *wādī*, f., *ādat* f., (all with *paiṇī*) : *see* custom : make h. of, special verbal construction, G. 68, 69 : *gazā pakk jāṇī* (*dī*) : *see* accustomed.
haggle, *mull dī bābat jhagaṛnā*.
hail, n., *candrā*, m., *gaṛā*, m., *aihṇ*, f.
hair, *wāḷ*, m. (single h.) : very fine hair on body, each hair, *lū*, m. : fur, *jatt*, f. (also goat's h. etc.) : long hair, *chatte*, m. pl. : plaited lock, *mēḍhī*, f., *mēṇḍhī*, f. : curl, (special kind), *kalam*, f. : Sikkh's hair, *kēs*, m. : Hindu's lock, *bōddī*, f. : white hair, *dhauḷe* (*auṇe*, M. 117. 10), *ciṭṭe* or *bagge wāḷ* : grey, *karṛ barṛe* or *karṛ barṛ wāḷ*, m. pl. : do one's h., *wāḷ suārne*.
hairless (on face) *khōddā* : beard, etc. not yet grown, *alū* : *see* bald.
half, *addhā*, *addh* : h. and h., *addh pacaddh*, approximately ; *addho addh*, exactly : in land tenure, *adhiāre te* : h. way, *adhwāṭe* : $1\frac{1}{2}$, $2\frac{1}{2}$, *see* one, two : above 2, *sāḍhe* w. number, G. 23 : *see* halve.
hall, in school, etc., *hāl*, m. : in house, *hāl kamrā*, m.
halo, round moon, *piṛ*, m., *cann piṛ malleā hoeā e*.
halt, *makām karnā*, *rāt raihṇā*.
halter, esp. cattle, *mohrak*, f. : horse, *talihārā*, m.
halve, *addho addh karnā*.
(1) hammer, *hathauṛā*, m. : wooden, *munghlī*, f. : sledge h., *wadān*, m.
(2) hammer, v., pegs, nails, *ṭhōkṇā* : poles, *gaḍḍṇā*.
(1) hand, *hatth*, m. : without one or both h., *ṭuṇḍā* : h. of

watch, clock, *sūī*, f.: by h. *dastī*: *see* tie.
(2) **hand**, v., *phaṛāṇā*, *dēṇā*: *leā* (imperat. only).
handbreadth, *cappā*, m.
handcuff, *hatthkaṛī*, f., *kaṛī*, f.
handful, single, *lapp*, f.: double, *bukk*, m.: fistful, *muṭṭh*, f., rarely *muṭṭhī*, f.
handkerchief, *rumāl*, m.
handle, w. hole through it, of cup, dish, *kuṇḍā*, m.: button of lid, *dūḍḍaṇ*, m.: latch -h., *lāṭū*, m.: others, *hatthā*, m., *hatthī*, f.: *muṭṭh*, f.: *dastā*, m.: cloth catch of chikk, *khūṭī*, f., *khuṭṭī*, f.
handsome, *see* beautiful.
hang, v. tr., *ṭaṅgṇā*, *lamkāṇā* (int. *lamkṇā*): h. person, *phāhe d.* (*nū̃*): h. oneself, *phāh laiṇā*: h. -ing frame for clothes, *ṭaṅgṇā* m.: hanging, *lamkdā*, *ṭaṅgeā hoeā*.
happen, *hōṇā*, *bītṇā*.
happy, *khush*, *rāzī*.
harass, *see* annoy.
harbour, *bandargāh*, f.
hard, *ḍāhḍā*, *sakht*.
hardly, *see* scarcely, difficulty.
hare, *saihā*, *sehā*, m.: also rabbit.
harm, *see* injure, loss, hurt.
harmless, *see* guiltless, innocent: also harm w. neg.
harmony, *see* tune, agreement.
harness, *sāz*, m. (*lāṇā*, int. *laggṇā*): v., also *jōṇā* (int. *juttṇā*, *juppṇā*).
harrow, *suhāggā*, m. (*phērnā*, int. *phirnā*).
harsh, *see* hard, rough.
harvest, *fasl*, m.: *see* reap.
(1) **haste**, n., *kāhl*, f.: *tāṛ*, f.: *utauḷī*, f.: *see* impatien-ce,-t.
(2) **hasten**, *kāhl* or *chētī* or *shtābī* or *jaldī* all w. *karnī*: *kāhḷā* or *utauḷā ṭurnā*: *see* headlong.
hasty, *kāhḷā*, *utauḷā*: *jaldbāz* (bad sense).
hat, *ṭōpī*, f.
hatch, *bacce kaḍḍhṇe*.
hatchet, *kuhāṛī*, f.: *see* axe
hate, *wair rakkhṇā*: *dushmaṇī rakkhṇī*: *see* dislike, disgust, envy.
haught-iness, -y.: *see* pride, proud.
haul, *see* pull.
have, *de kōḷ h.*: *see* keep: to h. to, inf. w. agent, G. 75, 97: or inf. w. *paiṇā* or aux. v. w. *hōṇā*, G. 96. 97: have something done, *see* cause: *see* possession.
hawker, *chābṛīwāḷā*
haze, *see* fog.
he, *eh*, *oh*: his, her, *ehdā*, *ohdā*: also *s. sū*, G. 82-6: to him, her, *ehnū̃*, *ohnū̃*, also *s. sū*, G. 82-6.
head, *sir*, m.: of inanimate things, *sirā*, m.: sheep, goat, for eating, *sirī*, f.: bed, *sarhāndī*, f.: door, *sērū*, m.: of canal *hēḍḍ*, m.
heading, *see* title.
headlong, on one's head, *sir parne*: h. flight, paraphrase, as *khurī karke* or *annhe wāh* or *khiṭṭ dēke bhajj jāṇā*.
headman, *caudhrī*: of village, *lambaṛdār*: *see* lead-, -er.
headquarters, *hēḍkuāṭar*, m.: of canal, *see* head.
headstrong, *see* obstinate
heal, *see* cure, treat.
health, *tandrustī*, f.
healthy, *wall*, *caṅgā*, *acchā*, *tandrust*.
heap, *ḍhēr*, m., *ḍhērī*, f.: of

sugarcane, straw, chaff, plastered over, *dhaṛ*, f.: *see* wood.

hear, *sunnā*: *sunāī dendā e*, he, she, they, etc., can hear: M. 238. 19.

hearing, of lawcase, *pēshī*, f.

hearsay, *sunī sunāī gall*, f.

heart, *dil* or *diḷ*, m. (lit. and gen.): *man*, m.

heartily, *dilō wajhō hōke*, *dil nāḷ*.

heat, *garmī*, f.: *tā*, m. (of fire): fever h., *bhakhā*, f.: pungent heat, *see* hot: v. tr., *garm k.*, *tāṇā*; *tā pāṇā*, put burning coal into fire: *tā d.*, make coal burn up: become very hot (of fire), *see* blaze and add tr. *bhakhāṇā*: *see* slow (fire), hot (fire)

heaven, *bihisht*, m. (gen.): *surg*, m. (H.).

heavy, *bhārā*.

hedge, *wāṛ*, f., *see* railing, enclose.

hedgehog, *jhāh cūhā*, m.

heel, *aḍḍī*, f.

height, *ucāī*, f.: of person, *ucāī*, *lamāī*, f.: *masātar*, f., height to tips of fingers above head (to estimate depth of water).

heir, *wāris*, m.

hell, *dozakh*, m. and *jahannam*, m. (M.): *nark*, m (H.).

help, v., *madat*, f. (*k.*, *dī*: *d.*, *nū̃*): *hatth phaṛnā* (*dā*): also caus. of v. w. dat. of pers. and acc. of thing. G. 109: without assistance, by himself, without being told to, *āpū̃*, *āpe*, *āpī*, *āpō*, G. 88.

helper, *wasīlā*, m.: *madadgār*, m.

helpless, *lacār*, *wacārā*.

hemorrhoids, *bawāsīr* f., bleeding, *khūnī*.

hemp, *saṇ*, f.: *saṇkukṛā*, m.: *sūjjo-* or *sajjo-bhārā*, m.: intoxicating h., *bhang*, f., *cars*, f.

hen, *kukkṛī*, f.

hence, *ētthō*, *ēttalō*, *edharō*.

henceforth, *edū̃ agge*, *agge nū̃*.

her, *see* he.

herb, medicinal, *būṭī*, f.

herd, cattle, *wagg*, m.: *see* flock.

herdsman, *wāggī*, *chēṛū*, *ḍāṅgrī*: *see* shepherd.

here, *ētthe*, *ēttal*, *eddhar*: *ure* or *urhā̃* (gen. of motion alone): here it is, *āh wekhā̃*: h. and there, *kitale kitale*, *kite kite*, *kidhare kidhare*.

hereditary, *maurūsī*.

hero, *bahādar*: *see* brave.

hesitate, *shakk wicc raihṇā*, *ḍōlṇā*, *ḍāwā̃ ḍōl raihṇā*: *see* desire.

hiccup, *hiḍkī laggṇī* (M. 124. 50) or *auṇī*, (both w. *nū̃*).

(1) **hide,** *lukāṇā*, *chapāṇā* (int. *lukkṇā*, *chappṇā*): hidden, *gujjhā*.

(2) **hide,** n., *see* skin.

hideous, *see* ugly.

high, *uccā* (gen.): person, *uccā*, *lammā*.

hill, *pahāṛ*, m.: small, *pahāṛī*, f.: v. small, *ṭibbā* m.: range of small hills, *pabbī*, f.

hilly, belonging to hills, *pahāṛī*.

him, *see* he.

hinder, *ḍakkṇā*, *rōkṇā*, *aṭkāṇā*: *see* stop, forbid, obstruct.

hindrance, material, *ḍakkā*, m.: abstract, *aṭkā*, m. *bāndhā*, m.: *rukāwaṭ*, f. (gen.).

hinge, *kabzā*, m.: *see* pivot [socket.

hint, *ishārā*, m. (*k., de wall*): *see* hit, point.
hip, *lakk*, m.: h.-joint, *cūknā* m., *cūlā*, m., *cūkļī*, m.: (carry) on hip, *ḍhākke*.
hippopotamus, *daryāī ghōṛā*, m.
hire, *bhāṛā*, m.: *karāyā*, m.: *see* wages.
hiss, snake, *shūkṇā*, *shūkarnā*: n., *shūkar* f., *shukāṭ*, f., (both [*pāṇī*).
history, *tawārīkh*, f.
hit, int. *laggṇā* (stone, bullet, etc.): *see* beat: h. at in speech, *nōk lāṇī* (*nū*, int. *laggṇī*, *wajjṇī*): *see* hint, point.
hither, *ure*, *urhā*: *see* here.
hoarse, become, *saṅgh* or *wāz baihṇā* (*dā*): M. 117. 15: *wāz* or *awāz bhārā h.* (*dā*).
hobble, v. tr., *ḍhaṅgṇā*: v. int., *see* lame.
hoe, *gōḍṇā*, *gōḍḍī karnī*: n., small, *rambā*, m.: large, *kahī*, f.
hold, *phaṛī rakkhṇā*, *see* have, keep, seize.
hole, *mōrī*, f., (*kaḍḍhṇī*): *chēk*, m. (*kaḍḍhṇā*): in roof, *maggh*, m.: in wall, made by rain, etc., *gharl*, m.: in water-channel, *ghukkā*, m. (these last three w. *paiṇā*): animal's burrow, *khuḍḍ*, f. (*kaḍḍhṇī*).
holiday, *chuṭṭī*, f. (leave): *see* leave, festival.
hollow, *pōllā* (soft inside), *kholā khōkhlā* (U.).
holy, *pāk* (M.): *pawittar* (H.): *see* pure: h. man (H.), *sādhū*, *sanyāsī*, *gusāī*, *jōggī*: (M.) *aulīā*, *sāī*, *fakīr*: *see* priest.
home, *see* house: at h., *ghare*: gone h., *ghar geā*.
homesick, feel, *oddarnā* (*mā khunō* or *bājhō* or *thō*, for his mother).
homesickness, *udrēwā*, m.
honest, *dyānatdār*, *imānwālā*.
honey, *shaiht*, m., *mākhyō*, *mākhyō*, f.: *see* bee.
honeycomb, *mākhyō* (f.) *dā khaggā* or *pakkhā* or *kharkṇā* (or *dī challī*).
honour, *izzat*, f. (*k.*): *ādar*, f. (*k.*): *pat*, f., *see* esteem, respect.
honorary, *bēlankhāh*: h. magistrate, *ānararī majasṭrēṭ*, m.
hoof, *khur*, m. (cloven): *sum*, m. (uncloven).
hook, *kunḍā*, m. (gen.): clothes, *hukk*, f.: fish-h., *kunḍī*, f.
hoop, boys', *reṛhā*, m., *cakkar*, m.
hoot, *oe oe karnī*: *see* clap.
hope, *umēd*, f.: *in shā Allā*, please God (M.): *see* expect: *umēd*, expectation, seldom used for hope: I h. he will soon get well, *Khudā kare shtābī wall ho jāe*: I h. it did not hit him, *wajj nehī nā baiṭhā su*? I h. you will not get wet on the way, *wāṭe bhijj nā nā jāē*: I h. your horse does not jib now, *huṇ te nehī ō nā ghōṛā aṛdā*?
horn, *siṅg*, m.: -ed, *siṅgā wālā*.
hornet, *ḍehmū* m.: *see* wasp.
horse, *ghōṛā*: *waihtar*, m. (beast of burden, horse, mule ass).
horse-breaker, *cābuksuār*, m.
horse-race, *ghuṛdauṛ*, f.
hospital, *haspatāl*, m.
hostile, *see* enemy.
hot, *tattā*, *garm*: pungent in taste, *garm* (not *tattā*: n., *garmī*, f.): feel h., *waṭṭ laggṇā*

(*nū̃*) : *garmī laggṇī* (*nū̃*) : *baṛā hussaṛ e* : cook at hot fire, *tēz tā̃ pakāṇā*.
(1) hour, *ghaiṇṭā*, m. : *ghaṛī*, f. (strictly 22½ min.).
houri, *parī*, f. : *hūr*, f.
(2) hourly, *see* repeatedly : *ghaiṇṭe ghaiṇṭe picche*.
house, *ghar*, m., *kōṭhā*, m., *makān*, m. : European, *kōṭhī* f., *baṅglā*, m. : *see* home, hut : cow-h., *kuṛh*, f. (for cattle) : pigeon -h., on pole, *kābuk*, f. : in ground, *ghumail*, f. : *see* roost.
how, *kīka-n*, *-nā̃*, *-r*, *-rā̃*, *kis tarhā̃*, *kiñ*, *kīkū̃* : *see* somehow.
howl, *rōṇā*, *cilāṇā*, *karlāṇā* : of jackal, *hawāṅknā*, *see* [scream.
hubbub, *see* noise.
huff, take, *russṇā*.
hug, *see* embrace.
hum, *see* buzz.
humble, neg. of proud : h. oneself, *apṇe āp nū̃ nīweā̃ k.* : h. another, *ohdī lamb kaḍḍhṇī*, *ohdī ākkaṛ bhannṇī* : be humbled, *ohdī lamb* or *phūk nikḷnī* : *see* humiliation.
humiliation, *ʾbeiztī*, f. : *namōshī*, f. : v., *see* humble, disgrace, dishonour, pride.
hunchbacked, *kubṛā*, *kubbā*.
hundred, *sau*, *sai*, *saikṛā* : -th, *sauwā̃*, *sauhwā̃* : G. 20, 22, 93, 123 : *see* per cent.
hunger, *bhukkh*, f. (*laggṇī*, *nū̃*, G. 108).
hungry, *bhukkhā*.
hunt, *shikār k.* and *khēḍṇā* : *see* search, prey.
hunter, *shikārī*.
hurry, *see* hasten.
hurt (from blow, accident, etc.), *saṭṭ* f. (*laggṇī*, *nū̃*) : *see* wound, pain, damage, injury : of new shoes, medicine, etc., *laggṇā* (*nū̃*) : *see* strike.
hurtful, *nuksān* or *zyān* (*jān*) *karnwāḷā*.
husband, *khasm*, *gharwāḷā* : h. and wife, *miā̃ bīwī*, *dowē jī*, G. 122, M. 128. 16.
hush, *see* quiet ; h. up, *see* screen. [peel.
husk, *chill*, f. : v., *chaṛnā* : *see*
hut, small house, *kullī*, f. : *jhuggī*, f. : thatched h., *chappar*.
hydrophobia, *see* rabies.
hypercritical, be, *ghutklā̃ cheṛnīā̃* or *kaḍḍhṇīā̃* : *see* criticize.
hypocrisy, *makārī*, f. : *pakhaṇḍ*, m. : *see* deceit.
hypocrite, *makār*, *pakhaṇḍī* : *see* deceitful.

I, *maĩ* : people like me or us, *hamātaṛ*, G. 28.
ice, *warf*, f. : *barf*, f.
idea, *khyāl*, m. : *see* thought, believe, opinion.
idiom, *muhāwrā*, m.
idiot, *see* mad.
idle, *sust*, *kamcōr* : out of work, *bekār*, *wehlā*.
idol, *but*, m. : *mūrat*, f. (picture).
idolator, *butparast*, *butā̃* or *mūratā̃ nū̃ pūjjaṇwāḷā*.
idolatry, *butparastī*.
if, *jē*, *agar*, *jēkar* : ask or see if, *pucch lai paī*, (never *jē*, *agar*).
ignite, *see* light.
ignorance, *añānpuṇā*, m. : *beilmī*, f. : *nawākfī*, f. : *see* foolishness, stupid.

ignorant, *beilm*, *anāṇā*, *jaihl*: *see* stupid.
iguana, *goh*, m.
ill, *bamār*, *wall nehī*; *māndā*, *rōgī* (habitually ill): out of sorts, *nimmā*, *nimmo jhūṇā*: of men, boys, animals, *maṭeā hoeā*, *ṭhaṅgreā hoeā*, *hanēkeā hoeā*.
illegal, *kanūn de khalāf*: *see* unlawful.
illegitimate, child, *harām dā*: *see* illegal.
illfeeling, *see* envy (not distinguished). [*rōg*. m.
illness, *bamārī*, f.: *auhr*, f.:
illusion, *waihm*, m.: *see* deceit.
imagin-e, -ation, *khyāl karnā*, *farz karnā* (suppose): *waihm*. m. (foolish fancy, *h*.).
imaginary, *khyālī gall*, *farzī gall*.
imitat-e,-ion, *nakl*, f. (*k*.): copy at school, *nakl mārnī*, *k*.: of clown, *nakl utārnī*, *sāṅg utārnā*: in i. of, *ohde wallō wēkhke*, *ohdī wēkhā wēkhī* (U.): *see* counterfeit, copy.
immediately, *hune*, *ese weḷe*, *jhaṭ paṭṭ*: past time, *ōse weḷe*, *owē*.
immodest, *bēhayā*, *belajjā*.
immovable, *nehī halldā*: *see* lasting.
impartial, be, *raī nā karnī*, *sabbhnā nū ikkī akkh nāḷ wēkhṇā*.
impassable, *laṅghaṇwāḷā nehī*.
impatience, *saur*, f., *kāhl*, f. (both *paiṇī*): *see* hast-e,-en.
impatient, *kāhḷā*, or *saurā* (*paiṇā*), *bēsabr*: *sabr*, m., or *hauslā*, m., *nā k*.
impediment, *see* hindrance.
imperfect, *kaccā*, *nākas*, *mukkā nehī*.
imperfection, *see* defect, fault.
imperious, be, *hukm cāṛhnā*, *zōrāwarī karnī*: adj., *hākamānā*.
impertinent, *gustākh*, *shōkh*: *see* forward, rude.
implore, *see* beseech.
important, *bhārā*, *zarūrī*.
impossible, *namumkin*, *unhōṇī*: as interj., *mērī majāl e*? *majāl geī e*? *tōbbā*!
impress upon, *pakkī karnī* (*nū*).
impression, *nishān*, m.: on mind, *asr*, m.
imprison, *kaid-k*.: be -ed, *bajjhṇā*, *kaid-h*: *see* prisoner.
improper, *nāmunāsib*.
improve, int., *suddharnā*, *saurnā*: tr., *sudhārnā*, *suārnā*: *see* correct.
improvement, *see* progress: in disease, *riait*. f., *arām*, m., *armān*, m.
imprudent, *sōcdā nehī*.
impure, *see* dirty, unclean.
in, *wicc*, *andar*: on the inside, *andarwār*: from inside, *wiccō*, *andarō*: pass by way of inside, *wiccō* or *andarō dī laṅghṇā*: of place, often loc., G. 9, 10, 77: in or after half an hour, three weeks, *addhe ghaiṇṭe* (*triūh hafteā*) *nū* or *picche*: within half hour, etc., *addhe ghaiṇṭe de andar*: often loc., *tinnī haftī*, in three weeks, so in the morning, evening, etc., G. 10, 34, 78.
inadvertently, *see* accidentally, carelessness.
inattentive, *dhiān nehī kardā*.
inauspicious, *see* auspicious.
inborn, *zātī*. A.
incantation, perform, *hāl khēḍ-*

ṇā, sir mārnā, mantar paṛhnā (K.).
incapable, incapacity, *see* able, worthless, useless.
incarnate, become, *deh dhārī h.* (H.): *autār dhārnā* (H.): *mujassam h.* (M.): *bandeā dī sūrat shakl wicc auṇā.*
incense, n., *dhūf*, m., *dhūkh*, m.
incessant, *see* always, repeatedly, daily.
inch, *incī*, f.: *see* wts. and meas.
incite, *cukkṇā, bhaṛkāṇā, macāṇā, paṭṭī paṛhāṇī* (*nū̃*): *kann wicc phūkṇā* (*de*): *see* induce, excite, urge, seduce.
incitement, *cukk*, f.
inclined to, *rūh* or *jī karnā*, (e.g. *cukkaṇ nū̃*, to lift, etc.): *see* desire, taste.
includ-ed, -ing, *de sane, wicc pāke, shāmil karke, raḷāke.*
incoherent, *bemaikne.*
income, *āmdanī*, f.
incompetent, *see* able, worthless, useless.
incomplete, *see* imperfect.
incomprehensible, *samajh wicc nehī̃ aundā, kujjh piṛ palle nehī̃ peā.*
incongruous, *raḷdā* or *phabbdā nehī̃.*
(1) inconvenience, *wakht*, m.: *taklīf*, f.: *bēarāmī*, f.
(2) inconvenienced, *khajjal, khajjal khuār, aukkhā*: *see* difficulty, trouble, straits.
(3) inconvenient, *sādde wāste mushkil e, eh wēḷā ṭhīk nehī̃*: *see* convenience.
increase, int. *waddhṇā, trakkī karnī*; tr., *wadhāṇā, trakkī dēṇī* (*nū̃*).
incredible, *mannaṇwāḷī gall nehī̃.*
incubate, *bacce kaḍḍhne.*
incurable, *koī ilāj nehī̃, lāilāj.*
indebted, *see* debtor: acknowledge obligation, *ahsān* or *ṭhāhrā mannṇā.*
indecent, of words, *fohsh*; of persons, *luccā.*
indeed, is it so? *halā, sacc e?*
indefatigable, *anthakk, thakkaṇwāḷā nehī̃.*
indefinite, *ṭhīk patā nehī̃, ṭhīk faislā nehī̃, kuccī gall, kac pakk.*
independent, *khudmukhtār, āpū̃ mālik e.*
index, *firist*, f.
indicate, *see* show.
indifferen-ce, -t, *see* carelessness.
indigent, *see* poor.
indigestible, *pacdā nehī̃.*
indigestion, *badhazmī*, f., *unpācā*, m.
indigo, *nīl*, f.
indistinct, *sāf nehī̃, maddham.*
induce, *manāṇā*: *see* incite, urge.
indulge (child), *lāḍ karnā* (*nāḷ*).
industrious, *mehntī.*
inevitable, *zarūrī, aṭall, kismat nāḷ nehī̃ laṇdā*, etc.
inexperienced, *aṇāṇā*: *kaccā*: *nāī tajrabakār* (U.): *tajrabā nehī̃, allhaṛ.*
inexpert, *aṇāṇā, kaccā*: *see* clever.
infant, *kucchaṛ wicc, duddh pīṇwāḷā.*
infer, *natījā kaḍḍhṇā.*
infidel, *see* atheist: *kāfar* (M.).
infidelity, *kufr*, m. (M.): *bedīnī*, f.: *see* adultery.
inflammation, *sōj*, f. (swelling): v., *sujjṇā.*
influence, *rōhb*, m. (half fear): *rusūkh*, m.: *asr*, m.

inform-, -ation, *itlāh dēṇī* ; *kaiṛ karnī* : *khabar dēṇī*, (all *nū̃*).
ingenious, *see* clever.
ingenuity, *hikmat*, f.
ingratitude, *nāshukrī*, f. : *kirt-ghaṇī*, f. : *see* ungrateful.
inhabit, *wassṇā*, *raihṇā* : being i.-ed, *wassō*, f. : caus. v., *see* people (2).
inhabitant, *raihṇwāḷā* : *see* resident.
inherit, *wāris h.* : i.-ed, *maurūsī*.
inheritance, *wirsā*, f. : *mirās*, f.
inhuman, *insān nehī̃*, *bandā nehī̃* : *see* cruel, oppression.
injure, *trattī cauṛ karnī* (int. *hōṇī*, both *dī*) : *see* damage, hurt, loss.
injustice, *bēinsāfī*, f. : *bēniāī*, f. (H.).
ink, *syāhī*, f. : coloured i., *rang*, \[m.
inkstand, *duāt* f.
(1) inn, *sarā̃*, f. : European rest-house, *ḍāk banglā*, m.
innings, *wār*, f. (both individual and side : *laiṇī*, *dēṇī*).
(2) innkeeper, *bhaṭhyārā*.
innocent, *masūm* : *see* guiltless, acquit.
innuendo, *nōk lāṇī* (*nū̃*) : *ishārā k.* (*de wall*) : i. be apposite, *nōk wajjṇī* (*nū̃*) : *see* hint.
innumerable, *angiṇā*, *bē-bahā*, *-shumār*, *-hadd*.
inoculate, *ṭīkā lāṇā* (int. *laggṇā*, caus., *luāṇā*) or *ukhṇāṇā* (int. *ukkhaṇṇā*).
inquire, *see* ask, discover : i. after health, *surt laiṇī* (*dī*), *patā karnā* (*dā*), *pucchṇā* (*nū̃*).
inquirer, *mutlāshī* (or catechumen).
inquiry, investigation, *takīkāt*, f. (*k.*, *dī*).

insane, *see* mad.
insect, *kīṛā*, m. (often snake) : large ants, *kīṛe*, *ḍhak makauṛe*, m. pl.
insensible, *behōsh* : *see* numb.
inside, *see* in.
insipid, *bēsuādda*, *phikkā* : without sauce, etc., *rukkhā*
insist, *see* obstinate : *takrār karnā*, *magar paiṇā* (*de*) : *gal paiṇā* (*de*).
insistence, *takrār*, m. : *see* obstinate.
insistent, *khaihṛā nehī̃ chaḍḍdā*.
inspection, school *muāinā karnā* (*dā*) : medical, etc., *mulāhzā karnā* (*dā*) : in gen. *phērā mārnā* (visit, etc.).
inspector, *inspiṭṭar*, *inspĕkṭar*.
instalment (money), *kishṭ*, f.
instance, *see* example. \[*kisht*.
instant, n., *sakinṭ*, m. : *dam*, m. : *jhaṭ*, m. : *palī*, m.
instead, *de thā̃*, *de badle*.
instigate, *see* incite.
instinctively, *see* intuitively.
instruct-, -ion, *see* teach.
instrument, *ṛacch*, m. *hathyār*, m. : *kalā̃*, f., *kalā*, f. musical, *wājā*, m. : *see* play, tune, \[tool.
insult, *see* disgrace.
insure, oneself, etc., *bīmā*, m. *karāṇā* (*dā*).
intelligent, *siāṇā*.
intelligence, *siāṇap*, f. : *see* sense, clever.
inten-d, -ntion, *manshā*, f. : *irādā*, m. : *nīyat*, f. : *matlab*, m. : *dalīl*, f. : *pucchaṇ pucchaṇ kardā sā̃*, intended to ask but hesitated, G. 112 : *see* object, desire.
intentionally, *see* deliberately, purposely.
intercede, *sifārish karnī* (*dī*) : *shafāt karnī* (*de-wāste*).

intercept, *rāh wicc pharnā.*
intercessor, *sifārish* or *shafāt karnwāḷā.*
intercourse, *sangat,* f. : *sohbat,* f. : *wāh,* m. : (*see* connection) : esp. eating, drinking, *wartō,* f., *wartāwā,* m., *wartṇā,* m. : coming and going, *auṇā jāṇā.*
(1) interest (gen. monthly), *byāj,* m., *sūd,* m. : *see* advantage, profit, benefit : self-i., *khudgarzī,* f. : *gaū,* m. : *see* object, intention.
(2) interested in, *dilcaspī,* f. (*menū̃ ehde nāḷ e*), *ohdā shauk h.* (*nū̃*).
interesting, *suādlā, dilcasp.*
interfere, *dakhl dēṇā* (*wicc*).
intermingle, mix : *see* mix.
internal, *wiclā, wishkārlā, andarlā, andrūnī* (U).
interpose, *see* mediator, interfere, interrupt
interpret, *tarjmā karnā* (*dā*).
interpreter, *tarjmā karnwāḷā, mutrajjim.*
interrupt, *gall tukknī* (*dī*), *dī gall wicc gall karnī* : *see* interfere.
interval, time, *cir,* m. : *mohlat,* f. (days of "grace") : *wakfā,* m. (U.) : space, *paindā,* m. : *khappā,* m., *witth,* f., *wāt,* f.
intervene, *see* interpose.
interview, *mulākāt karnī* (*nāḷ*).
intimate, *pakkā dōst* or *yār* : *see* friend.
intimidate, *see* fear.
intolerable, *jehṛā nā jareā* (or *saiheā* or *jhalleā*) *jāe.*
intoxicant, *nashā,* m. : *nashe wālī cīz,* f. [(*kaḍḍhṇā*).
intrench, *khandak,* f. or *toā,* m.
intricacy, *waḷ,* m., *pēc,* m. : *waḷ pēc,* m.
intricate, *pēcwāḷā, waḷ pēcwāḷā.*
intrigue, *see* plot.
introduce, person, *miḷāṇā* (*nāḷ*), *wākif karāṇā* (*nāḷ*) : *mēḷ karāṇā* (*dā*) : law, custom, money, *jārī karnā, tōrnā, kaḍḍhṇā.*
intrude, *see* interfere, interrupt.
intrust, *see* entrust.
intuitively, *uñ, āpū̃ khyāl āeā, apṇī* (*apṇe*) *akl nāḷ, khāhmakhāh.*
invade, *mulkh wicc hamlā karke warṇā.*
investigation, *see* inquiry.
invincible, *see* unconquerable.
invisible, *jehṛā nā disse.*
invit-e, -ation, *saddṇā, rōṭī ākhṇī* or *thākṇī* or *warjṇī* (*dī*), *dāwat karnī* (*dī*) : *sāḍḍī ohde wall roṭī e.*
invoke, *kise dī duhāī dēṇī.*
involuntarily, *khāhmakhāh* : *see* force.
iron, *lohā,* m. : adj., *lohe dā* : (ironing) *istrī,* f. : iron, v. tr., *istrī-k.*
irony, *tāhnā mārnā* (*nū̃*), *nōk lāṇī* (*nū̃*), *makhaul nāḷ ākhṇā.*
irrecoverable, *geā guātā.*
irregular-, -ity, *bēkaid-ā* (n -*agī,* f.), *bēkanūn-* (n. -*ī,* f.), *bētartīb-* (n., -*ī,* f.).
irrelevant, *ehdā tallak nehī̃* (*nāḷ*).
irreligious, *bedīn* (M.) : *bedharm* (H.) : nouns add -*ī.*
irremediable, *dā ilāj nehī̃.*
irrigate, *see* water.
irritable, *ciṛhnwāḷā, kiṛnwāḷā.*
irritate, *see* tease.
island, *ṭāpū,* m. : *jazīrā,* m.
issue, order, *jārī-k., kaḍḍhṇā.*

it, *see* he, she.
itch, n., v., *khurk*, f. (*h. paiṇī*).
item, *gall*, f.
itinerary, *safar*, m. : *safarnāmā*, m.
ivory, *dand khaṇḍ*, f.

J

jackal, *giddaṛ*, m.
jacket, *kōṭ*, m : *jākaṭ*, m.
jail, *see* prison.
jam, *jām*, m. (K., *baṇāṇā*) : *murabbā*, m. (*pāṇā*).
janitor, *capṛās-ī*, m. fem. *-an*.
January, *janwarī*, f. : *māhṅg*, *māh*, m. (about Jan. 13 to Feb. 12).
jar, *see* pot.
jasmine, *cambā*, m.
jaw, *khakhwāṛā*, m. : *haṛbāccī*, f.
jealous-, -y, *see* envy, suspicious.
jeer, *see* mock.
jerk, *see* jolt.
jester (excess implied), *makhaulīā*, *ṭokī*, *maskharībāz* : professional, *bhanḍ* : *see* joke.
Jesus, *Yĕsū*, *Īsā*, *Hazrat Īsā* (M.).
jet-black, v. black, *kāḷā syāh*, *kāḷā shāh*.
Jew, *Yahūd-ī*, fem. *-aṇ*.
jewellery, *gaihṇā*, m., *gaihṇe*, m. pl. : each piece, *ṭūmb*, f., also *gaihṇā*.
jib, *aṛnā*.
jingle, *chaṇ chaṇ k.* : *see* tinkle.
join, *jōṛnā* (int. *juṛnā*) : person, *ralṇā* (*nāḷ*), *milṇā* (*nāḷ*, *nū̃*) : army, *bhartī h.*
joint, body, *jōṛ*, m.
jointly, *raḷke*, *milke*, *katthe*.
joke, *hāsse dī gall* : *jugat*, f. (quibble w. slight sting) : rather objectionable, *makhaul*, m. : *maskharī*, f., *mashkarī*, f.
jokingly, *hāsse nāḷ*, *makhaul nāḷ*.
jolt, *hujjkā laggṇā* (*nū̃*) : *dhakkā khāṇā*.
journal, diary, *rōznāmcā*, m. (U) : *ḍairī*, f. ; *see* newspaper.
journey, *safar*, m. (*k.*) : *sair*, m. or *sail*, m. or *sail sapaṭṭā*, m., j. for pleasure, walk, etc. : *phērā*, m. (*pāṇā*, *mārnā*, int. *paiṇā*), esp. visit, useless j.
joy, *khushī*, f.
joyful, *khush*.
judge, n., *jaj*, *munsaf* (civil), *tasīldār*, (criminal and executive) : *see* magistrate : v., *faislā karnā*.
judgment-day, *kiāmat dā din*, m. (*kiāmat*, f., really resurrection).
jug, water or milk, *jagg*, m. : *see* pot.
juggler, *madār-ī*, fem. *-an*.
juice, *ras*, m.
juicy, *raswāḷā*.
July, *jaulāī*, f. : *julāī*, f. : *jaulā*, m. : *saoṇ*, m. (about July 13 to Aug. 12).
jumble up, *hēṭh utā k.*, *rauḷā mārnā*, *gaṛbaṛī karnī*.
jump, *ṭappṇā* (over, *nū̃* : on to, *utte*) : waves, water, *uchaḷṇā* : n., *chāḷ*, f. : *chalāṅg*, f. : *phalāṅg*, f. (all w. *mārnī*).
June, *jūn*, m. : *hāhṛ*, m. (about June 13 to July 12).
jurisdiction, *ikhtiār*, m.
just, *insāfwāḷā*, *niāī* : adv., *zarā* : j. now, *huṇe*.
justice, *insāf*, m. : *niā*, f.

K

kedgery, food, *khicṛī*, f.
keen, on sthg., *shukīn* : *see* desire, sharp.
keep, *rakkhṇā* ; in one's possession, *apṇe kabze wicc rakkhṇā* : animals *rakkhṇā* : k. seat, *see* engage : k. safe, *sāmbhṇā* : temporarily k. back money, wages, *heṭh rakkhṇā* (G. 91) : *see* detain, hinder : kept tame animal, *rākhwā* : k. feast, *īd karnī* ; *see* celebrated
keeper, *see* guardian, watchman.
keepsake, *yādgār*, f.
kernel, *girī*, f. : (cocoanut, *garī*).
kettle, *kētlī*, f.
key, *kunjī*, f. : *cābī*, f. : fit, *laggṇī* (tr. *lāṇī*, try).
kick, by person, *thuḍḍā lāṇā* or *mārnā* (int. *khāṇā*, *laggṇā*) : also *thuḍḍī mārnā* : football, *kik mārnī* : by horse, etc., *dulattā mārnā*.
kid, *bagrōṭā*.
kidney, *gurdā*, m.
kill, *mār chaḍḍṇā* or *saṭṭṇā*, *thā̃ mārnā*, *jānō̃ mārnā* : for food, *kohṇā* : *halāl-k.* (M.) : *takbīr paṛhnī* (*utte*, M.) : *jhaṭkā karnā* (*dā*, *nū̃*, H.).
kiln, *bhaṭṭhā*, m. : *āwā*, m. : *āwī*, f.
kilt, *ghaghrī*, f. : *see* skirt : k.-ed regiment, *ghāghrā palṭan*, f.
(1) **kind**, *mehrbān*.
(2) **kind**, n., *jins*, f. : *kism*, f.
kindness, *mehrbānī*, f.
kindred, *see* relati-ve,-onship.
king, *bādshāh* : *rājā*, *māhrājā*, *sultān*.

kingdom, *bādshāhī*, f. : *saltanat*, f. (rule, etc.) : *rāj*, m.
kiss, *cummṇā* : n. *cummā*, m. : *cummī*, f. (all gen. w. bad meaning) : *see* caress.
kitchen, *baurcīkhānā*, m. : village, *culhānnī*, f. (M.) : *rasōī*, f. (H) : He's square, *caukkā*, m., *caũkā*, m.
kite, boy's, *guḍḍī*, f.
kitten, *bilūṅgā*, m.
knack, *jāc*, f. : *thauh*, m.
knead, flour, *gunnhṇā* (pa. p. *guddhā*, *gunnheā* : int. *gujjhṇā*) : clay w. hands or feet, *gōṇā*.
knee, *gōḍḍā*, m. : -cap, *cappṇī*, f., *chūṇī*, f.
kneel, *gōḍḍe niwāṇe* or *ṭēkṇe*, *goḍḍeā̃ bhār* or *parne baiṭhṇā*.
knife, *churī*, f. : *kard*, f. : pen-k., *cakkū*, m. : large k., *churā*, m. : -board, *takhtī*, f.
knob, *see* handle.
knock, at door, *khaṛkāṇā* (lit. rattle) : k. down, *ḍhāṇā*, *ḍēgṇā* : k. against, gently, *khaihṇā* (*nāḷ*) : *see* collide : be k.-ed about, *dhakke* or *bhambalbhūse khāṇe*.
knot, n., (tied or in wood) *gaṇḍh*, f. : v., *gaṇḍhṇā*, *gaṇḍh dēṇī* (*nū̃*) : open, *kholhṇī*.
know, *jāṇṇā*, *patā hōṇā* (*nū̃*), *malūm hōṇā* (*nū̃*) : make known, *patā dēṇā* ; spread abroad, *dhumāṇā* (int. *dhummṇā*) : k. languages *jāṇṇā* ; adj., *-dān*, *fārsī-dān* knowing Persian, etc.
knowingly, *see* purposely.
knowledge, *ilm*, m.
knuckle (hand or foot), *gaṇah*, f.

L

label, *ciṭṭ*, f.

labour, *mehnat*, f. : *see* force, effort, labourer.

labourer, *mazdūr*, m. : fields, *kāmmā* : employer or employee, wages in kind, *sēpī*, fem. *sēpaṇ* : all-time employee, *āthrī* : one of menial classes, *kammī*, fem. *kamṇeāṇī* : condition of *sepi*, *sēp*, f. : *see* servant.

lace, boot, shoe, *waddhrī*, f. : *tasmā*, m. (U.).

lack, n., *thuṛh*, f. : *ghāṭā*, m. : v., *thuṛhnā*, *ghaṭṭṇā* (be insufficient).

ladder, *pauṛī*, f., *paṛsāṅg*, f. : *see* rung.

ladle, *see* spoon.

lady (European) *mēmsāb* : unmarried *miss sāb*, *miss*.

ladybird, *kumnihā kīṛā*, m.

lake, *jhīl*, f., *sar*, m., *ḍal*, m. : *see* pond.

lamb, *lēllā*, m.

lame, *laṅgā*, *laṅgṛā* : walk l., *laṅgāṇā* : *see* cripple.

lament, *see* mourn, weep.

lamp, *lamp*, m. : *battī*, f. : wall-l., *duālgīr*, m. : earthen, *dīwā*, m.

lamppost, *munnā*, m. : *waḷā*, m.

lampstand, movable, *dīurī*, f. : in wall, *duākhā*, m.

lance, *see* spear.

(1) **land**, *zamīn* or *zimī* or *jīwī* or *jiwī*, f. : *see* soil, country.

(2) **land**, v., of ship, *kaṇḍhe* or *dande laggṇā* : of person, *jahāz uttō utarnā*

landlord, *mālik*, m.

lane, *gaḷī*, f. [speech.

language, *bōlī*, f. : *zabān*, f. : *see*

lantern, *lālṭaiṇ*, f., *hatth battī*, f.

lap, *gadd*, f. : *see* arm : *jhoḷī*, f (front of garment, for carrying things in).

large, *see* big, roomy, loose.

(1) **last**, adj., *chekaṛlā*, *pishlā* : year, week, month, *see* year, week, month : last night, *ajj rāt nū̃*, *ajj dī rāt*, *rāt* : l. Monday, *pishle suār nū̃* : l. time, *aglī wārī*.

(2) **last**, v., boots, clothes, etc., *haṇḍhṇā* : last 2, 3 days, of food, *kaḍḍhṇā* (*dō trai din*) G. 118 : M. 119. 45 : of join in furniture, machinery, *khlōṇā*.

lasting, *pakkā*, *baṛā haṇḍhaṇ-wāḷā* : *see* permanent.

lastly, *see* finally.

late, adj., *cirkā*, *carākā* (but *carōkṇā*, of a long time ago), *pachētrā* : be l., *cir*, m., *ḍēr*, f. (both w. *lāṇā*, int. *laggṇā*), *paccharṇā* : *cirkā auṇā*, etc. (of train often *lēṭ auṇī*) : late, deceased, *marhūm* (M., U.), *bahishtī* (M), *surgī* (H).

lathe, *kharād*, f. : v., *kharādṇā*, *kharād k.* or *cāṛhnā*.

laugh, *hassṇā* : *hāssā auṇā* (*nū̃*), inclined to laugh, (M. 117, 6) : *guṭakṇā* (giggle) : derisive words, *mū̃h aḍḍṇā*, *dand kaḍḍhṇe* : *see* joke, ridicule.

law, *kanūn*, m. : relig., *sharā*, m. : *shariat*, f. (both M.).

lawful, *jāiz* : *halāl* (M., esp. food, money) : *see* legal.

lawsuit, *mukadmā*, m. : *see* case, lose, hearing : date of l., *tārīkh*, f. : *tarīk*, f.

lawyer, *wakīl*, m. : *bālishṭar*, m. : the practice or work, *wakālat*, f., *bālishṭrī*, f. : his pay, *mehntāṇā*, m.

lay, *see* place : eggs, *dēṇā*.

layer, fold, *taih*, m. f.: of bricks in building, *raddā*, m.

laziness, *ḍhill*, f., *ḍhill maṭṭh*, f.: *susti*, f.

lazy, *ḍhillā*, *maṭṭhā*, *sust*, *kamcōr*.

(1) lead, *sikkā*, m

(2) lead, *mohre calṇā*, *agge calṇā*, *lai calṇā*, *āggū* or *mohrlā h.*: *see* guide.

leader, *sardār*: *see* lead, headman.

leaf, *pattar*, m.: of book, *warkā*, m.: of door, *bhitt*, m.

leak, *see* drip, ooze

(1) lean, adj., *māṇā*, *patlā*, *lissā*.

(2) lean on, *de sahāre calṇā* or *khlōṇā*: l. back, *nāḷ ḍhāsṇā lāṇā*, *ḍhoh lāṇī*: *see* stoop.

leap, *see* jump.

learn, gen. *sikkhṇā*: study in gen., *paṛhnā*: lesson, *pakāṇā*, *yād-k.* (int. *pakkṇā*, *yād h.* or *auṇā*, M. 117. 4).

learned, *ālam*, *ilmwāḷā*: *maulwī* (M.): *paṇḍat* (H.): *see* expert.

lease, *paṭā*, m.: *ṭhēkā*, m. (contract): v., *paṭe* or *ṭhēke te dēṇā*.

least, *sabbhnā* or *sāreā tō nikkā* or *ghaṭṭ*: at l., *ghaṭṭo ghaṭṭ*, *ghaṭṭ tō ghaṭṭ*.

leather, *camm*, m.: *camṛā*, m.: untanned, *khall*, f.: l.-worker, *mōc-ī*, fem. *-aṇ*: *cameār-*, fem. *-ī* (fr. the U.P.)

(1) leave, *chuṭṭī*. f. (*laiṇī*, *dēṇī*): take l. of, *widyā -h.*, *rukhsat -h.* (send off, *widyā -k.*, *rukhsat-k.*): l. off, *see* abstain: l. off work, *chuṭṭī karnī*: *see* liberty.

(2) leavings of food, *jūṭhā*, any food once begun is *jūṭhā*, adj.: n., *jūṭh*, m.

leaven, *khamīr*, m.

lecture, *dars*, m. (*d.*): *likcar*, m. (*d.*).

leech, *jōk*, f.

left, *khabbā*: l.-handed, *khabbā*.

leg, *latt*, f.: *liṅg*, m.: of furniture, *pāwā*, m.: of mutton, *lēk*, f. (K.): *see* calf, shin, thigh. muscle.

legal, *kanūn wallō jāiz*: *see* lawful.

legend, *kahāṇī*, f.

legitimate (child) *halāl dā*: *see* legal, lawful.

leisure, *wehl*, f.: *wāndak*, f.: *wānd*, f.: *fursat*, f. (U.): *see* leave: at l., *wehlā*, *wāndā*.

lemon, *see* lime.

lemonade, *lamnēṭ*, m., *miṭṭhā pāṇī*, m.

lend, money, *udhār -d.*: *see* debt. borrow.

lender, *see* money-lender.

length, *lamāī*, f.: *lām*, m.: *lamittaṇ*, f.: l.-wise, *see* direction.

leopard, *cittrā*, m.

leper, *koṛhā*, fem. *koṛhī*.

leprosy, *koṛh*, m.: *waḍḍā rōg* or *dukh*.

less, *kamm*, *ghaṭṭ*, *kassā*.

lessen, *ghaṭāṇā*, *ghaṭṭ k.*, *kamm k.*: (int. *ghaṭṭ h.*, *kamm h.*, *maṭṭhā h.*): price, *riait karnī*.

lesson, *sabak*, m.: *see* learn, teach.

lest, *mate*, *cētā*, *ajehā nā howe paī*.

letter, *ciṭṭhī*, f.: *khaṭṭ*, m. (often postcard): note, *rukkā*, m.: *parcī*, f.: official l., *rōbkār*, m.: of alphabet, *harf*, m.: *akkhar*, m. (H.).

lettuce, *salāt*, m. : *salād*, m.
leucoma, *see* eye-ulcer.
level, *padhrā*, *suāhrā*, *sāf*, *barābar* : *see* flat, plain.
lever, *tul* (*dēṇī*, l. up, raise).
liable, *see* prone.
liar, *jhūṭhā*.
libel, action, *izzat dā dāhwā* : *see* slander, accuse.
liberal, *see* generous : thought, *azād khyāl wālā*.
liberty, gen. *azādī*, f. : l. to do something, *khullh*, f., *ijāzat*, f. : *izn*, m. : take l., be familiar, *see* familiar : act without leave, *ijāzat tō binā karnā* : (or *bē* or *bilā ijāzat*).
library, *laibrerī*, f. : room in house, *daftar*, m.
licence, *laisans*, f. (a written l.) : *see* liberty.
lick, *catṇā*.
lid, *ḍhakṇā*, m. : *ḍhakkaṇ*, m. : for vessel, *cappṇī*, f., *chūṇī*, f., *chūṇā*, m.
(1) lie, tell, *jhūṭh bōlṇā* or *mārnā*.
(2) lie, down, *lammā paiṇā*, G. 64 (tr. *pāṇā*) : *saūṇā* (sleep) : remain lying, *peā raihṇā* A.
lieutenant, *laftain* : L.-Governor, *lāṭ sāb*.
life, (animal) *jān* : course of, *hyātī*, f., *zindagī*, f., *jindṛī*, f. : eternal l., *hamēshā dī zindagī* : past l., *guzrī hoī* or *pishlī zindagī* : biography, *hāl*, m., *hawāl*, m. : conduct *cāl caln*, m.
lifeless, *bejān*. [carry.
lift, *cukkṇā*, *uṭhāṇā*, *cāṇā* : *see*
(1) light, n. *lō*, f. : *cānnaṇ*, m. : *cānṇā*, m. : *rōshnī*, f.
(2) light, adj., not heavy, *haulā* : colour, *hawāī*, *nīm*.
(3) light, lamp, fire, *bālṇā* (int. *balṇā* : begin to burn, *bal paiṇā*) : *see* fire, burn.
lightning, *baddal lishkṇā* : *bijlī*, f.
(1) like, adj., *see* similar.
(2) like, v., *caṅgā laggṇā* (*nū̃*) : *see* desire, taste.
limbs, gen., *naiṇ prāṇ*, m. pl. : *hatth pair*, m. pl. : *aṅg*, m. : *see* cripple.
(1) lime, lemon, large kind, *khaṭṭā*, m. : small, *nimbū*, m. : (thin rind) *kāgzī nimbū* : sweet, *miṭṭhā*, m. : small do., *nārgī*, f. : inferior l., *galgal*, f., *truñ*, f., *kimb*, m. : eat l., *cūpṇā*.
(2) lime, building, *cūnā*, m.
limestone, *rōṛ*, m.
line, *līk*, f. : *lakīr*, f. : in book, *satar*, f. : of poetry, *misrā*, m. : railway, *laiṇ*, f. : of boys, etc., *katār*, f. (U.) : draw l., *khiccṇā* : a few lines (letter) *dō* or *cār harf*, m. pl.
lineage, *nasabnāmā*, m. (genealogy) : *see* descendants. tree.
lining, *lailaṇ*, f.
link, of chain, *kuṇḍī*, m. : *saṅglī*, f. (rare).
linseed, *alsī*, f.
lion, *shēr babar*, *babar shēr*, m.
lip, *bull*, m. : *hōṭh*, m.
lisp, nearest word "stammer."
list, *firist*, f.
listen, *suṇṇā* : attentively, *kann lāke* or *dhyān karke* or *lāke suṇṇā* : l. for, *kaiṛ laiṇī* (*dī*).
literal, meaning, *lafzī*.
literary, *kitābī*.
literature, *kitābā̃*. f. pl.
litigious, *mukadmebāz*.
little, size, *see* small : quantity, *thōṛā jehā*, *zarā ku*, *kujjh*

kujjh, ghaṭṭ waḍḍh (G. 28) : v. l., *ruāḷ*, as *ruāḷ ku āṭā*, v. l. flour : too l., *kassā, ṭhōṛā*.

live, *jyūṇā* (pa. p. *jīweā*) : dwell, *raihṇā* : l. good life, *cāl caln acchā e* : l. in ease, *arām wicc* or *nāḷ raihṇā*.

livelihood, *rozī*, f. : *rōzgār*, m. : *guzārā*, m.

liver, *kalejā*, m. : of animal, *kalejī*, f., *kalejā*, m.

livery, *wardī*, f.

living, *see* alive, livelihood.

load, *bhār*, m. (*laddṇā*) : *bōjh*, m. (U.) : *see* wts. and meas.

loaf, Indian, *rōṭī*, f. : *capāṭī*, f. : *paraunṭhā*, m. : small, *gullī*, f. : European, *ḍabal rōṭī*, f. : *see* bread.

loafer, *awārā*, fem. the same.

loan, *see* lend.

loathsome, *ghinaoṇā* : words for disgust.

(1) lock, *jandrā*, m. : *tāḷā*, m. (both w. *mārnā*, *lāṇā*, int. *laggṇā*, *wajjṇā*) : unlock, *jandrā lāhṇā* (int. *laihṇā*).

(2) lock, hair, *see* hair : Hindu's, *bōdī*, f.

locust, *makṛī*, f.

log, *gēllī*, f. : v. short, for fuel, *mōchā*, m. (*pāṇā*, int. *paiṇā*) : *see* sleeper.

logic, *manṭak*, f.

(1) loincloth, *langōṭī*, f.

(2) loins, *see* waist.

lonel-y, -iness, use *kallā*, alone, and *see* homesick.

(1) long, adj., *lammā* : l. time, *cir*, m. : fr. l. time ago, *kadōknā*, *carōknā*, *jū* : *see* delay : longways, *see* direction : as long as, *jinnā cir*, *jicar*, *jicar tīkar* : long days (summer), *see* day.

(2) long for, *taṛafṇā* (great unrest) : *saihknā*, (*nū̃*), *tarsṇā* : cause to l. f., afflict, *tarsāṇā*.

(3) long-lived, *waḍḍī umr dā* : *see* old.

look, *wēkhṇā* (pa. p. *ḍiṭṭhā*, *wekheā*), *takkṇā* : glance, *nazr mārnī* (*utte*) : l. stealthily, *jhāttī mārnī* : *see* frown, search : l. after, *sāmbhṇā*, *sambhāḷṇā* : *see* watch, protect.

loom, *khaḍḍī*, f. : warp, *tāṇī*, f., woof, *pēṭā*, m.

loose, *ḍhillā* : get loose, machinery, masonry, *ukkhaṛnā* (tr. *ukhēṛnā*, *see* piece) : clothes, *mōkḷā*.

lopsided, *see* weight.

loquacious, *see* talkative.

lord it over, lordly, *see* imperious.

lose, *guāṇā*, *khaṛāṇā*, *gum-k*. (U.) : int. *guācṇā*, pa. p., *guātā* or *guāceā* : *khaṛācṇā*, pa. p. *khaṛātā*, *khaṛāceā* : *gum-h*., (U.) : also *jāndeā raihṇā* : l. game, *see* game : l. law-case, *ohdī* or *ohde-sir digrī hōnī*, *mukadmā khārij hōṇā* (*dā*), *mukadmā hārnā* (*dā*).

loss, damage, *nuksān*, m., *jān*, m., *zyān*, m., all w. *h*. : financial, *mōs*, f., *ṭoṭṭā*, m., both w. *laggṇā*, *khāṇā*, *paiṇā* : *harj*, m. (*h*.), *caṭṭī*, f. (*paiṇī*) : *ghāṭā*, m. (*khāṇā*, *paiṇā*) : make up l., *ṭōṭṭā* or *ghāṭā pūrā k*. : *kasr kaḍḍhnī* : pay for l., *nuksān bharnā* : *see* damage.

lot, *see* fate : lots, draw, *guṇe pāṇe*.

lottery, *lāṭarī*, f.

loud, *zōr dā*.

loudly, *ucci ucci*, *ucci ditti*, *dabbke*, *zōr nāḷ*, *kaṛakke* (angrily) : *see* aloud.
louse, *jū̃*, f.
love, *mhabbat*, f. : (*rakkhṇī* or *k.*, *nāḷ*) : *pyār*, m. (*k.*, *nū̃*, *nāḷ*) : *see* fondle, indulge : *ishk*, m., *āshik h.* (*utte*) : *see* lover.
lover and loved one, *āshik mashūk* : words *ishk*, *āshik*, *mashūk* gen. bad meaning.
(1) low, adj., *nīwā̃* : -er, *hēthlā*, *nīwā̃* : speak low, *see* gently : *see* mean.
(2) low, cattle, *aṛiṅgṇā*, *aṛāṇā*.
loyal, *khairkhāh*, *namakhalāl*.
luck, *see* fate, fortune.
lucky, *see* fortunate, rich.
lucrative, *baṛī khaṭṭī wāḷā*.
luggage, *see* baggage : -receipt, *biḷṭī*, f.
luggage-van, *see* brake.
lukewarm, *see* tepid.
lump, of earth, *ḍhehm*, f. : in flesh, *giḷhṭ*, m. : *sunḍhā*, m. : *see* boil (1) : of meat, *see* piece.
lunch, *tipan*, m.
lung, *phēphṛā*, m.
lust, *lucpuṇā*, m. : *shaihwat*, f. (U.).

M

macaroni, *makrūnī*, f.
machine, *mashīn*, f. : *kalā̃*, f. (mechanical device).
mad, *jhallā*, *pāgal*, *kamḷā*, *shudāī*. : *bā* or *mat* or *hōsh mārī jāṇī*, hence adj., *bā mārea*, etc. : *see* fool, foolishness : m. dog, *haḷkā kuttā* : *see* rabies.
magic, *jādū*, m. : *mantar*, m.
magician, *jādūgar*-, fem. -*nī* : *see* witch. [honorary.
magistrate, *majastrēṭ* : *see*

magnet, *miknātīs*, f.
magnificence, *see* splendour.
maiden, *see* girl, virgin, young.
mail, *ḍāk*, f. : m. train, *ḍāk gaḍḍī*, f. : Bombay, Calcutta m., *bambā* or *kalkattā mēl*, f.
maimed, *see* limb, cripple.
maintain, *pāḷṇā*, *parwarish karnī* (*dī*) : *kharc dēnā* (*dā* or *nū̃*) : *see* assert.
maintenance, *rōṭī kapṛā*, m. *kharc*, m., *parwarish*, f.
maize, *makaī*, f. : *see* cob.
make, *baṇāṇā* (int. *baṇṇā*) : *see* force, cause : ready-made, *baṇeā battreā*.
make-weight (for scales), *pāskū̃*, m. : *see* patch.
male, of animals, *nar* : adj., (men), *mardānā*.
malice, *see* envy.
mallet, *muṅglī*, f.
man, gen. *bandā*, *ādmī*, *insān*, m. : m.-kind, *insān* : m., not woman, *jaṇā* : my good m., *whaī*, M. 130. 32 : G. 125.
manage, *see* arrange : get along, *guzārā karnā*.
manager, *mainajar* : of land, *gumāshtā*.
mane, of horse, *jāddā*, f. pl.
manger, *khurlī*, f.
mango, *amb*, m. (tree and fruit) : eat m., *cūpṇā*.
manifest, *see* evident.
manner, *tarhā̃*, f. : *tarīkā*, m. : *ḍhaṅg*, m.
mansion, *mahall*, m. : *hawēlī*, f. : *waḍḍā makān*.
manufacture, *see* make.
manure, *mallhaṛ*, m. (*pāṇā*, int. *paiṇā*).
manuscript, *nuskhā*, m.
many, plur. of much : *see* much.

map, *nakshā* (*baṇāṇā*, *khiccṇā*).
marble, *saṅg marmar*, m.
(1) March, *mārc*, *mārac*, m.: *cēttar*, m. (about Mar. 13 to Apr. 12).
(2) march, v., *kūc karnā* (U.): *paindā mārnā*.
mare, *see* horse, pony.
margin, book, *hāshīā*, m.: *see* edge.
marine, *baihrī*, *samundar dā*.
mark, *nishān*, m.: exam., *nambar*: beating leaving no m., *gujjhī mār*, f.: Hindu m., *ṭikkā*, m., *tilak*, m.
market, *bazār*, m.: for special goods, *manḍī*, f: *see* purchases.
(1) marriage, whole celebration, *shādī*, f., *wiāh*, n.: actual m., *nikāh*, m. (M.): *see* marry
(2) marriage procession, *jañ*, f.: gathering, *mēḷ*, m.: member of *jañ*, *jāñī*: of *mēḷ*, *mēḷī*: m.-gift, *neōndrā*, m.: *bhāñī*, *bhāñjī*, f.: m. settlement, *maihr*, m. (M.).
marrow, *mikkh*, f.
marry, M. *shādī k.*. *wiāh k.*, *nikāh paṛhāṇā* (all w. *nāḷ*): of priest. *nikāh paṛhnā*.
H., *lāwā laiṇīā*, *phere laiṇe*: *wiāh k.*, *manḍū paṛhnā* (both w. *nāḷ*): of priest, *wiāh karāṇā* (*dā*). *wiāh paṛhnā* (*dā*): widow remarriage, *cādar pāṇī*, *cādrā pāṇā* (*nāḷ*), *karēwā*, m. (H.)
Gen. words, *khasm karnā* (marry husband), *zanānī karnī* (wife), or *karnā* w. person's name: *ghar wassṇā* (*dā*): man married second time, *duhājū* (no word for woman).
marsh, *jhīl*, f. (also lake).
martyr, *shahīd*, m.
martyrdom, *shahīd h.*
masculine, *muzakkar*.
mason, *rāj*, m.
massage, *see* shampoo.
mast, *mastaul*, m.
master, *see* owner, teacher, clever.
masterless, *see* ownerless.
mat, straw, *phūhṛ*, m.: *caṭāī*, f.: small *phūhṛī*, f.: for prayer, *masallā*, m. (M.): *see* rug, sack.
(1) match (lucifer), *tīllī*, f.: collective, *mācas*, m.: m.-box, *ḍabbī*, f.
(2) match, game, *maic*, m.
(3) match, v., *raḷāṇā*, int. *raḷnā*.
matchless, *sabbhnā̃ tō̃ caṅgā*, *waḍḍā*, etc.: *see* unique.
mate, *jōṛīdār*, *sāthī*: *see* companion.
materials of house, *malbā*, m.: minor m. for building, *masālā*, m.
mathematics, *hisāb*, m.: *riāzī*, f.
matter, *see* affair, pus: no m., *oh jāṇe*, *koī ḍar nehī̃*, *koī parwāh nehī̃*, *jāṇ dē*: *see* right (2).
matting, *see* mat.
mattress, *tulāī*, f.: *gadēlā*, m.: *see* quilt.
mature, *pūrī umr dā*, *pakkā*.
maund, *man*, m.: *see* wts. and meas.
May, *maī*, f.: *mēī*, f.: *jēṭh*, (about May 13 to June 12).
maxim, opinion, *maslā*, m.
maximum, *waddh tō̃ waddh* marks, *pūre nambar*.
me, *menū̃*.

meal, a, *khāṇā*, m. : one of two daily meals, *ḍang*, m. : flour, coarse, *āṭā*, m. ; fine, *maidā*, m.

(1) mean, *kamīnā* : stingy, *shūm*, *kanjūs* (U).

(2) mean, v. *see* signify.

meaning, of word, *maihṇe*, m. pl. : sense, intention, *matlab*, m.

meanness, *kamīnā kamm*, m. : stinginess, *shūmpuṇā*, m.

means, *wasīlā*, m. : *see* income, livelihood : by m. of, through, *oh de wasīle*, *ohdī rāhī̃* : by all m., *see* certainly : you're welcome, *jam jam*, *jī sadke*, *sir matthe te*.

meanwhile, *inne* or *ōnne wicc*, *hālī*, *hālā̃*, *ucarā̃ nū̃*, *icarā̃ nū̃*.

measles, *khasrā*, m. : (*nikḷṇā*, *nū̃*).

(1) measure, v., *minṇā*, *kacchṇā*, *mēcṇā* : be m.-ed. by tailor, shoemaker, *nū̃ mēcā dēṇā* : n., *nāp*, m. : *mēcā*, m. : *pamaish*, f. (*k.*).

(1) measuring-tape, *fītā*, m.

meat, for food, *mās*, m. : *gōshat*, *gōsht*, m. : *tarkārī*, f. : *laun*, m. : *see* mutton, beef, flesh.

meat-safe, *ḍōllī*, f.

mechanical, *kalā̃ nāḷ*.

mechanism, *kalā̃*, *kalā*, f. : *see* machine.

medal, *tagmā*, m. : *takmā*, m.

meddle, *see* interfere.

mediator, *wicōlā* : referee, *tarfain* : *see* umpire.

medicine, *duāī*, f. : *dārū*, m.

mediocre, *see* average, and add *mamūlī*, *aust darje dā*.

meditation, *dhiān*, m., *giān dhiān*, m

meek, use " not proud."

meet, *miḷṇā* (*nū̃*) : *ṭakkarnā* (*nū̃*, by accident) : *mulākāt karnī* (*nāḷ*, interview) : go to meet, *ohnū̃ aggōwāḷī* or *aggaḷwāhṇḍī miḷṇā*, *ohdī aggaḷwāhṇḍī nū̃ nikḷṇā*, *aggō lain jāṇā*.

meeting (someone), n., *ṭākrā*, m. : *mulākāt*, f. : relig. m., *mīṭiṅ*, f. : *see* assembly.

melody, *see* tune.

melon, musk, *khakkhṛī*, f. : water, *haduāṇā*, m. : Kabuli, *sardā*, m.

melt, v., int., *gaḷṇā* (also meat, rice, etc., getting too soft : tr. *gāḷṇā*) : *pagharnā* (esp. fat before fire : tr. *paghrāṇā*) : dissolve, as salt, sugar in water, tr. *ghōḷṇā*, *khōrnā* (int. *ghuḷṇā*, *khurnā*).

member, *sharīk*, m. : *mimbar*, m.

memorial, *yādgār*, f. : *see* memory.

memory, faculty, *cētā*, m. : (or *hāfzā*, m., U. : never *yād*) : bad m., *cētā kharāb* : within my m., *mērī hōsh sambhāḷ wicc* : *see* remember : in m. of, *dī yādgārī wāsté*, or *wicc*.

mend, *see* repair, shoe.

menial, member of lower caste, shoemaker, barber, carpenter, sweeper, etc., *kam-mī*, fem. -*ṇeāṇī* : *see* servant.

mention, *dā zikr k.*, *dā nā̃ laiṇā*, *dī* (or *dā*) *carcā k.*

mercantile, *sudāgarī dā*, *tajārat dā*.

merchandise, *saudā*, m. : *saudā sūd*, m. : *māl*, m.

merchant, *sudāgar*, *byōpārī*, *tajārat karnwāḷā*.

merciful, *see* compassionate, mercy.

mercury, *pārā*, m.
mercy, *raihm*, m. (*auṇā* or *k.*, *utte*): *see* pity.
merely, *nirā*, *sirf* (not *k͟hālī*).
merrymaking, *k͟hushī karnī*.
message, verbal, *sanēhā*, m.: *sanāh*, m.: work, *kamm* m.: *buttī*, m.: *wiḍḍī*, f.
messenger, use "man."
metal, *dhāt*, f. [*see* manner.
method, *tarīkā*, m.. *kaidā*, m.,
metempsychosis, *awāgaū*, m.: *āwāgauṇ*, m.: *curāsī*, m. (all H.).
mew, cat, *miaūkṇā*.
midday, *see* noon.
middle, *wishkār*, m.: *addh wishkār*, m.: adj., *wiclā*, *wishkārlā*.
middle-aged, *adhkaṛ*.
middleman, *dalāl*.
middling, *see* average, mediocre.
midnight, *addhī rāt*, f.
midwife, *dāī*.
might, *see* power, strength, strong.
milch, *lawērī* (cow or buffalo).
mild, person, *halīm*, *narmdil*, *see* kind, compassionate, merciful.
mildness, *halīmī*, f.: *narmdilī*, f.
mile, *mīl*, m.: 1½ m., *kōh*: m., roughly, *kuhāṭrā*, m.: *see* wts. and meas.
milestone, *mīl*, m.
milk, n., *duddh*, m.: for first few days after calf born, *bauhlī*, f., *bauhlā*, m.: buttermilk, *lassī*, f.: v., *dhār kaḍḍhnī* (*dī*); *cōṇā* (obj. both milk and cow): cow, etc. let herself be milked, *gā̃ milṇī*, M. 124. 1.
milkman, *dodh-ī*, fem. *-aṇ*; *duddhwāḷā*.

(1) mill, hand-, *cakkī*, f.: oxen, *khrās*, m.: water, *ghrāṭ*, m.: *see* millstone.
millet, *juār*, f.: *bājrā*, m.
million, *das lakh*: ten m., *karōṛ*, m.: ordinals, *das lakhwā̃*, *karōṛwā̃*.
millionaire, *lakhpatī*, *karōṛpatī*.
(2) millstone, *puṛ*, m.: to roughen m., *rāhṇā*.
mimic, *see* imitate, jester, grimace.
mince, *mins*, m. (*k.*, K.); *kīmā*, m. (*k.*).
mind, *dil*, m.: *jī*, m.: *man*, m.: *see* sense, intelligence: never m., *see* matter: not m. him, *ohdī parwāh nā karnī*.
mine, n., *khāṇḍ*, *khāṇ*, f.: *see* tunnel.
mingle, *see* mix.
(1) mint, herb, *pūdnā*, m.
(2) mint, for coin, *ṭaksāl*, f., *ṭaṅgsāl*, f.
(1) minute, n., *minṭ*, m.
(2) minute, fine, *see* fine. [m.
miracle, *karāmāt*, f.: *mohjzā*,
mirror, *shīshā*, m.
mischief, *sharārat*, f.
mischievous, *sharārtī*, *sharīr* (last three words applied to grown-up people mean wicked-, -ness).
miser, *shūm*, *kanjūs*, m.c.
miser-able, -y, *see* poor, straits.
miserliness, *shūmpuṇā*, m.: *kanjūsī*, f.
misfortune, *badkismatī*, f.: *badnasībī*, f.: *see* calamity.
misjudge, *galt k͟hyāl karnā* (*dā*, *dī bābat*).
mispronounce, *galt talaffaz bōlṇā* (*dā*)

mislay, *rakkhke bhull jāṇā.*
miss (aim), *ukknā, wār ēwē jāṇī, nishānā ēwē jāṇā, gōlī* etc., *nā laggṇī* or *khunjh jāṇī*; m. train, *gaḍḍīō khunjhṇā* or *ghussṇā* or *raih jāṇā*: m. way, *rāhō khunjhṇā* or *ghussṇā*: feel person's absence, *ohde khuṇō* or *bājhō dil ōddarnā*: m. day, *diṇ chaḍḍṇā diṇ khālī jāṇā.*
mission, *mishn*, f.
missionary, *mishnarī, pādrī sāb*: lady m., *mishn dī miss sab.*
misstate, *galt beān karnā (dā).*
mist, *see* fog.
mistake, *galtī*, f. (*k., h.*): *bhull*, f. (*h.*), *bhull cukk*, f.: *bhulēkhā*, m. (*laggṇā, nū*): *ṭapḷā*, m. (*laggṇā, nū*): *khunjhṇā, ghussṇā.*
mistress, *see* teacher.
misunderstanding, *galtfaihmī*, f. (U.)
mix, v. tr., *raḷāṇā, miḷāṇā* (int. *raḷṇā, miḷṇā*): int. *āpe icc miḷde juḷde* (or *giḷde*) *ne.*
mix-ed, -ture, *raḷā miḷā*: *khicṛī*, f., *see* adulterate-, -d.
moan, *see* groan.
mock, *see* imitate, jester.
mocker, *see* jester.
model, *see* pattern.
moderate, *see* average, mediocre.
modern, *inhā̃ diṇā̃ dā, ajj kall dā, hāl de zamāne dā*: *see* new.
modest. *nēkbakht*, or *see* good.
moist, moisten, *see* damp, wet.
moisture, *see* damp: in soil for ploughing, *wattar*. m., G. 122: M. 129. 26-8: *wattar hō geā*, rain has wet soil enough for ploughing: *jīwī wattar ā geī*, (after v. heavy rain) soil dried enough to be ready for ploughing: *hēṭhlā utlā wattar raḷ geā e*, the m. from rain has reached down to the soil m.: *rēj*, m. (m. in earth of house after rain).
Monday, *suār*, m.: *somwār*, m.
money, *rupayyā paisā*, m.: *see* wealth.
money-lender, *sāhūkār, shāhūkār, shāh.*
mongoose, *neōḷ, nyōḷ*, m.
monkey, *bānd-ar*, fem. *-rī.*
monotheis-m, -t, *ikko Khudā nū̃ mann-ṇā, -aṇwāḷā.*
month, *mahīnā*, m.: last m., *pishle mahīne*. *see* next.
monthly, *mahīne dā, mahīne de mahīne.*
moon, *cann*, m.: full m., *pandhrawī rāt dā cann*: light night, *cāṇṇī rāt*, f: *see* rise, set.
morals, *cāl caln*, m.
more, *waddh, wadhīk, hōr, zyādā, wadhērā.*
moreover, *nāḷe, te nāḷe*
morning, *subā*, f.: *waḍḍewelā*, m.: *sarghī weḷā, parbhāt weḷā*, 1½ hrs. before dawn: *namāz weḷā*, ¾ hour before dawn: *jhusmusṛā*, m., *muhānjḷā*, m., *mūh anhērā*, m., morning twilight: *dhammī weḷā*, m., time of dawn: *jhalānghe*, at sunrise: *fajr*, f., early m.: *see* forenoon.
morsel, *see* mouthful.
mortal, *fānī*: *see* deadly, fatal.
mortar for pointing, *pink*,

cūnā, m. : black, *sīmilt*, m. : *sīmint*, m. : *see* point (4), pestle.

mortgage, v., *gaihṇe pāṇā* : *see* pawn.

mosque, *masīt*, f.

mosquito, *macchar*, m. : *guttī*, f. : **-net**, *machairī*. f., *jāḷī*, f., do. w. rods, *macchardānī*, f.

most, *sabbhnā̃* or *sāreā̃ tõ waddh*, *waddh tõ waddh*.

moth, *bāhmaṇ baccā*, m.

mother, *bēbbe*, *mā̃*, *māī*, *wāldā* (U.) : m. in law, *sass* : m. in law's father, *naniauhrā* (his wife, *nanēhs*); m. in law's brother, *maliauhrā* (his wife, *malēhs*) : mothers of bride and bridegroom are *kuṛmṇī* to each other.

motion, *harkat*, f. : in meeting, *mōshn*, f. : *rā* f. : *see* move.

motive, *matlab*, m. : *wicclā matlab* ; *garz*, f.

(1) **mould**, bricks, *saccā*, m. : pudding, *sāncā*, m. (K.) : v. tr., *sacce wicc ḍhāḷṇā* (int. *ḍhaḷṇā*).

(2) **mould** (green), *ullī*, f. (*laggṇī*, *nū̃*).

mound, *ṭibbā*, m. : *ḍhērī*, f.

mount, *utte caṛhnā* (tr. *cāṛhnā*) : m. animal or vehicle, *suār h.* (tr. *k.*).

mountain, *pahāṛ*, m. : *parbat*, m. : *see* hill.

mountainous, belonging to mountains, *pahāṛī*.

(1) **mourn**, *mātam-k.*, *karlāṇā*.

(2) **mourners**, collective, *mukāṇ*, f.

(3) **mourning**, united, *mukāṇ*, f.

mouse, *cūhī*, f. (no word for male) : *see* rat

mouse-trap, *see* trap.

moustache, *mucchā̃*, f. pl. : beard and m., *daṛhī mucch*, f.

mouth, *mū̃h*, m. : at his m., through him, *ohdī zabānī*, G. 36, 37 : corner of m., *warāch*, f. : get sore m., *mū̃h pakk jāṇā* (*dā*) : do. horse, cattle, etc. *mū̃h auṇā* (*dā*), M. 117. 9 : *mū̃h pakk jāṇā*.

mouthful, liquid, *ghuṭṭ*, m. : solid, *barkī*, f., *burkī*, f., *garāh*, m., *garāhī*, f.

move, *hallṇā* (tr. *halāṇā*) : m. away, *haṭṇā* (tr. *haṭāṇā*) : m. a motion, *pēsh-k.* : without moving, gently, *aḍōl*, *malkṛī*.

moving, *see* pathetic, motion.

mow, grass, *ghāh mārnā* or *waḍḍhṇā*, *see* reap.

much, *cōkhā*, *bāhḷā*, *bauht*, *bathērā*, *ām*, *wāfar* : *see* more : many, use plur. of much : as m. as I, *mēre jinnā*, G. 91 92. : *see* number.

mucus, *balgam*, m.

mud, *cikkaṛ*, m., *cikkaṛ cambhaṛ*, m. : half-dry, *khobhā*, m. : cake of m., *carēpṛī*, f. : m. for building, w. straw, *ghāṇī*, f. : without straw, *gārā*, m. : get covered w. m., *bharnā*, *miṭṭī nāḷ bharnā* : M. 118. 22.

muddy (water), *gandhḷeā hoeā*, *gandhḷā*.

muffler, *see* tie (2).

mug, *magg*, m.

mulberry, tree and fruit, *tūt*, m. : large-fruited, *shatūt* m.

mule, *khac-rā*, fem. *-car* (masc. rare) : *waihtar*, m. (also horse, ass) : man in mule corps, *khaccarpātrī*.

multiply (educ.), *zarb dēṇī* (*nū̃*,

nāḷ) : *see* increase : multiplication table, *pahāṛā*, m.
multitude, *see* crowd.
murder, *khūn*, m. (*k.*, *dā*).
murderer, *khūnī*.
murmur, *hauḷī bōlṇā*, *see* grumble.
muscle, no word, use *mās*, m. : *gōsht*, *goshat*, m. : m. of forearm, *bā̃h dī machḷī*, f. : of lower leg, *pinnī dī machḷī*, f. : m. to right and left of aesophagus, *rag*, f. : *see* biceps.
museum, *ajaib ghar*, m.
mushroom, *khumb*, f. : toadstool, *padd bhaiṛā*, m.
music, *see* tune, play, instrument.
musician, professional and gen. disreputable, *mirās-ī*, fem. *-aṇ* : *ḍūm-*, fem. *-ṇī* : singer (good meaning), *gawayyā*, (no fem.) ; *gauṇwāḷā*.
musk-rat, *cakcūhndar*, m.
muslin, *malmal*, f.
mustard, *rāī*, f., *auhr*, f. : growing, *sarhō̃*, *sarheō̃*, f. : *tārāmīrā*, m.
mutineer, *bāgī*.
mutiny, *bagāwat*, f. (*k.*) : *gadr*, m. (*k.*).
mutter, *see* murmur, grumble.
mutton, word for meat w. *nikkā*, small, or *bākrā*, of sheep or goat, prefixed *maṭaṇ*, m. (K.).
muzzle, *see* snout, halter.
my, *mērā*.
mystery, *see* secret.

N

nail, finger, toe *naūh*, m. : small iron, *brinjī*, f. : *prēk*, f. : large, iron or wood, *killī*, f. : *kill*, m. : *mēkh*, f. : *see* hammer.
naked, *naṅgā*.
nakedness, *naṅg*, m.
name, *nā̃* m. : *nā̃wā*, m. (esp. in list) : v. tr., *nā̃ rakkhṇā* or *dharnā* : *see* call : get a n. for, *all paiṇī* (*dī*) : getting bad n., *bhaṇḍī*, *badnāmī*, f. (both w. *h.*, *dī*) : *see* named.
named, *musamm-ī*, fem. *-āt* : be called Kammo, *Kammo akhwāndī* or *sadāndī e* ; G. 109 : *Kammo, Kammo karke saddde ne.*
nape, *see* neck.
napkin, *mēz dā tauliā*, m. : for infant, *nāpkin*, m.
narrate, *see* relate.
narrow, *sauṛā*, *bhīṛā*, *taṅg* : *ghaṭṭ cauṛā e* : of cloth, *bar chōṭā e*.
native, *dēsī* (Indian) : n. language, *mādrī bōlī* : *see* country.
natural, *kudratī*
naturally, *uṅ ī*.
nature (around) *kudrat*, f. : *see* disposition.
naughty, *see* mischievous.
navel, *dhunnī*, f.
navigable, *jitthe kishtīā̃ yā jahāz jā sakaṇ.* [(in plur.).
navy, *jahāz*, m. : *jaṅgī jahāz*
near, *nēṛe*, *kōḷ*, *koḷe*, *nāḷ*, *karīb* : *see* distance : adj., *nāḷ dā*, *nēṛe dā*, *urlā*, fr. n., *nēṛeō̃*, *koḷō̃*, *nāḷō̃* : pass by n., *neṛe dū̃*, *nāḷdū̃* or *nāḷō̃ dī*, *kōḷdū̃* or *koḷō̃ dī* (*laṅghṇā*, *jāṇā*).
nearly, *karīban*, *karīb*, *kujjh ghaṭṭ* : *see* approximately.
necessary, *zarūrī*, *lāzarūrī* : *lōṛīdā* or *cāhīdā*, G. 67, 96 : *see* have to. [*līā̃ cīzā̃*.
necessaries, *zarūrī cīzā̃*, *lōṛwā-*

necessity, *lōṛ*, f. : *zarūrat*, f.
neck, nape, *gicī*, f. : *dhauṇ*, f. : *gāṭā*, m. : *muṇḍī*, f. : *gardan*, f. : front, *gaḷ*, m. : *see* throat, Adam's apple, aesophagus.
necklace, *haikaḷ*, f. : *hassī*. f. : *hass*, m. : *hasīrā*, m. : etc.
necktie, *nakṭāī*, f.
need, *see* necessity.
needle, *sūī*, f. : large, *sūā*, m.
neglect, *lāparwāhī*, f. : *gaflat*, f., *gāflī*, f. (all *k.*).
negotiation, *gall katth*, f. (*k*).
negro, *habsh-ī*, fem.-*aṇ*.
neigh, *hiṇakṇā*.
neighbour, *guāhṇḍ-ī*, fem. -*aṇ*.
neighbourhood, *guāhṇḍ*, f. : *āhṇḍ guāhṇḍ*, f.
neither, *dohā̃ wiccõ koī nā* : n. ..nor, *nā.. nā* : *nā te.. te nā* : *nā.. te nā*.
nephew, brother's son, *bhatrīā* : sister's son, *bhaṇēwā̃*, *bhaneā* : n.'s wife, *bhatrīõ nūh*. *bhaṇeweõ nūh*.
nest, *ālhṇā*, m.
net, fishing, *jāḷ*, m. : tennis n., *jāḷī*, f. : for straw, chaff, *traṅgaṛ*, m. : wire netting, *jāḷī* : *see* mosquito.
never, *kadī nā* : never! interj. *majāl e*, *tōbbā tōbbā* : of incredulity, *hēkkhā̃* ; (the reply is *hēkkhā̃ kī* ?)
new, *nawā̃* : fresh, *sajrā* : n. or unwashed cloth, unused paper, waterpot, *kōrā*.
news, *khabar*, f. : incorrect, *gapp*, f.
newspaper, *akhbār*, f.
next, *nāḷ dā*, *dujjā*, *aglā*, *agḷā* : n. week, month, year, *agḷe*, *auṇwāḷe hafte*, *mahīne*, *sāl* : *aunde sāl* : this day n. week, *ajj de* or *ajōke dihāṛe*.
nib, *cunjh*, f. : *par*, m.
nibble, *kutarnā* : *see* gnaw.
nice, *see* good, tasty.
niche, *āḷā*, m.
nickel, *ciṭṭā trāmmā*, m.
nickname (to annoy) *cēṛh*, f. (*paiṇī*) : otherwise, say *nā̃ pai geā*.
niece, brother's daughter, *bhatrī* ; sister's, *bhaṇēwī*, *bhaṇeī*. niece's husband, *bhatrīõ* or *bhaṇewīõ jawāī*.
night, *rāt*, f. (*paiṇī*) : by n., *rātī*. n. and day, *rātī diṇe*, *dēh rātī* : to-n., last n., *ajj rāt nū̃*, *ajj rātī* : n -clothes, *rāt de kapṛe*, m. pl. : *see* bedding.
nightmare, *ḍaraoṇī khāb*, f.
nine, *naū* : -th, *nauā̃*, *nāwā̃*.
nineteen, *unnī* : -th, *unnhīwā̃*, G 22.
ninety, *nawwe*, *nabbe* : -one, *ikānwe* : -two, *bānwe* : -three, *tarānwe* : four, *curānwe* : -five, *pac*- or *panj-ānwe* : -six, *cheānwe* : seven, *satānwe* · -eight, *athānwe* : -nine, *naṛinwe* : ordinals add -*wā̃* and high tone *h*, *nabbhewā̃*, *ikāhnwewā̃*, etc. : G. 20, 22, 123.
nipple, baby's indiarubber, *cūsṇī*, f., *cūpṇī*, f.
nitre, *shōrā*, m.
no, *nā*, *nehī*, *āhā̃* (w. glottal stop at end) : *see* nothing, nowhere.
no one, *koī nehī*.
nobility, *sharāfat*, f. : *see* noble.
noble, rank, *sharīf khāndān dā*, *āhlā raīs*.
nod, *see* sleepy.
noise, *rauḷā*, m. : *khapp*, f. : *ḍaṇḍ*, f. : *raṭṭā*, m. : *rēṛkā*, m. (all *pāṇā*, int. *paiṇā*) : *shōr*, m. (*k.*), *awāz*, f. (*auṇī* : *mārnī*,

call): *khṛāk*, m. (*auṇā*, of footsteps, cart, etc.): *see* splash, disturbance.
nomad, *pakkhīwās-*, fem. *-aṇ*: *ṭaprīwāḷā*; *see* tent.
nominal, *nirā nā ī e.*
nominate, *nā pēsh karnā* (*dā*).
nonsense: *see* never: *wāhyāt gall*, f.: *bakwās*, f.: *wāfrī*, f.: *wāfar gall*, f. (all *k.*): *yabbhā*, f. pl. (*mārnīā*): *fazūl* or *wāfar gallā*, f. pl. (*k.*): *gappā*, f. pl. (*mārnīā*): talker of n., *bakwās-ī*, fem. *-aṇ*.
noon, *dopaihr*, f.: at n., *dopaihrī*: *see* afternoon, forenoon.
nor, *see* neither.
north, *pahāṛ*, m.: *parbat*, m.: n.-wards, *pahāṛ* or *parbat pāse* or *wall*: n.-east, *pahāṛ te caṛhde dī gutth*: n.-west, *pahāṛ te laihnde dī gutth*.
nose, *nakk*; flat-nosed, *phīhnā*: blow n., *nakk suṇknā*.
nostril, *nās*, f.
not, *nā*, *nehī*.
note, *see* letter: bank-n., *nōṭ*, m.: make n. of, *likkhṇā*, *nōṭ k.*
notebook, *kāpī*, f.: *nōṭbuk*, f.
noteworthy, *sōccaṇ* or *suṇaṇ* or *yād rakkhaṇ jogā*.
nothing, *kujjh nehī*: n. at all, *kakkh wī nehī*: come to n., *guggaḷ jāṇā*.
notice, n, *ishtihār*, m.: v., *khyāl karnā* (*dā*): *dhiān karnā*: *see* advertisement.
notwithstanding, *bhāwē*.
nourish, *see* maintain.
novel, *see* new: book, *nāwal*, m.
November, *nawambar*, m.: *magghar*, m. (about Nov. 13 to Dec. 12).

now, *hun*, *huṇe*: at present, *hālī*, *hālā*: only n., *aje huṇe*: now now!, interj. (rebuke), *hāē*, *āhē*.
nowhere, *kitale nā* or *nehī*.
noxious, *see* injure, loss, hurt.
numb, *ṭhareā hoeā* (through cold, v. cold): *sunn* (also limb asleep).
number, *see* figure: *nambar*, m., of page, house, regiment, etc.: *tedād*, f., of people, etc.: what page? *kinnawā safā*? (so *jinnawā*, *innawā*, *ōnnawā*), also *kinnā*, *kehṛā*.
nurse, ayah, *āyā*, f.: European n., *nais miss sāb*: midwife, *dāī*.
nursery, of plants, *zakhīrā*.
nut, pistachio, *pistā*, m.: *see* walnut.

O

O, calling: woman to woman, *nī*, *aṛīe*: woman to man, *wē*: man to man, *ō*, *ōe*: man to woman, *ē*: all imply "*tū*": *see* oh.
oar, *cappū*, m.
oath, *saūh*, f.: *kasm*, f. (both *khāṇī*, *cukkṇī*): *Kurān cukkṇā*, take o. on Quran: administer o., *duāṇī*, *cukāṇī* (*nū*): be v. unwilling to, lit. take o. against, *eh kamm karn dī saūh hōṇī* or *cukkṇī*: M. 107. 17-9.
oats, *ganḍhaiḷ*, f.
obey, obedience, *tābedārī karnī* (*dī*); *ākkhe laggṇā* (*de*); *hukm mannṇā* (*dā*).
object, *garz*, f.: *see* intention, aim: secure o., *kamm* or *matlab kaḍḍhṇā*.
objection, *ehtrāz*, m. (*k.*): *uzr*, m. (*k.*), excuse.

obligation, favour, *ahsān*, m. (pron. *as-hān*) : *ṭhāhrā*, m. : admit o., *ahsān* or *ṭhāhrā mannṇā* (*dā*) : trade on another's o. to one, *ahsān* or *ṭhāhrā cāṛhnā* (*utte*) or *manā-ṇā* : *see* benefit.

oblige, *see* force. cause : *see* obligation.

obliterate, *see* delete, efface.

obscene, *gandā*, *fohsh*.

obscure, *see* dark, ambiguous : *matlab sāf nehī*.

observe, *see* notice, attend.

obstacle, *see* hindrance.

obstinacy, *zidd* (*bannhṇī*) : *khaih* (*rakkhṇī*) : *haṭṭh*, m., *aṛī*, f., *kabbpuṇā*, m. (all w. *k.*).

obstinate, *aṛyal*, *ziddī*.

obstruct-, -ion, *see* hinder, hindrance, and add *aṛekā*, m. : *mushkil*, f. : *aṛikk* or *aṛicc*, f. (all w. *pāṇā* : also *aṛicc ḍāhṇī*).

obtain, *labbh laiṇā*, *laiṇā* : *menū labbhā* or *mileā*, *mēre hatth āeā* : *see* secure, supply, produce.

obvious, *see* evident.

occasion, *maukā*, m. : *see* opportunity.

occur, take place, *see* place.

occurrence, *gall*, f.

ocean, *see* sea.

o'clock, what o ? *kī wajeā e*, *kinne waje ne* ? one o., *ikk wajeā e* : at 1 o., *ikk waje*, *ikk waje nāḷ* (about one) : M. 61.

October, *aktūbar*, m. : *kattē*, m. (about Oct. 13 to Nov. 12).

octroi, *see* tax.

odd, not even, *ṭāk* : *see* strange.

of, *dā* : material, *dā* : of himself, of his own accord, *see* help.

off, see o., *see* farewell : send o., *see* send : go o., *Allā Bēlī h.*, *alī panj h.*

offence, stumblingblock, *ṭhoh-kar* (*laggṇī*, *nū* ; *lāṇī*) : take o., *burā mannṇā* (at, *nū*) : *see* stumble, resent.

offer, *pēsh-k.*, *agge rakkhṇā* : sacrifice, *cāṛhnā*, *caṛhāṇā*.

offering, *caṛhāwā*, m. . *nazr*, f. (both at shrine) : *see* gift, sacrifice.

office, room, *daftar*, m.

officer, *afsar* (military or any superior in office). [*ohdedār*.

official, adj., *sarkārī* : n., *afsar*,

officiat-e, -ing. : *iwzī*, *kaim makām*, *ohde thā kamm kar-nā*.

often, *aksar* : *see* repeatedly.

oh, pain, *hāl oe*, *hāe hāe* : displeasure, *hāē*, *āhē* : surprise, *halā*, *see* astonishment : protest, *tōbbā*, *lai*, *see* never.

oil, *tēl*, m : paraffin, *miṭṭī dā tēl* : for food, for rubbing, *miṭṭhā* or *kauṛā tēl* (sweet or bitter, according to origin).

oilman, caste, *tēl-ī*, fem. *-aṇ*.

ointment, anoint, *malham*, f. (*lāṇī*, int. *laggṇī*) : *lēp karnā*, without bandage : *phāh lāṇā*, w. bandage (int. *laggṇā*) : *see* anoint.

old, *buḍḍhā*, *buḍhṛā*, *waḍḍā bandā* ; *see* great : ancient, *purāṇā* : three years old, *triūh sālā* or *warheā dā* . become o., *umar ḍhalṇī* (*dī*) : o. age, *pishlī umr*, *baṛī umr*, *buḍhēpā*, m.

old-fashioned, *purāṇe faishn* or *ḍhaṅg* or *namūne dā*.

oleander, *kaner*, m.
olive, *kaū*, m.
omen, *sagan*, m.: random sentence in sacred book, *fāl*, f. (*kholhnī*, *kaddhnī*, *pānī*): *see* auspicious.
omit, *chaddnā*: miss a day, *see* miss.
omniscient, God, *sabbho kujjh jāndā e*, *ālam ul gaib*: man, *auliā* (M.).
on, *see* upon.
once, *ikk wārī*, *ikk dang* (*see* meal): at o., *see* immediately: all at o., *see* suddenly.
one, *ikk*; G. 21: all at o. time, adv., *ikko rikkī*: adj., *ikko rikkā*: 1½ *dēdh*, *dūdh*: adj. from these, *deodhā*, *deorhā*.
onion, *gandhā*, m.
only, *nirā*, *sirf*: *see* emphasis: o. son, no word in nom., obl. *ikkse*: for "*ikko*" *see* son.
ooze, *simmnā*, *niklnā*: *see* drip, trickle.
open, v. tr., *kholhnā* (gen.: int. *khulhnā*): door, window, lock, *lāhnā* (int. *laihnā*): eyes, *ughērnā* (int. *ugghar-nā*): mouth, *addnā*: w. open doors, *see* door: o. school, shop, *kholhnā*.
openly, *khulham khulhā*, *sāf sāf*, *khulhī gall*: *see* publicly.
operation, surgical, *aprēshan*, m. (*k.*).
ophthalmia, *see* eye.
opinion, *rā*, *rai*, f.: *khyāl*, m.: *kiās*, f. m.: in his o., *ohde agge*, G. 91, *ohde bhāne*, *ohde wande dā*, *ohde bhā dā* M. 127. 4-6.
(1) **opium**, *afhīm*, f.: *pōst*, m. (poppy).
(2) **opium-eater**, *afīmī*, *pōstī*.
opponent, *mukhālaf*, *see* enemy.
opportunity, *maukā*, m.: *tāng*, m. (both w. *laggnā*, get): seek o., *maukā wēkhnā* or *jācnā* or *tārnā*.
oppose, *mukāblā karnā* (*dā*): *mukhālfat karnī* (*dī*): *see* enemy.
opposite, prep., *de sāhmne*: *see* face: the o. of, *ohdā ulṭ*, M. 279. 18.
oppression, *zulm*, m.: *sakhtī*, f.: *dāhdpunā*, m.: *taddī tōrī*, f.: *jabr*, m. f.: *sikkhā shāhī*, f.: (all w. *k.*, *utte* or *nāl*): *see* violence, confess.
option, *ikhtiār*, m.: *marzī*, f.
optional, *ikhtiārī*.
or, *ke*, *yā*: *see* either.
oral, *zabānī*.
orally, *mūh zabānī*: heard o. fr. him, *ohdī zabānī suneā*.
(1) **orange**, Indian, *santarā*, m.: Maltese, *mālṭā*, m.: eat o., *cūpnā*.
(2) **orange**, adj., *gutaī*.
ordain-, **-ed**, *see* preacher.
(1) **order**, written, *parwānnā* (for supplies, etc.): *see* command, method, class, rank, arrange: in o. to, *ēs wāste paī*, *paī*, *tā jo*: also inf. w. *wāste*, *laī*, *nū*, etc. (G. 95), or simple inflec. inf: in line 17 of G. p. 95, for "in the past tenses of verbs" read "in the case of trans. verbs". Out of o. (machine, cart, well, etc.) *hanēkeā* or *wigreā hoeā*: *see* disorder.
orderly, n., *ardalī*, *caprāsī*.
(2) **orders**, holy, *see* preacher.
ordinary, *see* common: every day, affair, *rōz dī gall*.
organ, *wājjā*, m.: play, *wajānā*.
origin, *asl*, f.: *see* beginning.

ornament, *see* adorn.
orphan, without father, *yatīm*, *pyō mhaitar* : without mother, *mā̃ mhaitar*.
orthodox, gen. *pakkā* : Hindu, *sanātanī*.
ostensible, *zāhrī* : only outwardly, *uttōwāḷī*.
ostentation, *see* show.
ought, *see* necessary, advisable, duty, require, have to.
other, *hōr*, *dujjā*.
otherwise, *nehī̃ te* : or use "lest."
out, *see* outside.
outbid, *wadhke bōlī dēṇī*.
outhouses, *naukarā̃ de ghar* : *see* stable, cowhouse.
outpost, *caukī*, f., *caū̃kī*, f.
outside, *banne*, *bāhr* : fr. o., *banneō̃*, *bāhrō̃* : by way of o., *banneō̃ dī*, *bāhrō̃ dī* : on the o., *bāhrwār*.
outwardly, *see* ostensible.
oven, *tanūrī*, *tandūrī*, f. : *bhaṭṭhī*, f., *tandūr*, m.
over, *see* above, upon, finish.
overawe, *see* threaten : be o.-ed, *dabbṇā*.
overcoat, *waḍḍā kōṭ*, m. : *brāṇḍī*, f. (waterproof).
overcome, *see* conquer.
overflow, in vessel, *ucchaḷṇā* : boil over, *ubbaḷ jāṇā*, *ubbaḷke paiṇā* : river, *ucchaḷṇā*.
overhear, deliberately, *cōrī* or *malkṛī suṇṇā* : accidentally, *sbabb nāḷ* or *ēwē̃ suṇṇā*.
overlook, *nā khyāl karnā* (*dā*).
overseer, of labourers : *see* superintendent.
overshadow, *see* shade, shadow.
overtake, *jā raḷṇā* or *phaṛnā* (*nū̃*) : *kōḷ appaṛnā*, *agge laṅghṇā*.
overturn, *see* upside down.
owe, he owes, *ōs dēṇā e* : he is owed, *ōs laiṇā e*, *ohnū̃ aundā e* : *see* debt.
(1) own, adj., *apṇā*.
(2) own, owner, *kih dā e*, *ehdā mālik kauṇ e*.
(3) ownerless, *lawāris*, *nikhasmā* : of animal temporarily separated fr. its owners, *luggā*.
(4) ownership, *mālkī*.
ox, *see* bull : pair for ploughing, *haḷ*, m., *jōg*, f.

P

pace, *kadam*, m. : *see* walk.
pacify, *rāzī-k.* : *sulhā karāṇī* (*dī*) : *see* calm (2), appease.
(1) pack, *asbāb teār-karnā* or *bannhṇā* : shove in, *tunnṇā*.
packet, postal, *pākaṭ*, *paikaṭ*, m. : *see* bundle, parcel.
(2) pack-horse, *lāddū ghōṛā*.
(3) pack-saddle, *sūṇḍkā*.
pad, on head, *innū̃*, m.
padlock, *see* lock.
page, *safhā*, m. : one double p., *warkā* (a leaf) : *see* sheet, paper.
pain, *pīṛ*, f. : *dard*, m. : griping, *watt* (*paiṇā*) : shooting, *trāṭ*, f. (*paiṇī*) : *see* grief, hurt.
painful, *dukhdā e*, *pīṛ kardā e*.
paint, *rang*, m. : (*lāṇā*, *nū̃* ; *k.*, *dā* or *nū̃* ; int. *laggṇā*).
painter, *taswīrā̃ baṇāṇwālā*.
pair, *jōṛā*, m. : of oxen, etc., *jōg*, f. : *hal*, m. (for ploughing) : the p. or fellow, *ehde nāḷ dā*.
palace, *mahall*, m.
palate, *tāḷū*, m.
pale, *pīlā* (*paiṇā*, *h.*) : *rang laihṇā* (*dā*) : *bhussā*, p. and ill : of colour, *see* light.

palm, hand, *tali*, f. : date-p., *see* date (1).
palpitate, fear, *dharaknā* : excitement, longing, *tarafnā*.
palpitation, *dharki*, f.
palsy, *adhrang*, m. : man w. p., *adhrangī*.
pamphlet, *rasālā*, m.
pankha, *see* punkah.
pannier, donkey's saddle-bags, *chatt*, f.
pant, *chetī chetī sāh lainā* : *see* breath, out of ; gasp.
pantry, *bōtalkhānā*, m.
paper, *kāgaz*, m. : sheet, *tā*, m. : *see* news-p., page.
paragraph (educ.) *pairā*, m.
paralysis, *see* palsy.
paramour, *yār*.
parapet, *banērā*, m.
parcel, *pārsal*, m. : *see* packet.
parch, v. tr., *bhunnnā* : int. *bhujjnā* : grain-parcher, *bharbhūjā*.
pardon, *see* forgive.
pare, peel, fruit, vegetables, *chillnā*, *chill lāhnī* (int. *laihnī*, *dī*) : nails, *lāhnā*, gen. *luhānā*, get them done (A.).
parents *māpe*, *mā pyō*, *wāldain*.
(1) **part**, n., *hissā*, m. : take p. in, *ralnā*, *sharīk* or *shāmil h.* (*wicc*) : fifth p., sixth p., etc., *see* time.
(2) **part**, v., *see* divide.
partake, *see* part, share.
partially, as p. blind, *kujjh annhā* : *see* partly, partiality.
partiality, *raī*, f. : *tarfdārī*, f. : *lihāz*, m. (all w. *k.* and *dā*, *dī*).
particular, *see* special : -s, *see* detail.
partition, *see* part, divi-de, -sion.
partly, *kujjh te eh..te kujjh eh*, *abbal te*.. or *ikk te*..*te phēr*.
partner, *sīrī*, *sānjhī*, *panjhāl*, *sāthī*, *jōrīdār*, *hissedār* : half and half p., *ādhī*.
party, *farīk*, m. : *dhir*, f. : *pāssā*, m. : quarrelling clique, *dharā*, m., *see* sect.
pass, *langhnā* (tr. *langhānā*) : p. money, *lānā*, *calānā* (int. *laggnā*, *calnā*) : p. exam., *pās h.* or *k.* : p. time, *welā tapānā* (int. *tappnā*), *jhat* or *wakat langhānā* (int. *langhnā*).
passage, in book, *ibārat*, f. : *see* tunnel.
passenger, *suārī*, f. : p.-train, *suārī gaddī*, f. : *see* traveller, train (2).
passport, *pās*, m. : *rāhdārī*, f.
past, *jehrā zamānā langh geā e.* : *purānā zamānā*.
paste, *lēwī*, f. (for gumming : *lānī*, int. *laggnī*) : for pudding, *krās*, m. (K.) : *see* gum, glue.
pasture, *see* graze.
pat, v. tr., *thāprī mārnī* or *dēnī* or *lānī*, (also *thāprā*, m.).
patch, cloth, leather, *tākī* (*lānī*, int. *laggnī*) : metal, *tānkā* (*lānā*, int. *laggnā*) : not a p. on him, *ohdā pāskū wī nehī*.
path, *paihā*, m. : *rāh*, m. : v. narrow (between fields, *see* boundary), *bannā*, m. : track, *ghāssī*, f. : *see* road, way.
pathetic, *rōn-* or *ruān-wālī gall*, f. : *see* sad, touching.
patience, *hauslā* m. : *sabr*, m.
patient, adj., *hausle* or *sabr wālā* : n., *bamār*, *marīz* (U.).

patriotism, *watan dā mhabbat*, f.
pattern, *namūnā*, m.
paucity, *thuṛh*, f. : *ghāṭā*, m. : *kamī*, f. : *see* deficient.
paw, *panjā*, m. : p. ground (horse), *khaurū kaḍḍhṇā*.
pawn, v. tr., *gaihṇe* or *bandhe pāṇā* or *rakkhṇā*.
pay, *tankhāh*, f. (*tārnī*, *dēṇī* : int. *tarnī*, *milṇī*) : p debt, *dēṇā*, *lāhṇā* (int. *laihṇā*) : p. fine, *bharnā* : *see* strike off.
peace, between parties, *sulhā*, f. : in country, *aman*, m. : rest, *arām*, m. : of mind, *tsallī*, f., *tsallā*, f. : M. salutation, (*as-*) *salām alaikum* : reply, *wā alaikum* (*as-*) *salām*.
peacemaker, *sulhā karāṇwālā*.
peach, *āṛū*, m (tree and fruit).
peak, of mountain, *cōṭī*, f. : *sirā*, m. : *ṭīshī*, f.
pear, *nākh*, f (tree and fruit).
pea, *maṭar*, m.
pearl, *mōtī*, m.
peasant, *see* farmer, villager.
pebble, *gīṭī*, f. : *gīṭā*, m.
peck, *cunjh* or *cinjh mārnī*, *ṭhūṅgā mārnā* : eat grain, etc., *cuggṇā*.
peculation, *gaban karnā*.
peculiar, *see* strange.
pedlar, *see* hawker.
pedigree, *nasabnāmā*, m. : tree, *shajrā*, m.
peel, *chill*, f. : v., *see* pare.
peep, *jhāttī mārnī*.
peepul tree, *pippal*, m.
peerless, *sāreā tō wadhīā* or *awwal*, *ohde jehā* or *barābar koī nehī* : *bēnazīr* (U.) ; *lāsānī* (U.), *see* matchless.
peevish, *shtābī ciṛhnwālā*.
peg, *see* nail.
pellet, (small for *gulēl*), *gulēlā*, m. : (large, for *kubhāṇī*), *ḍhīnḍhā*, m. : *see* sling, pebble.
pen, *par*, m. : *kalam*, f. : *see* nib : p. and ink, *kalam duāt*, f. : p.-tray, *kalamdān*, m.
pencil, *pinsal*, f. : *pilsaṇ*, f. : *rūl*, f. m.
penetrate, *see* enter, pierce, sink.
penknife, *cakkū*, m.
penman, *see* caligraphist.
pension, *pinshan*, f.
Pentateuch, *taurēt*, f.
(1) people, *lōk*, m. pl. : *lōkī*, m. pl. : Tom, Dick and Harry *jaṇā khaṇā*, *hamā shamā* : *see* common, everyone, all.
(2) people, v. tr., *abād-k*. (place) : *wasāṇā*, settle p. in a place
pepper, black, *kāḷī marc*, f. : *gōḷ marc*, f. : red, *lāl marc*, f.
per, *picche*, *sēṭī* (both after infl. noun) ; *fī* (before noun, U.) : in prices often loc., G. 78 : per man, *jaṇe sēṭī* : per house, *ghar picche* : at 6/- a maund, *chī rupaī maṇ* : *see* rate.
per cent, *saikṛā* (5%, *panj rupayye saikṛā*) : *fī sadī* : -age given to lambardar, zaildar, *panjōtrā*, m
peremptory, *see* imperious, urgent.
perennial, *jehṛā sārā sāl rawhe*.
perfect, *kāmal*, *pūrā* : *see* complete, guiltless.
perfection, *kamāl*, m.
perfid-ious, -y, *see* treacherous. treason.
perform, *see* do, finish.

perfume, *acchī bō*, f. : *khushbō*, f. (in villages this may mean also bad smell) : *caṅgī khushbō*, f. : *see* smell.
perfunctory, *kamm taraṅgaṛnā*.
perhaps, *shaid*, *shait*, *ho sakdā e*.
period, *zamānā*, m. : fixed p., *miād*, f., *mohlat*, f. : long time, *cir*, m. : *muddat*, f. : *bāmuddat*, f.
perish, *nās-h.*, *barbād-h.* : *see* destroy, downfall : perish !, *bēṛā ruṛhī* (abuse).
perjury, *jhūṭhī saūh* or *kasm*, f. : *see* oath.
permanent, *see*, lasting : service, *mustakil*, *pakkī* (*naukrī*).
(1) **permissible**, *jāiz*, *hukm*, m., or *ijāzat*, f., *haiwe*.
(2) **permi-t, -ssion**, *see* allow, liberty.
perpendicular, *siddhā*, (straight) : *khaṛā*, steep.
perpetual, *hameshā dā* or *wāste*.
perplex, *gallā nāḷ phasāṇā* (int. *phasṇā*) : *see* confuse.
perquisite, *dastūrī*, f., on purchases : *kamīshan*, m.
persecut-e, -ion, *see* oppression.
persevere, *khaihṛā nā chaḍḍṇā*, *chaḍḍū nehī*, *pakkā*.
persist, *see* persevere, obstinacy, -te.
person, *see* man, etc. : in p., *āpū*, *āpe* : *see* self : the Spirit is a p., *nirā asr nehī*, *Rūh we*.
personal, *zātī* ; not used for "my p. Saviour," which is *mērā apṇā*, *mērā ī* : p. work, *jaṇe jaṇe nāl gall karke*, etc.
perspiration, *muṛhkā*, m. (*wagṇā* w. *dā*, *auṇā* w. *nū*) : *trēlī*, f. (through weakness or fear, *auṇī*, *nū*). [*nā*.
persuade, *manāṇā*, *samjhā-*
perturb-, -ation, *see* perplex, confuse.
perverse, *puṭṭhā*, *ulṭā*.
(1) **pervert**, v. tr., *wagāṛnā*, *gumrāh-k* (int. *wigaṛnā*, *gumrāh-h.*) : *see* excite, incite.
(2) **pervert**, n., *murtadd*.
pestilence, *bamārī*, f. : *see* plague.
pestle and mortar, *daurī ḍaṇḍā*, m. : *caṭṭū waṭṭā*, m. : *hamām dastā*, m. : in ground, *ukhḷī mūhḷī*, f.
pet, child, *lāḍlā* (spoilt), *pyārā* : animal, kept, *rākhwā*, *pāltū*.
petal, *pattī*, f. : *phull dī pattī*.
petition, *arz*, f., *suāl*, m. : leg., *arzī*, f. (written).
petticoat, *ghagghrī*, f. : *pēṭikōṭ*, m. : *see* skirt, kilt.
pewter, *jist*, m.
philosopher, *failsūf* (U.).
philosophy, *failsūfī*, f.
photograph, *taswīr*, f. : *fōṭō*, m. f. (both *khiccṇā*).
phthisis, *tap dikk*, m.
physician, *see* doctor.
piano, *wājjā*, m. : play, *wajāṇā*.
pice, *paisā*, m. : half p., *dhēllā*, m. : quarter, *damṛī*, f. : third, *pāī*, f. : two p., *see* anna.
(1) **pick**, flowers, fruit, *khohṇā* (int. *khussṇā*), *cuṇṇā* : p. off sticky things, *lāhṇā* (int. *laihṇā*) : p. up, *cukkṇā* : *see* peck.
(2) **pick**, tool, *gaintī*, f.
pickle, *acār*, m. (*pāṇā* ; of, *dā*).
picture, *taswīr*, f. (*baṇāṇī*, *khiccṇī*), *mūrat*, f. (*baṇāṇī*).

piebald, *ḍabbā*, *ḍab khṛabbā*.
piece, *ṭōṭā*, m. : *ṭukṛā*, m : of meat, *bōṭī*, n : *dakkrā*, m. : take to pieces, undo, machinery, bed, masonry, *ukhēṛnā* (int. *ukkhaṛnā*) : *see* loose.
pierce, make hole, *see* hole : needle, thorn, *see* prick : pierce ears, nose, *winnṇā* (pa. p. *widdhā* : int. *wijjhṇā*)
piety, *see* pious.
pig, *sūr*, fem. *sūrnī* : *bāhrlā*, *bāhr dī shai* : G. 114.
pigeon-house, *see* dovecot.
pigmy, *see* dwarf.
pigtail, *see* hair.
pile, *see* heap.
piles, *bawāsīr*, f., (also *mohkā*, m.) : bleeding, *khūnī*.
pilgrim, to Makkah, *hājī* ; Hindu, *tīrthī*, *jātrī*.
pilgrimage, to Makkah, *hajj*, m. (*k*.) : to Muslim shrine, *ziārat*, f. : to Hindu shrine *tīrath*, m. : *jātrā*, m. (all *k*.).
pill, *gōḷī*, f. ; *ṭikkī*, f. (flattened).
pillar, masonry or wood, *thammh*, m. : small, *thammhī*, f. (wood) : of brick, in house, *kauḷā*, m. : *see* support, boundary.
pillow, *sarhāṇā*, m. : *takiā*, m. : p.-slip or case *takīe dā uchāṛ* m.
pimple, *phimhṇī*, f.
pin, *pinn*, m. : rolling-p., *wēllaṇ* or *wēlṇā* m. : *see* rolling-board.
pincers, *sannhī*, f. : *see* tongs.
pinch, *cūṇḍhī* *waḍḍhṇī* or *bharnī* (*nī*).
pine, *diār*, m. : *biāṛ*, m. (both cedar) : pinus longifolia or excelsa, *cīhṛ*, f. : *cīhl*, f.
pinion, arms (tie), *mushkā̃ bannhṇīā̃* (*dīā̃*).
pink, *gulābī*, adj : *see* red.
pinnacle, of building *kiṅgrā*, m. : *see* peak.
pious, *Khudā-parast*, *dīndār*, *parhēzgār*, *bhagat* (H.).
pipe, *hukkā*, m. : *paip*, m. (European).
pirate, *darvāī cōr*, *baihrī cōr*.
pistol, *pistaul*, m. : *tamā̃cā*, m. (both *calānā*. *mārnā*) : *see* shoot.
pit, *ṭoā*, m. (also ditch, *kaḍḍhṇā*) : *khāḍḍā*, m. (*lāṇā*, int. *laggṇā*) : *khāttā*, m. (gen. an old *khāḍḍā*).
(1) pitch, tar, n., *lukk*, f. : *see* tune.
(2) pitch, tents, *lāṇā* : *see* strike.
piteous, *see* pathetic.
pith, *girī*, f.
pitiful, *see* compassionate, pathetic.
pity, *tars*, m (*auṇā*, *k*., *utte*) : *see* mercy, compassionate : it's a pity that, *afsōs e paī*.
pivot, *cūthī*, f. : of bed, *cūḷ*, m. : *see* socket.
(1) place, n., *thā̃*, m. f. : *jaghā*, f. : out of p., *kuthā̃-*, *-e*, *kojhā* : in right p., *thā̃ sir* : *see* instead, awkward.
(2) place, v., *rakkhṇā*, *dharnā* : p. bed, chair, water (before animal), *ḍāhṇā* (int. *ḍaihṇā*, pa. p. *ḍatthā*) : *see* put A.
plague, *tāūn*, f. : *see* pestilence.
(1) plain, adj., *sāf* : *see* evident : simple, (both simple-minded and unornamented), *sādā*, *siddhā sādā* : *see* flat, level.
(2) plain, n., *madān*, m. : open space, no crops, *raṛā thā̃*, m., *raṛā*, m.
plainly, *sāf sāf*, *safāī nāḷ*.
plaintiff, *mudaī*.

plaintive, *see* pathetic, sad.
plait, v., *gundṇā* : rope, *waṭṭṇā* : n., *see* hair.
plan, *tajwīz*, f. : *hikmat*, f. (both *k.*) : *see* arrange : of building, etc., *nakshā*, m. (*baṇāṇā*).
plane, *randā*, m. (*phērnā*) : v., *randṇā*.
plank, *see* board.
plant, n., *būṭā*, m. : *būṭī*, f. : young for replanting, *panīrī*, f. (all w. *lāṇā*, int. *laggṇā*) : w. long tendrils, creeping, climbing, *wēl*, f. : *wall*, f.
plantain, *see* banana.
plaster, n., *see* mortar, mud : v., *limbṇā* : *lēmbī* or *lawāī karnī* (*dī*), *plastar karnā* (*dā*) : *see* mud, smear.
plate, gen. *bhāṇḍā*, m. : large, *plēṭ*, f. : smaller, *hāfplēṭ*, f. : still smaller, *kuāṭar*, m. : soup-p., *suplēṭ*, f. : Indian, *prāt*, f., *thāḷ*, m. : *thāḷī*, f. : *see* dish, drinking-vessel.
platform : *thaṛhā*, m. : *cabūtrā*, m.
(1) play, n., *khēḍ*, f. : drama, *nāṭak*, m.
(2) play, v., *khēḍṇā* : music, *wajāṇā* (int. *wajjṇā*).
player, *khaḍārī*.
playfellow, *see* companion.
pleader, *wakīl*.
pleasant, *dil nū̃ caṅgā laggṇā* : *see* good, tasty.
please, v. tr., *kh̲ush-k.*, *rāzī-k.* : int. *kh̲ush h.*, *rāzī h.* : p. do it, *mehrbānī karke* (very emphatic), *zarā* ; gen. omit : p. God, *in shā Allā*.
pleasure, *kh̲ushī*, f. : *marzī*, f. : w. p., *see* means.
plectrum, *mizrāb*, m.
pledge, *see* mortgage, pawn, promise.
plentiful, *see* much.
plenty, not famine, *sukāḷ*, m. : *see* much.
pliable, pliant, of thing, *lifaṇwālā*, *kūḷā* : person, *jaldī mannaṇwālā*, *jehṛe pāse bhuāīe bhauṇdā e* : *see* changeable, vacillate.
plinth, *kursī*, f.
plot, *garmathā*, m. or *gall*, f. or *matā*, m. (w. *pakāṇā* : int. *pakkṇā*), M. 125. 16.
plough, *wāhṇā*, *haḷ wāhṇā* (int. *waggṇā*) : each ploughing, *sī lāṇī* (int. *laggṇī*) : *see* cultivate, train (1) : p.-ed land, *warihāḷ*, f. : *wāhṇ*, f. : *see* fallow.
ploughman, *hāḷī*, *wāhk* (plougher) : *see* farmer, cultivator.
pluck, *see* pick.
plug, *ḍaṭṭ*, m. (*lāṇā*, int. *laggṇā*).
plum, *alūcā*, m. : (tree and fruit) : small, tree, *bērī*, f. ; fruit, *bēr*, m. : large grafted *bēr* (fruit or tree), *syō bēr* : small, *kāṭhā bēr* ; *bēr* bush, *maḷhā*, m.
plunder, *see* rob, steal.
plural, *jamhā*, f.
P.M. *see* A.M.
pocket. *bojhā*, m. : *jēb*, m.
pocket-book, *pākaṭ buk*, f.
pocket-money, *jēb kh̲arc*, m.
pod, *phaḷī*, f.
poem, *nazm*, f. : *shēhr*, m.
poet, *shairī*, *nazmā likkhaṇwālā*, *shāir* (U.).
poetry, *see* poem.
(1) point, *nōk* f. : p. of letter like *sīn* or *shīn*, *dandā*, *kiṅgrā*, m. : p. of story, etc., *matlab*, m. : be on the p. of, verbal form in *-wālā*, G. 98, 99 ; root of verb w. *caleā* G. 67 : *see* desire.

(2) point, v., *ishārā karnā* (*de wall*) : *see* hit at.
(3) point a building, *ṭīp karnī* (*dī*).
poison, *mauhrā*, m. : *zaihr*, m. : *wiss*, m.
poisonous, *zaihrī*.
poke, w. stick, goad, *hujj mārnī* (*nū̃*) : *see* goad.
poker, wooden, *kuḍḍhaṇ*, m.
pole, north, *kutab*, m. : pole-star, *kutab tārā*, m.
pole, *ḍaṇḍā*, m., *bā̃s*, m. : *see* stick, post.
police, gen., *puls*, f. : *polīs*, f. : -man, *pulswālā*, *kanstebal* : p.-station, *thāṇā*, m. : -post, *caukī*, f., *caũkī*, f.
polish, *pālash*, m. (esp. boot-p.), blacking, *syāhī*, f. both *lāṇā*, int. *laggṇā*) : *see* varnish.
polite, *shaistā* : *see* courteous.
pollute, *see* dirty, defile, unclean.
polytheist, *mushrik*.
pomegranate, tree and fruit, *anār*, m.
pomelo, tree and fruit, *cakōdhrā*, m.
pomp, *see* show.
pond, *chappaṛ*, m. : *chappṛī*, f. (small, often dry) : *ḍhāb*, m. (big depression) : *see* lake.
ponder, *sōcṇā* (*nū̃*) : *gaur karnā* (*utte*).
pony, small, *ṭaṭṭū*, fem. *ṭair*.
polo, *pōlō*, m.
pool, *see* pond.
poor, *garīb*, *muthāj* (seeking help), *maskīn*, *wacārā* (p. fellow) : *māṛā* (feeble, poor) : *daliddarī* (wretched) : *see* straits : of land, *niras*, *māṛī*, *raddī*, *matthī*, *narm* : *see* soil, waste : p. Panjabi, *ṭuṭṭī bhajjī* or *māṛī mōṭī Panjābī*, f., *see* smattering.
popcorn, *dhāhṇā*, f. pl. (barley).
poppy, *pōst*, m.
popular, *lōk baṛe khush ne ohde nāḷ* or *cāhnde ne* (*nū̃*) or *caṅgā jāṇde ne* (*nū̃*).
population, *abādī*, f.
populated, *abād*.
populous, *baṛī abādī*, *baṛe lōk*, *baṛā abād*, etc.
porcelain, *cīnī*, f.
porridge, *dalīā*, m.
porter, *kulī*.
portion, *see* part.
portmanteau, *thailā*, m.
possess-, -ion, get p. of, *kābū-k.*, *mallṇā* : keep in p., *apṇe kabze wicc rakkhṇā* : *see* have.
possible, *mumkin*, *hō sakdā e* : see able.
(1) post (mail), *ḍāk*, f. : by post, *ḍāk wicc* : p. letter, *ḍāke* or *ḍāk icc pāṇā* (int. *paiṇā*) : travel post, *ḍāk bannhke safar karnā*.
(2) post, telegraph-, *waḷā*, m. : short p., *munnā*, m. : lamp-p., *waḷā*, *munnā* : *see* pillar.
(3) post, situation, *asāmī*, f. : vacancy, *asāmī khālī e* : service, *naukrī*, f.
(4) postage, *masūl*, m. : *ḍāk dā masūl*.
(5) postman, *ḍākwālā*, *ciṭṭhī rasān* (U.) : *halkārā*, runner.
(6) post-office, *ḍāk khānā*, m.
posterity, *see* descendants.
postpone, *multawī-k.*, (U.) : p. a week, *aṭṭhā̃ diṇā̃ te gall pā dittī*, *aṭṭh din pāe* : *see* respite.
pot, earthenware, *ghaṛā*, m. : *jhajjar*, f. : large, *maṭṭ*, m.; *cāṭī*, f. : long-necked, *surāhī*, f. : for cooking (earthen)

hāṇḍi, f., *tauṛi*, f., *kunni*, f.: at well, *ṭinḍ*, f.: pot-stand (wooden), *ghaṛwanjī*, f., *ghaṛēthnī*, f.: metal pots, v. large, *kaṛāh*, m.; smaller, *kaṛāhī*, f., *dēg*, f.; small, *dējkī*, f.; *gāgar*, f. (for water): put on pot, *cāṛhnā* (int. *caṛhnā*).

potato, *ālū*, m.

potsherd, *ṭhīkrā*, m.: small, *ṭhīkrī*, f.

potter, *kumhyār-*, fem. *-ī*.

pounce, *see* snatch, seize.

(1) pound, *kuṭṭṇā*, *ghōṭnā* (w. liquid): (p. and husk) rice, grain, etc., *chaṛnā*: *see* grind, beetle, pestle, rolling-board.

(2) pound, n., for cattle, *phāṭak*, m.: coin, *pauṇḍ*, m.: weight, *see* w s. and meas.

pour, *lhṇā* (int. *ḍulhṇā*): *luddṇa*: p. out, *roṛhnā* (int. *ruṛhnā*): *see* spill.

poverty, *garībī*, f.: *muthājī*, f. (seeking help, *k.*, *dī*): *maskīnī*, f.: *tangī*, f.: *see* poor, difficulty, straits.

powder, gun-p, *barūd*, m.: *dārū*, m.: medicine, *puṛī*, f., *phakkī*, f.: no word for p. in gen.

power, *was*, m.: *mērī majāl e?* what p. have I (to do that)? *see* authority, strength: p. of attorney, *mukhtār-nāmā*, m.

powerful, *see* strong, strength.

practi-ce, -se, *mashk*, f (*k.*), *jāc*, f (knack, *auṇī*, *nū*): *see* use.

praise, *wadeāṇā*, *salāhṇā*, *waḍeāī k.* (*dī*), *tarīf k.* (*dī*), *hamad karnī* (*dī*, only of God).

praiseworthy, *baṛā laik*: *see* good, excellent.

pray, prayer, gen., *duā mangṇī* or *karnī*: *namāz paṛhnī* (M.): *prārthnā karnī* (H.): prayers, *bandgī karnī*, *namāz paṛhnī*: p. for person, *duā dēṇī* (*nū*); gen., *de wāste duā karnī* or *mangṇī*: call to p., *bāṅg dēṇī* (M.): *see* ask, beseech.

preach, in church, *wāhz* or *wāhd kar-nī* or *-nā*: to non-Christians, *manādī karnī*.

preacher, *wāhz* or *wāhd karn-wāḷā*, *pādrī*, *girjā karāṇ-wāḷā*: ordained person, *pādrī*; ordain, *pādrī baṇāṇā* (int. *baṇṇā*): *see* priest.

precaution, *khabardārī*, f.: *hōsh*, f., *ehtiāt*, (U.), all w. *k.*

precedent, *dastūr*, m., *rawāj*, m.: no p., *eṅ kadī nehī hoeā*: *see* custom, unexampled.

precept, *maslā*, m.: *see* advice.

precious, *pyārā*: *see* costly, good, excellent.

precipice, *khaḷā pahāṛ*, m.: *baṛī khaḍḍ*, f.

precipita-ncy, -te, -tion, *see* haste.

predestined, *Khudā dī marzī nāḷ* or *de hukm nāḷ*: *see* fate, fated.

preemption, right of, *hakk shufā*, m. (*k.*).

prefer, *eh menū ohdū caṅgā laggdā e*: *see* desire, like.

pregnant, woman, use *ohnū umēdwārī e*: animals, *sūṇ-wāḷī*, *wakkōḍī* (cattle).

prejudice, *tassab*, m.: *see* partiality.

prejudiced, *tassabī*: *see* partiality.

premature, *wakat tō paihlā*.

prepar-e, -ation, *teār-k.* (*nū*): *teārī karnī* (*dī*): *see* ready.

prescience, supernatural, *gaib-dānī*, f., *gaib dā ilm*, *ilhām*, m.
prescription, medical, *nuskhā*, m.
presence, *hāzrī*, f. (not absence): of superior, *huzūrī*, f.: *see* face, before: in p. of God, *Khudā dī huzūrī wicc*, *Khudā dī dargāh wicc*.
(1) present, adj., *hāzar* (esp. of inferior): *majūd*, (not absent): p. time, at p., *hāl dā zamānā*, m.: *hālī*, *hālā̃*.
(2) present, v., *dēṇā*, *pēsh-k*.
(3) present, n., *see* gift.
presentiment, *mēre dil wicc agdū eh gall āī sī* or *eh khyāl sī*.
preserve, *hafāzat nāḷ* or *sāmbhke rakkhṇā*: *see* jam: -d fruit, *murabbā*, m. (v., *pāṇā*).
(1) press, n., for books, clothes, plates, in wall or otherwise, *almārī*, f.: v. small in wall, *āḷā*, m.: for sugarcane, *wēlṇā*, m.: binder's p., *shakanjā*, m.: oil-p., *kolhū*, m.
(2) press, v., *dabāṇā* (int *dabbṇā*): *see* incite, urge, pressure, emphasise.
pressure, moral, etc., *dabā*, m.; *rōhb*, m. (both w. *pāṇā*, *utte*).
pretence, *bahānā*, m., *khēkhan*, m., *hīlā*, m., (all w. *k.*): *see* ostensible, put off, trifle.
pretty, *see* beautiful.
prevail, *phailṇā* (spread): *see* conquer, persuade.
prevaricate, *see* put off, trifle.
prevent, *see* stop, hinder, forbid.
previous, *aglā*, *paihlā*.
previously, *see* before.
prey, *shikār*, m.: dupe, v. tr. *jāḷ* or *shikār wicc phasāṇā* (int. *phasṇā*), *shikār-karnā* (int. *hōṇā*): *see* hunt, shoot.
price, *mull*, m., *kīmat*, f.: *see* rate, cost, expense, spend.
priceless, use v. costly.
prick (needle, thorn), *cubbhṇā* (tr. *cōbhṇā*): tr., *sūī mārnī*, p. w. needle: p. up ears, *kann khaḍe karne* or *khalhār-ne*.
prickly-heat, *pitt*, f.; come out, *nikḷṇī*; subside, *marnī*.
pride, (good) *fakhr*, m.: (bad) *magrūrī*, f., *shēkhī*, f., *ākkaṛ*, f., *mizāj*, f., *damāg*, m.: *see* proud, airs, conceit, take down p., *see* humble.
priest, Christian, *pādrī*; *fādar* (Rom. Cath.): M., *malwāṇā*, *miyyā̃*: H., *prōhat*: Cuhra, *gyānnī*, *fakīr*: Jewish, *kaihṇ*.
prince, *shāhzād-ā*, fem. -*ī*.
print, of printer, *chāpṇā*: caus. *chapwāṇā*: be p.-ed, *chapṇā*.
prison, *kaidkhānā*, m., *jēhlkhā-nā*, m.: *see* imprison.
prisoner, war or prison, *kaid-ī*, fem. -*an*: *see* imprison.
private, *sāḍḍī apnī gall*, *prāiwēṭ*, *parde dī gall*: in p., *pasitte hōke*, *nawēkḷe hōke*.
privet, *sanatthā*, m.
privilege, *hakk*, m. (right): *ijāzat*, f. (permission): *riait*, f. (easement).
prize, *inām*, m.: v., *see* value.
probably, *wīh wiswe*, *umed e pai*.
probe, a matter, *phōlṇā*.
procla-im, -mation (causal), *ḍaunḍī piṭwāṇī*, *ḍhanḍōrā duāṇā*, *manādī karāṇī*: of actual crier, *ḍhanḍōrā d.*: make known, *dhumāṇā*, *suṇāṇā*.

procrastinate, *see* delay, put off.
procurable, *milda e.*
procure, *labbh laiṇā*, *see* obtain, produce (2).
prod, w. stick or knuckles, *hujj mārnī* (*nū*), *see* goad.
(1) produce, n., *paidāwārī*, f. (of land), *see* crop: *jo kujjh bandā e.*
(2) produce, v., *paidā-k, banāṇā*: *see* secure, supply, obtain.
profan-e,-ity, *kufr bakṇā.*
profession, *kamm*, m. (men or women): *pēshā*, m., *kasab*, m. (these two not of women).
professor, *ustād*, *profēsar.*
proficient, *see* clever, able, intelligent.
profit, *khaṭṭī*, f., *labhat*, f., *nafā*, m: for his own advantage, *apṇe gaū nū*: p. and loss, *nafā nuksān*, m: *see* advantage, excess.
profligate, *luccā, badkār.*
progress, *trakkī*, f. (*k.*): *see* advance.
prominent, *see* famous, conspicuous.
promise, *wāhdā*, m., *sukhan*, m., *karār*, m., *gall*, f., *zabān*, f. (all w. k.): break p., *apṇe wāhde, sukhan*, etc., *dā* or *thõ jhūṭhā h.*, *wāhdā trōṛnā*: fulfil p., above words w. *pūrā k.*: *see* word.
promote, *trakkī dēṇī* (*nū*): a scheme, *calāṇā, madat dēṇī* (*wicc*).
prone, on face, *mūhdā, mūhdṛe mūh, mūh parne*: p. to, liable to, use *-wāḷā*; p. to forget, *bhullanwāḷā*: p. to fall, *ḍiggaṇwāḷā*: to sickness, *bamār hōṇwālā.*
pronounce, letter, word, etc., *bōlṇā, bulāṇā*: be p.-ed, *bōlṇā, bōleā jāṇā, bulāeā jāṇā.*
pronunciation, *talaffaz*, m., (*bōlṇā*).
proof, *sabūt* (*dēṇā, dā*): *dalīl*, argument, *dēṇī, dī*): *see* prove.
prop, *sahārā*, m. (*d.*, *see* lean): for trees, *thūhṇī*, f.: *see* support, pillar.
proper, *munāsib, ṭhīk*, *see* suitable, right (2), advisable.
property, *māl*, m., *māl asbāb*, m.: estate, *jāedāt*, f., *jāedād*, f.: *hasīat*, f., wealth: *see* wealth, rich.
prophecy, *nabuwwat*, f. (*k.*): *pēshīgoī*, f. (*k.*).
prophet, *nabī, pakambar, pagambar.*
propitiat-e, -ion, *see* conciliate, atone.
propos-e, -al, *rā* or *rai dēṇī, dassṇī*: in meeting, *rā* or *mōshn pēsh karnī*: *see* opinion, advise.
prose, *nasr*, f.
prosecute, *see* case.
prosper-, -ous, *see* advance, progress, rich: or say *ohdā kamm wāh wā caldā e.*
protect, *see* guard, preserve, save.
protector, *see* guardian, saviour.
protrude, *nikḷṇā, wadhṇā*: -ing, *nikḷeā* or *wadheā hoeā.*
proud, *magrūr, mizāj-* or *damāg-* or *ākaṛ- -wāḷā*: *see* pride.
proudly, words for pride w. *nāḷ.*
prove, *sābit-k.*: *see* proof.
proverb, *masāl*, f.: *akhāṇ*, m.
(1) provide, *see* obtain, supply, produce (2), secure.

(2) provided that, *jē* or *agar* (if): *jē te, hā par jē te*: *see* condition.
province, *sūbā*, m.
provision, rations, *rasad*, f., *rāsn*, f.
provo-ke, -cation, *see* annoy.
proxy, *wakīl*, m.
prune, v. tr., *chāṅgṇā*, *chaṅgāī karnī* (*dī*).
pry, *see* peep.
psalm, *zabūr*, m.; book of P., *zabūrā dī kitāb*, f., *zabūr*, m. pl.: a volume containing the Ps., *zabūr*, f.
publicly, *khulham khulhā*, *khulhā*, *khulhā ḍulhā*, *lōkā de sāhmṇe*: *see* openly.
publish, *chapwāṇā*: be p.-ed, *nikḷṇā*, *chapṇā*: *see* print, proclaim.
pudding, *puṭīn*, f.: *phuṭīn*, f.
pull, *khiccṇā*: punkah, *khiccṇā*: p. out hair, weeds, and other small things, *puṭṭṇā*: *see* drag.
pulley, *garārī*, f.: for well, *carakhṛī*, f.
pulpit, *mimbar*, m., *mēz*, *mēc*, m.
pulse, *nabz*, f. (*wēkhṇī*, caus. *wakhāṇī*, also *būh*, f.).
pump, *naḷkā*, m.: railway, etc., *pamp*, m., *papp*, m.
pumpkin, *kaddū*, m.
punctual, *weḷe sir auṇā*: *wakat dā paband* (U).
puncture, (bicycle) *pancar*, m. (*h.*, *nū*).
pungent in taste, *see* hot.
punish-, -ment, *sazā*, f. (*d.*): capital p., *phāhe* or *phāsī* or *maut dī sazā*.
punkah, *pakkhā*, m.: to fan, *pakkhā jhallṇā*: pull p., *khiccṇā*; p.-coolie, *pakkhe-wāḷā*.
pupil, of eye, *see* eye: of wrestler, *paṭṭhā*, m.: *see* disciple, scholar.
puppy, *katūrā*, m.
purchases, *saudā*, m.: *saudā sūd*, m.: *see* buy, obtain.
pure, *see* clean: ceremonially, *see* holy: unadulterated, *nakhākhrā*, *khālas*: pure Panjabi, etc., *theṭh*. [A.
Purgative, *julāb*, *m.* (*laiṇā*, *d.*).
purify, words for clean, pure, holy, w. *k.*: *see* wash.
purity, *pakīzgī*, f. (U.): *see* cleanliness.
purple, *kāshnī* (violet), *kirmzī kirmcī* (red purple or crimson): purplish, *see* somewhat.
purpose, *see* aim, object, intention: for the p. of, *see* order: to no p., *dhigāṇe*, *ēwē*: *see* useless.
purposely, *ucēcā*, *jāṇke*, *samjhke*: *see* deliberately.
purse, *guthlī*, f., *gutthī*, f., *thailī*, f., *baṭūā*, m.
pursue, *magar bhajjṇā*.
pus, *pāk*, f. [(*nū*).
push, *dhikkṇā*, *dhakkā dēṇā*
put, *rakkhṇā*, *dharnā*: *see* place: p. in, *pāṇā* (int. *paiṇā*): p. away w. care, *sāmbhṇā*: p. off, *see* delay: p. off w. excuses, promises, *lāre* or *lāre lappe dēne*, *ṭālṇā* (int. *ṭaḷṇā*), *ṭāḷ maṭoḷā karnā*, *ṭāḷ ṭapoḷe karne*: p. off w. semi-jocular remarks, *jugtā karnīā*: p. on clothes, on to oneself or child, *pāṇā*; to oneself, *utte laiṇā*; a shawl round one's head, *bukkaḷ mārnī*: make someone p. on clothes or let him put them on to oneself, *puāṇā*: *see* wear: p. out, *see* extinguish, annoy, eject.

putrid, *see* rotten, bad.
putty, *puṭīn*, f., *phuṭīn*, f.

Q

quadruple, *cauṇā*, *cār guṇā* : in four folds, *cauhrā* : *see* fold, time.
qualification, *liākat*, f. : *kī pās e*, what has he passed ?
quality of mind, *sifl*, f. (also Divine attributes, attributes of mind) : q. of thing, *darjā*, or simply good, bad, etc.
quantity, *kinnā*, how much ? *ēnnā*, *ōnnā*, *jinnā*.
quarrel, *takrār*, m., *jhagṛā*, m., *laṛāī*, f. (all *k.*, *h.*) : mild q., *āpe icc rinj rāzī h.* : *see* disturbance, discord.
quarrelsome, *jhagṛnwālā*, *laṛākā*, *takrārī*. [*kiā*.
quart, about *ikk sēr panj chaṭā-*
quartan fever, *cauthā*, m.
quarter, G. 23, *cauthāī*, f. : *cuhāī*, f., (esp. land) : *cauthā hissā*, m. : *pā*, m. (of *ser*, *see* wts. and meas.) : q. more than, *sawā*, as 3¼, *sawā trai* : adj., *suāyā*, used for one and q. : q. less than, *pauṇe*, as 1¾, *pauṇe dō* : q. of orange, etc., *see* section : ¾ of, *muṇnā*.
queen, *rāṇī*, *malkā*, f.
quench, fire, *bujhāṇā* ; int., *bujjhṇā* : thirst, *see* slake.
question, *suāl*, m. (*k.*), *see* ask.
quibble, *jugat*, f. (*k.*), *huṭṭar*, m. (*k.*), *hujjat*, f. (*k.*) : *see* argument, excuse.
quick, *see* swift, quickly.
quickly, *shtābī*, *chēti*, *jabde*, *jhabde*, *jhaw*, *shapāshapp* : of action *hallke*, *hilā karke*, *wag tag* : go q., *khurī karnī*, *khiṭṭ dēṇī* or *mārnī*.
quicksilver, *pārā*, m.
quiet, *cup*, *cupkītā*, *cup cupītā*, *sun munn* : keep q., *aman karnā*, *sāh laiṇā*, *ḍanḍ nā pāṇī*, etc. (noise w. neg.), *cup k.* ; *see* screen.
quietly, *malkṛī*, *aḍōl*, *anchōp* : *see* gently, slowly.
quilt, *lēf*, m., *jullā*, m., *razāī*, f., *gudṛī*, f. : *see* mattress.
quince, fruit and tree, *bahī*, f.
quintuple, *panj guṇā*, *panjauṇā* : *see* fold, time.
quire, *dastā*, m. (24 sheets).
quite, *see* absolutely, altogether.
quiver, *see* tremble, shake.
quorum, *kōram*, m.
Quran, *kurān*, m. : one who knows by heart, *hāfaz* : for *hāfaj* *see* blind : Q-stand. *rehl*, f.

R

rabid (dog, etc.), *halkā*.
rabies, *halak*, m. (get, *kuddṇā*, *nū̃*).
race, *dauṛ*, f. : horse-r *ghuṛdauṛ*, f.
racquet, tennis, racquets, *ballā*, m.
radish, *mūlī*, f.
raft, *bēṛā*, m.
rag, *līr*, f. : *cithṛā*, m.
rage, get into r., *agg laggṇī* (*nū̃*) : be angry inwardly, *lūsṇā* : *see* anger, enrage.
ragged, garment, *pāṭā hoeā* : man, *pāṭeā kapṛeā wālā*, *līrā pāṭīrā wālā*.
railing, *jaṅglā*, m. : *see* hedge, enclose.
railway line, *lain*, f. : *rēl dī sarak* ; sometimes *pakkī sarak* (also Grand Trunk Road) : *see* station, train.

rain, *mīh*, m. (*wassṇā*) : *jhaṛī*, f., (continued r., *laggṇī*) : *pāṇī*, m. (*paiṇā*) : *kaṇīā*, f. pl. (*paiṇīā*) : *kaṇī muṇī*, f. (*h.*) : *kaṇman*, f. (*laggṇī*) ; last three words mean slight rain : *bārish*, f. (U., continued r., *h.*) : *see* drizzle, storm.

rainbow, *pīṅgh*, f., *guḍḍī guḍḍe dī pīṅgh*, f. (*paiṇī*).

raise, *cukkṇā*, *uṭhāṇā* (int. *uṭṭhṇā*) : r. stick, *uggarnā* : r. wall, *usārnā* (int. *ussarnā*) : r. dead, *jawāḷṇā*.

raisin, *sauṅgī*, f., *mewā*, m., (collective).

rake, *jandrā*, m. (*lāṇā*) : r. up a matter, *phōlṇā*.

ram, *chatrā*, m.

rampart, *duār*, f., *duāl*, f., *fasīl*, f.

ramrod, *gaz*, m.

rancid, *see* bad, rotten, smell.

random, at, *uṅ*, *ēwē*, *bin sōceā* ; *see* guess, reason.

rank, *darjā*, m., *ohdā*, m. : *see* line.

rankle, *dil icc khaṭakṇā*.

ransom, *fidyā*, m. : *see* save.

rap, *see* knock.

rapid, *see* swift.

rare, *ghaṭṭ wēkhīdā e* or *miḷdā e*.

rash, *jaldbāz* (U.) : *see* hasty.

rashness, *jaldbāzī*, f. (U.) : *see* haste.

rasp, *see* file.

(1) rat, *cūhā*, m. (no word for female) : *see* mouse.

(2) rat-trap, *see* trap.

rate, *bhā*, m., *nirkh*, m. : at r. of, *caūh ānnī waṭṭī*, 4 lbs. for 4 annas, G. 78 : *rupayye dā cār ser*, 4 ser a rupee : *see* tariff, per.

rather, *see* prefer, than : r. white, etc., *ciṭṭā jehā*, G. 27, 92 ; or add *-ērā*, *waḍērā*. biggish : G. 18 : *see* somewhat : rather than, *nāḷō*.

ratify, *tasdīk karnī* (*dī*) : *see* confirm.

rations, *rāsn*, f., *rasad*, f.

(1) rattle, v. int., *khaṛkṇā*, *khaṛ khaṛ-k.*, tr. *khaṛkāṇā*.

(2) rattle, toy, *chaṇkṇā*, m.

raw, *kaccā* : *see* uncertain.

ray, of sun, *kirn*, f. (U.), *rashm*, f. (U.), also of cloth.

raze, *ḍhā chaḍḍṇā*.

razor, *ustrā*, m.

reach, *appaṛnā*, *paūhcṇā* : *hatth nehī appaṛdā*, cannot reach it : *see* obtain.

read, *paṛhnā* : r. it out, *paṛhke suṇāṇā*.

readmit, to rel. privileges, *see* excommunicate.

ready, *teār* : r. to do, *karn nū teār* : r. made, *baṇeā battreā* : *see* prepare.

real, *aslī* : r. gold, silver, *succā* : r. reason, *wiclā matlab*, *asl gall*, f.

reality, *hakīkat*, f., *aslīat*, f. : in r., *asl wicc*, *hakīkat wicc* : *see* root.

really, *see* reality.

reap, *waḍḍhṇā*, *wāḍhīā karnīā*, *lāīā karnīā* or *lāṇīā*.

reaper, *wāḍhā*.

reaping-hook, sickle, *dātrī*, f.

(1) rear, v tr., *pāḷṇā*, *parwarish karnī* (*dī*).

(2) rear, of horse, *sīkhpā-h*.

(3) rear, n., *pishlā pāsā*.

reason, *dalīl* (argument) : *see* cause, purpose, therefore, without any reason, *bēsbabb*, *uṅ*, *ēwē*, *dhigāṇe* : *see* random.

reasonable, *mākūl*. [(U.).

rebel, *bāgī* ; *sarkash*, rebellious

rebellion, *bagāwat*, f., *gadr*, m.: *see* riot.
rebuke, *see* reprimand, forbid.
receipt, *rasīd*, f. (*likhṇī*, *dēṇī*): railway r., *bilṭī*, f.
(1) receive, *milṇā* (*nū*), also for r. visitors.
(2) receiver of stolen goods, *cuṅg cōr*.
recent,-ly, *jabde*, *jhabde*, *jhaw jhaw*, *nawā*, *ajj kall dā*, *hun dī gall*, *thōṛeā dihāṛeā dī gall*, *thoṛā cir hoeā*.
reciprocal, *āpe icc*.
recite, *ākhṇā*, *sunāṇā*.
reckless, *lāparwāh*.
reckon, *see* count, estimate.
recluse, *gōshā-nishī*, (M. relig. term).
recognise, *sihāṇṇā*, *sañhāṇṇā*, *pachāṇṇā* (pa. p. *sihātā*, *sāñhātā*, *pachā-ttā* or *-ṇeā*).
recognition, *sihāṇ*, f., *sañhāṇ*, f., *pachāṇ*, f.
recoil, *pishā haṭṇā* (go back).
recollect, *see* remember.
recommend, no exact word, *safārish karnī*, beg for (*dī*); *cāl caln dī ciṭṭhī dēṇī*, give letter of character: *see* advise.
recompense, *badlā*, m., *iwzānā*, m. (both *d.*): *see* damage.
reconcile, *sulhā karāṇī* (*karnī*, *hōṇī*), *rāzī-k.*: be r., *āpe icc rāzī h.*; *hun rāzī e koī shikait nehī kardā*, now r.-ed, no complaint.
record, *likhṇā*: n., *sanad* (f.) *rawhe*, that there may be a r
recover, get back, *phēr milṇā*, *phēr laiṇā*: get well, *wall* or *caṅgā h.*: r. oneself, *sambhalṇā*.
recruit, *raṅgrūṭ*: *see* enlist.

red, *lāl*, *sūhā*, *rattā*: v. red, *lāl sūhā*: of cattle, *gōrā*. A.
redeem, *chuḍāṇā* (from pawn, seizure, etc.): rel., *see* save.
Redeemer, *see* Saviour.
reduce, *see* degrade.
reduction in price, *riait*, f.
reed, *kānnā*, m.: various kinds. *kāhī*, f., *naṛ*, m., *sarūṭ*, m., *sirkī*, f., *ḍibb*, f.: *dabb*, f. (v. long grass).
reel, *ḍōlṇā*, *ḍōldeā jāṇā*.
reference, *hawālā dēṇā* (*dā*).
refined, *shāistā* (manners).
reflection, in mirror, *parchāwā*, m. (*paiṇā*): *see* thought, shadow.
reform, v. tr., *sudhārnā*, int., *suddharnā*.
refrain, *parhēz karn-ī* or *-ā* (*tō*): leave off, give up idea of, *muṛnā* (*tō*), *chaḍḍṇā*: *see* abstain.
refuge, *panāh*, f.: *see* shelter.
(1) refuse-e, -al, *mukkarnā*, *namukkarnā*, *inkār karnā* (*dā*), *inkārī karnī* (*dī*), *nāh karnī*: *madē*, *machaḍḍ*, one who refuses to give, leave: *see* reject: receive refusal, *juāb milṇā* (*nū*): flat refusal *sukkā juāb*: answer back, *gall partāṇī*, *aggō bōlṇā*.
(2) refuse, n., *see* rubbish.
refute, *jhūthā sābit-k*: *radd-k.* or *raddṇā* (*ohdī gall nū*): *see* reject.
regard, *see* esteem, considera-tion, honour, respect.
regeneration, *see* conversion.
regiment, *palṭan*, f.: cavalry, *rasālā*, m.: artillery, *tōpkhā-nā*.
register, v. tr., *rajistrī karāṇī* (*dī*, said of sender: *karnī*,

of clerk): -ed letter, *rajistrī*, f.
regret, *pachtāṇā*; *afsōs*, m. (*k.*), sorrow in gen.: *see* grief, repent, remorse.
regrettable, *afsōs dī gall*, or words like, *burī gall*, etc.
regular, *kaide nāḷ*, *kaide dī gall*, etc.: a r. thief, *pakkā cōr*.
regulation, *kaidā*, m., *hukam*, m.
reign, *saltanat*, f., *rāj*, m.
rein, *wāg*, f.
reinstate, *bahāl-k.*, *phēr rakkhṇā*.
reject, *radd-k.*, *raddṇā*, *raddī-k.*, *nāmanzūr-k.*: *see* refuse (1), refute.
rejoice, *khushī karnī* (*dī* of cause): *see* delight.
relate, *beān karnā* (*dā*), *sunāṇā*.
relationship, *sākādārī*, f., *rishtedārī*, f.
relative, n. *sāk*, *rishtedār*: *see* full: be related to, word for relative w. verb subst. or *hōṇā*. G. 119, M. 121. 11
release, *chaḍḍṇā*; *azād-k.* (U.): *see* acquit, free.
relent, *see* pity, mercy, compassionate.
reliable, *mohtbar*, *pakkā*, *imānwāḷā*: A: *see* untrustworthy.
reliance, *wasāh*, m., *māṇ*, m. (both w. *k.*, *dā*): *see* confide, trust, faith, untrustworthy.
relief, *see* ease, rest.: military, *badlī*, f.
relieve, *see* ease, rest.: of one's duty, *ralīw-k.* (int. *ralīw-h.*), *kamm chuḍāṇā* (*koḷō*).
religion, *mazhab*, m. (gen.): *dīn*, m. (M.): *dharm*, m. (H.).
religious, *dīndār* (M.), *namāzī* (praying much, M.): *dharmī* and *bhagat* (H.).

relinquish, *see* abandon.
relish, *see* enjoy, like, taste.
reluctant, use not wish, not desire, *rūh nehī kardā*: *see* wish, oath, desire, sick of.
rely, *see* reliance, trust, confide.
remain, be left over, *bacṇā*. *wadhṇā*, *bākī raihṇā*: r, behind, *picche raihṇā*: r. in one place, *tikṇā*: *see* stay.
remainder, financial, mathematics, *bakāyā*, m.: gen., *jehṛā bākī e*.
remedy, *see* treat, cure, recompense.
remember, not forget, gen., *cētā*, m. (*auṇā*, *raihṇā*, *nū*, M. 117. 11): *thauh*, m. (*raihṇā*, *nū*), *yād-raihṇā* (*nū*): suddenly r., *yād auṇā* (*nū*), M. 117. 4: r. is also *yād rakkhṇā* or *karnā*: note *yād rakkhṇā* is keep in mind: *yād karnā* is (1) r. a person, think of him: (2) used speaking respectfully of calling someone: (3) learn lesson: (4) r. after an interval: *see* memory.
remembrance, *see* memorial, memory.
remonstrance, *see* objection, reprimand, reproach.
remiss, *see* lazy, delay.
remorse, *pachtāwā*, m. (*laggṇā*, *h.*, *nū*), *afsōs*, m. (*auṇā nū*, *k.*): *see* regret.
remote, *see* distant.
remove, v. tr., *dūr-k.*, *laijāṇā*, *khaṛnā*, *haṭāṇā*: int., to another house, city, *uṭṭh jāṇā*.
renegade, *murtadd* (M., rel.): *see* treacherous.
rennet, *jāg*, f. (*lānī*, int. *laggṇī*): tablet of r., *ṭikkī*, f.

renounce, *see* abandon: r. claim, *dāhwā chaḍḍṇā* (*dā*). A.

repair, *marammat karnī* (*dī*): *see* shoe, require.

repeal, laws (of God), *mansūkh-k.* (M.): *see* abolish, cancel.

repeat, *phēr ūkhṇā*: r. after me, *mēre picche picche ākh, mērī gall durhāndā jā, jo maī ākhā tū wī ākhdā jā*: r. or recite poetry, etc., *ākhṇā, paṛhṇā*.

repeatedly, *bhaū caū, jhaṭe binde, ghaṛī ghaṛī, ghaṛī muṛī, jhaṭe jhaṭe, bauht wārī, baṛī wārī, kinnī wārī* (for *wārī* also *wērī*): do thing repeatedly, special verbal construction. *see* G. 68, 69.

repent, *tobā karnī* (*dī, tō*): *pachtāṇā* (*tō*): *kannā nū hatth lāṇā, nakk nāl līkā* (or *hadīsā*) *kaḍḍhṇīā* (caus. *kaḍhāṇīā*). [f. (*k.*).

repentance, *tobā*, f.: *pacchōtāp*,

repetition, *see* repeat, repeatedly.

report, *khabar*, (*d., dī*): *rapōṭ*, f. (*d., dī*). [delegate.

representative, *see* ambassador,

reprieve, *see* forgive, respite.

reprimand, *jhiṛak*, f., *jhāṛ*, f., *taṛī*, f., *ghurkī*, f. (all w. *d., nū*): also *ohnū jhāṛ kītī* or *pāī*, or *ohdī jhāṛ kītī*: *jhāṛ-nā, jhiṛknā, ghurknā, dābbā cāṛhnā* or *d.* (*nū*), *ṭhākṇā*: *see* reproach, sit upon.

reproach, *ulāhmā dēṇā* (*dā* of cause, *nū* of person): *phiṭkā dēṇīā* (v. mild abuse).

reprove, *see* reprimand.

republic, *jihde wicc kamēṭī kamm calāndī e, bādshāh koī nehī*: (U., *jamhūrī riāsat*, f.).

repudiate, *see* renounce, refuse (1), abandon.

request, *see* ask, beseech.

require, *see* ask, desire, advisable, necessary: r. to be done, often verbal part. in *-wāḷā, juttī gaṇḍhanwāḷī e*, shoes r. to be repaired, G. 45.

resemblance, *āpe icc raḷde ne, ikko jehe ne, miḷde juḷde ne*: of face, *muhāndrā raḷdā e*: *see* same.

resent, *burā mannṇā* (*gall nū*): *see* offence.

reserve, *rakkh chaḍḍṇā*.

resident, *raihnwāḷā*; *wassan-wāḷā*: leg. *sākan*, fem. *saknā*: *see* dwell, inhabit.

resign, *istīfā dēṇā* (*kamm tō*): *kamm chaḍḍṇā*, sometimes *chuṭṭī mangṇī*.

resin, *gūnd*, f., *rāḷ*, f.: *see* gum.

resist: oppose, objection, fight.

resolute, *ḍāhḍā, rāth, pakkā*.

resolution, *faislā*, m. (decision): firmness, *ḍāhḍpuṇā*, m., *daḍhippaṇ*, m.: *see* intend.

resolve, *see* decide: in meeting, *faislā karnā* (int. *hōṇā*): *tajwīz karnī* (int. *hōṇī*).

respect, *adab*, m., *izzat*, f., *ādar*, f., (all w. *k.* and *dā, dī*): word of respect, *horī*, m. pl., G. 27, 73. 82.

respectable, *izzatdār, sharīf, ashrāf* and words for good.

respectful, *adab wāḷā, adab nāḷ kūṇā*.

respite, give r. of two months, *do mahīne pāe*; M. 126. 23: *mohlat*, f., (U): *see* postpone, forgive.

responsible, *zimmewār*: make oneself r. for, *zimmā cukkṇā*,

(*dā*), *zimmewārī cuk'ṇī* (*dī*), *bīṛā cukkṇā* (*dā*) : hold someone r. for, *ohde pete pāṇā*, G. 34 : *ohde zimme lāṇā* : *ohde matthe lāṇā* (blame for).
rest, *arām*, m. (*k*.), *cain*, m. (of mind, U.) : *tsallī*, f. (mind) : take a r., *sāh laiṇā* : give person r. by doing his work for short time, *sāh kaḍhāṇā* (*nū̃*) : let animal r., *sāh duāṇā* (*nū̃*) : for these three *see* G. 122, 109 ; M. 129. 22 ; 118. 32 : give person r., also *chaḍḍṇā* : *see* ease, convenience.
resthouse, *baṅglā*, m. or *ḍāk-baṅglā* : village, *dārā*, m. : a serai, *sarā*, f.
restless, *bēkarār*, troubled in mind ; *becain*, uneasy (both U.).
restlessness, *cintā*, *bēkarārī*, f. (U.), *becainī*, f. (U.) : *bēarāmī*, f. [hinder.
restrain, *see* stop, forbid,
resurrection, *jī utthṇā*, *kiāmat*, f. (often used for judgment-day) : *see* rise.
retail, *see* wholesale.
retinue, *nāḷ de bande*, *nāḷ de suār*.
retire, go back, *pishā haṭṇā* : *naukrī chaḍḍṇī*, *raṭair hō jāṇā* (*tō*).
return, v. int., *partṇā*, *part jāṇā*, *part auṇā*, *muṛnā*, *pishā muṛnā* : v. tr., *partāṇā*, *pishā mōṛnā*, *mōṛnā* : article that may be returned, *mōṛwā* : r. fare, *wāpsī karāyā*, m. : r. post, *wāpsī ḍāk*, f. : *see* turn back.
revenge, *badlā laiṇā* (*de kolō*, *gall dā*) : *sijjhṇā* (*nū̃*).
revenue, *āmdaṇ*, f.
revere, *see* acknowledge, respect, honour.
reverse, v. tr., *putthā-k*. ; turn back, *pishā bhuāṇā* : *see* upside down, defeat.
revile, *burā ākhṇā* (*nū̃*), *gāhḷā kaḍḍhṇiā* (*nū̃*).
revise, lesson, etc., *durhāṇā*, *rawaiz-k*. (*nū̃*) : look over again, *nazr sānī karnī* (*dī*, U.).
revive, *jān wicc jān auṇī*, *hōsh auṇī* (*nū̃*).
reward, *inām*, m. : *ajar*, m. (of God, U.).
rhyme, *kāfyā*, m (*bannhṇā*, int. *bajjhṇā*).
rib, *pasḷī*, f : I'll break your ribs, *babbar bhannū̃gā*.
ribbon, *fītā*, m. : *rēshmī fītā*, silk r.
rice, growing, *munjī*, f., *dhān*, m. : grain, cooked or not, *cauḷ*, m. pl. : r. cooked w. milk, *khīr*, f. : cook r., *rinnhṇā* (pa. p. *riddhā* : int. *rijjhṇā*) : get soft in cooking, *baihṇā*.
ricochet, ducks and drakes, *tatto tārī*, f. (*khēḍṇī*).
rich, *amīr*, *bakhtāwar*, *saukhā*, *paise-wāḷā*, *hasiat-wāḷā*, *dhanī* (H.), *daulatwand*.
riches, *see* wealth.
riddle, *kahāṇī* (*pāṇī*) : *bujhārat* (*pāṇī*) : *see* secret.
ride, *suār h*., *suār hōke jāṇā*, *ghōṛe te jāṇā* : get ride, carriage, boys' back, anywhere, *hūṇṭe laiṇe* (*de*).
ridicule, mock, *makhaul karnā* (*nū̃*) : *hujtā karniā* (*nū̃*) : milder, *jugtā karniā* (*nū̃*) : *kise dīā maskhriā karniā* : *oh de wallō wēkhke hassṇā* (also means laugh w. pleasure) :

ohnū̃ tauṛī mārnī : *see* taunt, imitate, laugh, jester, clap.
rifle, *rafal*, f., *bandūk*, f.
(1) **right**, not left, *sajjā* : r.-handed, *sajjā*.
(2) **right**, not wrong, *ṭhīk*, *durust* ; and words for good, etc. : all right, *khair sallā*, *khair mehr e*, *caṅgā*, *halā* : *see* matter.
(3) **right**, n., *hakk*, m. : person w. a. r., *hakdār*.
righteous, *nēk* : *see* religious, good.
rigid, *sakht*, *ḍāhḍā*, *jehṛā nā life*.
rind, *see* peel, pare.
(1) **ring**, n., large or small, without stone, *challā*, m. : small w. stone, *mundrī*, f., *chāp*, f. (see stone) : ear-r., *wālī*, f., *murkī*, f. : thumb-r., *ārsī*, f.
(2) **ring**, v. tr., small bell, etc., *chaṇkāṇā* (int. *chaṇakṇā*) : large bell, gong, coin or pot to see if sound, *wajāṇā* (int. *wajjṇā*) : also *bulāṇā*, *khaṛkāṇā* : coin, etc., rings, *wajjdā e*, *bōldā e* : does not r., *bōlā e*. *nehī bōldā*, or *wajjdā*, *ḍorā e*.
ringworm, *dhaddar*, *daddar*, m.
rinse, mouth, *kurlī karnī* : vessel, etc., *haṅgālṇā*.
riot, *balwā*, m. (*k.*, int. *h.*) : *see* disturbance.
rip, *see* undo.
ripe, *pakkā* : half r., *āhbū* ; *ḍaddrā* (also half cooked).
rise, *uṭṭhṇā* : note following pairs : *uṭṭhke bauh*, get up into sitting posture : *uṭṭh bauh*, get up (gen. implying "and go away") : *uṭṭhke khlō*, (also *khlō jā*), stand up : *uṭṭh khlō* rise (and move away) : *uṭṭhke geā*, he rose and went away ; *uṭṭh geā*, he removed (to another house) : r. fr. dead, *jyū paiṇā*, *jī uṭṭhṇā* (*murdeā̃ wiccō̃*).
rise, sun, moon, stars, *caṛhṇā*, *nikḷṇā* : r. late, of moon on 15th day, *gōḍḍā mārnā* or *lāṇā* (int. *gōḍḍā laggṇā cann nū̃*), G. 119 : M. 121. 17.
rise, of price, *wadhṇā* : dearness, *maṅghāī*, f., *maiṅg*, f., *tēzī*, f., *pyār*, m. : *see* dear.
rise, of wind, *wagaṇ lagī e*.
rise, originate, *shurū-h*.
risk, *khatrā*, m.
rites, *rīt rasm*, f. (*pūrī karnī*).
rival, *jehṛā mukāblā kare*.
river, *daryā*, m. : *see* stream.
rivet, *kāblā*, m. : r.-screw, *dhibrī*, f. : *see* patch.
(1) **road**, metalled, *pakkī sarak* : unmetalled, *kaccī sarak*, f. : village, *paihā*, m. : *see* path, way : centre of metalled r., *goḷā*, m. : sides, *paṭrī*, f. : dip in metalled r. for water-flow, *gaib*, f. : *see* roughness.
(2) **road-metal**, *rōṛ*, m.
(3) **road-mender**, *māhwārīā*, m.
roar, of animal, man in anger, *gajjṇā*.
roast, *bhunnṇā*, int. *bhujjṇā* : r.-meat in bazar, *kabāb*, m. : r. vegetables or rice, *bhuññā*, m.
rob, *luṭṭṇā*, *dhāṛā mārnā*, *luṭṭ mārnī* or *macāṇī* : metaph. *ṭhaggṇā* : *see* steal.
robber, *ḍākū*, *dhāṛwī*, *luṭērā* (esp. metaph.).
robbery, *ḍākā*, m. (*mārnā*, int. *paiṇā*).
robust, *taṛ*ᵃ*ā* : *see* strong.

rock, no word, *caṭān*, f. (U.), *see* stone.
rocket, *hawā*, f. (*calāṇī*, *calnī*).
rod, *see* stick: iron r., *kandlā*, m., *sīkh*, f.
rogue, *see* blackguard.
(1) roll, call, *see* attendance and call.
(2) roll, v. int. *riṛhnā* (tr. *reṛhnā*).
(3) roller, iron, *rūl*, m., *rōlar*, m.
(4) rolling-board, *phaṭṭā*, m.: -pin, *wēlṇā*, m.; of stone, for grinding, *sil* f., *waṭṭā*, m.
roof, *chatt*, m., *kōṭhā*, m.: v. tr., *chattṇā*.
(1) room, *kamrā*, m.: in village house, *kōṭhṛī*, f.: front r. in do., *pasār*, m.: spare-r., *musāfar kamrā* or *khānā*, m.: r. on roof, *cubārā*, m.: *see* bath-, bed-, dining-, drawing-r.
(2) room, space, *thā̃* m. f., *jaghā*, f., *gunjaish*, f.
roomy, *mōklā*: non-r., *sauṛā*, *taṅg*.
root, *jaṛ*, f.: *see* uproot: get to root of thing, *kuṇh kaḍḍhṇī* (*dī*), *asliat* or *hakīkat dā patā lāṇā*.
rope, *rassā*, m.: for drawing water, *lajj*, f.: round the *bair*, *baraṛ*, m.. round *baiṛ* for *tinḍā*, *māhl*, f.: for well, gen., *khabbaṛ*, m., *chillaṛ*, m. (also *dullaṛ*, *tillaṛ*, m.): for horse's heels, *pachāṛī*, f.; for his forelegs, *agāṛī*, f.: *see* string, thong.
rosary, *tasbī*, f. (M., *phērnī*, *ralṇī*): *mālā*, f., (H., *phērnī*, *simarnī*, *ralṇī*).
rose, *gulāb*, m.: colour, *gulābī*.
rot, decompose, *trakkṇā*: begin to r., *bō chaḍḍṇī*: get soft, *galṇā*: allow to rot, decompose, *tarkāṇā*.
rotten, *see* rot, bad.
rough, *kharhwā*: r. work, *mōṭā kamm*: r. and ready, *jaṭkā*, *jaṭkā hisāb*, m.: *ḍagg jehā*: r. road, *see* roughness.
roughness, unevenness, in ground, *aḍḍokhōṛā*, m., *khṛappā*, m., *khṛōc*, m.
(1) round, adj., *gōl*: adv., *duāḷe*, *āḷe duāḷe*, *cufere*, *cār cufere*, *cāre pāse*, *sabbhnī pāsī*.
prep., *de duāḷe*, *de āḷe duāḷe*, *de cufēr*, *de cār cufēre*. *dī caũh pāsī*.
pass by way of round, *duāḷeõ dī laṅghṇā*, pass beyond and round, *walṇā*: go r. and r., esp. involuntarily, *cakkar khāṇā*.
(2) round, n., a long round, *walā* (*paiṇā*, *nū̃*): *waḷe wāḷā rāh*: *cakkar laggṇā* (*nū̃*): of ladder, *see* rung.
roundness, *guḷeāī*, f.
rouse, *see* wake, incite, excite, urge.
rover, *awārā* (bad sense), fem. the same: *see* nomad.
row, *see* line.
royal, *bādshāhī*, *shāhī*.
rub, *malṇā*, *mālish karnī* (*nū̃*); *ragaṛnā* (roughly): gently in passing, *khaihṇā* (*nā̃*): skin get rubbed and sore. *ucchṇā ambṇā*: *see* chafe; rubbed off, *chill ghattṇā*: anything get rubbed, *ghasar laggṇī* (*nū̃*): get rubbed away, *ghass jāṇā*: r. out, *see* delete.
rubber, *rabaṛ*, m., *rabaṭ*, m.
rubbish, refuse, *kūṛā*, m.: r.-heap, *rūṛī*, f.: *see* nonsense.
ruby, *lāl*, m.

rude, *see* impertinent, forward: answer back, *gall partāṇī*, *aggō bōlṇā*: rough and r., *waihshī*: *see* rough and ready.

rudeness, *gustākhī*, f., *shōkhī*, f.: *see* rude.

rug, *galīcā* m., *namdā*, m.

(1) ruin, *see* destroy, downfall, perish: add *tabāhī*, f., *kharābī*, f.

(2) ruins, of house, only walls, *khoḷe*, m. pl.

(1) rule, *kaidā*, m., *kanūn*, m. (both *baṇāṇā*): *tarīkā*, m. (method): *see* custom, govern. [*fuṭṭā*, m.

(2) rule, foot-rule, *dufuṭṭā*, m.,

(1) ruler, *hākim*, m.

(2) ruler, wooden, *rūl*, f. m.

rumble, of wheels, etc., *khṛāk auṇā*: noise of *hukkā*, camel, *buṛhkṇā*.

ruminate, *chew cud*, *ugālī karnī*.

rumour, *afwāh*, f. (*uḍḍṇī*, tr. *uḍāṇī*): *see* spread.

run, *bhajjṇā*, *dauṛnā* (caus. *bhajāṇā*, *duṛāṇā*): r. away, *bhajj jāṇā*, *maḷ jāṇā*, *nass jāṇā* (caus. *nasāṇā*), *khisknā* (caus. *khaskāṇā*): go off quickly, *wag jāṇā* (caus. *wagāṇā*); *see* swift: run, of water, *wagṇā*: run, of sore, nose, *wagṇā*: of eyes, *akkhīā wiccō pāṇī wagdā e*.

rung of ladder, *ḍaṇḍā*, m.

rupee, *rupayyā*, m., *rupeā*, m., jocular, *chill*, f., *chillaṛ*, f.: r.'s worth of change, *rupayye dā bhanghaṛ*, or *bhān*: but bring back the change, *bākī lai ā*.

ruse, *dā*, m., (*lāṇā*, int. *laggṇā*, *khāṇā*): *see* deceit, trick.

rush at, *ṭuṭṭke paiṇā* (*nū*): *hatthī paiṇā* (*oh dī*): *mārn paiṇā* (*nū*).

rust, n., *jaṅgāḷ*, m.: v., *jaṅgāḷ laggṇā* or *khāṇā* (*nū*).

rut, of wheels, *gail*, f.: metaph., paraphrase w. habit, custom.

S

sabre, *see* sword.

sack, *bōrā*, m.: *bōrī*, f.: *gūṇī*, f.: -cloth, *trappaṛ*, m.: *see* pannier.

sacred, *pawittar* (H.): *pāk*, *mukaddas* (M.).

sacrifice, n., *kurbānī*, f. (M.): *balidān*, m. (H.): v., *kurbān-k.*, *balidān-k.*

sad, *udās*, *nimmo jhūṇā*: *see* sorry, grief.

saddle, *zīn*, f., *kāṭhī*, f. (wooden): put on s., *pāṇī*: to s. something on anyone, *see* responsible.

saddle-bags, *see* pannier.

sadness, *udāsī*, f.: *gacc*, m. (*auṇā*), almost weeping.

safe, *salāmat*, *sahī salāmat*. A.

safety, *salāmtī*, f., *bacā*, m.: *see* guard, preserve, save.

sago, *sāgū*, m.

sail, n., *bādbān*, m.: v., *jahāz wicc sail* or *safar karnā*.

sailor, *beṛīwālā malāh*.

saint, *see* holy and add *pīr*, (M.): *rishī*. *munī*, *warāgī* (H.).

sake, *de wāste*, *de wāte*, *de laī*, *dī khātar*: in prayer *Masīh dī khātar*.

sale, *wikrī*, f., *farōkht*, f. (U.).

saliva, *thukk*, m.: *lab*, m.

salt, *lūṇ*, m., *namak*, m. (U.): s.-cellar, *lūṇ-* or *namak-dān*, m.: s. water, *khārā pāṇī*, m.: s. opposed to sweet in food,

salūṇā : without s., of something which should have s., *phikkā* (*see* insipid) : s. meat, *namkīn* : to s., *namkīn-k.*
saltpetre, *shōrā.*
salute, salutation, *salām*, f. m. (*k.*) : *bandgī*, f. (*k.*) : acknowledge s., *salām dā juāb d.* : s. with guns, *salāmī*, f.
salvation, *najāt*, f. (M.) : *muktī*, f. (H.).
same, *īho*, *īhoī*, *ūho*, *ūhoī*, *oh ī* : *ose* or *ese tarhā dā*, *eho-* or *ūho-jehā* : of same age, *see* equal : *see* resemblance.
sample, *namūnā*, m.
sanction, *manzūrī*, f. : obtain, *laiṇī* : grant, *dēṇī*, also *manzūr-k.*
sand, *rēt*, f : stretch of s. in water, *barēt-ā*, m., *-ī*, f.
sandy, *rētlā.*
sarcasm, *see* taunt.
Satan, *shatān.*
satiat-e, -ed, -y, *see* satisfy, etc., appease (hunger) in A.
satin, *see* silk.
satisfaction, *tsallī*, or *tsallā*. f. (comfort) : *rāzī* or *khush h.* : having had enough food, drink, water (said of land, trees, people, cattle), of someone's society, etc., *rajj*, f. : *see* satisfy, satiate.
satisfactor-y, -ily, *khātarkhāh* : *see* good.
satisfy, *rāzī* or *khush k.*, (int. *h.*), *tsallī* or *tsallā hōṇī* (*dī*) : w. food, etc. (*see* satiate, satisfaction) *rajāṇā*, *sēr-k.* (U.), be s.-ed, *rajjṇā*, *sēr-h.* (U.):
Saturday, *haftā*, m. : *abbal haftā*, m. : Hindu words, *saniccar*, *saniccarwār*, *chanicchar*, *chanicharwār*, *chiṇchiṇ*, *chiṇchiṇwār*, all m.
sauce, *sās*, f. : *grēbbī*, f. (gravy), chutney, *catnī*, f.
saucer, *pirc*, f.
savage, *waihshī*, *jāṅglī.*
save, *bacāṇā* : of Christ, *bacāṇā*, *najāt dēṇī* (*nū*) : be s.-ed, *bacṇā*, *najāt milṇī* (*nū*).
Saviour, *bacāṇwāḷā* (also human), *Najāt Dēṇwāḷā.*
saw, n., small, *ārī*, f. : large, for two men, *kalwattar*, m., *ārā*, m. : large, in frame, two men, *parnāhī*, f. : v., *cīrnā* (*ārī nāḷ*, etc.).
sawdust, *būrā*, m.
say, *ākhṇā*, *ākhṇā wēkhṇā*, *kaihṇā* : caus., *akhwāṇā*, *bulāṇā*, G. 109.
saying, n., *akhāṇ*, m.
scab, *khrīṇḍ* (*bajjhṇā*) : *see* scar.
scabbard, *miān*, m.
scald, *sāṛnā*, int. *saṛnā.*
scales, small, *trakkṛī*, f. : large, *kaṇḍā*, m. : weighing machine at station, etc., *kaṇḍā*. m. : goldsmith's, *kaṇḍī*, f., one side of basket s., *chābbā*, m.
scandal, use slander and spread, *see* spread, slander.
scar, *zakhm dā nashān* or *dāg*, m. (both also of fresh mark) : *see* scab.
scarce, *see* rare.
scarcely, *masā*, *masā kiwē*, *masē kiwē* : *see* difficulty.
scarcity, *see* famine, rare.
scarecrow, *ḍaraoṇā*, m.
scarlet, *shōkh lāl*, *lāl sūhā*, *gul anārī.*
scatter, v. tr., *khalārnā*, *khanḍāṇā* ; int. *khillarnā*, *khinḍṇā.*
scattered, few, *see* few.
scene, *see* sight, view : s. of crime, *maukyā*, m.

scenery, *see* scene.
scent, *see* perfume, smell.
scholar, learner, *paṛhnwāḷā*, *tālib ilm* (U.) : *skūl dā muṇḍā* : learned, *see* learned.
scholarship (money), *wazīfā*, m. : learning, *ilm*, m. : *see* learned, know.
school, *skūl*, m., *madarsā*, m. : special Hindu, *pāṭhshālā*, m. (for girls, *puttrī pāṭhshālā*).
schoolboy, *see* scholar.
schoolfellow, *jamāt-ī*, fem. *-aṇ*.
school-master, -mistress, *see* teacher.
science, gen., *ilm*, m : physical s., *sains*, f.
scissors, *kaincī*, f.
scold, *see* reprimand.
scorch, v. int., *saṛnā*, *jhalūhṇā* : tr., *sāṛnā*. [93.
score, twenty, *wīh*, G. 21, 22.
scorn, *hikārat dī nazr nāḷ wekhṇā* : *see* despise.
scorpion, *ṭhūhā*, m.
scoundrel, *see* blackguard.
scrape, *khurcṇā*, *khōtarnā* (esp. clean by scraping).
scraper, for horse, *kharknā*, m.
scratch, for itch, *khurkṇā*. get a s., *jharīṭ paiṇī* (*nū̃*) : *see* scrape.
scream, *cīkṇā*, *cīk mārnī*, *caṅghāṛnā*, *caṅghāṛ mārnī* : *see* howl.
screen, *see* chikk, curtain : anything to s. fr. sight, wind, etc., *ohlā*, m. : v. tr., *see* save, preserve, guard : hush up, *paṛdā pāṇā*, *pōcā phērnā* (both *gall utte*) : *see* quiet.
screw, *pēc*, m. (*lāṇā*, *kassṇā*).
screw-driver, *pēckass*, m.
scrub, *kūcṇā* : metal vessel, *mānjṇā* : table, chair, etc., *dhōṇā*, *ragaṛke dhōṇā*.
scuffle, *āpe icc hatthī paiṇā* or *khaihṇā* : *see* rush.
scullion, *masālcī*.
scum, *jhagg*, f.
scythe, *see* sickle.
sea, *samundar*, m. : *see* shore.
seal, *mohr*, f. (*lāṇī*, int. *laggṇī*).
sealing-wax, *lākh*, f. (*lāṇī*, int. *laggṇī*).
search, *labbhṇā*, *ḍhūṇḍhṇā*, *talāsh karnī* (*dī*) : turn over things, *phōlṇā* : police s. of house, person, for stolen goods, *talāshī*, f. (*laiṇī*, *dī*).
season, *bahār*, f., *mausam*, m.
(1) seat, n., in railway carriage, *banc*, f., *thā*, m. f. : *see* chair, stool, bench.
(2) seat, v. tr., *bahāṇā*, *bahāḷṇā* : *see* teach, sit.
(1) second, *dujjā*, *dūsrā*.
(2) second, motion, *tāīd karnī* (*dī*).
second-hand, *purāṇā*.
second-sight, n., *gaibdānī*, f. : possessing s., *gaibdān*.
secret, *bhēt*, m., *bhēt wāḷī gall*, f. : *see* hide : adj., *gujjhā* : s. agent or one in the s., *bhēt-ī*, fem. *-aṇ*.
secretly, *cōrī*, *cōrī chappī*, *bhēt nāḷ*.
sect, *firkā*, m. : *see* party.
section, *see* part : of orange, lime, lemon, pomelo, etc., *phāṛī*, f.
secure, firm, *pakkā*, *ṭhīk*, *tagṛā*, *huṇ khlōwegā* : *see* safe, servant.
security, *see* bail, safety, trust.
sedition, *see* mutiny.
seduce, *baihkāṇā* (pron. *bak-hāṇā*), *wagāṛnā*, *warglāṇā* : *see* incite.
(1) see, *wēkhṇā* (pa. p. *ḍiṭṭhā*,

wēkheā), wēkhṇā cākhṇā : we shall see, wēkhī jāpegī : be seen, *see* visible : able to see, not blind, *sujākhā*.

(2) seeing that, *see* since.

seed, *bī*, m. : (v. tr. s. cotton, [*wēlnā*.

seek, *see* search.

seem, *jāpṇā*, *malūm h.*, *zāhr h.* : *see* visible, evident.

seize, *phaṛnā*, *phagaṛnā*, *khōhṇā* (int. *khussnā*), *nappṇā*, *napaṛnā*, *mallṇā*, *zore laiṇā* : *see* snatch, confiscate.

seldom, *ghaṭṭ*, *ghaṭṭ waddh* : *see* sometimes.

select, *cuṇṇā*, *pasand-k*.

(1) self, myself, himself, etc., *āpī*, *āpū*, *āpe*, *āpõ* : genit. *apṇā* (when distributive, *apṇā apṇā*, *āpo dhāpṇā*, *āpo apṇā*) : acc. *apṇe āp nū* : G. 27, 28, 87, 88.

(2) self, n., (relig. sense, evil self), no word, use, *apnī marzī*, *apṇe khyāl*, *gunāh*, m.

selfish, *khudgarz*, *matlabī*, *garzī*.

selfishness, *khudgarzī*.

sell, v. tr., *wēcṇā* : int. *wikṇā*.

semolina, *samlīnā*, m. (K.).

send, *ghallṇā*, *ṭōrnā*, *apṛāṇā*, *pucāṇā* : s. for person, *sadd ghallṇā* : thing, *maṅgā ghallṇā*, *maṅg ghallṇā* : s. and ask, *pucch ghallṇā* : send message, *ākh ghallṇā*, *sanēhā ghallṇā*.

senior, *waḍḍā*.

sensation, *see* feeling, astonish, surprise.

sense, *hōsh*, f., *akl.*, m. f., *sudh*, f., *budh*, f., *magz*, m., *ṭhēṭh*, f. : *see* understanding : come to senses, *hōsh auṇi (nū)*, M. 117. 7 : out of senses, *see* mad, fool : meaning, *see* meaning.

senseless, *behōsh* (unconscious) : *see* mad, fool.

sensual, *luccā*, *shaihwatī*.

sentence, in book, *jumlā*, m., *fikrā*, m. : of judge, *hukm*, m.

sentry, *santrī*, *paihrewāḷā*.

separate, adj., *wakhrā*, *aḍrā*, *aḍḍ*, *wakkho wakkh*, *aḍḍo aḍḍ*, *waḷo waḷī*, *nawēkḷā*, *alaihdā*, *alagg* : *see* apart.
 v., *nakheṛnā* (int. *nikkhaṛnā*), also any adj. for s. w. *karnā* : int. *wiccharnā* (w. sadness), or any adj. for s. w. *hōṇā*.

separation, *alaihdgī*, f., *judāī*, f. : *wachōṛā*, m. (w. sadness).

September, *satambar*, m., *assū*, m. (about Sept. 13 to Oct. 12).

series, *silsilā*, m.

serious, solemn, *sanjīdā* : important, *bhārā*.

sermon, *wāhz*, f. m. : *wāhd*, f. m. : *khutbā*, m. (M) : *see* preach.

servant, *naukar* (fem. do), *ṭaihlīā* : Govt. s., *mulāzam* : s. of God, *Khudā dā bandā*, *sēwak*, (H.) : person rendering services for fixed amount of grain, *sēp-ī*, fem. *-aṇ* (master also called *sēpī*) : night and day s. of farmer, *āthṛī* : farm s., *kāmmā* (fem. *kāmmī*) : secure s., *banāṇā*. A.

serv-e, -ice, *naukrī*, f., *ṭaihl*, f., *mulāzmat*, f., *khidmat*, f., *sēwā*, f. : s. of *sēpī*, *sēp*, f. : all w. *k.* : day labour, *mazdūrī karnī*, *dihāṛīā karnīā* : relig. service, *bandgī*, f., *duā bandgī*, f., *girjā*, m. (church) : all w. *karāṇā* of clergyman, *karnā* of worshippers : *see* attend. A.

set, *lāṇā*, int. *laggṇā* : *see* place, put : s. limb, *jōṛnā*, int. *juṛnā* : s. jewel, *jaṛnā* : of sun, moon, stars, *ast h.*, *ḍubbṇā* : s. table, *see* table : of cement, etc., *ḍāhḍā h.*, *pakkā h.*

settle, *see* arrange, decide : dispute, *faislā karnā*, *see* umpire : s. matter, *nabēṛnā*, int. *nibbaṛnā* ; *bhugtāṇā*, int. *bhugtṇā* : of earth in water, *baihṇā*, *see* clear : of building, earth (sink), *baihṇā* : dwell, *wassṇā* : debts, *see* pay : not quite settled, *see* uncertain.

settlement, *faislā*, m. : land-s, *bandobast*, m. (*k.*) : *see* assess-, -ment, tax. [m.

settler, *raihṇwālā*, *wassaṇwālā*,

seven, *satt* : -th, *satuā̃* : G. 19.

seventeen, *satārā̃* : -th, *satāhrwā̃* : shoe s. fingers long, *satāhrī juttī* : G. 19–24, 123.

seventy, *sattar*, *s-hattar* : -one, *ak-hattar* : -two, *bahattar* : -three, *tihattar*, *tarhattar* : -four, *cuhattar*, *curhattar* : -five, *panjhattar* : -six, *chĕhattar* : -seven, *satattar*, *sathattar* : -eight, *aṭhattar*, *aṭhhattar* : -nine, *unāsī*, ordinals add *-wā̃* : 79 adds high tone h, *unāhsīwā̃* : G. 19–24, 123.

several, *kaī*, *kujjh* : *see* few.

severe, *ḍāhḍā*, *sakht*, *zōr dā*.

severity, *ḍāhḍpuṇā*, m., *zōrāwarī*, f., *sakhtī*, f. : *see* oppress.

sew, *syūṇā*, pa. p. *sītā*.

sewing, *salāī*, f. : -machine, *mashīn*, f., *syūṇwālī mashīn*.

sex, *jins*, f. : use man, woman ; for animals, *see* male, female.

shade, *chā̃*, f. : in the s., *chā̃we* : *see* shadow.

shadow, *parchā̃wā̃*, m. : overshadow, of tree, *sāyā pāṇā* (int. *paiṇā*, *utte*).

shady, *chā̃wāḷā*.

shaft, of carriage, *bamb*, m.

shake, v. tr., *halāṇā*, int. *hallṇā* : *see* wobble, tremble : s. hands, *hatth malāṇā* or *suṭṭṇā* (*nāḷ*), *panjā suṭṭṇā* (*nāḷ*).

shallow, water, *pāṇī thōṛā e* or *langhaṇwāḷā e* : of person, *kaccā*, *sōcdā nehī̃*.

sham, *see* pretence, imitation : adj., *naklī*.

shame, *sharm*, f. : *namoshī*, f. (humiliation) : both w. *auṇī*, *uā̃*, M. 117. 3 : feel ashamed, *bhaiṛā paiṇā*, M. 125. 7 : *see* shy : for s. ! *tōbbā tōbbā*, *hoe hoe*, and words for bravo used ironically.

shameless, *besharm*, *behayā* (strong words, of woman mean immoral).

shameful, *sharm dī gall*, f.

shampoo, *mutthiā̃ bharnīā̃* (*nū̃*) : w. feet, *laṭāṛnā*.

shape, *see* form.

share, *hissā*, m. : *see* part, divide, partner, common.

sharp, not blunt, also of sight, intelligence, *tēz*.

sharpen, knife, axe, etc., *canḍṇā*, *tēz-k* : *see* grindstone.

sharpness, *tēzī*, f.

(1) **shave**, *munnṇā* : get shaved, *munāṇā* (w. word for beard, head, etc.) : -ed patch on head, *tāḷū* (*kaḍḍhṇā*, caus. *kaḍhāṇā*).

(2) **shavings** of wood, *sak*, m., *sakṛā*, m.

shawl, *see* sheet : *loī*, f., *cutahī*, f., *khēs*, m., *dushāllā*, m. : wrap s. round head, *bukkaḷ mārnī*.

she, *eh*, *oh*.
sheath, *see* scabbard.
shed, *dhārā*, m.: railway s., *chidd*, m.
sheep, *bhēḍ*, f., *bhēḍī*, f.: fat-tailed, *dumbā*, m.: *see* ram: adj., *bākrā* (or goat's).
sheepfold, *wāṛā*, m.
sheeshum tree, *ṭāhlī*, f.
sheet of paper, *tā*, m.: of cloth, *cādar*, f. (*palangh dī*, *manjī dī*, of bed): pull s. over one, *cādar utte laiṇī*: *see* cloth.
shelf, niche, *ālā*, m.: on wall, *ṛaṛchattī*, f.: in wall-press, *drāz*, f.
shell (sea, river) *sippī*, f.: cowrie *kauḍḍī*, f.: explosive, *gōlā*, m.: *see* husk, peel.
shelter, *ōhlā*, m. (esp. against something coming from side): *dakkā*, m. (gen.): *bacā*, m. (gen.): *sāyā*, m. (someone's protection): *see* guard, save, preserve.
shepherd, *ājṛī*, *chēṛū*, *ayāḷī*.
shield, *ḍhāl*, f.
shin, *sukṛanj*, f.
shine, *lishkṇā*, *camakṇā*.
ship, *jahāz*, m.
shipwreck, *jahāz ṭakkar khāke ṭuṭṭ geā*.
shirker, *kamm cōr*, *see* lazy.
shirt, *kamīz*, f., *jhiggā*, m., *kuṛtā*, m.
shiver, *see* tremble, chatter.
shock, sorrow, etc., *saṭṭ* (*laggṇī*, *nū̃*), *sadmā*, m. (U. *h.*, *nū̃*), *see* grief, collide.
shoe, *juttī*, f.; English, *būṭ*, m.: pair of s., *juttī*, *jōṛā*, m., *būṭ*: G. 73, 74: Hindu wooden s., *paūā*, m., *khṛā*, f.: repair s., *gaṇḍhṇā*: put on, *pāṇā*: take off, *lāhṇā*: horse-s., *khurī*, f., *nāḷ*, m.: cattle-s., *khurī*, f.: old worn-out s., *chittar*, m.: size, of s., thirteen, fourteen to eighteen finger-breadths, *tehrī*, *cauhdī*, *pandhrī*, *sohḷī*, *satāhrī*, *aṭhāhrī*, G. 123; small 14, *narm cauhdī*: large 16, *pakkī sohḷī*.
shoeless, *see* bare.
(1) shoot, *see* fire (2), and add following: *calāṇā* (int. *calṇā*) and *mārnā* used of both gun, cannon, etc., and missile (bullet, arrow, etc.), also *chaḍḍṇā* of gun, cannon, etc.: but *calāṇā* and *chaḍḍṇā* mean merely "fire," "fire off," whereas *mārnā* implies hitting (w. *nū̃* of thing, person hit): go shooting, *shikār khēḍṇā* or *karnā*: *see* stone.
(2) shoot, of tree, *gullā*, m.
shop, *haṭṭī*, f., *dukān*, f.: keep s., *haṭṭī* or *dukān karnī*: start s., *haṭṭī pāṇī* or *kholhṇī*.
shopkeeper, *haṭṭīwāḷā*, *baṇīā*, *dukāndār*.
shore, *kanḍhā*, m., *dandā*, m. (lit. edge).
(1) short, things in gen., *see* small: person, *madhrā*, *mandhrā*, *nikkā*: *see* dwarf: letter, speech, *see* brief: in short, *muddā*, *gall kāhdī*: in s. time, soon, *thōṛe cir nū̃*, *zarā ku nū̃*.
(2) short-lived, *thōṛe cir dā*, *chōṭī umar icc moeā*, *thōṛā cir rehā*: *see* transient.
shot, grains of, *charrā*, m.: *see* shoot (1).
shoulder, n., *mōnḍhā*, m.: v., *mōnḍheā te* or *kandhāṛe* or *dhangāṛe cukkṇā*: *see* back, also back in A.: s. one's

way, *dhakke nāḷ laṅghṇā* (also means by force): *see* shove.
shout, *awāz mārnī, kūk mārnī*: *see* call, scream: speak loudly, *uccī* or *zōr-nāḷ* or *dabbke kūṇā, uccī dittī bōlṇā*: loudly or angrily, *kaṛakke kūṇā*.
shove, *dhakkā dēṇā* (*nū̃*), *dhikkṇā*: s. off (esp. in water), *ṭhelhṇā*, int. *ṭhillhṇā*.
shovel, *bēlcā*, m.: *kaṛch*, m. (v. large iron spoon).
(1) show, v., *dassṇā, wakhāṇā*.
(2) show, n., *wakhāḷī*, f., *dakhāwā*, m.: for s., *wakhāṇ wāste, apṇī izzat wadhāṇ wāste*: display, grandeur, *chūkā shākī*, f. (*k.*): *ṭash* or *ṭash ṭush kaḍḍhṇī*: *ḍaddh kaḍḍhṇī* (affect style) M. 120. 48: *see* splendour, sit.
shriek, *see* scream, shout.
shrill, *tēz*.
shrine, (M.) *khāngāh*, f. (tomb): (H.) *sthān*, m., *mandar*, m. (temple).
shrink, v. int., cloth, etc., *saṅgaṛnā*: through pain, *sī karnī*: s. back, *pishā haṭṇā*.
shrivel, *see* wither, wrinkle.
shroud, n., for burial, *khapphaṇ*, m.
shrub, *jhāṛī*, f.: small, *bucc*, m.
shun, *parhēz karn-ī,-ā* (*tõ*, esp. of food, actions): *bacṇā* (*koḷõ*): *dūr raihṇā* (*tõ*): *see* avoid, abstain.
shunt, train, *shanṭ karnā*.
shut, *band-k.*: s. door, window, *mārnā* (int. *wajjṇā*): fasten hook of door, etc., *kunḍī mārnī* (*dī*): *hukk mārnī*, (*dī*): *kunḍā mārnā* (*dā*): close door, etc., *see* close: s. u , *band-k.*

shy, be, *saṅgṇā*. *jhakṇā, jhijhakṇā*: adj. *saṅgā wāḷā*: *see* ashamed, shame, shyness.
shyness, *saṅgā*, f.: *jhākkā*, m. (both w. *auṇā, nū̃*): *see* shy.
sick, *see* ill, sorry, vomit: be s. of, *jī* or *rūh* or *dil caṛhnā* (*tõ*): *see* tire, (tired of).
sickle, *dātrī*, f.
side, direction, *pāsā*, m., *lāhmb*, f., *bāī*, f., *bāhī*, f., *guṭṭh*, f. (corner): get to one s., *lāhmbe* or *ikkī pāse hōjā*: in what direction, *see* direction: on all sides, *sabbhnī pāsī, cawhī pāsī*; everywhere, *sabbh dare, har kite*: round, near, *āḷe duāḷe*: *see* round: on this s., *urār*: on that s., *pār*: s. of body, *wakkhī*, f.: *see* party, bed, door.
sideboard, *sālbōṭ*, *m.* (K.).
side-dish, *ḍōṅghā*, m.
siege, *muhāsrā*, m. (*k.*), *ghērā*, m. (*pānā*).
sieve, *chānnī*, f.
sift, *chāṇṇā*: separate husk fr. grain, *chaṭṭṇā*.
sigh, *hāhukā mārnā*.
sight, eyesight, *nazr*, f.: view, *nazārā*, m.: spectacle, *tamāshā* (*see* entertainment): of holy place or person, *see* visit.
sign, *nishān*, m. (*k.*, mark): *ishārā*, m. (*k.*, sign): *see* effect, proof, result.
signal, railway, *saṅgaḷ*, m.: go down, *hōnā ḍaun h. hatth*, m. (*ḍiggṇā*:) *see* sign.
signature, *daskhaṭṭ*, m.
signet, *mohr*, f. (*lāṇī, laggṇī*): engrave, *see* engrave.
signify, *ohde maihṇe kī ne, ohdā matlab kī e*: *see* meaning: it does not s., *see* matter.

silence, *cup-cāp*, f., *khamōshī*, f. (U.).
silent, *cupcapītā*, *cup*, *cupkītā*.
silently, *cup capītā*, *cup cāp*, *m ikṛī*, *hauḷī hauḷī* : *see* secretly.
silk, *paṭṭ*, f., *rēsham*, m., *ṭassar*, m. : adj., these words w. *dā*, also *rēshmī*, *ṭassarī*.
silly, *see* fool.
silver, *cāndī*, f., *ruppā*, m.
silversmith, *sunyārā*.
similar, *wāṅgar*, *wāṅgū*, *wargā*, *hār*, G. 35 : *jehā*, G. 91, 92 : *ajehā*, *ehojehā* : like what ? *kehā*, *kehojehā* : relative, *jehā*.
simmer, *maṭṭhe tā pakknā*.
simple, *sādā* (not ornamented) : of person, *bholā*, *siddhā*, *sādā*, sometimes *bātshāh*.
simultaneously, *ikse weḷe*. *nāḷo nāḷ*, *katthā*.
sin, *gunāh*, m. (*k.*) : *pāp*, m. (*k.* H.) : *see* evil, wickedness.
since (1), time, *jadō dā*, *jis weḷe tō* : *jadō dī oh āī e*, *maĩ ohnū nehī diṭṭhā*, I have not seen her since she came : time since, pa. p. with *nū* : *ohnū khote tō ḍiggeā dō dihāṛe hoe ne*, it is two days since he fell from the donkey ; G. 79, last line : *see* ago.
(2) reasoning, *see* because, also *jis hāl wicc*, *jadō*.
sincere, *saccā*, *dilī*.
sincerely, *dil nāḷ*, *dilō wajhō hōke*.
sinew, *nāṛ*, f. (also vein, artery).
sinful, *see* sinner.
sing, *gauṇā*.
singer, *see* musician.
singe, v. tr., *sāṛnā*, int. *saṛnā*.
single, one fold, *akāhrā*, *ighrā*, *see* fold, bachelor.
singly, *ikk ikk karke*.
singular (grammar), *waihd*, f. : *see* strange, wonderful.
sink, in water, *ḍubbṇā* (also of sun, etc. : tr. *ḍōbṇā*) : in something soft, mud, etc., *khubbhṇā*, tr. *khōbhṇā* : *see* drown.
sinless, *bēgunāh* ; faultless, *beaib*, *bēkasūr* : innocent, *masūm*, *mashūm*.
sinner, *gunāhī*, *pāpī* (H.).
siris tree, *see* acacia.
sister, *bhaiṇ*, *hamshīrā* (U.) : s.-in-law : wife's s., *sāḷī* : wife's brother's wife, *sāḷehā-r*, *-j* : brother's wife, *bhāhbī*, *bharjāī* : husband's sister, *naṇān*, *naṇāṇ* : husband's elder brother's wife, *jaṭhāṇī* : younger do., *darāṇī*.
sit, *baihṇā*, pa. p. *baiṭhā*, G. 64 : sitting, *baiṭhā hoeā*, G. 108 : *see* squat : s. on eggs, *baihṇā* : sit up, *see* rise : at someone's feet as scholar, *baihṇā*, M. 117. 13, 19 : *see* teach : sit upon, reprimand severely, (jocular), *khabar lainī* (*dī*), *makkū ṭhappṇā* (*dā*), *lamb kaḍḍhṇī* (*dī*), *sukṛanjū bhannṇīā* (break shins, *dīā*), *babbar bhannṇe* (break ribs, *de*), *ākkaṛ bhannṇī* (take down pride, *dī*). N.B.—In some places *lamb kaḍḍhṇī* means "affect style" : *see* reprimand, reproach.
site, *jaghā*, f.
sittingroom, *baiṭhak*, f. : *see* drawingroom.
situated, simply say *kitthe we*, [etc.
situation, service, *naukrī*. f. ; *asāmī*, f. (vacancy) : place, *jaghā*, f. (also for service).

six, *chē* : -th, *chēwā* : G. 19–24.
sixteen, *sōḷā* : -th, *sohḷwā* : sixteen finger shoe, *sohḷī juttī* : G. 19–24, 123.
sixty, *saṭṭh* : -one, *akāhṭh* : -two, *bāhṭh* : -three, *trehṭh* : -four, *cauhṭh* : -five, *paĩhṭh* : -six, *cheāhṭh* : -seven, *satāhṭh* : -eight, *aṭhāhṭh* : -nine, *unhattar* : ordinals add *-wā*, *saṭṭhwā*, etc., G. 19–24, 123.
size, of person, *kadd*, m. (U.) : of boot, shoe, *see* shoe : in gen. no word, use *ēḍḍā*, *ōḍḍā*, so large ; *kēḍḍā*, how large ; *jēḍḍā*, as large : *see* big.
skein, *gunjī*, f.
skeleton, *pinjrā*, m., *pinjar*, m.
skewer, *sīkh*, f (also iron bar).
skill, skilful, skilled, *see* clever-, -ness.
skim, milk, *malāī lāhṇī*.
(1) skin, n., *camm*, m. : *camṛā*, m. : hide, *khall*, f. : water-s., *mashk*, f. ; do. for crossing river, *sarnāhī*, f. : of fruit, vegetable, *see* peel.
(2) skin, v. tr., *camm lāhṇā*, *khall lāhṇī*, *khullṇā* (used by scavengers) : *see* pare.
skirmish, *laṛāī bhiṛāī*, f.
skirt, *ghagghrī*, f., *laihngā* m., *kōrā*, m. (2nd and 3rd ornamented) : worn by men and women, *taihmat*, m., *lunṅī*, f., *lācā*, m., *dhōttī*, f. (H.).
skull, *khōprī*, f.
sky, *asmān*, m. [careless.
slack, *ḍhillā*, loose : *see* lazy,
slake, thirst, *treh maṭṭhī karnī* or *bujhāṇī*.
slander, use *jhūṭhā*, false, w. "accusation" : *bakhīlī k.* (*dī*), *tohmat* (*lāṇī*, *utte*, U.), *nakhiddhṇā*, *mukālā k.* (*dā*), *kulāhṇā*.
slant, m., *urēb*, m., *see* slope, sloping.
slanting, *kuāsā* ; *ḍiṅgā*, crooked, *see* slope.
slap, *capēṛ*, f., *caṇḍ*, f., *dhapphā*, m. (*mārnā*, *khāṇā*).
slate, *slēṭ*, f. : wooden, *takhtī*, f.
slaughter, *see* kill.
slave, *gulām* : slavery, *gulāmī*, f.
sledge-hammer, *see* hammer.
(1) sleep, n., *nīndar*, f. (sleepiness), *see* sleepy.
(2) sleep, v., *saũṇā*, pa. p. *suttā*, G. 64 : fast asleep, *ghūk suttā hoeā* : sleeping, *suttā hoeā*, G. 108 : to have just fallen asleep, *akkh laggṇī* (*dī*) : to be getting up fr. s., *suttā peā uṭṭhṇā*, M. 125. 8 : go to s., of limb, *saũṇā*.
sleeper, wooden, *gellī*, f., *see* log.
sleeplessness, *unīndrā h.* (*nū*) : *jagrāttā kaṭṭṇā* : *see* vigil.
sleepy, feel, *nīndar auṇī* (*nū*), M. 117. 5 : *unghlāṇā*, *uglhāṇā*, nod drowsily : *jāgo mīṭī*, half asleep on one's bed.
sleeve, *bāh*, f.
slice, of bread, *tōs*, m. (whether toasted or not) : of fruit, *phāṛī*, f. (whether cut as in melon, or section of orange, etc.).
sling, n., *gulēl*, f. (like bow) : *kubhāṇī*, f. (real sling) : *see* pellet.
slip, *tilhkṇā* : down, *riṛhnā*.
slipper, *gurgābī*, f : *slīpar*, m.
slippery, *tilhkaṇwālā*, *cīhknā*.
slit, n., *trēṛ*, f., (*paiṇī*, *nū*) : v. tr., *cīrnā*, *pāṛnā* (also tear) : *see* cut.
slope, *nuāṇ*, m., *salāmī*, f., *ḍhalwāṇ*, m., *urēb*, m. : *see* slanting.

sloping, *ḍhāḷwā*, and words for slope w. *-wāḷā*.
slow, *ḍhillā*, *maṭṭhā* : *see* lazy : s. fire, *maṭṭhe tā* (*pakāṇā*, *see* simmer).
slowly, *hauḷī hauḷī*, *saihje* : go s. *jū dī tōr turnā* : *see* steadily.
slowness, *ḍhill*, f., *ḍhill maṭṭh*, f.
slur, *dhabbā*, m., *dāg*, m. (both *lāṇā*, int. *laggṇā*).
small, *nikkā*, *chōṭā* : of person, *see* short, dwarf.
smallpox, *mātā*, f. (*nikḷnī*).
(1) smart, adj., *sajā sajāeā*, in appearance; and words for show : *cust* in action.
(2) smart, ache, *see* pain, hurt.
smartly, *custī nāḷ*.
smash, v. tr., *ṭōṭe ṭōṭe k.*, *phīṭe phīṭe k.*, *cūr cūr k.* (all *nū̃*) : int., same words w. *h.* : *see* collide, knock.
smattering, speak language badly, *ṭis mis karnā* : *see* poor.
smear, w. oil, butter, etc., *cōpaṛnā* : *see* plaster.
(1) smell, v. tr., *sunghṇā* : int. (bad s.) *bō chaḍḍṇī* or *karnī*, *bō auṇī* (*tō*).
(2) smell, n., sweet, *see* perfume : bad, *mushk*, f. : *bō*, f. (by itself means bad s.).
smile, *muskṛāṇā* : jocular words, *guṭaknā*, *guṛhkṇā*.
(1) smoke, n., *dhū̃*, m. : *see* soot.
(2) smoke, v. int., *dhū̃ nikḷṇā* : s. pipe, hukka, tobacco, etc., *pīṇā* : of hukka also *chikkṇā* : have turn at hukka, *sūṭ*, m., *sūṭā*, m., *wārī*, f. (all w. *lāṇā*), *wārī laiṇī*.
smooth, to touch, *kūḷā* : road, ground, *padhrā* : gen. *sāf*, *suāhrā*.

smother, *sāh band karke mārnā*, *saṅgh ghuṭṭke mārnā* : *see* choke, strangle, stifle.
snaffle, *kazāī*, f.
snake, *sapp*, fem. *sappṇī* : -skin, cast off, *sappkunj*, f.
snake-charmer, *sapyādhā*.
snap, fingers, *cuṭkī mārnī*. [A.
snare, *phandhā*, m. : net, *jāḷ*, m.
snatch, kite, cat, hand, *jhuṭāh mārnā*, *jharāṭ* or *jharuṭṭ mārnī* : *see* seize.
sneer, *tāhne mārne* (*nū̃*) : *mehṇā dēṇā* or *mārnā* (*nū̃*).
sneeze, *nicch mārnī* : severe w. cough, *dhrañṇā*, *drāsṇā*.
snore, *ghurāṛe mārne*. [f.
snout, *būthī*, f. : pig's, *thunnī*,
snow, *warf*, f., *barf*, f. : fall, *paiṇī*.
snuff, *naswār*, f.
so, *see* thus : so and so, *falāṇā*, *see* such and such : so so, *ajehā kajehā* ; in indifferent health, circumstances, *heṭhā uṭā*.
soak, v. tr., *bheõṇā*, int. *bhijjṇā* : *see* wet.
(1) soap, *sabūṇ*, m. : *sāban*, m. (U.).
(2) soap-nut, *rēṭhā*, m., *rēṭhṛā*, m.
sob, *haṭghōre laiṇe* or *bharne*, *bilkṇā*.
sober, *hōsh wicc* : *sanjīdā* (solemn).
sociable, *milṇwāḷā*, *maḷāpṛā*.
society (also *a* society), *susaiṭī*, f. : M. *anjuman*, f. : H. *sabhā*, m., *samāj*, m.
sock, *julāb*, f., *jurāb*, f., *jarēb* f., *mauzā*, m. : *massī*, f.
socket, *ghūā*, m. : *see* pivot.
soda, *sōḍā*, m. : s.-water, *sōḍā*, m., *khārā pāṇī*, m. : bottle of, *khārī bōtal*, f., *sōḍe dī bōtal*.

sofa, *waḍḍī kursī*, f. : *kauc*, m.

soft, *kūḷā*, tender of flesh, meat, skin, trees, shoots, leaves, bones (of children, young animals), smooth of skin, cloth : *narm*, soft of heart, cloth, skin, leather, also of meat if result of cooking : *pōllā*, of earth, soil.

softly, not loudly, *see* gently.

(1) **soil,** *zamīn*, f., *jīwī*, f., *bhoē*, f., *miṭṭī*, f. : good, damp s., *chambh*, f., *rohī*, f. : also good, *mairā*, m., *pakkī jīwī* : not good, *rētā*, m. : barren, *rakkaṛ*, m., *banjar*, m., *kallar*, m.

good, adj., of soil, *saras*, *caṅgī*, *missī*, *bhōrī* : bad, *māṛī*, *niras*, *karlāthī*.

(2) **soil,** soiled, *see* dirty.

solder, *kaṭī karnī* (*nū̃*) : *see* patch.

soldier, *sipāhī*, *faujī ādmī* : English, *gōrā* : *see* officer.

sole, of foot, *taḷī*, f. : of boot, shoe, *taḷā*, m.

solemn, *see* serious, sober. [U.).

solid, *piḍḍā*, *ṭhōs* (not hollow,

soliloquise, *sōcṇā*, *see* think, meditation.

solitude, *see* alone, lonely.

solve, sum, problem, *hall-k.*, *kaḍḍhṇā* : riddle, *bujjhṇā* (guess).

some, *kujjh*, *bāze*, *koī*, *koī koī* (G. 87), *ikknā* (only oblique), G. 28 : some . . . others, *koī* . . . *koī*, G. 87 : *see* few.

somehow, *kiwē̃*, *kise tarhā̃*, *masā̃* : *see* difficulty, scarcely.

someone, *koī* : s. or other, *koī nā koī*.

something, *kujjh* : s. or other, *kujjh nā kujjh*.

sometimes, *kade*, *kade kade*, *kadī kadāī* (implies seldom).

somewhat, rather, -ish, *jehā*, G. 27, 92 : or add *-ērā*, as *waḍērā*, biggish, G. 18 : colour, yellowish, blackish, etc., *pīḷī* or *kāḷī bhai mārdā e*.

somewhere, *kite*, *kitale*, *kidhare* : s. else, *hōr kidhare*, *hōr dare*.

son, *puttar*, *bētā*, leg. *wald* : Europeans', *bāwā* : s.-in-law, *juāī*, *juātrā*, *majmān* : *ikko puttar mar geā*, only one son died : *ikkse puttar dī saūh*, oath by only son.

song, *gauṇ*, m., *gīt*, m.

soon, *jabde*, *jhabdē*, *jhaw jhaw*, *thōṛe cir nū̃*, *zarā̃ ku nū̃*, *huṇe*, *jaldī*.

soot, *kāḷakh*, f. : *dhū̃*, m. (smoke).

soothe, *see* comfort, condole, add *dalāsā dēṇā* (*nū̃*), *piṭ maṭṭhī karnī* (*dī*).

soothsayer, *najūmī*, *see* astrologer, magician.

soporific, *suāṇwāḷī duāī*, f.

sorcerer, *see* magician, astrologer, soothsayer.

(1) **sore,** n. (wound), *phaṭṭ*, m., *zakhm*, m : (blow), *saṭṭ*, f., on back of horse, mule, etc. *lāggā* (*laggṇā*, M. 121. 14) : *see* boil (1).

(2) **sore,** adj., *see* chafe, painful.

sorrow, *see* grief.

sorrowful, *see* sad.

sorry, *see* sad, grieve, regret : s. for oneself, *nimmā* (*jāpṇā*).

(1) **sort,** n., *jins*, f., *kism*, f.

(2) **sort,** v. tr., *chāṇṭṇā*.

so so, *see* so.

soul, *rūh*, m : often *dil*, m., heart ; *jān*, f., life.

(1) sound, n., *ăwāz*, f., *wāz*, f. : *see* noise.

(2) sound, adj., horse, etc., *bilkul taġṛā*.

(3) sound, v. int. *ăwāz dēṇī*, *shōr karnā* : v. tr., a person, *patā lāṇā* (*koḷō* of person, *dā* of thing) : coin, pot (to test it), *see* ring : a letter, *see* pronounce.

soup, *shuruā*, m. : -plate, *suplet*, f. (K.).

sour, *khaṭṭā* : milk become s., *phiṭnā*, *saurnā* (G. 113), *kharāb hō jāṇā*, *wigaṛnā*.

source, spring, *cishmā*, m., *cashmā*, m. : origin, *jaṛh*, f., *asl*, f., *mundh*, m.

sourness, *khaṭeāī*, f.

south, *dakkhaṇ*, *dakkhaṇ pāsā*, m. : -wards, *dakkhaṇ wall* or *pāse* : south-west, *dakkhaṇ te laihnde dī gutth* : south-east, *dakkhaṇ te caṛhde dī gutth*.

sovereign, *see* king : coin, *pauṇḍ*, m., *asharfī*, f.

sovereignty, *rāj*, m., *bādshāhī*, f., *saltanat*, f., *hukūmat*, f.

(1) sow, n., *see* pig.

(2) sow, v. tr., *bījṇā* : sowing, n., *biāī*, f., *bijāī*, f.

space, *khappā*, m., *witth*, f., *thā̃*, m. f. (place) : *wāṭ*, f., *paiṇḍā*, m. (distance).

spacious, *mōkḷā* : *waḍḍā* (big).

spade, *bēlcā*, m : inverted, *kahī*, f.

span, *giṭṭh*, f.

(1) spare, adj., *fāltū*, *waddh*.

(2) spare, v. tr., do without, *ohde bājhō guzārā karnā* : *see* forgive.

sparingly, *sarfe nāḷ*, *thōṛā*.

spark, *cingāṛā*, m. (from fire) : *ciṇag*, f., from. flint, iron, etc., also small fr. newly kindled fire.

sparkle, *lishkṇā*, *camakṇā*.

sparse, *wirlā*, *ṭāwā̃ ṭāwā̃*, *thōṛā*.

spatter, *chiṭṭā̃ pāṇīā̃*. int. *paiṇīā̃* : *chaṭṭe mārne* : *see* splash, sprinkle.

spavin, *haḍḍ mūtrā*, m.

speak, *kūṇā* (pa. p. *koyā*), *kūṇā saihnā*, *bōlṇā*, *bōlṇā cālṇā*, *gall karnī*, *kuskṇā* : also note *maĩ ohde nāḷ ā̃*, I am speaking to him : *see* speech : s. against, *see* accuse, slander.

spear, *barchā*, m., *barchī*, f., *nēzā*, m.

special, *ucēcā*, *khāss*.

specially, *ucēcā* (of set purpose), *khāskar* (U.).

species, *jins*, f., *kism*, f.

spectacle, *see* sight, entertainment.

spectacles, *aiṇak*, f. ; wear, put on, *lāṇī* : take off *lāhṇī*.

spectator, *wekhaṇwāḷā* : *see* audience.

speech, *see* language, and add speak lang., *bōlṇī* ; know, *jāṇṇī*, *auṇī* (*nū̃*), M. 117. 2 : speak badly, *see* smattering : make a s., *spīc dēṇī* : *see* conversation.

speed, *kinnā tēz*, *kinnī jaldī* : *see* swift.

spell, *see* charm : s. a word, *jōṛ karnā* (*dā*), *hijā karnā* (*dā*).

spelling, *jōṛ*, m., *hijā*, m., *spēl*, m.

spend, money, *kharc-k.*, *lāṇā*, *puṭṭṇā* : be spent, *laggṇā*, *kharc-h.* : s. time, *weḷā laṅghāṇā* (pass time), *wakat lāṇā*, *dihāṛe lāṇe* (int. *laṅghṇā*, *laggṇā*) : *see* squander.

spices, *masālā*, m.

spider, *bambohyā*, m.
spike, *see* nail.
spill, v. int., *ḍulhṇā*, *ruṛhnā* (in tr. mean pour, *see* pour): tr. *ḍulhaṇ* or *ruṛhan dēṇā*.
(1) spin, *kattṇā* (object thread or spinning wheel): *see* spinning-bee, spinning-wheel, turn, top.
spinach, *sāg* m., *pālak*. f.
spindle, *see* spinning-wheel.
spine, *kaṅgrōṛ*, f. [*bhohrā*, m.
(2) spinning-bee, *triñan*, m.,
(3) spinning-wheel, *carkhā*, m: needle, *trakḷā*, m.
spirit, *rūh*, m: Holy Spirit, *Pāk Rūh*, m.: in phrases like "s. of pride" or "faithfulness," omit "spirit": intoxicating, *sharāb*, m., *nashā*, m.
spirited, poor-s., *dil chōṭā*, G. 122: M. 128. 9.
spiritual, *ruhānī*.
spit, *thukkṇā*: *see* saliva, vomit.
spite, *see* envy, hate.
splash, n., *chaḷak*, m.: noise of, *ghṛam*, m.: v. int., *chaḷakṇā*, *chittā paiṇā* (drops): tr. *chaḷkāṇā*, *chatte mārne*, *chittā pāṇā*: *see* spatter, sprinkle.
spleen, *tilī*, f., *lif*, f.
splendour, *bhaṛak*, f., *rauṇak*, f. (many people): *see* show, glory.
splice, *bannhṇā*: village style, *gāṇḍhā lāṇā* (*nū*, int. *laggṇā*).
splinter, wood, *chiltar*, f.: brick, stone, *citth*, f.
split, *pāṛnā* (int. *pāṭṇā*), *cīrnā*: *see* tear, cut, chop.
spoil, *wagāṛnā*, int. *wigaṛnā*; *kharāb-k.*, int. *h.*: be spoiled, of matter, affair, *guggaḷ jāṇā*: *see* destroy, rob, steal.
spoilt, child, *lāḍḷā*.
spoke, in wheel, *ār*, m.
sponge, spane, m. [*āpō*.
spontaneously, *āpū*, *āpe*, *āpī*,
spoon, *cimcā*, m., *cammac*, m., *doī*, f. (wooden), *karchī*, f., *karch*, m. (v. large).
sport, *khēḍ*, f. (game): shooting, fishing, etc., *shikār khedṇā*.
sportsman, *shikārī*: player, *khaḍārī*.
spot, *see* stain: drop, *chiṭṭ*, f. (*paiṇī*): *see* spatter, splash.
spotted, *dāgwāḷā*, *ḍabbā*, *ḍab khṛabbā*.
spout, of teapot, etc., *ṭūṭī*, f.: on roof for rainwater, *pāṛchā*, m., *parnāḷā*, m.
sprained, be, foot, *moh ghattṇā*, *mohcā jāṇā*, *moh nikḷnī* (*dī*): other parts, *waḷ paiṇā* (*nū*): *see* strain.
spread, carpet, cloth, *wachāṇā*, int. *wichṇā*: separate out, *khalārnā*, int. *khillarnā*: s. abroad, *phalāṇā*, int. *phailṇā*: s. rumour, *dhumāṇā*, int. *dhummṇā*.
(1) spring, season, *cētar wasākh*, m., *basant*, f.
(2) spring, steel, etc., *kamānī*, f.
(3) spring, water, *sōtā*, m., *sumb*, m., *cishmā*, m., *cashmā*, m.
(4) spring, *see* jump.
sprinkle, *chiṇakṇā*, *traūkṇā*; *see* splash, spatter.
sprout, *phuṭṭṇā*, *puṅgarnā*: grow, *uggṇā*.
spur, *kāṇṭā*, m. (*mārnā*).
spurious, *jhūṭhā*, false; *jāhlī*, forged.
spurn, *see* scorn, despise.
spy, *jāsūs*; *mukhbar* (informer): *see* espionage.

squander, *uḍāṇā, phūk chaḍḍṇā, ujāṛnā, luṭāṇā* (often of extravagant alms): *see* waste, destroy.
square, *cauras, murabbā*: of land, *murabbā*, m.
squash, *citthṇā, napiṭṭṇā*; *cūr-k.*, into small pieces: *see* squeeze, burst, crush.
squat, on heels, *pairā bhār baihṇā*: cross-legged, *caukṛī mārke*: w. legs stretched out, *nisḷīā karke*: on knees and feet, *gōṭh mārke, kutte baihṇī baihṇā, ūṭh baihṇī baihṇā, goḍe mūdhe mārke baihṇā*.
squeak, *cī cī karnī*, rats, mice, etc.: *see* creak.
squeeze, *ghuṭṭṇā*: wring, *nacōṛnā, napīṛnā*; press, *dabāṇā*: so as to burst, *phehṇā*, int. *phissṇā*, *see* burst: s. sugarcane, oil, etc., *pīṛnā*; of fruit, *nacōṛnā, napīṛnā*: *see* squash, press, crush.
squib, *paṭākā* (*calāṇā*, int. *calṇā*).
squint (eyed), *bhaiṅgā*: v., *bhaṅgāṇā*.
squirrel, *gālhaṛ*, m.. *gālhaṛ cūhā*, m.
stab, *talwār*, f., *khanjar*, m., *churī*, f.: all w. *mārnā* and *nū* [*astabal*, m.
stable, *tawēlā*, m., *stabal*, m.,
stack of hay, *kupp*, m.
staff, *see* stick.
stag, *harn*, fem., *harnī*: *bārāsiṅgā*, m.
stage, *paṛā*, m., *manzal*, f.
stagger, *ḍōlke ṭurnā, ḍigdeā ṭurnā*.
stagnant, *khlōtā hoeā, gandā* (dirty).
stain, both moral and lit., *dāg*, m., *dhabbā* (moral), m.: both w. *lāṇā*, int., *laggṇā*: *see* delete.
stair, *pauṛīā*, f. pl.: one step, *pauṛī*, f.
stake, for impaling, *sūḷī*, f., *sīkh*, f.: *see* nail.
stale, *behā* from yesterday; *tarbehā* from day before: *behā*, also gen.
stalk of wheat, barley, *nāḷī*, f., millet, maize, sugarcane, *ṭāṇṇā*, m.
stallion, *sāhn*, m.
stammer, *thathlāṇā*.
stammerer, *thatthā*.
stamp, seal, etc., *mohr*, f. (*lāṇī*, int. *laggṇī*): postage, *ṭikaṭ*, m. f. (*lāṇā*, int. *laggṇā*).
(1) stand, *khlōṇā*, pa. p. *khlōtā*, *khaḷā*: standing, *khlōtā*, *khaḷā*, G. 108: caus. *khalhārnā*: *see* rise.
(2) stand, I won't stand that; paraphrase: *eh mēnū manzūr nehī*; *maī tēnū ēs tarhā nehī karn dēṇ lagā*; *maī ēs tarhā nehī hōṇ dēṇ lagā*; *ēs tarhā mērī tērī nehī nibhaṇ lagī*.
(3) stand, n., for tumtums, carriages, etc., *aḍḍā*, m.
standard, *see* flag.
star, *tārā*, m.: *see* rise, set, comet: for names *see* A.
starch, *kalf*, f., *māyā*, m.
stare, *tāṛī lāṇī*; angrily, *ghurākī wēkhṇī, ghūrnā*.
(1) start, be startled, *traihṇā* (pa. p. *traṭṭhā*), *trāh nikḷṇā* (*dā*): *see* startle.
(2) start, set out, *ṭur paiṇā*, *ruānā h.*, *Allāh bēlī h.* (God be your, his friend, farewell): *alī panj h.*
startle, v. tr., *trāhṇā*, *see* start (1).
starvation, *baṛī bhukkh*, f.

starve, *baṛā bhukkhā h., bhukkh nāḷ marnā, bhukkhā marnā.*
state, *hālat,* f., *hāl,* m., *hāl hakīkat,* f.: Native State, *riāsat,* f.: *rāje dā rāj.*
stately, building, *waḍḍā te sohṇā.*
statement, *beān,* m., *ākhṇā,* m
statesman, *bādshāh dā salāhkār.*
station (railway), *ṭeshn,.* m., *sṭēshn,* m.
stay, *ṭhaihrnā, raihṇā, ṭikṇā:* *see* wait: place where one can stay, friend's house, etc., *ṭhāhr,* f. A.
steadily, go slowly but s., *raṛakdā jāṇā.*
steal, *cōrī karnī,* gen.; *curāṇā* (must have object): *see* stealthily, receiver.
stealthily, *cōrī, cōrī chappī* (or *chappe*), *cup capītā:* *see* quiet- -ly, silent-, -ly.
steam, real or vapour from kettle or hot food, *hawāṛ,* f.: from ground, *bhaṛās,* f.
steamer, *jahāz,* m.
steel, *aspāt,* m., *fulād,* m.
steep, *siddhī caṛhāī,* f.; *siddhā uttā jāndā e; sakht caṛhāī,* f.
stench, *see* smell.
(1) **step,** *kadam,* m.: stepping-stone, *paintṛā,* m.: *see* stair, ladder.
(2) **step,** in s.-son, brother, etc., *matrēā,* fem. *matrēī:* step brother or sister on father's side, *pyōō mātar;* on mother's, *māō mātar:* wife's child by former husband, *pishlagg.*
stew, n., *ishṭū,* m. (K.): v., *rinnhṇā,* (pa. p. *riddhā,* int. *rijjhṇā*).
(1) **stick,** n., *sōṭī,* f.: cane, *baint,* m.: stout, s., *sōṭā,* m. (short), *ḍaṅgōrī,* f. (for old people); *ḍāṅg,* f. (long), *ḍanḍā,* m. (short): *see* switch.
(2) **stick,** v., gen. *laggṇā,* tr. *lāṇā:* s. in mud, etc., *khubbhṇā,* tr. *khōbhṇā.*
sticky, *see* viscous.
stiff, dough, *ākrā:* proud, *ākaṛwāḷā, ākṛeā hoeā.*
stifle, v. int., *baṛā waṭṭ laggṇā* (*nū̃*): *see* sultriness: tr., *see* smother.
(1) **still,** yet, *aje, phēr wī, tā̃ wī.*
(2) **still,** *halldā nehī̃, see* quiet, calm (1).
sting, *ḍaṅg mārnā,* (*nū̃*), int., *laggṇā* (*nū̃*); *laṛnā* (*nū̃*).
stingy, *see* miser-, -liness.
stink, *see* smell.
stipulation, *shart,* f., *karār,* m. (promise).
stir, *see* excite, disturbance: fire, *bhakhāṇā.*
stirrup, *rakāb,* f.
stitch, *trōppā,* m. (*lāṇā,* int. *laggṇā*): *see* patch.
stocking, same as sock, or add *lammā,* long.
stomach, *ḍhiḍḍh,* m., *pēṭ,* m.
(1) **stone,** *waṭṭā,* m., *patthar,* m.: *see* pebble, limestone: in bladder, *patthrī,* f.: in fruit, *giṭak,* f., *hikkaṛ,* f.: pip of orange, apple, etc., *bī̃,* m.: in ring, *thēwā,* m.: throw s., *saṭṭṇā, mārnā* (hitting some-one or -thing).
(2) **stone,** v. tr., fruit, *giṭkā̃ kaḍḍhṇīā̃:* person, etc.: *see* stone (1).
stony, *waṭṭā̃wāḷā.*
stool, *ṭūl,* m., *caukī,* f.: village, *pīṛhī,* f., *pīṛhā,* m.: of reeds, *mūṛhā,* m.: *see* chair, seat.
stoop, *uṛnā, nyūṇā, jhukṇā,*

nīwā h., *sir jhukāṇā*: *see* bend, lean (2), crooked.

stop, v. tr., *see* hinder, forbid, leave off, and add *mōṛnā*, int. *muṛnā*; *ṭhākṇā*: int. *rukkṇā*.

stopper, in bottle, plug, *ḍaṭṭ*, m.: *see* lid, cork.

store, *zak͟hīrā*, m., *k͟hazānā*, m. (treasure): stores, *saudā*, m.; European, *shṭōr*, m. (K.).

store-room, -house, *gudām*, m.

storey, *see* story (2).

storm, wind, *hanērī*, f., *jhānjhā*, m.: gust, *jhakkhaṛ*, m.: heavy rain, *phāṇḍā*, m., heavy squall of rain, *sharlāṭā*, m.

(1) story, narrative, *kahāṇī*, f. (*pāṇī*, *suṇāṇī*): *bĕān* (*karnā*).

(2) story, of house, *chatt*, m. (ceiling), *manzal*, f.: two-, three- four-storied, *du-*, *tar-*, *cu-chatta* or *-manzlā*.

stove, *aṅgīṭhī*, f.

straight, *siddhā*, *suāhrā*.

(1) strain, (sift), *chāṇnā*: strain through cloth, *puṇṇā*: cloth for straining, *pōṇā*, m.

(2) strain, arm at socket, through throwing, etc., *bāh* w. *chanak jāṇī*, *cuṭak jāṇī*, *chaṇ jāṇī*, *chaṇkī jāṇī*, *chanak ghaṭṭṇī*.

straits, in, *awāzār*, *taṅg*, *aukkhā*, *k͟hajjal* (going here and there), *k͟hajjal k͟huār*: *see* knock, difficulty.

strange, *ōprā*; *bagānā* and *parāyā* (not one's own): *ajīb*, *ajaib*, *anōkhā*; *see* stranger wonderful.

stranger, *ōprā*, *obbhaṛ*, *parāyā*, *pardēsī*.

strangle, *saṅgh* or *gaḷ ghuṭṭṇā*: *see* hang, smother, choke.

strap, *waddhrī*, f., *tasmā*, m.

stratagem, *dā* (*lāṇā*, int. *laggṇā*, *khāṇā*): *see* trick, deceit.

straw, *see* chaff.

straw-coloured, *kakkā*.

stray, v. int., *khunjhṇā* (*rāhō*, etc.), *ghussṇā* (*rāhō*, etc.), *ṭhaṛukṇā*: *see* astray, wander.

stream, *nadī*, f., *nāḷī*, f.: *see* river.

street, *bazār*, m., *gaḷā*, m.: lane, *gaḷī*, f.

strength, *zōr*, m., *tākat*, f.: *see* power, strong.

stretch, *see* spread, pull: s. oneself, *ākaṛnā*, *ākaṛ auṇe* (*nū*).

strict, *kaide dā paband*, *sak͟ht*, *ḍāhḍā*, *karṛā*.

(1) strike, *see* beat, blow, mark, prod: add *saṭṭ lāṇī*: of missile, *laggṇā* (*nū*): M. 244. 26: of stick, etc., *wajjṇā* (*nū*), *laggṇā* (*nū*): s. tent *puṭṭṇā*: s. off name, *see* delete; do. on payment of debt, *nāwā waḷṇā* or *lāhnā* (int. *laihṇā*), *āgat pāṇā* or *karnā* (int. *painā*).

(2) strike, refuse to work, *kamm chaḍḍṇā*.

(1) string, *rassī*, f., *ḍōrī*, f., *sūṭrī*, f.: on bed, *wāṇ*, m.: on *ṭiṇḍ* at well, *warhī*, f.: bundle or ball of, *pinnā*, m., *gunjī*, f.: as sold. *charā*, m.

(2) string, together papers, *natthī-k*.

strip, clothes, bark, etc., *lāhnā*.

stripe, *dhārī*, f.: mere line, *līk*, f.

strive, *see* effort.

stroll, *sail*, m., *sair*, m., *sail sapaṭṭā*, m. (all *k.*).

strong, *tagṛā*, *tākatwāḷā*: of things, *mazbūt*, *ḍāhḍā*: of

tea, *sañhṇī*, *gūhṛī* : *see* strength, power.
struggle, *see* scuffle, effort.
stud, collar, shirt, *gudām*, m. : *see* button.
student, *see* scholar, disciple.
studious, *mehntī*.
study, v., *paṛhnā*, *sṭaḍī karnī* : n. (room), *daftar*, m.
stuff in, *tunnnā*.
stumble, *thuḍḍā laggṇā* (*nū*) or *khāṇā*.
stumblingblock, *see* offence.
stump of tree, *munḍh*, m. : jagged bit of wood, *khuṅghī*, f., *muḍḍhī*, f., *munḍhī*, f.
stun, *behōsh-k.*, int. *h.*
stupid, *beakl*, *allhaṛ* (inexperienced), *ḍhaggā* : *see* fool.
stupidity, *see* foolishness.
subject, n., persons, *raīyat*, f., *parjā*, f. (both always sing.) : of book, letter, *mazmūn*, m.
submerge, *ḍōbṇā* : *see* sink.
submission, *see* obedience.
subordinate, *mataiht*.
subscri-be, -ption, give, *candā dēṇā* : raise, *ugrāhṇā* (int. *uggharnā*).
subside, building, *baihṇā* : *see* collapse, lessen.
subsist-, -ence, *guzārā*, m. (*k.*, *h.*).
substitute, *iwzī* : *see* exchange, change, relief.
subterfuge, *see* trick, deceit, stratagem.
subtract, *tafrīk karnī*, *minhā-k.* (educ.), *ghaṭāṇā*.
(1) succeed, *kamm tōrnā*, *matlab kaḍḍhṇā*; *kāmyāb h.* (U.).
(2) succeed, *ohde thā auṇā*, *ohde magar auṇā*.
such *ajehā*, *ehojehā* : s. and s., *falāṇā*.

suck, *cuṅghṇā*, *cūpṇā* (fruit) : *see* eat, suckle.
suckle, *duddh piāṇā* or *cuṅghāṇā*.
suddenly, *acāṇcak*, *cāṇcakke*, *accaṇcēt*, *awāghatt*.
suffer-, -ing, *see* endure, pain, grief.
sufficient, *see* enough.
suffocate, *see* choke, hang, smother.
sugar, *miṭṭhā*, gen. : ground fine, *būrā khanḍ*, f. : not so fine, *dāṇedār khanḍ* (or both simply, *khanḍ*, f. ; European variety, *cīnī*, f.) : tablets, *mishrī*, f. : unrefined, *guṛ*, m. : finer than *guṛ*, *shakkar*, f. : without s., of tea, etc., *phikkā*.
sugar-cane, *kamād*, m. : each cane, *gannā*, m. : different kinds, *pōnnā*, m. (very thick), *pēṭkū*, m., *trēṛū*, m., *dhauḷū*, m., *ciṇkhā*, m. (v. thin, also called *kāṭhā*, m.) : s. juice, *rauh*, f. : eat s., *cūpṇā*.
suggestion, *see* hint, say.
suicide, *phāh laiṇā*, hang oneself ; *gaḍḍī agge baihke marnā*, sit before train : gen. *khudkushī*, f. (U.).
(1) suit, in law, *mukadmā*, m. : *see* case, lose.
(2) suit, clothes, *jōṛā*, m., *sūṭ*, m.
(3) suit-, -able, v., *phabbṇā*, *munāsib h.*, *caṅgā laggṇā* also *de gōcrā*, *de jogā*, *de laik*, G. 38 ; *jogā* w. infl. infin. *see* proper, right, advisable.
sulk, *russṇā*, *mūh waṭṭṇā* : *see* displeased.
sulphur, *gandhak*, f.
sultriness, (outside) *gummā*,

gōmmā, gum, ghummā, ghōmmā, cumāsā (all m., *laggṇā, nū̃*): (in room or outside), *watt* (*laggṇā, nū̃*): physical feeling, *hussaṛ*, m. (*h., nū̃*), and v. *hussaṛnā*.
sum, in arithmetic, *suāl*, m.: of money, *rakam*, f.: total, *jōṛ*, m., *jamhā*, f., *mizān*, f. (U.). [m., *samrī*, f.
summary, *nacōṛ*, m., *khulāsā*,
summer, *garmīā̃*, f. pl.: often *hāṛh*, m. (lit. the month June 13–July 12), *unhāḷ*. m.
summer-school, *paṛhāī*, f.
summit, *see* pinnacle, peak.
summon, *see* call.
summons, leg., *samman*, m.
sun, *sūraj*, m., *dyū̃h*, m., *diṇ* or *din*, m.: s. come out fr. cloud, *dhupp laggṇī*: have five or six days of sunshine, *panj che dhuppā̃ laggṇīā̃*, G. 125: M. 129. 27: warm oneself in sun, *see* bask: put it in the sun, *dhupp icc rakkhṇā, sukṇe pāṇā*: *see* sunshine.
sunday, *aitwār*, m.
sunshine, *dhupp*, f: *see* sun.
superfluous, *wāfar, wādhū, fāltū*; *fazūl* (useless).
superintend, *kamm wekhṇā* (*dā*), *nigrānī karnī* (*dī*, U.), *nigābānī karnī* (*dī*, U.).
superintendent, *kamm wekkhanwāḷā, mainajar*: head workman, *mēṭ*.
superior, *see* good, better, one's s. officer, *afsar*.
superstition, *waihm*, m.
superstitious, *waihmī*.
supervise, *see* superintend.
supine, lying or fallen on one's back, *utāṇā, kaṇḍ parṇe* or *bhār*.
supper, *safar*, m. (K).
supplant, *dhokhe nāḷ thā̃ mallṇā*.
supple, *lifaṇwāḷā, kūḷā*.
supply, *apṛāṇā, pucāṇā*: *see* produce, obtain, secure.
support, *see* prop, pillar, lean: gen. *sambhāḷṇā, madad dēṇī* (*nū̃*): hold up, *cukkī rakkhṇā*: provide for, *pāḷṇā, parwarish karnī* (*dī*): *see* endure.
suppose, *farz karnā*: *see* think, guess, calculate, what if.
suppress, *see* hide, stop, hinder.
suppurate, *pakkṇā, pāk paiṇī*.
sure, *see* certain.
surety, *see* bail, certain.
surgeon, *see* doctor, operation.
surpass, *wadhṇā, de nāḷō cangā h*.
surprise, *see* astonish-, -ment.
surrender, *hār mannṇī*: *hathyār saṭṭṇe*.
surreptitiously, *see* stealthily.
surround, *waḷṇā, ghērnā, gherā pāṇā* (*de duāḷe*).
surveillance, *nazr*, f.: keep under s.. *nazr icc rakkhṇā*: *see* detenu.
survey, measure land, *kacchṇā pamaish karnī* (*dī*): *see* look, measure.
suspect, *see* suspicion.
suspend, *muattal-k*. (U.).
suspicion, *shakk karnā* (*dā*), *zan karnā* (*dī bābat*), *badgumāṇī karnī* (*dī bābat*).
swagger, *ākaṛke calṇā*.
swaddling-clothes, *pōtṛe*, m. pl.
swallow, *nigaḷṇā, langhāṇā*: *see* anger.
swamp, *see* marsh.
swarm, of bees, *ghaṇ*, m.: of flies, *ḍār*, m.: *see* flock.
swear, *see* oath.

sweat, *see* perspiration.
sweep, *jhāṛū phērnā* or *dēnā* : s. up leaves, papers, etc., *hūnjṇā*.
sweeper, *mehtar*, *jhāṛū dēṇwālā*, addressed often as *jamādāṛ* : caste, *Cūhṛā*, *Kāḷakh dās* : one who has become Muhammadan, *musall-ī*, fem. *-aṇ* ; Sikkh, *mazbhī Sikkh-*, fem. *-ṇī*, or simply *mazbh-ī*, fem. *-aṇ*.
sweet, *miṭṭhā*, both of people and things : s. drink, *sharbat*, m.
sweets, gen., *miṭhāī*, f. : many kinds.
swell, flesh, etc., *sujjṇā* : something hollow, as stomach, *āpharnā*.
swelling, *sōj*, f. : *aphrā*, m. : *see* swell : fr. bite of insect, *dhrapphaṛ*, m. : *see* lump.
swift, *trikkhā*, *tēz* : in a hurry, *kāhḷā* : go swiftly, *khurī karke jāṇā*, *khiṭṭ dēṇī* or *mārnī*.
swim, *tarnā* : water deep enough to s. in, *tārū pāṇī*, m.
swimmer, *tārū*.
swimming, the art, *tārī*, f. (*aunī*, *nū*)
(1) swing, n., *pīṅgh*, f.
(2) swing, on a swing, *pīṅgh caṛhāṇī*, *pīṅgh de hūṇṭe laiṇe* (tr. *dēṇe*) : gen., *ṭaṅgke halāṇā* (int. *hallṇā*) : *see* hang.
switch, little stick, *chamak*, f. *chūjak*, f., *shūshak*, f. : *see* stick.
swoon, *see* faint.
swoop, *see* pounce.
sword, *talwār*, f. (*mārnī*, int. *laggṇī*, *nū*).
sympathiser, *dardī*.
sympathise w., *ohdā dard karnā*, *ohnū ohdā dukkh hōṇā* (this may mean envy) ; G. 125 : M. 130. 34–6 : *hamdardī karnī* (*nāḷ*) : or *ohnū ohdā dard hōṇā* or *auṇā*.
sympathy, *see* sympathise.
sympathetic, *dardī* ; *hamdard* (U.).
symptom, *nishānī*, f.
syringe, *pickārī*, f. [*ṭrīkal*, m.
syrup, *shīrā*, m. : golden,
system, *kaidā*, m. : *tarīkā*, m.

T

table, *mēz*, m., *mēc*, m. : lay, set t., *mēz lāṇā* (int. *laggṇā*) : take away things, *mēz cukkṇā*.
tablecloth, *mēz dī cādar*, f.
tablet, *takhtī*, f.
taciturn, *gall nehī kardā*, *cuppū*, *mūh wattdā raihndā e*.
(1) tack, n., *brinjī*, f. : *see* nail.
(2) tack, sew, *kaccī suāī karnī*, *kaccā karnā* (*nū*).
tail, *pūshal*, f. : of bird, fish, *būṇḍā*, m. : tailless, *luṇḍā*.
tailor, *darz-ī*, fem. *-aṇ*.
tainted, be, *bō chaḍḍṇī*, *trakk caleā*, *wigaṛ caleā*, *muss caleā* ; of milk, *wigaṛ caleā*, *phiṭ caleā* : *see* bad, sour. A.
take, *laiṇā*, G. 64 : t. away, *khaṛnā*, *lai jāṇā* : *see* seize, conquer ; t. out stain, *see* delete : t. off clothes, hat, shoes, *lāhṇā*, sometimes, *wadhāṇā*, G. 113.
talc, *abrak*, m. (mica).
tale, *see* story : t.-bearer, *cugalkhōr* (U.), *bakhīlī* or *cuglī karnwālā* : *see* accuse, slander.
(1) talent, money, *tōṛā*, m. (1000 rupees).

(2) talent, *see* ability, able, clever.
talisman, *tilism*, m. (U.).
talk, *see* conversation.
talkative, *galāhdaṛ*, *gappī* (esp. of what is untrue), *bakwāsī*, *baṛīā gallā karnwāḷā* : *see* chatter.
tall, *lammā*, *uccā*.
tallow, *see* fat.
talon, *see* claw.
tamarind, *imblī*, f.
tambourine, *ḍaph*, f., smaller, *ḍaphṛā*, m., *ḍaphḷī*, f., *khanjarī*, f. : *see* drum.
tame (quiet), *asīl*, *garīb* : kept, not wild, *rākhwā*.
tank, *talā*, m.
tap, *naḷkā*, m. : *see* spout.
tape, *fītā*, m. : for beds, *nuār*, f. (adj. *nuārī*) : for fastening drawers, *nāḷā*, m. : *see* measuring -t.
tapioca, *ṭāpiū*, m. (K.).
tar, *lukk*, f.
target, *takhtā*, m.
tariff, *nirkh*, m. : *bhā*, m. : t.-list, *nirkhnāmā*, m
tassel, as in fez cap, *phummaṇ*, m. : as in the cloth called *khēs*, *bumbaḷ*, m.
(1) taste, *suād*, m., *mazā*, m. (U.) : t. for, inclination towards, often used in connection with stealing, *jhass*, m., *caskā*, m. (both *paiṇā*, and *dā*) : *see* desire.
(2) taste, v. tr., *cakkhṇā*.
tasteless, *see* inspid, add *alūṇā*, *belūṇā*.
tasty, *suādḷā*, *mazedār*, *karārā* (well-spiced).
tattoo, *ukkhaṇṇā guddṇā*, both w. thing tattooed as obj.
taunt, *tāhne mārne* (*nū*), *mehṇā dēṇā* or *mārnā* (*nū*, *kise gall dā*), *nōk lāṇī* (*nū*, int. *wajjṇī*, *laggṇī*) : *see* ridicule.
taut, *see* tight.
tax, *masūl*, *maihsūl*, m. : octroi, *cuṅgī*, f., *cuṅgī dā masūl* : (octroi post, *cuṅgī*, f. : octroi official, *masūlīā*, *cuṅgīwāḷā*) : land-t., *muāmlā*, m. : (collect t., *laiṇā*, *ugrāhṇā*) : on sales, *āṛhtaḷ*, f., *dhaṛth*, m. : *see* collect, assess, settlement.
tea, *cāh*, f. : *see* teapot.
teach, *paṛhāṇā*, *sikhāṇā*, *talīm dēṇī* (*nū*), *sikkhyā dēṇī* (*nū* H.) : sit at feet of teacher to learn, *baihṇā* (caus. *bahāḷṇā*).
teacher, *ustād*, *māstar*, *munshī* : of Persian, Arabic, *maulwī* : of Sanskrit, *panḍat* : relig. t., M. *murshad*, *maulwī* : H. *gurū*, *panḍat* : female t. in school, *ustādṇī*.
teaching, *see* teach and add *paṛhāī*, f.
teapot, *cāhpōcī*, f. : vessels of similar shape, *astāwā*, m., *satāwā*, m., *lōṭā*, m.
(1) tear, v. tr., *pāṛnā*, int. *pāṭṇā*. [pl.
(2) tear, n., *atthar*, f., *hanjū*, f.
tease, *chēṛnā*, *satāṇā*, *dikk-k.* : t. by disappointing, *jhakhāṇā* : *see* annoy.
teat, animal, *thaṇ*, m. : *see* nipple.
teaze, *tumbṇā* : *see* card (1).
telegram, *tār*, f.
telegraph, *tār ghallṇī* or *dēṇī* : -wire, *tār*, f. : -post, *waḷā*, m.
telescope, *dūrbīn*, f.
tell, *ākhṇā*, *dassṇā*.
temper, tempered good-, *caṅge subhā wāḷā*, *saihndaṛ* (patient) : bad-, use easily angry, annoyed.

temperament, *tabīat*, f.
temperate (person), *parhēzgār*.
temperature, *garmī*, f. (heat): of body, do., and *bukhār*, m. (fever).
temple, *mandar*, m., *shiwālā*, m.
temporary, *thōṛeā dinā wāste*, *ārzī* (of employment, U.): t. piece of work, *calāwā kamm*, m.
tempt, v. difficult idea, *azmāṇā*, *warglāṇā*, *bakāṇ dī kōshish karnī*, *khiccṇā* (draw): *see* incite, test, seduce.
temptation (idea difficult), *azmaish*, f., *partāwā*, m., *khics*, f. (drawing).
ten, *das*: -th, *daswā*: G. 19–24.
tenaciously, *cambaṛke*, *khaihṛā nā chaḍḍke*.
tenant, *sāmī*, f., *asāmī*, f.
tender, soft, *kūlā*, *see* soft: loving, *mhablī*.
tendon, *see* sinew.
tendril, *wall*. f., *wēl*, f.
tenet, *akīdā*, m., *asūl*, m.: point of doctrine, *maslā*, m.
tent, *tambū*, m., *ḍērā*, m., servants' t., *chōldārī*, f.: nomads' small, *pakkhī*, f., *tapṛī*, f.: *see* nomad: wall of t., *kanāt*, f.: put up t., *lāṇā*: strike, *puṭṭṇā*.
tentatively, *wēkkhan wāste*, *azmāṇ wāste*.
tepid, *kōssā*, *khūh-nuāyā*.
terrible, *ḍarnwālā*, *jis tō ḍar āwe*, *ḍarauṇā*.
terrify-, -ing, *see* fear, terrible.
terror, *khauf*, m., *ḍar*, m.
tertian fever, *treā*, m. (*caṛhnā*, come on: *laihṇā*, go off).
test, *azmāṇā*, *parkhṇā*, *wēkhṇā*, *azmaish karnī* (*dī*): examine, *imtihān laiṇā* (*dā*): test exam., *ṭēst*, m., *tēst* or *azmaishi imtihān*, m. (educ.).
testament, *see* will: New T., *Nawā Aihdnāmā*, m., *Injīl*, f., *Anjīl*, f.: Old T., *Purāṇā Aihdnāmā*, m.: *see* Pentateuch, Psalms.
testi-fy, -mony, *see* witness, evidence.
testimonial, *sāṭifkaṭ*, m., *sanad*, f.
than, *nālō*, *thō*, *tō*, *thī*, G. 18: *see* rather, comparison, time.
thank, *shukr karnā* (*dā*): t. you: *tuhāḍḍī mehrbānī e*: t. God, *shukr e*, *Khudā dā shukr e*: the strange phrase *Rabb dā bhalā howe* is often heard.
thankful, *shukrguzār*: *see* obligation.
(1) that, conj., *pai*, *ke*: sometimes *akhe*, *makhe*, G. 121, 40: M. 127–42.
(2) that, pron., *oh*, *parlā*, *pailā*: that is, *yānī*.
thatch, *chappar*, m.
the, *eh*, *oh*, or omit.
theft, *cōrī*, f.: *see* robbery.
their, *ohnā dā*, *ehnā dā*, *ne*, *ṇe*, G. 82–6.
them, *ohnā nū*, *ehnā nū*, *ne*, *ṇe*, G. 82–6.
then, reasoning, *whalā*, *tā*, *te*, *phēr*, *khā* (only with imperat.), *tadde*: time, *odō*, *odū*, *ōsweḷe*, *ōtweḷe*, *tadō*, *tadū*.
thence, *ōtthō*, *see* there.
theolog-y, -ical, *see* A.
theory, *maslā*, m., *dalīl*, f.
there, *ōtthe*, *oddhar*, *parhā*; *ōttal* (gen. motion to): there it is, le voilà, *oh wekhā*.
therefore, *ēs wāste*, *ōs wāste*, *tā ī*, *tadde*, *tā karke*, *tāhīē*.
they, *eh*, *oh*.

thick, liquid, *gūṛhā*, *gāṛhā*, *sañhnā*: dirty water, *gandhleā hoeā*, *see* dirty: dense, trees, crowd, *sañhṇā*: close friendship, *gūṛhī* or *pakkī dōstī*: not thin, *mōṭā*.

thickness (not thinness), *muṭeāī*, f.

thief, *cōr*: *see* robber, receiver.

thigh, *paṭṭ*, m.

thimble, *aṅgūṭhī*, f.

thin, not fat or thick, *patlā*; *lissā* (persons, animals only): not coarse, *mhīn*: fine and small, *barīk*: ill-looking, *māṛā*, *lissā*.

thing, *cīz*, f., *cīz wast*, f., *shai*, f.

think, *sōcṇā*, *gaur karnā* (consider), *dhiān karnā* (meditate): I believed or thought, *maĩ ākheā*, *maĩ samjheā*.

third, *see* three: t. day fever, *see* tertian.

thirst, *treh*, f., G. 108: (intense) *bhaṛkī*, f.: *andar saṛdā e*.

thirsty, *trihāyā*.

thirteen, *tērā*: -th, *tehrwā*, G. 19–24, 123: thirteen-finger shoe, *see* shoe.

thirty, *trīh*: -one, *akattī*, *akattrī*: -two *battī*, *battrī*: -three, *tētī*, *tētrī*: -four, *cauttī*, *cautrī*: -five, *paĩtī*, *paĩtrī*: -six, *chattī*, *chattrī*: -seven, *saĩtī*, *saĩtrī*: -eight, *aṭhattī*, *aṭhattrī*: -nine, *unṭālī*, *unṭālī*.
ordinals add *-wā* with tonic *h*, (*trīh* already has it): as *akattīhwā*, *untāhḷīwā*, G. 19-24, 123.

this, *eh*, *urlā*.

thither, *see* there.

thong, *wadhrī*, f.

thorn, *kaṇḍā*, m.: t.-branch, *ḍhīṅgar*, m., *ḍhīṅgrī*, f., *moṛhā*, m., *moṛhī*, f.: tiny thorny plant injurious to rubber tyres, *bhakkhṛā*.

thorny, *kaṇḍeāwālā*.

thoroughly, *bilkull*, *pūrī tarhā*, *pūre taur nāḷ*: *see* absolutely, altogether.

thou, *tū̃*: people like thee or you, *tumhātaṛ*, G. 28.

though, *bhāwē*, *bhāwē jīkar*.

thought, gen., *sōc*, f., *sōc wacār*, f.: *khyāl*, m., idea, opinion: *gaur*, m., consideration; *dhiān*, m., meditation: *dalīl*, f., reasoning: *see* anxiety.

thoughtful, *sōcā icc*, *dalīlā icc*.

thoughtless, *lāparwāh*, *sōcdā nehī*: *bēparwāh*, beyond need of caring, as God, rich man.

thousand, *hazār*: -th, *hazārwā*: hundred t., *lakkh*: -th, *lakkhwā*: G. 20–4, 93.

thread, *dhāgā*, m., *tand*, f.: sacred Hindu t., *janeo*, m.: three-fold t., *paṛkatteā*, *dhāgā*: *see* string.

threat-, -en, *dhaũs dēṇī* (*nū̃*), or *cāṛhnī* (*utte*) or *wakhānī* (*nū̃*), *dhamkī dēṇī* (*nū̃*), *dabbā dēṇā* (*nū̃*), *dabkāṇā*, *ghurkī dēṇī* (*nū̃*), *ḍarāṇā*: *see* reprimand, frown.

three, *trai*, *tinn*: third, *trījjā*, *tīsrā*: G. 19–24: t.-fold (actual layers), *treohrā*; three times as big or much, *trīṇā*, *trai hisse waddh*: *see* time, thread: thrice, *trai wārī* or *werī*.

thresh, v. tr., *gāhṇā*, int. *gaihṇā*.

threshingfloor, *piṛ*, m. A.

threshold, room at, *ḍeoḍhī*, f.: of door, *brū̃*, f., *dalhīz*, f.

throat, outside, *gaḷ*, m., *gāṭṭā*, m.: inside, *saṅgh*, m.: *see* neck and add *saṅghī*, f.

throne, *takht*, m.: of ruling princes, *gaddī*, f.
throttle, *see* strangle.
through, *wiccdū*, *wiccõ dī*: t. Jesus Christ, *Yesū Masīh dī rāhī* or *de wasīleõ*: t. door, window, *see* way: *see* because of, means.
throw, *saṭṭṇā*, *suṭṭṇā*, *mārnā*: t. away, *suṭṭ* or *saṭṭ charnā* or *chaḍḍṇā*): t. away liquid, *roṛh charnā*, *ḍolh charnā*: t. at, strike w., *mārnā* (acc. of missile, *nū* of person.)
thrust, stuff in, *see* stuff in: t. out, *dhikkṇā*, *kaḍḍhṇā*.
thumb, *aṅgūṭh*, m., *aṅgūṭhā*, m.: affix t.-mark, *aṅgūṭhā lāṇā* (int. *laggṇā*).
thunder, v. int., *baddal gajjṇā* (sometimes *kaṛakṇā*).
Thursday, *jumerāt*, f., *wīr* or *wīrwār*, m. (H.).
thus, in this way, *eñ*, *iñ*, *aiñ*, *eõ*, *eñ karke*, *aikkaṇ*: in that way, *owẽ*, *aukkaṇ*, *uñ*: (*owẽ* also just then, immediately).
thy, *see* you.
(1) tick, n., in dogs, etc., *ciccaṛ*, m.
(2) tick of clock, etc., *ṭik ṭik*, f. (*k*.).
ticket, *ṭikaṭ*, m. f.: return t., *wāpsī ṭikaṭ*, *auṇ jaṇ dā ṭikaṭ*: (travel) without t., *baraṅg*, *betiktā*.
tickle, v. tr., *kutkutāṛī kaḍḍhṇī* (*dī*), int. *nikḷṇī* (*dī*), often in plur.
tidy, *sāf suthrā* (clean), *ṭhīk sāhmke rakkhṇā*, *koī shai kuthāẽ nā howe*, *thā pathāī rakkhṇā*: *see* untidy.
(1) tie, v. tr., *bannhṇā*, pa. p., *baddhā*, int. *bajjhṇā*: *see* knot: tie arms or hands behind back, *mushkā̃ bannhṇīā̃* (*dīā̃*).
(2) tie, n., muffler, *gulūban*, m.: *see* neck-tie.
tiffin, *ṭipan*, m.
tiger, *shēr*, fem. *shērnī*.
tight, *kasseā hoeā*, *ghuṭṭeā hoeā*: *see* narrow.
tighten, *kassṇā*, *ghuṭṭṇā*.
tightly, *kasske*, *ghuṭṭke*.
tile, *khaprail*, f. (U).
(1) till, v. tr., *see* plough, cultivate.
(2) till, up till, *ṭikar*, *tāṇī*, *toṛī*, *tāṛī*, *tāī*, *tākar*, *sīdhā*.
(3) till, conj., *jicar ṭikar* (or *tāī*, etc.), *jicar nū*, *jicar .... nā*.
tilt back, of carriage, *ullarnā*: *see* weight.
time, gen., *wakat*, m., *weḷā*, m.: the present, past or future age, *zamānā*, m., *samā*, m.: fixed period, *miād*, f.: length of t., *cir*, m.: short t., *jhaṭ*, m., *ghaṛī*, f. (*see* short, long): in t., at the right t., *weḷe sir*, *wakat sir*; at the wrong t., late, *kuweḷe* (*see* late): this t., *aitkī*, *aitkā̃*, *es wārī*, *es werī*, *es phēre*: *see* meanwhile, o'clock: for A.M., P.M., *see* A.M.
time in four, five times, etc., *wārī*, *werī*: the first, second t., *paihlī*, *dujjī wārī* or *werī*, *paihlā phērā*, etc.
five, six times as big, *panj hisse waddh*, etc., or reversing it, *ohdā panjwā̃ hissā* (a fifth part of it): fr. two to five, special words, *dūṇā*, *trīṇā*, *cauṇā*, *panjauṇā*.
time-server, *matlabī*, *garzī*.
timid, *see* coward.

tin, material or a tin, *ṭīn*, m. : for soldering, *kalī*, f. (*k.*) : canister. *kanastar*, m., *pīpā*, m. : bath-tin. *bhabkā*. m.

tinkle, *chanakṇā*, *wajjṇā*, *chan chan karnī*.

tip, *nōk*. f.

tiptoe, on. *pabbā bhār* (*pabb*, m., is ball of foot).

tire, v. int., *thaknā*. *thakāṇā*) : tired, *thakeā hoeā* : *see* faint : get tired of, *akkṇā* (*tō* tr. *akāṇā*), *see* sick of.

title, of book. etc., *nā*, m. : heading, *surkhī*, f. : of person, *lakab*, m. : honorary t. given by Government, *khatāb*, m.

to, dat., *nū̃* : of place, *nū̃*, often loc. case, G. 9, 10, 77 : of purpose, infin w. *wāste*, *laī*, *nū̃*, up to, *see* up.

toast, n., *tōs*, m. (slice whether toasted or not) ; v., *tōs sēkṇā rōṭī sēknī* : foment or heat limb at fire, *sēk karnā* (*hatth nū̃*, *latt nū̃*, hand, leg) : *see* warm.

tobacco, *tamākū* (*pīṇā*, *chikkṇā*).

to-day, *ajj* : a week fr. t., *see* week : emphatic, *ajjo*, *ajjo ī*, *ajje ī*.

toe, *uṅgaḷ*, f. : big t., *aṅgūṭh*, m., *aṅgūṭhā*, m. : little t., *cīccī*, f. : fleshy part of t., *pōttā*, m. : ball of toe, *see* tiptoe.

together, *katthe*, *ralke*, *nālo nāḷ*.

toilsome, *taklīfwāḷā*, *see* difficult.

toll, *masūl*, m. : *see* tax.

tomato, *ṭamāṭar*, m.

tomb, *see* grave, shrine.

to-morrow, *bhaḷke*, *kall* : *see* yesterday (last clause) : day after t., *parsõ* : day after that, *cauth* : fifth day, *panjauth* : sixth day, *cheauth* : (*satauth*, *aṭhauth*, seventh, eighth day, are perhaps jocular) ; also *panjwā din*, etc. : t. week, *see* week.

tonga, *ṭāṅgā*, m.

tongs, *uccā*, m., *cimṭā*, m. : *see* pincers.

tongue, *jībh*, f., *zabān*, f. : *see* language : t. of bell, *see* bell.

to-night, *ajj rātī*, *ajj rātnū̃*, also last night.

(1) **too**, as in too much. etc., gen. omit, show by context, *bauhtā tattā*, too hot, etc.

(2) **too**, also, *wī*, *bī*, *see* moreover.

tool, *hathyār*, m. : pl., *racch kāṇ*, m. : barber's t., *racch*, m.

tooth, *dand*, m. : double t., back t., *hanhū̃*, f. : show teeth (dog in anger, or derisively of person laughing), *dand kaḍḍhne* : tooth in saw, *dandā*, m. : *see* dentist in A.

toothbrush, *dāttan*, f.

toothed, *dandeāwāḷā*.

(1) **top**, of box, lid, *ḍhakkaṇ*, m. : of chest of drawers, bookcase, etc., *chatt*, m. : of page, *sirā*, m., *see* bottom, foot.

(2) **top**, plaything, *lāṭū*, m. : spin t., *lāṭū sattnā*, *wagāṇā* or *bhuāṇā* ; int. *wagṇā*, *bhaūṇā*.

topsy turvy, *hēṭh utte* (one on top of other) ; *ugrā dugrā*, *agaṛ dugrā*, *wigleā shigleā* : *see* untidy, upside down.

torch, *mashāl*, f. : t.-bearer in marriage, *mashālcī*.

torment, *see* tease, annoy, torture.

tortoise, *kaccukummā*, m., *khacōprā*, m.

torture, *puls ohde nāḷ burī kītī*, (not used of woman); *mār-nā*; *sakhtī karnī* (*nāḷ*): *see* tie.

total, *jamhā*, f., *mizān*, f. (U.), *jōṛ*, m.

totter, *see* stagger.

touch, *hatth lānā*, *chohṇā*: feel, *ṭohṇā*: t. heart, *dil utte asar karnā*.

touching, *see* pathetic, sad, and add *afsōswāḷā*, *dil te asar karnwāḷā*.

touchstone, *ghaswaṭṭī*, f.

tough, no word; say *camm wāṅgar* or *lif jāndā e par uṇ ḍāhdā e*, *pāṭdā nehī*.

tour, on duty, *daurā*, m. (*k.*): pleasure, *sail* or *sair*, m. (*k.*): very brief, *phērā*, m. (*mār-nā*)

tow, *see* hemp.

towards, *de wall*, *de wallō* (only w. look, see, otherwise *wall*); *dī sedh*, *de pāse*.

towel, *tauliā*, m.; *nhauṇwāḷā tauliā*, *gusl dā tauliā*: t.-horse (or rail) *tauliā dī ghōṛī*.

tower, *burj*, m.: small, *burjī* f.

town, *shaihr*, m., *naggar*, m. (large village).

toy, *khaḍauṇā*, m.

trace, *patā*, m. (for verbs, *see* discover), *nishān* (*labbhṇā*, *dā*); *sūh* (*kaḍḍhṇī*, *dī*): *see* track, path.

track, of wheels, *gail*, f.: of feet, hoofs, etc., *khurā*, m.: v. tr., *khurā kaḍḍhṇā*, *see* path, trace.

tracker, *khōjī* (chiefly for cattle, horses, etc.).

trade, *tajārat*, f., *byopār*, m., *wanj byopār*, m., *sudāgrī*, f. (all w. *k.*): *see* profession, merchandise.

trader, *see* merchant.

tradition, gen., *rawait*, f.: *hadīs*, f. (M.): *waḍḍeā dī gall*.

traffic, *auṇā jāṇā*, m.: *rauṇak raihndī e*.

(1) **train**, v. tr., *see* teach: t. animals for ploughing, also metaph. boy for work, *hāḷī kaḍḍhṇā*, int. *nikḷṇā*: for burden bearing, *lādū kaḍḍh-ṇā*, int. *nikḷṇā*.

(2) **train**, n., *gaḍḍī*, f.: mail, t., *ḍāk gaḍḍī*; Bombay mail, *bambā mēl*, f.; Calcutta mail, *kalkattā mēl*, f.: passenger t., *suārī gaḍḍī*, *psanjar*, f.: local t., *lōkal*, f., *nōkal*, f.: goods t., *māl gaḍḍī*: the Lahore, Wazirabad, t. has come, gone, *Lahaur* (*Wazīrā-bād*) *āeā e*, *ṭur geā e*.

trait, *sift*, f.

traitor, no good word, *see* treacherous, treason.

trample, upon, *mindhṇā*, *min-dhāṛnā*, *latāṛnā*, *utte ṭurnā*, *utte pair rakkhṇā*, *see* crush.

transaction, *kamm*, m., *laihṇ dēṇ*, *laiṇ dēṇ*, m.

transfer, *badlī karnī*, *hōṇī*.

transfigured, be, *sūrat badal jāṇī* (*dī*).

transform, *sūrat*, *shakl badalnī* (*dī*).

transient, *fānī*, *caũh dihāṛeā dā*; *see* shortlived.

translate, *tarjmā karnā* (*dā*, int. *h.*).

translation, *tarjmā*, m.: literal t., *lafzī tarjmā*.

translator, *tarjmā karnwāḷā*, *mutrajjam* (for *mutarjim*).

transmigration, *awāgaũ*, m., *āwāgauṇ*, m., *curāsī*, m. (all H.).

transport, *bārbardārī*, f. : man engaged in mule t., *khaccar-pātrī* : sentence to transportation, *kāle pāṇī dā hukm dēṇā* (*nū*), *kāle pāṇī ghallṇā*.
trap, *kuṛikkī*, f., *pinjrā*, m.
trash, *raddī cīz*, f. : *see* useless, worthless, nonsense.
travel, *safar karnā*; for pleasure, *sail* or *sair karnā* : t. distance, *paiṇḍā mārnā* or *k*. (esp. walking) ; go a stage, *paṛā jāṇā* (but *paṛā karnā*, halt).
traveller, *rāhī*, *musāfar*.
traverse, *see* travel.
tray, *trēḷ*, f. (K.) : t.-cloth, *trēḷ dī cādar*.
treacher-ous, -y, no good word, *namak-harām*-(n., *-ī*, f.), *dil icc bāgī*, *beīmān*-(n., *-ī*, f.) : *see* treason.
treacle, *ṭrīkal*, m. (also golden syrup).
tread, *see* trample.
treason, use *bagāwat*, f., *bādshāh* or *sarkār dā badkhāh* : *see* treacherous.
treasure, *khazānā*, m.
treasury, *khazānā*, m.
treasurer, *khazāncī*, m.
treat, well, badly, kindly, *kise de nāḷ caṅgā*, *burā*, *mehrbānī dā salūk k.* : t. disease, sick person, *alāj karnā* (*dā*) ; be treated (sick person), *duāī karnī* (by, *dī*), *alāj karāṇā* (by, *koḷō*).
treatment, *see* treat.
treaty, *aihd*, m., *āpe icc likhke karār karnā*.
treble, *see* three.
tree, *rukkh*, m., *būṭā*, m., *darakht*, m. : bark, *chill*, f., *chillaṛ*, f., *raṅg*, m. : piece of bark, *sakk*, m., *sakṛā*, m. : family tree, *shajrā*, m.
tremble, *kambṇā*, *kambṇī lagg ṇī* (*nū*) : *kambṇī chiṛnī* (*nū*), begin trembling.
trial, leg., *mukadmā*, m. : each appearance, *pēshī*, f. : send up for t., *calān k.* (*dā*) : *see* test, try, examine.
triangular, *targuṭṭhā*, *tarnukrā*.
tribe, *kaum*, f.
tributary of river, *shākh*, f., *sūā*, m. : *see* canal.
trick, n., v. *pakhaṇḍ*, m. (*khēḍṇā*, *nāḷ*), *chaḷ*, m. (*khēḍṇā*, *nāḷ*) ; *dā*, m. (*lāṇā*, *nū*, int., *khāṇā*, *laggṇā*) ; *dā fareb karnā*, *nū*) ; *khuṭṭar*, m. (*k.*, *nāḷ*) ; *waḷ pēc*, m. (*k.*, *nāḷ*) ; *luṭṭ*, m., or *luṭṭ*, *khruṭṭ* (*k.*, *nāḷ*) ; *dhōkhā* m (*d.*, *nū*), (int., *khāṇā*) ; *hīlā*, m. (*k.*, *nāḷ*), *ḍhaṅg*, m. (*k.*, *nāḷ*).
trickle, *cōṇā* : n., *coā*, m. (*paiṇā*) : *see* drip, ooze. *ḍhaṅgī*.
tricky, *pakhaṇḍī*, *khuṭṭarī*,
trident, *tarsūl*, m.
trifle, n., *nikkī cīz*, f., *nikkī gall*, f. : v. small amount, *ruāḷ jehā* : he's only trifling w. you, *hujtā* or *jugtā* or *huṭṭar kardā e* : *see* waste.
trigger (also cock), *ghōṛā*, m.
trim, hair, *katrnā* : trees, plants, *chāṅgṇā*, *katṛnā*.
Trinity, *Taslīs*, f.
trip, make stumble ; v. tr., *ṭhuḍḍā lāṇā* (*nū*, also kick), int. *laggṇā* (*nū*).
triple, *see* three.
trivial, *see* trifling.
trolly, on railway, *ṭhēllā*, *ṭhelhā*, m , *ṭrāllī*, f.
trooper, *suār*.
trot, *duṛkī calṇā* or *turnā* : tr *lāṇā*, *ṭōrnā*, *calāṇā*.
trouble, *taklīf*, f., *janjāḷ*, m , *kazīā*, m., take t., *taklīf k.*,

sir khapāṇā (mental): experience t. in getting something done, *khajjal h.*, *khajjal khuār h.*, *bhambal bhūse khāṇe*: give t., *taklīf d.*: *see* inconvenience, difficulty, straits, annoy.

trough, same as manger.

trousers, Indian for men, *tambī*, f., *salwār*, f. (baggy), *sutthaṇ*, f. (baggy), *ghuṭannā*, m., *pajāmā*, m.: for women, *sutthaṇ*: English, *patlūn*, f.

trowel, *rambā*, m., *khurpā*, m.

true, *saccā*: t. to his word, *gall dā pakkā*, *see* promise, word: t. friend, *pakkā* or *saccā* or *dilī* or *jānī dōst*: t. Sahib, *pakkā Sāhb*: *see* real, truthful.

truly, *saccī muccī*.

trumpet, *turam*, m., *turī*, f., *bigal*, f., all *wajāṇā*, int. *wajjṇā*.

(1) trunk, of tree, *pōrī*, f.: of men, animals, *dhaṛ*, m.

(2) trunk, of elephant. *sunḍ*, f.

(3) trunk, *see* box.

trust, n., *wasāh*, m., *bharosā*, m., *āsrā*, m.: in t., *amānat wicc*: v., t. to sthg., *ohdā mīṇ k.*: *see* faith, believe, confide, reliance, untrustworthy. [*see* worthy.

trustworthy, *ehtbārwālā*, *pakkā*,

truth, veracity, *sacāī*, f., *saccāī*, f.: reality, *hakīkat*, f.: *see* real, reality.

truthful, *saccā*, *see* true.

try, *koshish karnī*, *kōsht karnī*: t. hard, *see* effort, difficulty: t. one's best, *apṇe wallō ghaṭṭ nā karnī*.

tube, *naṛī*, f. (of reed): *phūknī*, f. (blowpipe); *nalkā*, m.: bicycle t., *ṭūp*, f., *ṭyūb*, f.

tuft, of Hindu's hair, *bōddī*, f.: *see* crest.

Tuesday, *mangal*, m., *mangalwār*, m.

(1) tumbler, acrobat, *naṭṭ-*, fem. *-ṇī*: *bāzīgar-*, fem. *-nī*.

(2) tumbler, glass, *gilās*, m.: *see* drinking-vessel.

tumour, *gilṭī*, f.: *rasaulī*, f.: *see* boil (1)

tumult, *see* disturbance, riot.

tune, air, *rāg*, m.: pitch, *sur*, f.: in t., *ṭhīk sur nāl*, *sur raḷāke*: out of t., *besur*, *besurā*, *sur nehī raḷdī*, *sur ṭhīk nehī*: being out of t., *besurī*, f.: tune, v. tr., *sur raḷāṇī*, *sur ṭhīk karnī*; *see* play, instrument. Note also *mērī ohde nāl sur nehī*, we are not friendly.

tunnel, *ṭanḍal*, m., *surangh*, f.: for water, *saifal*, m.

turban, *pagg*, f., *pagṛī*, f., *sāfā*, m.: red or black, *cīrā*, m.: blue and white, *luṅṅī*, f.: put on t., *bannhṇā*: take off, *lāhṇā*, *wadhāṇā*, G. 113.

turbulent, *fasādī*: *see* rebel, rebellion, riot.

turmeric, *hardal*, f., *wasār*, f.

(1) turn, n., *wārī* f.: my t., *mērī wārī*: take one's t., in game, *wār laiṇī*: by turns, *wārī wārī*, *wāro waṭṭī*: t. in canal, road, *mōṛ*, m., *goshā*, m.: t. or twist in road, *waḷā*, m., *warānglā*, m. (all four *paiṇā*, tr. *pāṇā*).

(2) turn, v., *bhaūṇā*, G 64 (tr. *bhuāṇā*); *phirnā* (tr. *phirāṇā*, *phērnā*): tr. also *ghumāṇā*: t. in lathe, *see* lathe: t. cattle, horses, by heading them off, *walṇā*, *walke leauṇā*: t. wheel, esp. well, *gēṛnā* (int.

girnā, caus. *garāṇā*); *see* spin: t. out., *see* expel and add *hikkṇā*, *see* excommunicate: t. out, prove, *nikḷṇā* (t. out thief, *cōr nikḷṇā*): t. back, *muṛnā* (tr. *mōṛnā*), *see* return: t. over papers, etc., *phōlṇā*: t. round (head), *see* dizzy: t. upside down, *see* upside down.
turnip, *gōṅgḷū*, m.
turnscrew, *pēckass*, m.
turquoise, *firōzā*, m.
turtle, *kaccūkumhā*, m., *khacoprā*, m.
twelve, *bārā*: twelfth, *bārhwā*, G. 19–24, 123.
twenty, *wīh*: twentieth, *wīhwā*, G. 19–24, 93, 123.
twice, *see* two.
twig, *see* branch.
twilight (morning), *mūh anhērā*, m., *muhānjḷā*, m.: (evening) *hanēre paie*.
twins, *jauṛe*, m. pl.: he is one of t., *jauṛeā dā e*, *jauṛeā wiccō e*, *jauṛeā dā bhrā* or *puttar* (t. brother or son). A.
twine, v., *see* twist, cling: n., *see* string.
twinkle, *camakṇā*.
twist, *marōṛnā*, *waṭṭṇā* (t. round and round, esp. of rope, etc.).
two, *dō*, *see* second: t. and a half, *ḍhāī*: adj. fr. *ḍhāī* is *ḍhāyā*: G. 19–24: t.-fold, actual layers, *dohrā*, *see* fold: double, *see* double: twice, *dō werī*, *dō wārī*; twice as big as, *dūṇā*, *dō hisse waddh*, *see* time.
typewriter, *likkhaṇwāḷī mashīn*, f.
tyranny, *see* oppress.
tyrant, *see* cruel.
tyre (bicycle, etc.), *ṭair*, m.

U

udder, *hawānnā*, m.: *see* teat.
ugly, *kojhā*, *bhairī sūrat wāḷā*: *see* awkward.
ulcer, *see* boil (1), eye-ulcer.
ultimate, *see* last (1).
ultimately, *see* finally.
umbrage, *see* offence.
umbrella, *chatrī*, f.: u.-cover, *uchāṛ*, m.: put up u., *lāṇī*: take down, *band-k*.
umpire, *tarfain*, m.: in game, *ampair*, m.: *see* mediator.
unadulterated, *see* adulterat-e, -ed, pure.
unanimous, use *sāreā dī salāh* or *rā*: *itfāk nāḷ*, *mutfik hōke* (U.).
unanimity, *itfāk*, m. (U.).
unaspiring, *choṭe dil wāḷā*.
unaware, *bekhabar*, *patā nehī*: *see* ignorant.
unbeliever, *kāfar* (M.).
unblemished, *beaib*, *bedāg*: *see* defect, fault.
uncertain, *shakk e* (*wicc*), *pakkī khabar nehī*.
uncertainty, *kacc pakk*, m.
uncharitable, *badzan*.
uncivilised, *waihshī*, *jāṅgḷī*, *ḍhaggā jehā*.
uncle, father's elder brother, *bābbā*, *tāeā* (H.): father's younger do., *caccā*: mother's brother, *māmmā*: father's sister's husband, *phupphaṛ*: mother's sister's do., *māssaṛ*: husband's or wife's uncle, *see* father.
unclean, *see* dirty: ceremonially, *palīt*, *napāk*, *mlēcch* (H.): morally, *napāk*, *palīt*: *see* pure, holy, clean.
uncleanness, *palītī*, f., *napākī*, f.

uncommon, *see* strange.
unconquerable, *jehṛā nā hāre*.
uncooked, *kaccā*: half-cooked, *ḍaḍḍrā*: *see* ripe.
uncover, any word for lid or covering with *lāhṇā* or *uttõ lāhṇā*: *naṅgā-k*. [*raṛā*, m.
uncultivated, *pei hoī zamīn*,
under, underneath, *see* below.
undergo, *see* suffer. [*bhohrā*, m.
underground room, cellar,
understand, *samjhṇā*, *samajh auṇī* (*nū̃*), M. 117. 4: be understood, of thing, *sujjhṇā* (*menū̃*, etc.); *palle paiṇā*, *piṛ palle paiṇā*, M. 129. 10: G. 112 (last two only in negative and interrogative sentences).
understanding, n., *samajh*, f., *thauh*, m.: *see* sense, wis-e, -dom, intelligen-ce, -t, clever.
undertake, *zimmā cukkṇā* (*dā*), *bīṛā cukkṇā* (*dā*), *zimmewār h*. (*dā*).
undo, sewing, *udhẽṛnā* (int. *udhaṛnā*): gen. *kholhṇā*: bed, machinery, *ukhẽṛnā* (int. *ukkhaṛnā*): *see* destroy.
undress, *kapṛe lāhṇe*, *wadhāṇe* G. 113: caus. *luhāṇe*.
undutiful, of children, *kuputtar*: servants, *see* lazy, unfaithful.
uneas-iness, -y, *see* restlessness.
uneducated, *anpaṛh*.
uneven, *see* rough, level, smooth.
unexampled, *es tarhā̃ dā hōr koī nehī̃*, *eñ kadī nehī̃ hoeā*: *see* unique.
unfaithful, gen. *bẽwafā*: of subordinate, *namak-harām*.
unfavourable, opinion, report, *de khalāf*, *de barkhlāf*, *caṅgā* or *acchā nehī̃*.
unfit, *laik nehī̃*, *dī laik dā nehī̃*, *nafiṭṭ*: *see* able.
unfortunate, gen., *wacārā* (v. mild word): unlucky, *badkismat*, *mandeā̃ bhāgā̃ wālā*.
unfortunately, *afsōs e pai*, *badkismatī nāḷ*: the opposite is *abihāre*, luckily.
unfounded, *ohdī bunyād* or *as līat koī nehī̃*.
unfruitful, trees, etc., *apphaḷ*: morally, *apphaḷ*: *see* barren.
unfurnished, *samān koī nehī̃*, *bussā*: *see* empty.
ungrateful, *nashukrā*, *kirtghan*.
ungrudgingly, *khushī nāḷ*, *khulhe dil nāḷ*.
unhappy, *see* sad.
unholy, *see* holy, unclean.
uniform, *wardī*, f.
uninhabited, of house, *khālī*: *see* unoccupied: of place, desolate, *suñā*, *bẽabād*.
uninteresting, *suād koī nehī̃*, *besuādā*: *dilcasp nehī̃* (U.).
uninvited, *bin saddeā̃*, *saddeā̃ binā*.
unique, *bẽnazīr* (U.), *lasānī* (U.): *see* unexampled, matchless, peerless.
unjust, *bẽinsāf*, *bẽniā̃*.
unjustly, *nahakk*, *bẽinsāfī nāḷ*.
unkind, *beraihm*; *betars*.
unknowable *bandeā̃ dī samajh wicc nehī̃ aundā*.
unlawful, gen., *najaiz*: *harām*, forbidden by religion, gen. food (M.): illegal, *kanūn de khalāf*.
unlimited, *behadd*: *see* endless, innumerable.
unload, *bhār lāhṇā*.
unlock, *see* lock.
unluck-y, -ily, *see* unfortunate-, -ly.
unmarried, *kuārā*, fem. *kuārī*:

charā, charā chānḍ, charā murā (last three also "alone"), *see* alone.
unmentionable, *dassaṇ de laik* (or *dī laik dā*) *nehī̃, jihde ākkhaṇ tõ sharm aundī e,* (*gall*) *karnwālī nehī̃.*
unmerciful-, -ly, *beraihmī nāḷ, betarsī nāḷ*: *see* unkind.
unmindful, *see* careless.
unnecessary, *loṛīdā nehī̃, ohdī lōṛ nehī̃, zarūrī nehī̃*: (spare) *fāltū, wadhīk, wādhkū.*
unoccupied, house, *wehlā, khālī*: out of work, *wehlā, wāndā benaukar* (out of service).
unpleasant, of matter, word, etc., *mandī gall* (or *kauṛī, maṭṭhī, burī*)
unpopular, *oste koī khush nehī̃, sāre ohdī shikait karde ne.*
unravel, *see* solve, undo.
unreliable, *see* untrustworthy.
unripe, *kaccā*: half-ripe, *see* ripe.
unruly, *sarkash* (U.): *see* disobedient.
unsafe, *see* danger-, -ous.
unseasonable, *see* untimely.
unstable, *see* shake, vacillate, wobble.
unsteady, *see* unstable.
untidy, *see* topsy turvy, and add *samān ēwē̃ peā hoeā e, cīzā̃ ēwē̃ peīā̃ hoīā̃ ne, betartībī nāḷ.*
until, *see* till.
untimely, adv., *kuweḷe, bewakt*: n., *kuweḷā*, m., *kuwēḷ*, f.
untrustworthy, *beatbārā, wasāh de laik nehī̃.*
unused, leather, blank paper, water-pot, cloth (or unwashed), *korā*: *see* new.
unventilated, *wā dā koī rāh nehī̃, bārī nehī̃, see* ventilate.

unwilling-, -ly, *see* force, reluctant, sick of, oath.
up, *utte, utā̃*: up to, *ṭikar, ṭāṇī, toṛī, tākar, sīdhā, tāī̃*: *see* upon.
upbraid, *see* reprimand, reproach.
uphold, *see* maintain, support.
upon, *utte, de utte, te*: upon arriving, *see* while.
uppermost, *utlā.*
upright, *see* perpendicular, stand, good, honest.
uproot, *ukhēṛnā* (int. *ukkhaṛnā*), *jaṛhõ puṭṭṇā.*
upset, *ḍēgṇā, garānā* (U.).
upside down, *mū̃hdā, puṭṭhā*: on one's face, *see* face: turn u., *mū̃hdā mārnā* or *k.*, *puṭṭhā k.*; of bricks, bread, *thullṇā*: *see* topsy turvy.
upwards, *see* up.
urge (warn against forgetting), *pakkī karnī* (*nū̃*), *jhī karnī* (*nū̃*): (emphasise) *gall utte zōr dēnā*: (annoy) *tang-k*: (keep on) *khaihṛā nā chaḍḍṇā, picche paiṇā*: *see* excite, incite, emphasise.
urgent, *zarūrī*: of command, *takīdī.*
us, *sānū̃*: *see* we.
usage, *see* custom, treat.
use, v. tr., *wartṇā, istemāl-k.* (U.): u. unnecessarily, of big words, etc., *wāhṇā*, G. 121, M. 127. 34: have no u. for, *maī̃ jarebā̃ kī karnīā̃ ne*, what use have I for socks? G. 118: be used of road, *wagṇā*: become used to, state of being used to, *see* accustom.
useful, *baṛe kamm dā e, baṛā kamm dendā e*: *waddhrīā̃ baṛe* or *baṛīā̃ kamm aundīā̃ ne*, thongs are v. useful.

useless, *kisc kamm dā nehī, raddī*: *see* worthless.
uselessly, *dhigāṇē, ēwē.*
usual, *see* custom, common, ordinary.
usually, *aksar, ām, bauht karke.*
usurp, *hakk mārnā* or *dabāṇā* or *laiṇā* or *dabbṇā*: *see* seize.
utmost, *jitthō toṛī hō sake, apṇe wallō ghaṭṭ nā karnī.*
utterly, *see* absolutely, altogether, thoroughly.

V

vacancy, *see* post.
vacant, *see* empty, unoccupied, uninhabited.
vacation, *see* leave.
vaccinate, *ṭīkā lāṇā,* int. *laggṇā*; caus. *luāṇā, ukhṇāṇā.* A.
vacillate, *galle galle phirnā, dalīlā badaldeā raihṇā, ḍōldeā raihṇā, ḍāwāḍōl, lāi lagg* (easily persuaded): *etthe kujh te otthe kujh, see* back out, wobble, changeable, pliable.
vagabond, *awārā* (fem. the same), *see* nomad.
vain, *nazākti, nakkhreā wālā, baṛī mizāj wālā, baṛe damāg wālā*: *see* conceit, delica-cy, -te, air, proud: in v., *mufl dā* (or *mukkhat dā*), *ēwē, dhigāṇe, befaidā.*
valet, *baihrā.*
valid, *ṭhīk, jāiz, kamm dā, aje caldā e,* still current, etc.
valley, *wādī,* f. : pass, *darā,* m.
valuable, *see* costly, good, excellent.
value, n., *see* cost: v., *mull ṭharhāṇā* (fix price), *kadr pāṇā* (*dā*); esteem, hold dear.
valueless, *see* useless, worthless.

vanish, *see* disappear.
vanquish, *see* conquer, defeat, win: in argument, *lājuāb-k, bōlan jogā nā chaḍḍṇā.*
vapour, *see* steam. [able.
variable, *see* vacillate, change-
variation, *wādhā ghāṭā,* m.: *see* change.
varicose vein, *see* vein.
variety, *kism,* f., *jins,* f. ; *see* various, change, variegated.
variegated (colours), *rang barangī.*
various, *kism kism dā, bauht kism dā, wakkho wakkh*: *see* variety, change, variegated.
varnish, n. and v., *rogan karnā* (*nū*).
veer, *see* vacillate, changeable.
vegetable, *salūṇā,* m., *sabzī,* f., *bhājī,* f., *sāg pattar,* m. (*tarkārī* means meat): v.-bed, *see* flower-bed: v -curry, *chichkī,* f. (K.).
vehemently, *zōr nāḷ, zore*: *see* force.
vehicle, *see* carriage, cart, train.
veil, *cādar,* f.: H. woman's, covering body, *addhaṛwanjhā,* m., *sāṛhī,* f.: M. woman's, all over, *bhurkā, burkā,* m.: v. oneself, *ghunḍ kaḍḍhṇā*: draw v. over, *see* screen.
vein, *nāṛ,* f. (also sinew, artery): varicose v., *phullī hoī nāṛ.*
velvet, *makhmal,* f.
venerate, *mannṇā*: *see* honour.
vengeance, *see* revenge.
venomous, *zaihrī.*
ventilate, *būhe bārīā lāhṇīā, wā nū andar auṇ dēṇā*: *s.* sultry.
venture, *himmat karnī, dalērī karnī, haūslā karnā* (all *dā, dī*).

venturesome, *dalēr, bekhauf.*
veracity, *see* truth.
verandah, *barāṇḍā*, m.: on the v., *barāṇḍe icc.*
verb, *fehl*, m.
verbal-, -ly, *zabānī*: hear v. from him, *ohdī zabānī suṇṇā*: G. 37.
verbatim, *lafaz lafaz.*
verdant, *see* green, verdure.
verdigris, *ullī*, f. (*laggṇī, nū̃*).
verdure, *hariaul*, f., *harā*, m., *sabzī*, f.
verge, *see* edge: on the v. of doing, *see* about, almost, nearly.
verif-y, -ication, *tasdīk karnī* (caus. *karāṇī, dī*).
vermicelli, *warmselī*, f.: native, *sēwīā̃* (*waṭṭnīā̃*, make).
verse, of Bible or other sacred book *ait*, f.: *see* poem: of poetry, *wars*, m. (educ.).
very, *baṛā* (G. 34, never *waḍḍā*), *dāhdā, bauht, bāhlā, cokhā, bauhtā, tagṛā, pujjke, parle darje dā, sagō*: also *wāhwā* (used of good things alone); *see* emphasis.
vessel, domestic, *bhāṇḍā*, m., *bartan*, m.: *see* ship, boat.
vest (under-), *banyāṇ*, f., *banain*, f.: *see* waistcoat.
vestige, *see* trace.
veterinary, surgeon (native), *salōtrī.*
vex, *see* annoy, tease, angry, displeased.
viâ, *de rāh, hoke.*
viaduct, *pul*, m.
(1) vice, *burī ādat*, f.: *see* sin, evil, bad.
(2) vice, blacksmith's, *jamūr*, [m.
Viceroy, *mulkhī lāṭ* (also Lt.-Gov.), *waḍḍā lāṭ*. Lt.-Gov. is often *choṭā lāṭ.*
vicinity, *see* neighbourhood, near.
vicious, *see* bad, blackguard: of horse, *cak mārnwālā* (biter), *dulatte mārnwālā* (kicker).
victory, *jitt*, f., *fatāh*, f.
view, scene, *nazārā*, m.: *see* opinion.
vigil, *jagrātā* (*kaṭṭṇā, raihṇā*): *see* wake, sleeplessness.
vigilance, *hushyārī*, f., *khabardārī*, f: *see* care.
vigorous, *see* vigour.
vigour, *tākat*, f., *zōr*. m.: *see* power. strong.
vile, *makrūh*, *see* bad, unclean, dirty.
village, *piṇḍ*, m., *grā̃*, m.: large, *naggar*, m.
villager, *piṇḍ dā, pēṇḍū* (slightly contemptuous).
vindicate, *saccā sābit-k.*
vine, *dākh*, f., *angūr dī wēl* or *dā būṭā.*
vinegar, *sirkā*, m.
vineyard, *dākh dā bāg.*
violence, *see* oppression and add *dhakkeshāhī*, f.: by v. (physical or mental), *dhakke nāl, zore*: *see* confess, force.
violent, *see* violence, severe.
violet, flower, *binafshā*, m., *binashkā*, m.: colour, *kāshnī.*
virgin, *kuārī.*
virtue, *see* goodness.
virtuous, *nēk, pāk, bhalā lōk*: *see* good.
viscosity, *lēs*, f.
viscous, *lēslā.*
visible, to be, *dissṇā, nazrī paiṇā, labbhṇā, wakhālī dēṇī*: come into sight, *huṇ dissaṇ* (or other verb) *lagā* or *lagg peā*: cease to be v., *see* disappear and add *akkhīā̃ thī*

ohle hō jāṇā, nazrō ghuss jāṇā, chāī mārī hō jāṇā.

visit, *miḷṇ jāṇā* (*nū̃*), *mulākāt nū̃ jāṇā* (*dī*) : go away from home, *wāhṇḍā jāṇā* : v. holy place or person, *ohde didār* or *ohdī ziārat* (M.) or *ohde darshaṇ* (H.) *nū̃ jāṇā* : v. of inspection, often simply *phērā mārnā* : *see* inspect.

visitor, *mulākātī* : on a visit, *wāhṇḍā* : *see* guest.

vital, *nāzck thā̃* (v. place) : *see* important

viva voce, *zabānī*, *mū̃h zabānī*, *takrīrī* (U.).

vivid, of colour, *see* bright, colour.

vocabulary, *firist*, f., *see* dictionary.

voice, *awāz* or *wāz*, f. m. : *see* call, hoarse.

void, make, become, *see* abolish, cancel, repeal : fizzle out, *guggaḷ jāṇā*, *fisk hō jāṇā*.

volcano, *ātshī pahāṛ*, m., *agg wāḷā pahāṛ*, m.

volley, *wāṛ*, f. (firing).

volume, *jild*, f.

voluntarily, *apṇī marzī* or *khushī nāḷ*, *āpū̃*, *āpō*, *āpī*, *āpē*, *khushī razāī* : *see* gladly.

volunteer, v., use words for voluntarily w. *jāṇā*, go, etc. : n., *wālanṭīr*.

vomit, *ulṭī auṇī* (*nū̃*), *uttō suṭṭṇā*, *kai karnī* ; *jī utā̃ auṇā*, feel inclined to v. (*dā*), G. 117, M. 117. 7 : v. up, *ugaḷṇā*, *ugḷācṇā* : vomiting and diarrhoea, *haizā*, m. (*h.*, *nū̃*).

vote, n. and v., *rā dēṇī*, *wōṭ dēṇā*.

vow, n., *manl*, f., *nazr*, f. : make v., these words w. *mannṇī* : fulfil v., same w. *pūrī karnī*, *cāṛhnī*.

voyage, *samundar dā safar*, m.

vulgar, of person, *waihshī jehā*, *jaṭkā*, *kamīnā* : of word or thing, *ḍagg*, *jaṭkā*, *moṭā*.

W

waft, *uḍāke laijāṇā*.

wager, *see* bet.

wages, *tankhāh*, f. : of day labourer, *mazdūrī*, f. : each day's, *dihāṛī*, f.

wagon, *see* carriage, cart.

wail, *see* weep, mourn.

waist, *lakk*, m.

waistcoat, *phatūhī*, f., *salūkā*, m., *kuṛtī*, f., *wāskaṭ*, f.

wait, *uḍīkṇā*, *ṭhaihrnā*, *baihṇā* (sit), *khlōṇā* (stand) : w. for, *uḍīkṇā*, *uḍīk rakkhṇī* (*dī*), *rāh wekhṇā* (*dā*, look out for) : caus., *uḍīk karwāṇī*, or use *uḍīkṇā peā* : lie in w., *dhrumbhḷā hōke baihṇā* : w. at table, *khidmatgārī karnī* : *see* attend, serve : w. a bit, *khlō jā* : *see* waiting.

waiter, *khidmatgār*, m.

waiting for, n., *uḍīk*, f. : *see* wait.

wake, waken, v. int., *jāgṇā* : w. up, *nīndar uggharṇī* (*dī*), *jāg auṇī* (*nū̃*), *jāg uṭṭhṇā* : v. tr., *jagāṇā*, *uṭhāṇā* : to stay awake, *unīndrā raihṇā* (*nū̃*) : observe vigil, *see* vigil : to have just got up fr. sleep, *suttā peā uṭṭhṇā* : half-awake, *jāgo mīṭī*, *jāgo mīṭā*, *jāgo nūṭā*.

(1) walk, v., *turnā* : *see* go : go for w., *wā bhakhṇī*, *sair* or *sail karnā*, *sail sapaṭṭe jāṇā* : walking, on foot, *ṭur-*

dā, paidal: to w. a horse, *kadmī lāṇā* or *ṭōrnā* (*nū*).

(2) walk, n., style or rate of walking, *ṭōr*, f.: garden-w., *rāk*, m., *paṭṛī*, f.

walking-stick, *sōṭī*, f.: *see* stick.

wall, *kandh*, f.: *duāl*, f.: roofless, crumbling w., *khoḷā*, m.: w. of tent, *see* tent.

walnut, *khrōṭ*, m., *akhrōṭ*, m.: w. very thin shell, *kāgzī khrōṭ*.

wander, *bhaundeā raihṇā*, *awārā phirnā* (idle and useless, fem. *awārā*); *see* astray, stray: be knocked about, *see* knock.

wanderer, wandering, *see* nomad and add *pharautū*.

wane, *ghaṭṇā*: *see* lessen.

want, *see* desire, long for, lack: be wanting, *nā hōṇā*: for w. of, *khuṇō*, sometimes *bājhō*, *see* without.

war, *laṛāī*, f. (also battle): *lām*, m., expedition, (occ. f., *laggṇā*): *jaṅg*, m (U.): H. holy war, *judh*, m.; M., *jihād*, m.: civil w., use *āpe icc*, among themselves: go to the w., *lām icc jāṇā*.

wardrobe, *kapṛeā wāḷī almārī*, f.

warehouse, *gudām*, m., *māl gudām*, m.: *see* storeroom.

warm, *see* hot, tepid: w. oneself at fire, *agg sēkṇī*; in sun, *siyyā sēkṇā*, *dhupp sēkṇī*.

warn, *khabrdar-k.*: *see* tell, inform, caution.

(1) warp, v. int., of frame, bed, etc., *kāṇō pai jāṇī* (*nū*), *ḍiṅgā h.*: tr. *ḍiṅgā k.*: *see* twist, crooked, bend.

(2) warp, n., *see* loom.

warrant, for arrest, *waranṭ*, m. pl. (*kaḍḍhṇe*, *nikḷṇe*): authority, *see* authority: guarantee, *see* bail, responsible.

wart, kind of, *mohkā*, m.

wary, *hushyār*, *samajhdār*: *see* caution.

(1) wash, clothes, separate parts of body, things in gen., *dhōṇā* (int. *dhuppṇā*, *dhuccṇā*): *see* bathe: ceremonial, *see* ablution: *see* scrub, clean.

(2) washerman, *chīmbā*, *dhōbbā*, *dhōbbī*: fem. *chīmbī*, *dhōbbaṇ*.

(3) washing, single w., set of clothes for one w., *jugān*, f.

wasp, *dhamūṛī*, f.: long, thin, *ghuraiṇ*, f.: *see* hornet.

(1) waste, adj., gen., as w. paper, *raddī*; *see* useless, worthless: w. land, *ujāṛ*, m., *raṛā* (not used), *kallar*, *banjar* (both barren), *see* soil, barren, desert.

(2) waste, v., *see* squander, destroy, devastate, lose.

(1) watch, timepiece, *ghaṛī*, f.

(2) watch, v., *see* look, guard, wait, wake.

(3) watchful, *see* wary.

(4) watchmaker, *ghaṛīsāz*.

(5) watchman, *see* sentry, guardian; village w., *barwāḷā* (caste), *rabṭī* (lit. reporter), *caukīdār*.

(1) water, n., *pāṇī*, m.: in eyes, blister, etc., *pāṇī* (*paiṇā*): in food, *pāṇī*, *tarī*, f., *shōrā*, m. (soup), *lās*, m. (soup): *see* shove off.

(2) water, v. tr., land, *piāṇā* (int. *pīcṇā*), *chiññā*: w. basket by hand, *jhaṭṭā jhaṭṭṇā* or *chiññā* (the basket is *jhaṭṭā*, m.): *see* sprinkle; cattle,

larger animals, *pāṇī ḍāhṇā* (*nū*); human beings, smaller animals, *pāṇī piāṇā* or *dēṇā* (*nū*): also *pāṇī dassṇā* (animals); place for giving people water free as charity, *chabīl*, f. (*lāṇī*, int. *laggṇī*): land watered by rain (not irrigated), *barānī*; by well, *cāhī*; by canal, *naihrī*.

(3) water-carrier, M. *māshk-ī*, fem. *-aṇ*; caste, *mācch-ī*, fem. *-aṇ*: H. *jhiūr-*, fem. *-ī*.

(4) water-channel, -course, in fields, from canal, *khāḷ*, m. (*khāḷṇā*): v. small w., *āḍ*, f. (*kaḍḍhṇī*): drain, *see* drain.

(5) water-fowl, *see* dabchik, duck, etc., under heading "bird."

(6) watering-can, *phuhārā*, m.

(7) water-man, *see* water-carrier, sailor.

(8) water-melon, *see* melon.

(9) water-mill, *ghrāṭ*, m.: *see* mill.

(10) waterpot, *see* pot.

(11) waterproof (material), *barsātī*, f.: coat, *barsātī*, *brāṇḍī*, f.

(12) water-tax, *ābyānā*, m.

watery, gen. and food, *jihde wicc pāṇī baṛā e*: food, *patlā*: *see* damp, moisture, wet.

(1) wave, n., *ṭhallh*, f., *ṭhāṭh*, f.: v. small, *laihr*, f.

(2) wave, v. tr., *halāṇā*.

waver, *see* hesitate.

(1) wax, n., *mōm*, m.: sealing-w., *lākh*, f.: in ears, *kannā dī maiḷ*, f.

(2) wax-candle, *see* candle.

(3) wax-cloth, *mōmjāmā*, m.

way, actual and metaph., *rāh*, m.; *see* path, road: manner, *see* manner, method: half way, *adhwāṭe*: show the w., *see* guide: off the w., lose w., *see* astray, stray: by w. of the door, window, *būhe rāh*, *bārī rāh*; by w. of the house, well, *ghar*, *khūh de uttō dī*.

wayfarer, *rāhī*.

waylay, *see* wait, lie in.

we, *asī*: people like us, *hamātaṛ*, G. 28.

weak, gen. *māṛā*; *kamzōr*: of people, animals, *māṛā*, *lissā*: w. in character, *kaccā*, *gallā dā kaccā*, *see* vacillate: w. tea, *patlī*: heart become w or faint, *dil ḍubṇā* or *chapṇā* or *ghaṭṇā*.

weaken, words for weak w. *karnā*.

weal, on body, *laūs* or *lās* (*paiṇī*).

wealth, *daulat*, f., *māl*, m., *hasiat*, f., *dhan*, m.

wealthy, *see* rich.

wean, child, *duddh chuḍāṇā* (*dā*): from habit, fault, *chuḍāṇā*.

weapon, *hathyār*, m.

(1) wear: put on, *pāṇā*, *lāṇā*: he wears a waistcoat (is in the habit of putting on), *phatūhī pāndā hondā e*: is wearing trousers, has put on, *tambī pāī hoī e*; or *pāke lagā jāndā e*, etc.: put on, bed-clothes, shawl, etc., *utte laiṇā*: v. int., wear (well or badly), *hanḍhṇā*: tr. *hanḍhāṇā*, wear out or for certain time (only of things that one wears): *see* wear out.

(2) wear away, *see* rub.

(3) wear out, int., *hanḍh jāṇā*, tr., *hanḍhāṇā*, *hanḍhā chaḍḍṇā*: (n., *hanḍhepā*, m.), of non-wearable things, *purāṇā*

hōjāṇā : wear out a person w. words, *sir khapāṇā* (*dā*), *kann khāṇe* (*de*); int. *sir khappṇā* (*dā*) : *see* tire, weary.

wearisome, *thakāṇwāḷā*, *akāṇwāḷā*, *see* weary, tire, sick of.

weary, *thakkā hoeā* : *see* tire, sick of.

weather, no word, *see* climate, season, spring, summer, autumn, winter, rain : fine w., *kharā*, after rain, *wānd laggṇī*, *nimbaḷ h.*, *kharā ho jāṇā*, *ṭarakkā laggṇā*.

weave, *uṇṇā*, *khaḍḍī uṇṇī* : *see* loom.

weaver, *julāh-*, fem.-*ī*.

web, **cobweb**, *jāḷā*, m.

wed, **wedding**, *see* marriage, marry.

wedge, *phaṇṇā*, m., *cappar*, f.

Wednesday, *buddh*, m., *buddhwār*, m.

weed, v. tr., *gōḍḍī karnī*, *gōḍṇā* : n., *būṭī*, f., *jāṅgḷī būṭī*. Names of common weeds :—

(i) occasionally eaten : *bughāṭ*, m., *jaūsāg*, m., *maināā*, m., *maiṇī*, f., *mrikkaṇ*, f., *papoḷī*, f., *saūcaḷ* f.

(ii) not eaten : *āthū bāthū*, m., *billī būṭī*. f., *dodhak*, f., *katittan*, f. (dock-leaf), *lēlhī* f., *madhrāṇī*, f., *naṛī dodhak*, f.

week, *haftā*, m., *aṭṭh din*, m. pl., *athwārā*, m (rare) : next w., *agle hafte* : last w , *pishle hafte* : this day next or last w , *ajj dā dihāṛā*, *ajōkā dihāṛā* : tomorrow w., *bhaḷak de dīhāṛe*. A.

weekly, adv. *atthwē de atthwē dihāṛe* or *din*, *aṭṭhī dinī*, *aṭṭhī dī aṭṭhī dinī* : adj., use adv., also *haftewār* (U.).

weep, *rōṇā*, *atthrū wagāṇīā*, *karlāṇā* (gen. aloud) : slightly, *atthrū wagṇīā* (*dīā*) : sadness, almost crying, *gacc* (*auṇā*, *nū̃*) : w. for person or thing, *rōṇā* (*nū̃*).

(1) **weigh**, *tōlṇā* (int. *tulṇā*) : estimate weight by lifting, *hāṛnā*, *jācṇā* : w. anchor, *cukkṇā* : metaph., *see* consider, think.

(2) **weighing-machine**, at railway station, *kaṇḍā* : *see* scales.

weight, *bhār*, m., *wazn*, m. : weight too much forward, *dābū*, m. : too much back, *ulār*, m. : weight for scales, *waṭṭā*, m. ; two-ser w., *dusērī*, f., *waṭṭī*, f. : weights and measures, *see* A.

welcome, v., *wēkhke khush h.*, *mhabbat* or *khushī nāḷ milṇā* (*nū̃*) : welcome! *jī āeā nū̃*, *see* means, gladly, willingly.

welfare, *khair*, f., *khariat*, f., *sukkh sāṇd*, m. (ask after, *pucchṇ-ā*, *-ī*) : *see* health, healthy, well (2).

(1) **well**, n., for irrigation, *khūh*, m. : for drawing water, no Persian wheel, *khūhī*, f. : deserted w , *ḍall*, f. : w. steps down, *baolī*, f. : the chief parts of a w. are vertical cogged wheel, *ḍhōl*, m. : horizontal do., *carhakḷī*, f., *cuhakḷī*, f : wheel w. pots, *baiṛ*, m. : pole through last two, *laṭṭh*, f. : earthen wall, *cannā*, m. : pole across above, *kāṇan*, f. : rope for pots, *māhl*, f. : pot, *ṭiṇḍ*, f. : ox-walk, *paḍāṇā*, *purāṇā*, m. : hand-pulley, *carakhṛī*, f. : work w. *wāhṇā* (int.

wagnā): turn by hand, *gēṛnā* (int. *giṛnā*).

(2) well, adv., *caṅgī* or *acchī* or *wall tarhā̃ nāḷ*: adj., in good health, *wall*, *caṅgā bhalā*, *rāzī*, *caṅgā*: *see* welfare, health, healthy: all's well, *khair e*, *khair mehr e*: all being well, e.g. where are you going, all being (I hope) well? *kitthe khair nāḷ* or *khairī mehrī* (H. *sukkh nāḷ*) *caleā ẽ*? well done! *see* bravo: v. well, all right, *halā*, *caṅgā*, *acchā*.

(3) well, particle of reasoning, *khair*, *whalā*.

well-bred, *see* courteous, polite.

well-dressed, use *acche kapṛe*, m. pl.: *see* fop.

well-known, *mashāhūr*: *see* common, famous.

well-meaning, *nēknīyyat*.

well-wisher, *khairkhāh*.

west, *laihndā*, *laihndā pāsā*: westwards, *laihnde*, *laihnde wall* or *pāse*.

wet, adj., *wattreā hoeā*, *see* damp, moisture: v. tr., *bheõṇā* (int. *bhijjṇā*).

wet nurse, no word, use *duddh piāṇwāḷī*, etc.: occ *dāī*.

wharf, *ghāṭ*, m.: *bandargāh*, f. (harbour).

what, *kī*: (obl. *kāh*, *kās*): what if (depreciatory), lest, *mate*, *cētā*, *par je*: but what, *kī par*: what else (often means why not), *te hōr*.

whatever, *jō kujjh*.

wheat, *kanak*, f.: different kinds, *dāgar* f., *nikkī kaṇak*, f., *waḍāṇāk*, f., *kaṇkū*, m.: *see* grain.

wheedle, *dhokhā dēke manāṇā*, *gallā̃ icc phasāke manāṇā* *see* coax.

wheel, *piñ*, m., *pahīā*, m., *cakkā*, m.: Persian w., *see* well, w.-barrow, *reṛhī*, f.

when, *jad*, *jadõ*, *jis weḷe*, *jis ghaṛī*: inter. *kadõ*, *kad*.

whence, inter. *kitthõ*: rel. *jitthõ*.

whenever, *jad kadī*, *bhāwē kadõ*.

where, inter. *kitthe*: motion to, *kitthe*, *kittal*, *kiddhar*: rel. *jitthe*, *ji'tal*, *jiddhar*.

wherever, *jitthe kite*, *bhāwē jitthe*.

whet, whetstone, *see* sharpen, grindstone: metaph., *wadhāṇā*.

whether, conj., *pai*: w. . . . or, *bhāwē* . . . *bhāwē*, *cāhe* . . . *cāhe*.

which? *kehṛā*? which, *jehṛā*.

while; repetition of infl. pres. part.: w. walking, *ṭurdeā ṭurdeā*. G. 80: w. going, returning, *jāndī wārī*, *partdī wārī*, M. 239. 22; 268. 17: while or upon; upon arrival, *appaṛdeā sār*, G. 91, *appaṛdeā ī*, M. 273. 40, 41 (and so w. other verbs): cf. *lō laggdeā*, while it was getting light; *lo hondeā*, while it was light: *see* when.

whimper, *ū̃ ū̃ karnī*, *see* groan.

whine, *see* whimper.

whip, lash, *traṭṭ*, m., *chāṭ*, m.: wooden part, *parāṇī*, f.: English w., *cābak*, m.: v. tr., these words w. *mārnā*, *nū̃*: *see* bea flog, strike: w. cream, beat eggs, etc., *phēnṭnā*.

whirlpool, *cakkī* f., *ghummaṇghēr*, m.

whirlwind, *wā warōḷā*, m.

whisper, no real word: *kann*

icc ākhṇā: *koī kuskeā wī nehī*, no one even whispered.
whistle, *sīṭī* (*mārnī*). both the sound and the instrument.
white, *ciṭṭā*, *baggā*, *safēd*: whitish, *see* somewhat: w. of egg, *safēdī*, f.: w. hair, *see* hair: w. and black, *see* A.
whitewash, *safēdī*, f. (*karnī*): brush for w.-ing, *kūcī*, f. (*phērnī*).
whither, *see* where.
whitlow, *phimmhṇī*, f.: *see* boil (1).
who, *kauṇ*, obl. *kih-*, *kis-*.
whoever, *jehṛā koī*, *jō koī*.
whole, unbroken, *sābat*, *sābat sabūt*: all, *see* all, complete.
wholesale (sell), *katthā* (*wēcṇā*); *thōk* (U., *wēcṇā*): retail, *parcūṇ* (*wēcṇā*).
wholesome, *see* good, advantageous, profit.
wholly, *bilkul*, *see* altogether.
whooping-cough, *kāḷī khangh*, f. (*h*, *nū*).
why, *kāhnū*, *kāhde jogā*, *kāhde laī*, *kāhde wāste*, *kyū*, *kis karke*, *kehṛī galle*.
wick, *battī*, f. (also lamp)
wicked, *see* bad, blackguard, sinner, and add *ucakkā* (especially robber).
wickedness, *see* badness, evil, sin, and add *sharārat*, f.
wide, *cauṛā*, *caiṛā*, *mōktā*.
widow, *ranḍī*, *bewā* (villagers use former).
widower, *ranḍā*.
width. *cuṛāī*, f., *pēṭ*, m.: of cloth, *bar*, m.
wife; *wauhṭī*, *suāṇī*, *ṭabbar*, m., (*mēre*, etc. *gharō̃*); *zanānī*, *bīwī* (w. educated people first three uncommon); sometimes *wāsf*, wife: co-wife, *saukaṇ*. Note that *ṭabbar* (lit. family) is masc.
wild, *waihshī*, *jānglī*: of plants, animals, *jānglī*.
wilderness, *see* desert (1), wood, forest.
wilful-, -ness, *see* obstina-te, [-cy.
will, n. (written), *wasīatnāmā*, m.: *see* bequeath, inheritance.
willing, *rāzī*, *mannaṇwāḷā*.
willingly, *khushī nāḷ*, *see* voluntarily: by all means, *see* means.
willingness, *razā*, f., *khushī*, f.: *see* pleasure.
win, *jittṇā*: game, *see* game.
wince, *see* flinch.
(1) wind, *wā*, f., *hawā*, f.: east w., *purā*, m., west, *pacchō̃*, f.: hot summer w., *lō*, f.: blow, of w., *wagṇā*: in the w., open air, *waule*: absence of w., *see* sultriness: strong w., *see* storm; contrary w., *wā sāhmṇī e*: favouring w., *wā picche we*.
(2) wind, watch, clock, v. tr., *cābī* or *kunjī dēṇī* (*nū*): twist, *see* twist.
winding-sheet, *khapphaṇ*, m.
window, *bārī*, f.: through the w., *bārī rāh*: *see* open, shut.
wine, *sharāb*, m., *dārū*, m. (both any wine or spirit, latter also medicine), *nashā*, m. (any intoxicant).
wing, *par*, m.
winged, *parāwāḷā*.
wink, *akkh mārnī*.
winnow, in open fields, *uḍāṇā*: with basket in hand, *chaṭṭṇā*: winnowing, *uḍāiā*, f. pl.: winnowing basket, *chajj*, m.: *see* sift.
winter, *siāḷ*, m., *pōh māh*, m.

wipe, *pūnjhṇā*.

wire, *tār*, f.: wire gauze or netting, *jāḷī*, f.

wisdom, *danāī*, f., *akl*, f. m., *siāṇap*, f.: *see* sense, intelligen-ce, -t, understanding, philosophy.

wise, *danā*, *aklwāḷā*, *siāṇā*: *see* wisdom, clever.

wish, *see* desire.

wits, *see* wisdom, sense.

witch, *cuṛel*, *ḍaiṇ*, *jādūgarnī*.

with, along with, *nāḷ*, *sane sang*, *see* together: instrument, *nāḷ*; for parts of body existing in pairs, loc. plur., as *akkhī*, *kannī*.

wither, plants. etc., *kurmāṇā*, *kumlāṇā*.

within, *see* in.

without, *bin*, *binā*, *de binā*, *tō binā*, *bājhō de bājhō*, *bagair*, *de bagair*, *khuṇō*: do without, *see* do.

witness, person, *guāh*, *see* eye-witness: from hearsay, use *suṇī suṇāī gall*: evidence, *see* evidence.

wizard, *see* magician.

wobble, *ḍōlṇā* (tr. *ḍulāṇā*): *see* vacillate, changeable, back out, shake.

wolf, *bhageāṛ-*, fem. *-ī*.

woman, *zanānī*, *janānī*, *buḍḍhī* (married, of any age), *aurat*: "womankind," *khodā mhaiṇ*, m. (slightly jocular): my good woman, *whaī*, M. 130. 32: G. 125: adj. *zanānā*, as *zanānī gaḍḍī*, carriage for women only: *zanānā kamm*, women's work.

womanish, *zanānī tabīat dā*.

womb, *kukkh* f., *dharn*, f., *rehm*, m. (U., all uncommon). *ḍhiḍḍh*, m., *pēṭ*, m., both meaning stomach, may be used.

wonder, feeling of, *see* astonish-, -ment: wonderful thing, *tajjab dī gall*, *harānī dī gall*: I w. if he'll come, *patā nehī khabre āwe ke nā*, *wēkhīye āwe ke nā*.

wonderful, *ajaib*, *acarj*, *anōkhā*: *see* strange.

wood, gen., *lakkaṛ*, f, *lakṛī*, f., *kāṭh*, m.: firewood, *bālaṇ*, m.: heap of for sale, *ṭāl*, m.: piece of split firewood, *phāṅg*, f. (*k*.), out across, *mochā*, m. (*pāṇā*); any piece, *ṭōṭṭā*, m.: *see* log, beam: saw w., *cirnā*, *see* chop: lot of trees, *see* forest, copse: forest of dhak trees, *ḍhakkī*, f., *see* dhak: wood and grass land near river, *bēllā*, m.

wood-boring insect, *ghuṇ*, m.

wooded, use *baṛe rukkh ne*.

wooden, *lakkaṛ dā*, *kāṭh dā*.

woof, *see* loom.

wool, *unn*, f.: soft hair or fur, *jatt*, f.: silky w., *pashmīnā*, m.

(1) woolly, *unn dā*: *pashmīne dā*, of silky wool.

(2) woolly insect, destroys clothes, *lehā*, m.

word, single word *lafaz*, m., *lafs*, m.: phrase, matter, thing, speech, *gall*, f.: one's w., promise, *see* promise and add *kalām*, f. m., *kaul karār*, m.: Word of God, *Khudā dī Kalām*: w. by w., *see* verbatim, literal: a few words, written, *dō cār harf*; of conversation, *see* converse.

(1) work, n. *kamm*, m., *kamm dhandā*, m. *kamm kāj*, m.: literary w., use *kitāb*, f.,

book; *rasālā*, m., pamphlet, etc.: work involved in message, *see* message: w. turn up to be done, *kamm paiṇā* (*nū*), M. 125. 6: G. 120: w. go on, *calṇā*, *ṭurnā* (tr. *calāṇā*, *ṭōrnā*) M. 126. 29: out of w., *see* unoccupied: leave off w., *see* leave: permanent w., *see* permanent in A.

(2) work, v., *kamm karnā*, *kamm kāj*, *kamm dhandā karnā*: literary, *likhṇā*: finish work badly, w. carelessly, *traṅgaṛnā*: he has begun working, is at work, *oh kamm lagg peā e*: work out at per rupee, maund, etc., *baihṇā*, M. 117. 12, 14: G. 117: work, be working, of machine, etc., *calṇā*, *ṭurnā*; of well, *wagṇā*.

workman, skilled, mason, builder, etc., *rāj*: unskilled, *kulī*, *mazdūr*: paid by day, *dihāṛīdār*: *see* labourer, servant, clever.

workmanship, *kamm*, m., *kārīgarī*, f., *banāwaṭ*, f.

workshop, *kārkhānā*, m.

world, earth and people, *dunyā*, f., *jahān*, m.: H. sometimes *jagat*, m., *jagg*, m.: the earth, *dunyā*, f., *zamīn*, f., H. *dhartī*, f.: the next w., *aglā jahān*, *parlōk*, m. (H.): *aglā jagg* (H.): *see* heaven.

worldly, *dunyāwī*, *dunyā dā*.

worm, *kīṛā*, m.: blindworm, slow-worm, *dumūhī*, f.: *see* ant, snake.

worry, worried *see* annoy, angry, bore, displease, tease, trouble, inconvenience, difficulty, straits.

worship, Christian, *bandgī karnī*, *duā bandgī karnī*, *girjā karnā*, *duā namāz karnī* (of officiating person, *karāṇī*, *karāṇā*), occ. *namāz paṛhnī*: H. and M., *see* pray: *pūjā karnī* (*dī*), w. idols.

worshipper, use words for worship w. ending *-wāḷā*, or paraphrase: *pujār-ī*, fem. *-an*, worshipper of idols.

worth, *see* value, cost.

worthless, *see* useless and add (things) *bakār*, *bakārā*, *nikammā*, *kujjh nehī*: matter, words, *see* nonsense: persons, *raddī*, *kucajjā* or *becajjā* (doing things badly), *nighreā hoeā*, *nāmurād*, *bēhadzitā* (rather strong word): *see* bad, etc.

worthy, man, *bhalāmāṇas*, fem. *bhalīmāṇas*, *see* deserve, right.

would that, use *Khudā kare paī*; *kadī kare* (*kare ā*, *kardā*) *kehī sohṇī gall howe* (*howe ā*, *hondī*), what a good thing, if he does it, did it or were to do it: M. 270. 36, 37.

wound, *phaṭṭ*, m., *zakhm*, m.: blow, *saṭṭ*, f: v. tr. use beat, strike, etc.. *ohde lāṇ* or *mārn nāḷ phaṭṭeā geā* or *zakhm hoea*: be w., *phaṭṭeā jāṇā*, *zakhm h.* (*nū*), w. the feelings, *dil dukhāṇā*: *see* grieve.

wrap, *waḷhēṭṇā*: *see* fold.

wrath, *see* anger.

wreak, *see* revenge.

wreck, of ship, *ṭuṭṭṇā*, *ṭakkar wajjī te ṭuṭṭ geā*: *see* ruin, destroy, downfall.

wrestle, *ghuḷṇā*: wrestling match, *ghōḷ*, m.

wrestler, *ghuḷāṭīā*, *palwhāṇ*.

wretch, *kambakht*: *see* bad, wicked.

wretched, *see* poor, straits.

wring, out water, etc., *nacoṛnā*: twist round, *maroṛnā*: *see* squeeze.

wrinkle, in face, *jhuṛī* (*paiṇī*); gen. plur.: *see* crease, fold, frown.

wrist, *guṭṭ*, m.: w. and forearm, *wīṇī*, f.

writ, *samman*, m.

(1) **write**, *likhṇā*: enter in book, *likhṇā*, *darj-k.*: *see* calligraph-y, -ist, copyist.

(2) **writer**, *see* author, clerk, copyist: petition-writer, *arzī nawīs*: appeal-w., *apīl nawīs*.

(3) **writing**, handwriting, *khatt*, m.: act or price of w., *lakhāī*, f.

wrong, adj., *galt*: *see* bad.
v., *hakk mārnā* (*dā*), *see* damage. [loss.
n., *see* damage, injure,

wrongfully, *nahakk*, *dhigāṇe*, *befaidā*, *ẽwẽ*.

Y

(1) **yard**, length, *gaz*, m.: *see* wts. and meas. A: a yard measure, *gaz*, m.

(2) **yard**, *see* courtyard.

yawn, *ubāsī laiṇī*, M. 122. 35 · *ubāsī auṇī* (*nū̃*), M. 117. 5.

year, *warhā*, m., *sāl*, m.: of era, *san* m.: every y., *sāl de sāl*, *warhe de warhe*, *warhe dinī* (G. 78), *har sāl*: in a y., *warhe dinī*, *warhe nū̃*, *sāl nū̃*, *warhe din icc*: next y., *aunde sāl*: last year, *par*, *parū̃*, *par de sāl*, *parõke sāl*: y. before last, *parār*.

yearly, *sālānnā*, adj., *see* year.

yearn, *see* long (2).

yeast, *khamīr*, m.: *see* rennet.

yell, *see* scream, shout.

yellow, *pīḷā*: pale y., *khaṭṭā*: dark, *see* orange: of egg, *see* yolk: yellowish, *see* somewhat.

yes, answering question, *āho*, *ākho*, *āh*, *hā̃*: answering call, *hā̃*: G. 93, 94.

yesterday, *kall* (never *bhaḷke*): day before y., *parsõ*: day before that, *cauth*: fifth day, *panjauth*: sixth, *cheauth*: seventh, eighth *see* week, tomorrow: *satwẽ*, *aṭṭhwẽ dihāṛe* or *din*, etc., are also used.

yet, *see* still (1), besides.

yield, *see* give in, surrender: owing to threat, *dabb jāṇā*: n., *see* produce.

yoke, n., *panjāḷī*, f.: v., *jõṇā*, *jõtṇā* (int. *juppṇā*, *juttṇā*), *haḷ jõṇā* (for ploughing).

yolk, of egg, *zardī*, f.

you, *tū̃*, *tusī*: acc. *tenū̃*, *tuhānū̃*: your, *terā*, *tuhāḍḍā*: for acc., and your, also pronom. suff. (sing.), *ū̃*, *-ī*, *-ā*, *-ī*: (plur.), *je*: G, 82–6.

young, *thoṛī umr dā*, *nikkā*, *chõṭā*: the y. of anything, *baccā*, m.: *see* child: y. man, *gabhrū*, *juān*: y. woman, *muṭeār*, *juān aurat*.

youth, state of, *juānī*, f.

Z

zeal, *sargarmī*, f., *jõsh*, m.

zealous, *sargarm*, *joshwāḷā*.

zero, figure, *sifar*, m.

zest, *shauk*, m. (desire, keenness,): *suād*, m., *mazā*, m. (both taste): *see* taste.

zinc, *jist*, m.

zoological gardens, *ciṛīā ghar*, m.

APPENDIX I.

ADDITIONS TO PANJABI MANUAL: Second Part, Grammar.

GENDER.

p. 1. To words both masculine and feminine add the following:—

lām, expedition, war.
kadr, value.
kiās, opinion.
manshā, intention.
taih, fold.
Panjāb, the Panjab.

awāz, *wāz*, voice, sound is fem. except in the expression *wāz bhārā hōṇā (dā)*, become hoarse.

Note.—sarkār, meaning either the Government or "your honour," is always fem. sing.; *hazūr*, your honour, is generally masc. plur., but villagers sometimes make it fem. sing; *ādmī*, occasionally used for wife, woman, and *waihtar*, beast of burden, are masc.; *mukāṇ*, mourners or mourning, is fem.

p. 2, paragraph (3). Gender different from Urdu: omit *magz*, which is masc. and means intelligence: add

sharāb, m., wine, spirit.
fasl, m., harvest.
Urdū, m., Urdu.
gār, f., cave.
jaṅg, m., war.
lām, gen. m., war, expedition.
gūnd, f., gum.
takrār, m., fuss, quarrel.

p. 10, paragraph (4). Add *fajrī* or *fajrī*, in the morning: *ḍīgarī* or *ḍīgarī*, in the afternoon.

After the word *Bāgṛīē* read "and adjectives in agreement, which would have ended in -ī, also change to -īē." For *cāḷīē*, *cāḷī*, read *cāhḷīē*, *cāhḷī*.

p 11, paragraph (2). Vocative: instead of the first four lines read "A feminine in the sing. generally makes the vocative by adding -*e*."

p. 15. Doublets. Many other examples will be found in the vocabulary.

p. 16. The genitive prep. *dā* always has *dī* for the loc. plur. See p. 9 of Grammar.

sabbh: one sometimes hears *hamhnū acchā* for *sabbhnā tō acchā*, *habbhe weḷe* for *sabbhe weḷe*, and *samhnā*, *samhnī*, for *sabbhnā*, *sabbhnī*.

p. 22. Ordinals, see also note on p. 123. The tonic h is omitted in 60, 80 and by some people in 79, 81–8.

p. 27, line 19 read:—*hōr*, other, has *horī* or *hōr* in the sing. oblique.

p. 34. *baṛā* and *waḍḍā*. *waḍḍā* means big in size, great in age or dignity.

VERBS.

p. 43. Add (see also causal verbs near end of App. I.).

udhaṛnā, be ripped (sewing, etc.), *udhēṛnā*, rip.

ukkhaṛnā, get loose, come to pieces, of machinery, masonry, *ukhēṛnā*, loosen, etc.

uggharnā, be collected, of money, *ugrāhṇā*, collect.

wagṇā, *wagṇā*, flow, *wagāṇā*, cause to flow, etc.

wagṇā, *wagṇā*, be ploughed, be worked, of well or cattle, *wāhṇā*, plough, etc.

With *bajjhṇā*, be fastened, imprisoned, *bannhṇā*, tie, cf. *wajjṇā*, be struck, etc., *wajāṇā*, strike, etc.

Infinitive: after *l*, *lh*, the ending is *-ṇā* if the accent is on the last syllable of the root, otherwise it is *-nā*, as

kholhnā. open: *ḍōlṇā*, wobble, shake: *ḍulhṇā*, be spilt, but *badalnā* change.

p. 48. Add *rōṇā*, weep, pa. p. *runnā*, *roeā*.

dhōṇā, wash, pa. p. *dhōttā*.

With *gunnhṇā*, knead, pa. p. *guddhā*, compare *gundṇā*, plait, pa. p. *gundeā*.

p. 50. Imperative, plur. also *takkeā je*. This form *must* have *je*.

p. 52, line 2. *kardīē* or *kardī*.

line 6, *kardīo* is correct; omit note on p. 126.

p. 59, line 8: passive part. *dasseā hoeā*, or in Siāḷkōṭ and Jammū *dasseādā*, see p. 49, lines 6–9.

p. 62, last line but two. *tū dassdī* or *dassdīē*.

„ last line but one. *dassdīo* is correct; omit note on p. 126.

p. 65, (1). Emphasis or thoroughness: add " or completeness.

Habit.

p. 69 first line. After (i), add *karnā* :

,, under (ii) read :—*hōṇā*, tenses formed from the present part. ; both verbs in the same tense, the verb substantive (auxiliary verb) when it occurs, inserted only once.

To the examples add—

maĩ wehnnā honnā wā̃. I am in the habit of looking.

Note.—The idea of habit may be expressed also by means of *gijjhṇā* or *hiḷṇā*, to get accustomed :

oh iṭṭā̃ ḍhōṇ gijjhā̃ hoeā e or *hiḷeā hoeā e*, he is accustomed to carrying bricks, he has got used to it, is in the habit of doing it.

jāṇā, go.

p. 70. Paragraphs (2) and (3) may perhaps be better expressed thus :—(2) when *jāṇā* is used with the root of intransitive verbs to express completeness it does not add the idea of "going," but the idea may be inherent in the root itself.

Exception : *uṭṭh jāṇā*, go away, move to another house or city.

(3) With transitive verbs *jāṇā* adds the idea of "going."

Exceptions : *samajh jāṇā*, understand : *pī jāṇā*, drink up or drink and go.

The Repetition of Words, p. 71.

Another meaning expressed by repetition is that of the English word "nice" in phrases like "nice and fresh," "nice and warm", always something agreeable.

pāṇī leā, ṭhaṇḍā ṭhā̃ṇḍā leā,	bring water, bring it nice and cool.
ṭhaṇḍī ṭhaṇḍī wā wagdī e,	a nice, cool breeze is blowing.
sajrī sajrī malāī,	nice, fresh cream.
tatte tatte cauḷ,	nice, hot rice.
jhaw jhaw ā,	come (nice and) soon.

It will be noticed that in this connection it never has a bad meaning.

p. 74, last line. Instead of *phaṛāī dittī* we may have *phaṛā dittā* with the accent on the first syllable of *phaṛā*. This must be distinguished from *phaṛā dittā* with the accent on the second syllable which is the causal of *phaṛnā*, seize.

saṇḍhe phaṛā nehī dittā (accent on *phaṛ*),	the buffalo did not allow itself to be caught.
os saṇḍhā phaṛā dittā (accent on *ṛā*),	he caused the buffalo to be caught.

The first *phaṛā* is a noun, meaning catching, the second a verb.

Locative Case, p. 78.

The use of the loc. to indicate instrument or means appears to be confined to those parts of the body which are found in pairs.

goḍī arkī riṛhdā sī peā,	he was crawling on knees and elbows.
akkhī ḍitthā te kannī suṇeā,	he saw with his eyes and heard with his ears.
hatthī cukkeā,	he lifted it with his hands.

p. 82. *Horī* may also suggest the family a person serves, as *Jhaṇḍe horā̃ diā̃ pleṭā̃*, the plates of Jhanda's master. For *horī*, *horā̃*, some people say *warī*, *warā̃*.

Pronominal Suffixes, pp. 82–6.

To avoid confusion it should be remembered that, while these suffixes never indicate the nominative case, they do indicate the agent case, which Europeans often think of as the nominative. As the use of the suffixes is always found difficult it will be well to give the conjugation of the whole verb with the suffixes attached. Some parts do not usually take a suffix, but usage on this point is not invariable.

With Auxiliary Verb or Verb Substantive.

Examples :—

maĩ sajjaṇ ū̃?	I ask thee, am I a friend?
maĩ sajjaṇ sū,	I am his friend.
tū̃ naṇā̃n sū?	art thou her sister-in-law?
asī̃ jhalle ū̃,	I tell thee we are mad.

Present Tense.

Person.	*Possible suffixes.* SINGULAR.	*Possible suffixes.* PLURAL.
First ..	(*maĩ*) *ū̃*, *je*, *sū*, *ne*,	(*asī̃*) *ū̃*, *je*, *sū*, *ne*.
Second ..	(*tū̃*) *sū*, *ne*,	(*tusī̃*) *sū*, *ne*.
Third ..	(*oh*) *ī* (or *ā̃*), *je*, *sū*, *ne*,	(*oh*) *nī*, *je*, *sū*, *ne*.

Emphatic :—

First ..	*hai ū, je,*	*hai ū, je.*
Second..	none,	none.
Third ...	*hai ī, je, sū, ne,*	*haiṇ nī, je, sū, ne.*

Past Tense.

First ..	(*maĩ*) *sāje, sāsū, sāṇe,*	(*asī*) *sāje, sāsū, sāṇe.*
Second..	*tū*, none,	*tusī*, none.
Third ..	(*oh*) *sāī, sāje. sāsū, sāṇe,*	(*oh*) *sāṇī, sāje, sāsū, sāṇe.*

WITH TRANSITIVE VERBS.

Suffixes with *dassṇā*, show.

Imperative.

tū dass or *dassī sū, ne,*   *tusī dasso* or *dasseo sū, ne.*

Present Conditional, I may show, etc.

maĩ dassū, dassā je, sū, ne,	*asī dassiye je, sū, ne* (not *ū*).
tū dassẽ sū, ne,	*tusī dasso sū, ne.*
oh dassī, dasse je, sū, ne,	*oh dassaṇ ī, je, sū, ne.*

Future, I shall show.

maĩ dassā-gā (fem. *-gī*) *je, sū, ne* : also *dassū-gā* (fem. *-gī*), *dassje-gā* (f. *-gī*).

tū dassẽ-gā (f. *-gī*) *sū, ne.*

oh dasse-gā (f. *-gī*) *je, sū, ne* : *dassīgā, dassjegā, dasssūgā, dassṇẽ-gā* (f. *-gī*).

asī dassāge je, su, ne (f. *-giā*) : *dassūge, dassjege* (f. *-giā*).

tusī dassoge sū, ne (f. *-giā*).

oh dassange je. sū. ne (f. *-giā*) : *dassṇīge. dassjege, dasssūge, dassṇẽge* (f. *-giā*).

The future may also end in *-dā, -dī, -de, -diā.*

Past Conditional, I should show, if I showed, etc.

Suffixes are used only with the *-o* forms : see Grammar, pp. 104–7.

maĩ dass-do (f. *-dīo*) *ī, je, sū, ne.*
tū dass-dõ (f. *-dīõ*) *sū, ne.*
oh dass-do (f. *-dīo*) *ī, je, sū, ne.*
asī, none.
tusī dass-deo (f. *-dīo*) *sū, ne.*
oh dass-dẽo (f. *-dīõ*) *nī. je, sū. ne.*

Present Indicative, I am showing, I show.

maĩ dass-nā ũ, dass-dā je, sū, ne : f. *-nī ũ, -dī je, sū, ne.*
tū̃ dass-dā sū, ne : f. *-dī sū, ne.*
oh dass dā ī, je, sū, ne : f. *-dī ā, je, sū, ne.*

Imperfect.

maĩ dass-dā (f. *-dī*) *sāje, sāsū, sāṇe.*
tū̃ dassdā sāsū : f. *dassdī sāsū.*
oh dass-dā (f. *-dī*) *sāĩ, sāje, sāsū, sāṇe.*
asī̃ dass-de (f. *-dīā̃*) *sāje, sāsū, sāṇe.*
tusī̃ dass-de (f. *-dīā̃*) *sāsū, sāṇe.*
oh dass-de (f. *-dīā̃*) *sāṇī, sāje, sāsū, sāṇe.*

In the past indefinite, present perfect, pluperfect and future perfect of transitive verbs, tenses in which the passive participle is used, agreement is with the logical object (except, of course, where agreement is blocked by *nū̃*), and the use of pronom. suff. is generally confined to the 3rd sing. and plur. suffixes to indicate the agent. Occasionally the 2nd sing. and plur. suffixes are used when the logical nominative is *maĩ* or *asā̃* to express the idea "I am (or we are) speaking to thee" or "you."

Note.—To express the simple past with a suffix we must use the *-o* form or the pluperfect. The ordinary past if followed by a suffix, has the force of a present perfect.

Present Perfect.

The following cases therefore arise :—

maĩ ṭukkar khādhā ī (*je*),	I tell thee (you) that I have eaten my food.
maĩ roṭī khādhī ā (*je*),	I tell thee (you) I have eaten bread.
maĩ dō paraunthe khādhe nī (*je*),	. . . . two chapatis (masc.).
maĩ dō roṭīā̃ khādhīā̃ nī (*je*),	. . . . two chapatis (fem.).

Instead of *maĩ* we may have *asā̃*, we.

ṭukkar khādhā sū (*ne*),	he has (they have) eaten food.
roṭī khādhī sū (*ne*),	. . . . bread.
dō paunthe khādhe sū (*ne*),	. . . . two chapatis (masc.).
dō roṭīā̃ khādhīā̃ sū (*ne*),	. . . . two chapatis (fem.)

For the simple past use *-o* forms or pluperfect, *ṭukkar khādho sū* (*ne*), he (they) ate food : *roṭī khādhīo sū* (*ne*), he (they) ate bread.

Pluperfect (also means simple past).

The above sentences will become—

maĩ or *asā̃ khādhā sāi* (*sāje*),	I etc. ate or had eaten.
maĩ or *asā̃ khādhī sāi* (*sāje*),	do. do.
maĩ or *asā̃ khādhe sāṇī* (*sāje*),	do. do.
maĩ or *asā̃ khādhīā̃ sāṇī* (*sāje*),	do. do.
khādhā (fem. *khādhī*) *sāsū* or *sāṇe*,	he (they) ate or had eaten.
khādhe (f. *khādhīā̃*) *sāsū* or *sāṇe*,	do. do.

Future Perfect.

maĩ khādhā howīgā (*hojegā*),	I tell thee (you) that I shall have eaten.
maĩ khādhī howīgī (*hojegī*),	do. with fem. sing. object.
maĩ khādhe hoṇīge (*hojege*),	do with masc. plur. object.
maĩ khādhīā̃ hoṇīgīā̃ (*hojegīā̃*),	do. with fem. plur. object.

So also with *asā̃*, we.

khādhā hosūgā (*hoṇegā*),	he (they) will have eaten.
khādhī hosūgī (*hoṇegī*),	do. fem. sing. object.
khādhe hosūge (*hoṇēge*),	do. masc. plur. object.
khādhīā̃ hosūgīā̃ (*hoṇēgīā̃*),	do. fem. plur. object.

If the future in *-dā* is used the forms will be *howīdā*, *howīdī*, *hosūdā*, *hoṇēdīā̃*, etc., with *d* substituted for *g*.

The suffixes may also follow the verb as mentioned above.

Infinitive.

maĩ ṭukkar khāṇā ī (*je*),	I tell thee (you) I have to eat food,
maĩ roṭī khāṇī ā (*je*),	do. fem. sing. object,
maĩ khāṇe nī (*je*),	do. masc. plur. object,
maĩ khāṇīā̃ nī (*je*),	do. fem. plur. object,

and so on. The infinitive may be used all through the present, past and future exactly in the same way as *khādhā* except that *khāṇā*. *khāṇī*, *khāṇe*, *khāṇīā̃* occur instead of *khādhā*, *khādhī*, *khādhe*, *khādhīā̃* : thus—

asā̃ roṭīā̃ khāṇīā̃ sāje,	we tell you that we had to eat chapatis.
parauṇthe khāṇe sāṇe,	they had to eat chapatis (masc. plur.)
maĩ caul khāṇe hoṇīge,	I tell thee I shall have to eat rice.
roṭīā̃ khāṇīā̃ hosūdīā̃,	he will have to eat chapatis.

WITH INTRANSITIVE VERBS.

The only difference is in the past tenses where with intransitive verbs the agent case is not used. It must be observed that even in intr. verbs the agent case is regularly found with the agent-infinitive, thus—

kikaṇ turnā sāsū ? how was he to walk ?
roṭīā laike jāṇīā ne. they have to take the chapatis and go.

Here we should have expected *jāṇā ne*, but the infin. is attracted into the form of the noun which is the object of *laike* : see Grammar, p. 98.

Present Perfect.

Examples :—

maĩ geā ū̃, I tell thée I have gone.
maĩ geā sū ghar, I have gone to his house.

We get the following forms (using *geā*, went)—

maĩ geā ū̃, je, sū, ne, *asī gae ū̃, je, sū, ne.*
tū̃ geā sū, ne, *tūsī gae sū, ne.*
oh geā ī, je, sū, ne, *oh gae nī, je, sū, ne.*

Fem. change *geā* to *geī* and *geā* to *geīā* otherwise exactly the same except that 3rd sing. is *geī ā*, not *geī ī*.

Simple past : use *-o* forms :—

jaṇā geo sū ghar, the man went to his house.
janānī geīo sū ghar, the woman went to his house.

Pluperfect (also means simple past).

maĩ geā (f. *geī*) *sāje, sāsū, sāṇe,* *asī gae* (f. *geīā*) *sāje, sāsū, sāṇe.*
tū̃ geā (f. *geī*) *sāsū, sāṇe,* *tusī gae* (f. *geīā*) *sāsū, sāṇe.*
oh geā (*geī*) *sāī, sāje, sāsū, sāṇe,* *oh gae* (f. *geīā*) *sāṇī, sāje, sāsū, sāṇe.*

Future.

In addition to the following forms we may have *maĩ geā howā̃gā ī, oh geā howegā je* etc., with the pronom. suffixes after the verb.

maĩ geā hoū̃gā, hojegā : fem. *geī hoū̃gī, hojegī.*
tū, none.
oh geā howīgā, hojegā, hosū̃gā, honēgā : fem. *geī howīgī*, etc.
asī gae hoū̃ge, hojege : fem. *geīā hoū̃gīā, hojegīā.*
tusī, none.
oh gae honīge hojege, hosūge, honēge : fem. *geīā honīgīā*, etc.

Pronominal Suffixes in Negative Sentences.

With the negative nā: (for the interrogative *nā*, and *nehī̃ nā* see lower down). The rule is the same as for affirmative sentences. *nā* comes before the verb as a rule, occasionally after the suffix, in which case it is strongly accented.

je nā mārdo sū,	if he had not struck him.
ḍitthā sū nā,	he has *not* seen him.
ākhī̃ sū nā,	do *not* say it to him.

The second and third sentences, if *nā* is unaccented, will mean "he has seen him, hasn't he?" and "just say it to him, won't you?"

With the negative nehī̃. Two cases arise—

(1) Tenses not containing the past auxiliary *sā̃*, *saē̃*, *sī*, etc

(i) *First rule*. The suffix follows *nehī̃* (almost always).

nehī̃ je bhanneā?	did you not break it?
nehī̃ sū hikkaṇ lage,	they will not drive it out.

(ii) *Second rule*. The 2nd sing. suffix is always *õ*, no matter what it was in the affirmative sentence

labbhā ī? hast thou found it?	*labbhī ā?* (fem. object).
nehī̃ õ labbhā (*labbhī*)?	hast thou not found it?
labbhe nī̃ (fem. *labbhīā̃*)?	hast thou found them?
nehī̃ õ labbhe (*labbhīā̃*)?	hast thou not found them?
maĩ dassnā ū̃,	I am telling thee.
maĩ nehī̃ õ dassdā,	I will not tell thee.

(2) Tenses with past auxiliary.

Rule. The suffix is attached to *sā̃*, *sī*, etc. which become, as in affirmative sentences, *sāī*, *sāṇī*, *sāje*, *sāsū*, *sāṇe*. These words are preceded by *nehī̃*.

nehī̃ sāī muṛnā?	wert thou not going to stop?

Unaccented interrogative nā.

Rule. The *nā* follows the suffix.

huṇe chā̃ngṇā ī, nā?	you're going to prune now, aren't you?

Interrogative nehī̃ nā.

Rule. The suffix generally comes between *nehī̃* and *nā*; *nehī̃ õ nā ḍiggā?* I am asking thee, it has not fallen, has it? Cf. *nehī̃ ẽ nā ḍiggā*, thou hast not fallen, hast thou?

p. 84 end of paragraph third. *Add* Exception: the 1st sing. or plur. agent with 2nd sing. or plur. pronominal suffix, is fairly common in the pluperfect and infin., and is sometimes heard in the past indef. and pres. perf. Examples have been given above pp. 146–7.

INFINITIVE.

p. 94, line 12 from foot. For second "nominative" read "infinitive."

p. 95, middle of p. The two lines beginning "In the past tense" should read thus:—The infinitive in agreement often expresses purpose. It may occur with any tense.

-o FORMS.

p. 106, middle of p. After the two lines beginning "Sometimes we find," add "This is common in the 3rd pers. of trans. and 2nd pers. of intrans. verbs."

Additional examples:

kyũ geõ (geĩõ. geo. geĩo) ? Why didst thou go (thou, f., you, m. pl., you, f. pl.) ?

But we hear also

bhrā geo ī ?	did thy brother go ?
kī kīto ī ?	what didst thou do?
gall eñ hoīo je,	I tell you, the matter happened thus.

COMPOUND VERBS, p. 110.

chaḍḍṇā, as the second verb of a compound, is often pronounced *charṇā*, *sarnā* or *sharṇā*, but when it has its separate sense of "leave" it is always *chaḍḍṇā*.

ōs khēḷ gōḍ sarī e,	he has hoed the flower-bed.

Europeans employ intensive compound verbs to excess. The general rule is that they are uncommon in interrogative sentences and very rare in negative ones.

āeā e ? *ā geā. aje nehī āeā,*	has he come ? He has. He has not.
ḍāhn waḍḍhe nī ?	hast thou cut off the branches ?
nehī waḍḍhe,	I have not (cut them off).
waḍḍh chaṛe ne,	I have.

If the compound is used in an interrogative sentence it rather definitely implies completion or thoroughness. Thus we might have *ḍāhn waḍḍh sare nī* ? have you finished cutting off the branches ?

p. 126, omit the notes referring to pp. 52 and 62.

AGREEMENT OF ADJECTIVES.

Panjabi frequently uses adjectives where we should have adverbs, as in phrases like "he plays well," "he writes well." The question of their agreement causes some difficulty. The rules are—

(i) Intrans. verbs with no object. The adjective agrees with the nominative.

oh caṅgī khēḍdī e, she plays well.

(ii) Trans. verbs with no object. The adjective is masc. governed by the verb.

oh baṛā caṅgā likhdī e, she writes very well.

(iii) Trans. verbs with an object or intrans. verbs with a cognate object. The adjective agrees with the object.

oh kāpī caṅgī likhdā e, he does his copy well.
oh kirkaṭ caṅgā khēḍdī e, she plays cricket well.

USES OF *calṇā.*

(i) Accompany: *mēre nāḷ cal,* accompany me.
(ii) Start .. *cal, āeā ū,* start off, I am coming.
cal pher, start off then.
kadō̃ cale sao, when did you start?

(iii) With roots of verbs to express "almost" or "about to," see Grammar, p. 67.

mukk caleā e, it is almost finished.
mērā hatth lagg caleā sī, my hand was just about to touch it.

(iv) In negative sentences to express ability, Grammar, p. 112.

mēre koḷō̃ nehī̃ puṭṭeā caleā, I shall not be able to dig it.

(v) Like the English go or work (intrans.), go on, do its work, perform its functions, etc.

kaṃm caldā e, the work is going on (well).
mashīn caldī e (nehī̃ caldī), the machine is working (won't work).
dārū nehī̃ caldā, the powder or medicine is not working, i.e. is not efficacious.
rupeyyā caldā e, the rupee passes or circulates (i.e. is not bad).
ohdā mukadmā nehī̃ lagā calaṇ, his case will not go on, he has no case.
paṭāke or *goḷe ṇehī̃ calde,* the fire-works (special kinds) will not go off.

(vi) *Cal, cal whai, calo,* or *calo jī* often means "that's all right now", "there that's settled", etc.

USES OF *paiṇā* (see also G. 120, M. 124, 125).

It expresses—

(1) The idea of actually doing a thing at the moment spoken of, G. 67, 68: *oh gōḍḍā e peā, oh peā gōḍḍā e* (never *gōḍḍā peā e*), he is hoeing.

(2) Indifference (with the pres. subj.): *peī uḍīke*, let her wait (I do not mind). (1) and (2) only with past part. *peā*.

(3) Beginning or suddenness: *bhakh paiṇā*, blaze up: *akk paiṇā*, get tired of: *ḍigg paiṇā*, fall: *phull paiṇā*, blossom: *mil. paiṇā*, meet: *ral paiṇā*, join oneself to, and many more.

(4) Necessity, to have to, must, G. 67 *otthe aṭakṇā pawīdā*. you will have to wait there.

(5) Fall, in a wide sense of the word: *ralā paiṇā*, be adulterated: *peā hoeā*, fallen, lying (of ground), fallow: *lammā paiṇā*, lie down: *sutā peā*, asleep: hence also with words for rain, drops of water, etc., dew, shadow, reflection (in water, etc.), night, darkness, cold, famine: also of blows, abuse, and of instrument with which blows are administered as stick, cane, shoe.

(6) Worry, annoy, attack: *mārn paiṇā, ṭuttke paiṇā, hatthī paiṇā*, all mean rush at or attack: *kuttā paindā e*, the dog attacks: *magar* or *picche paiṇā*, follow annoyingly, not to cease following: *gal paiṇā*, harass, etc.

It expresses mental or physical feelings or conditions.

(7) Mental feelings: words for habit as *hiltar gējh* or *ādat paiṇī*: *saur* or *kāhl paiṇī*, be in a hurry: hence also with *sāṛā*, envy: *jhass* or *caskā*, taste: *rohb*, influence: of a person, *bhairā paiṇā*, become ashamed: *sauṛā, kāhlā p.*, impatient, etc.

(8) Physical conditions: with words like *chāllā*, blister: *bakhōṛ*, cramp: *trāṭ, waṭṭ, pīṛ*, all meaning pain or kinds of pain: *phollā, ciṭṭā*, white ulcer in eye: *pāṇī*, water (in eyes): *laūs, lās*, weal: *jhurrī*, wrinkle: *pāk*, pus (in wound, etc.): *khurk*, itch: of person, *pīlā paiṇā*, become pale.

(9) Happen, occur, with words for love, friendship, discord, noise, disturbance, loss, also hole, hollow, indentation, turn.

(10) Happen, occur, become, and meanings difficult to classify: *walā paiṇā*, long way round: *pherā paiṇā*, have to pay visit: *phal* or *phull paiṇe*, fruit or flowers be formed: *ḍālīī*

paiṇā, argue, hesitate : *bhann paiṇī*, become creased : *pir palle nā paiṇā*, not understand : *kurāhe paiṇā*, go astray : *warhā paiṇā*, get respite for year : *jādū paiṇā*, be bewitched : *peṭe paiṇā*, be responsible for : *wāh paiṇā*, have to do with : *kamm paiṇā*, work turn up : *tarīk paiṇī*, date be appointed : *nazrī paiṇā*, become visible : *pīṅgh paiṇī*, rainbow be formed : *āgal paiṇā*, name be struck off list of debtors : *kāṇō paiṇī*, get warped : *wagāṛ (phuṭṭ) paiṇā (-ī)*, discord, dispute occur : *moche paiṇe*, short logs be cut up : *wagyār paiṇī*, forced labour.

Past Participle in *-eā* or *-ā*.

Past participles end in *-eā* or *-ā*, and occasionally in both. It is not possible to give such rules as will enable students to decide in every case which form to use, but the following will perhaps be of some use. (The presence or absence of *h* makes no difference to the rules).

(1) Irregular past participles, whether transitive or intransitive, end in *-ā*, not *-eā* : *traihṇā*, be startled, *tratthā* : *sihāṇṇā*, recognise, *sihāttā* (but note *sihāṇeā* in *-eā*, a regular past part.). See Grammar, pp. 47, 48.

Exceptions : *marnā*, die, *moeā* : *jāṇā*, go, *geā*.
Slight vowel changes are not here considered irregularities.

(2) The following intransitive verbs whose roots end in a consonant have past parts. in *-ā* :—

bujjhṇā, be extinguished (but note the transitive *bujjhṇā*, guess, solve, *bujjheā*) : *ḍiggṇā*, fall : *ḍubbṇā*, sink : *juttṇā*, be yoked, harnessed : *labbhṇā*, be found (cf. below *labbhṇa*, find) : *laggṇā*, be applied, begin : *pāṭṇā*, be torn : *ṭuṭṭṇā*, break : *bhajjṇā*, break (cf. below *bhajjṇā*, run) : *ḍhukkṇā*, draw near.

The following intrans. verbs have either *-ā* or *-eā* :—

bhajjṇā, run : *bhijjṇā*, get wet : *bajjhṇā*, be fastened : *dhuccṇā*, be washed : *gijjhṇā*, become accustomed : *rijjhṇā*, be cooked : *rujjhṇā*, be busy : *wajjṇā*, strike : *wijjhṇā*, be pierced : *chuṭṭṇā*, escape : *khubbhṇā*, stick (in mud, etc.) : *gijjhṇā* and *rujjhṇā* have also irreg. past parts. which of course end in *-ā*, *giddhā*, *ruddhā* : with *bhijjṇā -eā* is rare.

(3) All regular verbs with roots ending in a vowel, and all regular transitive verbs (whether the roots end in a vowel or not) have past parts. in *-eā*, not *-ā* : *khṛāṇā*, lose, *khṛāeā* : *dhrūhṇā*, drag, *dhrūheā*.

Exceptions : *cubbhṇā*, pierce, *cubbhā*, and *cubbheā* : *labbhṇā*, find, *labbhā* and *labbheā*.

Verbal Roots ending in *g*, *kh*.

Confusion is sometimes caused by the change of *g* into *g̱*, and *kh* into *k̲h̲*. The following general rules will be a guide :—

(1) Verbs with roots ending in a single *g* or *kh* change *g* to *g̱* and *kh* to *k̲h̲* in the simple imperative sing. (not in the -ī form), and when *d*, *k* and *n* (but not *ṇ*) follow : thus—

wēkhṇā, *wēkhaṇ*, *wekhāgā*, but *wēk̲h̲*, *wēk̲h̲dā*, *wek̲h̲ke*, *wekheā*, *wek̲h̲nā*.

wagṇā, *wagaṇ*, *wagegā*, *wagī*, but *wag̱ jā*, *wag̱dā*, *wag̱ke*, *wag̱nā*.

So also *ākhṇā*, say.

Some people use *g̱* throughout in *wag̱ṇā* : others say *wagke*, not *wag̱ke*.

(2) Verbs with double *g* or *kkh* tend to keep *gg* or *kkh* throughout : so *ḍiggṇā*, fall ; *rakkhṇā*, place ; *sikkhṇā*, learn. It is, however, not uncommon to say *rak̲h̲dā*, *rak̲h̲*, *sik̲h̲dā*. *laggṇā*, begin, generally has past part. *lagā*. *likhṇā*, write, *bhak̲h̲ṇā*, blaze, do not come under either rule. They have *k̲h̲* in every part.

(3) The causal forms have *g̱* and *k̲h̲* : *wak̲h̲āṇā*, show ; *ak̲h̲wāṇā*, be called, cause to be said ; *sik̲h̲āṇā*, teach ; *rak̲h̲āṇā*, have placed ; *wag̱āṇā*, cause to flow.

Exception : *ḍēgṇā*, make fall.

The causal of *laggṇā* drops the *g* altogether, *lāṇā*, attach.

These rules are not strictly adhered to.

Formation of Causal Verbs : G. pp. 41–43.

Some difficulties are removed if one observes the following vowel changes which frequently occur in forming causal or transitive verbs. A double consonant becomes single.

a and *ai* become *ā* : *baḷṇā*, burn, *bāḷṇā* : *traihṇā*, be startled, *trāhṇā* : so also *saṛnā*, be burnt, *caṛhṇā*, ascend ; *marnā*, die ; *waṛnā*, enter ; *dhaḷṇā*, be poured in mould ; *uddhaḷṇā*, elope ; *ubbaḷṇā*, boil ; *paiṇā*, fall ; *dhaiṇā*, fall ; *laihṇā*, descend ; *gaihṇā*, be threshed ; *ḍaihṇā*, be placed (bed, etc.).

a in second unaccented syllable of root sometimes becomes *ē* : *ukhaṛnā*, be loosened, *ukhēṛnā* ; so also *nikkhaṛnā*, be separated, *nikhēṛnā* ; *uggharnā*, open (eyes, etc.), *ughēṛnā* ; *uddhaṛnā*, be ripped, *udhēṛnā* : *nibbaṛnā*, be settled, *nabēṛnā* : the double consonant of course becomes single.

i becomes *ē* : *rirhnā*, roll, *rēṛhnā* : so also *chiṛnā*, go to pasture; *girnā*, be turned (wheel, etc.); *ḍiggṇā*, fall, *ḍegṇā*: note too *wikṇā*, be sold, *wēcṇā*.

u becomes *o*: *ghulṇā*, melt, *ghōlṇā*: so also *dubbṇā*, sink, *dōbṇā*; *muṛnā*, turn: *ruṛhnā*, flow away; *cubbhṇā*, pierce; *khubbhṇā*, sink (in mud, etc.): *juṛnā*, be joined; *khurnā*, melt; note also with change of consonant, *tuṭṭṇā*, break, *tōṛnā*, *trōṛnā*; *ḍhukkṇā*, draw near, *ḍhonā*; *khussṇā*, be seized, *khohṇā*; *dhuccṇā* or *dhuppṇā*, be washed, *dhōṇā*; *juppṇā*, be yoked, *joṇā* (sometimes *juttṇā*, be yoked, *jōtṇā*).

A few Hints.

(i) Translate ideas not words. See Manual, p. vi, where this is insisted upon. In parts II and III of the Manual the translation is free, not literal. This is deliberate. We should note the necessity of avoiding the literal translation of epigrammatic phrases such as "Look up, not in"; "if you're right with God you will not be wrong with man." As an illustration we may take the word "personal." The coined word *shakhsī* means "possessing the attributes of personality": hence *mērā shakhsī Najāt-dēṇwālā* means a personal Saviour as opposed to an impersonal one, it does not suggest one personal to me. Again *shakhsī kamm* is devoid of meaning, for work cannot possess personality. In all these expressions the best rule is: Express the idea in other and simpler English words and then translate the explanation. Thus one would explain "personal work" as if one were talking to an educated non-Christian who did not understand the use of the word "personal," and then translate.

(ii) It is always wrong to omit the words for am, is, are, etc., except in negative sentences. The error is very common with Europeans, who constantly say *mundā kitthe*? for *kitthe we* (where is the boy?): *oh kī ākhdā* for *kī ākhdā e*, (what is he saying?): *kihdīā citthīā* for *kihdīā citthīā ne* (whose letters are they?): *māshkī teār* for *teār e* (is the water-carrier ready?).

(iii) In English we use "do" to avoid some other verb already used. Thus: put them away. I have *done* so. In Panjabi this can never be *maĩ kītā e*. The two sentences would be *ohnā nū sāhmke rakkh*. *maĩ rakkh chaḍḍe ne*. The same verb must be used again. In this case it is *rakkhṇā*.

(iv) Similarly we are fond of an unnecessary "like that." We say:—don't cry like that: don't shout like that. If we translate by *es, turhā* it means: do not cry or shout in that particular way, do it in some other way. The words should simply be omitted.

(v) We are addicted to a great use of possessive pronouns. We say: "we read in our Bibles." In parts of the British Isles people say "he's having his tea," "I'm going to my bed." All these must be omitted.

Baibal wicc likheā hoeā e, we read in our Bibles.
maĩ saun caleā wā, I am going to (my) bed.

(v) The future is not much used in negative sentences. The following will show the common usage.

maĩ bawhā̃dā, I shall sit down: *maĩ nehĩ baihndā* or *nehĩ baihṇ lagā,* I will not sit down.

Yet sometimes we do hear the future with the negative, especially in promises, as—

edū̃ agge maĩ nehĩ karā karā̃dā, in future I will not do so.

(vi) Interrogative words: the position of interrogative words should be noted.

The nominative of the sentence must never come between the interrogative word and the verb. Europeans accustomed to the English order "where are you going?", "what have you done?" are apt to say *kitthe tū̃ calea ẽ, kī tū̃ kitā e.* This is quite wrong. The following show the order:—

oh kā̃hde jogā kūndā e? why is he speaking?
bhrā kadõ āwīdā? when will your brother come?

Sometimes conversationally the nominative is brought to the end as: *kūndā kā̃hde jogā e oh, kadõ āwīdā bhrā,* but this does not violate the rule given above

(vii) Excessive use of Compound Verbs: see p. 150.

APPENDIX II.

ADDITIONS TO VOCABULARY.

absolutely, add *ukkā mukkā*: *see* altogether, thoroughly.
adulterate, add *khōṭ pāṇā* (*wicc*): *see* mix.
allow, add *see* permit, liberty.
angry, *lūsṇā* suggests inward, not outward anger.
anklet, add *bā̃k* f., *lacchā*, m., *sā̃ṭ*, f., *saglā*, m.
annul, *see* cancel, abolish, repeal.
apologise, add *koḷō* of person a.-ed to, and *dā* of thing a.-ed for.
appease, add *ṭhaṇḍā-k.*: a.-hunger. *lāhṇī*, int. *laihṇī*: *see* satisfy: quench thirst, *see* slake.
arm, of chair, *bā̃h*, f.: of coat, *bā̃h*, f.: *see* next word.
armlet, *ṭāḍḍ*, f., *ṭaḍḍ*, f.

back (1), (lying) on back, *utānā*: (carry) on shoulders or high up on b., *kandhāṛe*, *dhaṅgāṛe*: lower down, also pick-aback, *magar picche*.
bracelet, add *kaṛā*, m.: *see* armlet in A.
bride, add *wauhṭī*, wife.
butterfly, add *titrī*. *tittrī*, f.
buttermilk, milk and water, *kaccī lassī*: boiled and curdled, *pakkī lassī*.

cajole, *see* coax, wheedle.
cantankerous, *see* irritable.
card(1), *piññā* is softening before spinning, *jhambṇā* softening before seeding: to seed cotton is *wēlṇā*.
cargo, *māl asbāb*, m., *asbāb*, m.
carniverous, *māskhōr*, *mās* or *gōsht khāṇwāḷā*.
cash, v., add *trōṛnā*. *bhannṇā*.
cataract in eye, add *motīābind*, m.
catch, *phaṛā dēṇā*, *see* explanation on pp. 143-4.
chaff, fr. rice, *parāḷī*, f.
chain, on door, *kuṇḍī*, f.
(1) **chink**, opening, split, *trēṛ*, f.
(2) **chink**, sound, *see* tinkle.
compensation, *see* damage A.
cook (2), *rōṭī lāṇī* (int. *laggṇī*), means to slap the "*chupattee*" on to side of oven.
cud, chew, *see* ruminate A.
cut teeth, *dandīā kaḍḍhṇīā* (int. *nikḷṇīā*), of children; but back teeth, *haṇū* (*kaḍḍhṇīā*, *nikḷṇīā*): animals, *dand* (*kaḍḍhṇe*, *nikḷṇe*).

damage, legal, *harjā*, m., *harj*, m.: damages, *harjānnā*, m.: ordinary compensation, *iwzānnā*, m.
dark, *see* Errata.
dentist, *dand baṇāṇwāḷā*.
dismiss, add *chuṭṭī dēṇī* (*nū̃*), discharge, also give leave: *makūf-k.*, dismiss.
disqualify, add *nā̃wā lāhṇā* (*dā*, int., *laihṇā*).

divine, *Rabb dā*, *Khudā dā*, *Parmeshwar dā*, etc., *see* God : also *ilāhī* (U.).
divinity, godhead, *khudāī*. f. : *see* theology A.

feed, dogs, cats, etc., *ṭukkar pāṇā* (*nū*): cattle, *paṭṭhe pāṇe*, *ghāh pāṇā*, *guṭāwā pāṇā* (all *nū*) : horses, *ghāh pāṇā*, *nihāri dēṇī* (both *nū*).
fellow, *see* pair.
fever, *see* also quartan, tertian
fire (2), *see* shoot.
forget, add *menū ohdā thauh nehī rehā*, I forgot it.
free, adj., add *marzī dā mālak*.

gallop, v. tr., *poīā* or *sarpaṭṭ ṭōrnā* : *cakhurīā* or *caukhurīā saṭṭṇā* (*nū*).

hereabouts, *etthe jaie* : thereabouts, *otthe jaie* : whereabouts (inter.), *kitthe jaie*, (rel.) *jitthe jaie* : (*jaie* for *jaihe* fr. *jehā*).

immoral, *see* blackguard.
inborn, add from birth, *jamāhndrū* : deaf from birth, *jamāhndrū ḍōrā*.

lie down, for woman use *lēṭṇā*, not *lammā paiṇā* : lying down, *leṭī hoī e*.
luckily, *abihāre*.

permanent (resident, servant, service, work), *naṭhāhū*, *nāṭhehū*.
pip, of orange, apple, etc., *see* stone.
place (2), *daihnā* not used for water.
purgative, take effect, *laggṇā*.

reddish, *see* somewhat.
reliable, add *atbār wāḷā*.
renounce, add *hakk chaḍḍṇā* (*dā*, *apṇā*).
ruminate, chew cud, *ugāḷī karnī* : see meditate, think.

safe, add *rāzī bāzī*.
serv-ant, -ice, *see* permanent A.
sharpen, pencil, *ghaṛnā*.
snare, add *phāhī*, f.
stars ; Bear, the Great, *palhang pīhṛā*, m.
Canopus, *agath*, m.
Orion's Belt, *trangaṛ*, m.
Pleiades, *khittīā*, f. pl.
Procyon and Sirius, *lohnde*, m. pl.
Pole Star, *kutub tārā*, m.
Venus (evening star), *shām dā tārā*, m. : (morning star), *waihṛ tārā*, m.

tainted, be, of meat, add *humh jāṇā*.
theology, *Khudā* or *dīn dā ilm*, *fikā*, m. (U.) : *see* divinity in A, God
thereabouts, *see* hereabouts A.
threshing-floor, add *khalāṛā*, m.

whereabouts, *see* hereabouts A.
white and black, piebald, *ḍabbā*, *ḍabb khṛabbā* : small spots, lines, *tetrā metrā*.
work, *see* permanent A.

Weights and Measures.

Measures of Length.

inch, *incī*, f.
about 3 inches, *cappā*, m. (hand-breadth).
about 8 inches, *giṭṭh*, f. (span).

Cloth.

2¼ inches one *girhā*, f
16 *girha's* one yard.

Distance.

12 inches one *fuṭ*, *fiṭ*, m. (foot).
3 feet one *gaz*, m. (yard).
220 yards one *farlāṅg*. m. (furlong).
8 furlongs one *mīl*, m. (mile).
1⅛ miles one *koh*, m. (*kuhāṭrā*. m., approximately, or less than, a *koh*).

Land Measure.

5½ feet one *karū*, m.
22 feet one *jarīb*, f. (chain).

Square Measure (*land*).

one sq. *karū* is one *sarsāhī*, f.
9 sarsahi's one *marlā*, m.
20 marla's one *kanāl*, f.
4 kanals one *wighā*, m. (half acre).
8 kanals one *ghumā*, m. (acre) or *killā*. a killa is 40 karu's long by 36 broad.
25 acres one *murabbā*, m.

Weight (*precious metals or stones*).

1/240 oz. (nearly) one *rattī*, f.
8 ratti's one *māssā*, m.
12 massas one *tolā*, m.
5 tolas one *chaṭākī*.
16 chataki's or 80 tolas one *sēr*, m. (2 lbs. 0·914 oz.).

Food and general.

about 2 oz. one *chaṭākī*, f.
16 chatakis one *sēr* as above).
2 chatakis *addh pā*.
4 chatakis one *pā*, m. (quarter ser): 8 chatakis *addh sēr*.
6, 10, 12, 14 chatakis *ḍeḍh* or *ḍūḍh*, *ḍhāī trai*. *sāḍhe trai pā*.
40 ser one *man*, m. (maund).

Grain, etc., actually measured by toppas (*see below*).

20 ser one *man*, m.
3 man one *paṇḍ*. f.
4 pands one *māṇī*, f. (12 *man* of grain),
also the following :—

Capacity (*chiefly grain, etc.*).

4 cuha's one *paṛōppī*, f. (*cuhā*. m.: accent on second syllable).
2 paroppis one *ṭōppā*.
2 toppas one *daṛōppā*, m.
The weight of a toppa of grain varies from village to village. A 1¼ ser toppa is called *suāeā ṭōppā* (from *sawā sēr*) : a 1½ ser toppa is *ḍeḍh serā ṭōppā* : a 1¾ ser toppa is *sat pāeā ṭōppā* : a 1⅞ ser toppa is *sāṛhsutpāeā ṭōppā* (from *sāḍhe satt pā*), while a 2 ser toppa is called *dusērā ṭōppā*.